Delphi By EXAMPLE

que

Blake Watson

Delphi By Example

Copyright © 1995 by Que™ Corporation

All rights reserved. Printed in the United States of America. No part of this book may be used or reproduced, in any form or by any means, or stored in a database or retrieval system, without prior written permission of the publisher except in the case of brief quotations embodied in critical articles and reviews. Making copies of any part of this book for any purpose other than your own personal use is a violation of United States copyright laws. For information, address Que, 201 W. 103rd St., Indianapolis, IN 46290.

Library of Congress Catalog Card Number: 95-67673

ISBN: 1-56529-757-1

This book is sold *as is*, without warranty of any kind, either express or implied, respecting the contents of this book, including but not limitied to implied warranties for the book's quality, performance, merchantability, or fitness for any particular purpose. Neither Que Corporation nor its dealers or distributors shall be liable to the purchaser or any other person or entity with respect to any liability, loss, or damage caused or alleged to be caused directly or indirectly by this book.

98 97 96 95   4 3 2

Interpretation of the printing code: the rightmost double-digit number is the year of the book's printing; the rightmost single-digit number is the number of the book's printing. For example, a printing code of 95-1 shows that the first printing of the book occurred in 1995.

Publisher: *Roland Elgey*

Associate Publisher: *Joseph B. Wikert*

Director of Product Series: *Charles O. Stewart III*

Managing Editor: *Kelli Widdifield*

Product Marketing Director: *Lynn Zingraf*

Acquisitions Editor
Lori A. Jordan

Acquisitions Coordinators
Patricia J. Brooks, Angela C. Kozlowski

Product Director
C. Kazim Haidri

Production Editor
Mike La Bonne

Technical Editor
Jim Riesebeck

Associate Product Marketing Director
Kim Margolius

Book Designer
Sandra Schroeder

Cover Designer
Dan Armstrong

Graphic Image Specialists
Becky Beheler, Steve Carlin, Brad Dixon, Teresa Forrester, Jason Hand, Denny Hager, Clint Lahnen, Cheri Laughner, Michael Reynolds, Laura Robbins, Dennis Sheehan, Craig Small, Jeff Yesh

Production Team
Daryl Kessler, Bob LaRoche, Beth Lewis, Barry Jorden, G. Alan Palmore, Kaylene Riemen, Clair Schweinler, Kris Simmons, Michael Thomas, Jody York

Indexer
Michael Hughes

Composed in *Palatino* and *MCPdigital* by Macmillan Computer Publishing.

Dedication

This one is for Mom, and for George, for always being there.

About the Author

Blake Watson started programming at an early age and has never stopped studying the latest advances or writing useful and entertaining computer programs. He writes routinely for several magazines, including *PC Techniques* and *Toolbox* magazine. You can contact Blake on CompuServe at 70303,373.

Acknowledgments

Let me first acknowledge Borland for creating this amazing product, and the people who helped me technically and directly or indirectly, which contributed to my understanding of this amazing new contribution: Borland's **Zack Urlocker**, **Charlie Calvert**, **Leslie Kew**, **Linda Jeffries**, and especially **Danny Thorpe**, who answered many a panicked question in a timely fashion.

You probably wouldn't believe the number of people who come in and out of an author's life during the course of writing a book. Besides many people at the publishing company whom he may get to like but only know fleetingly, his life is filled with people in transition and social interaction becomes a constant flow of ships passing in the night, in the day, and at ungodly hours of the morning.

But, on Jan. 17th, 1994, at 4:31 a.m., when the earthquake shook my house and split its foundation, when every piece of glass I owned shattered, and when all the modern civilities like water, electricity, and gas were taken away from me (if only temporarily) I knew where to go. I knew who I could count on to be there. That's why this book is dedicated to my mother and stepfather. Few people can gracefully accept a man, his wife, his daughter, and their two largish dogs into their home for a period of several weeks without ever once pressuring them into leaving, or even suggesting it by word or deed.

Most of all in this book, I must acknowledge those people who were *there* at a volatile time in my life, or who have always been there: my wife, **Adriane**; my daughter, **Sarah**; my oldest and dearest friend, **Adam**; my newest and dearest friend, **Nolcha**; my backup mothers **Patty**, **Linda**, and **Rochelle**; my friends at the SDFORUM pub (always glad to recommend good places to relocate); and the dozens of other people whom I know I can count on in a pinch, and who I hope know that they can count on me.

Trademarks

All terms mentioned in this book that are known to be trademarks or service marks have been appropriately captialized. Que cannot attest to the accuracy of this information. Use of a term in this book should not be regarded as affecting the validity of any trademark or service mark.

Overview

Introduction 1

I Programming in the Age of Graphics
1 The Modern Computer and the Programmer 9
2 Traditional Programming 21

II Working in the Delphi Environment
3 Introducing Delphi 37
4 What's On-Screen? 49

III Approaching Delphi
5 Working with Pascal 75
6 Variables 95
7 Using Numbers 111
8 Subroutines 127
9 Data Conversion 155

IV Taking Charge of Delphi
10 On One Condition 169
11 A Special *Case* 195
12 Repeating Yourself 207
13 Pascal Math 231

V Additional Data Types
14 User-Defined Types and Enumeration 261
15 The Set Type 283
16 The Record 297
17 The Array 321

VI File Handling
18 File Basics 347
19 Typed Files and Random Access 367

VII Advanced Programming Concepts
20 Units 385
21 Objects 415
22 Better By Design 439

Appendixes
A ASCII and Extended ASCII Codes 471
B Answers to the Review Questions 481

Index 499

We'd Like To Hear from You!

As part of our continuing effort to produce books of the highest possible quality, Que would like to hear your comments. To stay competitive, we *really* want you, as a computer book reader and user, to let us know what you like or dislike most about this book or other Que products.

You can mail comments, ideas, or suggestions for improving future editions to the address below, or send us a fax at (317) 581-4663. For the on-line inclined, Macmillan Computer Publishing now has a forum on CompuServe (type **GO QUEBOOKS** at any prompt) through which our staff and authors are available for questions and comments. In addition to exploring our forum, please feel free to contact me personally on CompuServe at 74143,1574 to discuss your opinions of this book.

Thanks in advance—your comments will help us to continue publishing the best books available on computer topics in today's market.

Chris Haidri
Product Development Specialist
Que Corporation
201 W. 103rd Street
Indianapolis, Indiana 46290
USA

Contents

Introduction **1**
Who Should Use This Book? 1
    What Do I Need? 2
    Why Learn About Programming? 2
The *Modus Operandi* of This Book 2
    How Much Should I Know About Windows? 3
    Mouse Operations 4
    Conventions 4
    Icons Used in This Book 5
Overview 6

Part I Programming in the Age of Graphics   7

1 The Modern Computer and the Programmer   9
Looking at Hardware 10
    The Central Processing Unit 10
    Random-Access Memory 11
Looking at Software 15
    Program vs. Data 15
    Operating Systems 16
    DOS and Windows 16
Summary 20
Review Questions 20

2 Traditional Programming   21
The Machine's Language 21
The Assembler 22
Compilers 23
The World's Shortest Pascal Program (Almost) 24
A Brief History of the User Interface 24
User-Controlled Programs 26
Introducing the Object 27
    Real-World Objects 29
    Object Classes 29
    Object Properties 30
    Object Behavior 32

Contents

Summary 33
Review Questions 33

Part II Working in the Delphi Environment   35

3 Introducing Delphi   37

Installing and Running Delphi 37
Elements of a Delphi Program 38
    The Form 39
    The Code Editor 40
    Units and Forms 41
    The Project 41
    Working with the Project Manager 42
    Ending Delphi 46
Summary 47
Review Questions 47
Review Exercises 47

4 What's On-Screen?   49

The Standard Objects 50
The SpeedBar 50
The Form and Unit Selectors 52
The Form and the Component Palette 53
    Selecting Multiple Components 55
    Sizing Multiple Components 55
    Aligning Components with Each Other 56
    Removing Components from the Form 58
    Other Objects 58
The Object Inspector 59
    Properties 60
    Behavior 63
Using the Code Editor 63
Summary 71
Review Questions 71
Review Exercises 72

Part III Approaching Delphi   73

5 Working with Pascal   75

The World's Shortest Pascal Program, Revisited 75
    Your First Pascal Lesson 78
    Punctuation 80

Punctuation Errors	81
Getting Help	82
Debugging	83
Breakpoints	86
Object Methods	87
Objects in Pascal	87
Automatically Generated Code	88
Altering Object Behavior	90
Summary	91
Review Questions	92
Review Exercises	92

6 Variables — 95

Deciding on Variable Names	95
Restrictions on Variable Names	96
Using Numbers in Variable Names	97
Forbidden Identifiers	98
The Variable Type	98
When to Declare a Variable	99
How to Declare a Variable	100
The String Type	101
Declaring Strings	101
Declaring Shorter Strings	102
Assigning Values to a String	103
Summary	108
Review Questions	109
Review Exercises	110

7 Using Numbers — 111

Numbers in Delphi	112
Expressing Integers	112
Numeric Types	112
Working with Integers	114
Range Checking	120
Wrapping Around	122
Summary	123
Review Questions	124
Review Exercises	125

8 Subroutines — 127

What Are Subroutines?	127
Simple Subroutines	129

Contents

Subroutine Parameters 132
Watching What Happens Inside a Procedure 133
    Scope 134
    More Elaborate Procedures 137
    Long Lines 139
    Routines That Change Variables 140
    Debugging Your Program 141
    The *var* Parameter 141
    Const 143
The Global Variable 144
The Function 146
The Pascal Library 149
Summary 150
Review Questions 151
Review Exercises 152

9   Data Conversion   155

Why Is Data Conversion So Important? 156
Incompatible Integers 160
Summary 163
Review Questions 164
Review Exercises 165

Part IV   Taking Charge of Delphi   167

10   On One Condition   169

The Boolean Type 169
    Working with Boolean Variables 170
    Comparisons 170
    Logical Operators 172
The *If-Then* Statement 176
    Complex Logic 177
    Random 180
    Randomize 181
    Or Else… 182
    The Orphaned *Else* 183
Blocks 183
    The Orphaned *Else* Revisited 184
    Elements of Style 185

Summary 191
Review Questions 191
Review Exercises 192

11 A Special *Case* — 195

The *Case* Statement 196
    When Can I Use *Case*? 197
    What Can I Do with a Matching Selection? 199
    Ordinal Types 199
    Case Limitations 200
Summary 204
Review Questions 204
Review Exercises 205

12 Repeating Yourself — 207

Delphi and the GoTo 208
The Loop Concept 209
The *For* Loop 211
    For Loop Variations 212
    For Loop Limitations 214
The Listbox and List Objects 216
The *While* and *Repeat* Loops 219
Break and Continue 225
Summary 229
Review Questions 229
Review Exercises 230

13 Pascal Math — 231

Simple Math 231
    Integer Subroutines 239
Real Types 242
    Real Functions 244
Real vs. Integer 246
    Scientific Notation 247
    Generic Subroutines 248
Operator Precedence 254
Summary 255
Review Questions 256
Review Exercises 257

Contents

Part V Additional Data Types — 259

14 User-Defined Types and Enumeration — 261
Enumerated Types 262
    Declaring a User-Defined Data Type 262
    Ordination 264
Radio Buttons and the Group Box 267
The Radio Group 271
Enumeration Limitations 279
Summary 280
Review Questions 281
Review Exercises 282

15 The Set Type — 283
Declaring the Set Type 284
Set Operators 285
    Set Tips 287
Check Boxes 288
Set Limitations 293
Summary 295
Review Questions 295
Review Exercises 296

16 The Record — 297
The Record Data Type 298
    Declaring a Record 299
    Using Records 300
    Choosing Data Types 301
    The *SizeOf* Function 302
    Considerations When Using Multiple Forms 305
Record Limitations 306
The *With* Keyword 309
Summary 316
Review Questions 316
Review Exercises 318

17 The Array — 321
The Array Data Type 321
A Deck of Cards 327
Complex Arrays 338
Array Limitations 339
    The Character Array 340

Summary 341
Review Questions 341
Review Exercises 342

Part VI File Handling   345

18   File Basics   347

The Text File 347
    File Handling 348
    Declaring a File Variable 348
    Opening the File 349
    Closing a File 352
Write and *WriteLn* Revisited 353
Appending to Text Files 355
Read and *ReadLn* 355
    EOF 357
    A Note on Text Files 357
Summary 362
Review Questions 363
Review Exercises 364

19   Typed Files and Random Access   367

Typed Files 367
    Declaring 368
    Opening, Creating, Appending 369
    Random Updates 371
    Deletes 372
Summary 380
Review Questions 380
Review Exercises 381

Part VII Advanced Programming Concepts   383

20   Units   385

Unit Structure 388
    Interface 389
    Implementation 390
The *Uses* Clause 392
    Circular References 395
    Relationship of the Unit to the Project 396
Constants 397
The Typed Constant 399

Scope Revisited 402
Unit Design 403
Standard Units 406
The Timer 406
The Open Dialog 407
Summary 412
Review Questions 413
Review Exercises 414

21 Objects — 415

What Is an Object? 415
    Inheritance 417
    Constructors and Destructors 419
    Replacing Object Methods 420
    Object Type Compatibility 421
    Typecasting 424
Restricting Access to Object Features 431
Summary 437
Review Questions 437
Review Exercises 438

22 Better By Design — 439

Hacking 439
    Design 441
The Problem 441
    A Modest Proposal 442
The Description 442
The Prototype 444
The Objects 446
Defining the Objects 447
Miscellaneous Subroutines and Data Types 453
Implementation 454
Summary 466
Review Questions 467
Review Exercises 467

Appendixes   **469**

A   ASCII and Extended ASCII Codes   **471**

B   Answers to the Review Questions   **481**
    Chapter 1 481
    Chapter 2 482
    Chapter 3 483
    Chapter 4 483
    Chapter 5 484
    Chapter 6 484
    Chapter 7 485
    Chapter 8 486
    Chapter 9 487
    Chapter 10 487
    Chapter 11 488
    Chapter 12 488
    Chapter 13 489
    Chapter 14 491
    Chapter 15 492
    Chapter 16 492
    Chapter 17 493
    Chapter 18 494
    Chapter 19 495
    Chapter 20 495
    Chapter 21 496

Index   **499**

Introduction

Delphi By Example is a Que book based on the learn-by-doing principle, where learning is best done by actually doing rather than just reading. This principle is sound on the face of it—you wouldn't just read a book about repairing your car's transmission and then expect to install a new transmission. However, through a combined program of reading and "hands-on" application, you probably could change the transmission.

Delphi By Example is a "hands-on" book. By the time you finish this book, you'll have read about and worked directly with Delphi on many occasions, enough so that you will be comfortable with the program and excited about what you can accomplish with it.

Who Should Use This Book?

This book is about the Pascal language as it is realized in the Delphi product. If you don't know any computer language, then this book is for you. If you need to learn standard Pascal, then using a graphical product such as Delphi can make the process more enjoyable. If you already use a visual product such as Visual Basic or one of the many REXX products, you'll find this book an easy way to harness the power of Delphi. Be forewarned, however, that Borland has defined the standard for Pascal for years and that the Pascal taught in many schools pales by comparison.

Delphi By Example follows a simple format: Each chapter contains several features. With each feature, you first get an explanation of how and possibly why it works, then you get to work directly with the feature. At the end of each chapter is a summary, followed by review questions and exercises covering each feature.

This approach is designed to serve a broad range of readers from novice to advanced. If you've never programmed before, the learn-by-doing approach will

Introduction

help you move quickly and easily through this book. If you have programming experience, you'll find plenty of material in this book to refine and enhance what you already know, and to give you a solid understanding of how Delphi works.

Although definitions are provided for many of the terms used in this book, you should keep close at hand a standard English dictionary and a dictionary of computer terminology such as *Que's Computer Programmer's Dictionary* or *Que's Computer User's Dictionary*. (It's surprising how often computer programmers get into arguments over issues simply because they're both using the same word to mean two different things.)

What Do I Need?

Pascal is the basis for this book—you need to have it, and you need to have a computer that can run it. This book was written by running Pascal under OS/2 2.1 and 2.11's WinOS2 without difficulty. Pascal will probably run under any operating system that has decent Windows emulation.

Why Learn About Programming?

Maybe you still don't know whether this book is for you. Maybe you're just looking for an answer to the question, "Why learn to program at all?" Following are several reasons to learn more about programming:

- As a possible source of income and employment.

- For fun. Programming is a combination of an artistic, creative process and a never-ending series of puzzles.

- To get something done that you otherwise couldn't do. For example, despite the many commercial computer programs available, you may not be able to buy exactly what you need, or the products you can buy are too expensive or too complicated for the task at hand.

- To satisfy your curiosity. If you're curious about programming and what it entails, this book will help you decide whether or not it is something you want to pursue.

The *Modus Operandi* of This Book

Modus Operandi, a Latin term for "method of operation," often is used in police dramas to describe the specific way a crime is committed. This book, although not associated with anything criminal, has its own *modus operandi*.

First, this book is not extremely technical. Precise definitions of the Pascal language are available from numerous sources—one source is available through Delphi's on-line help system. However, such descriptions are useful only after you understand how and why certain things are done. Otherwise, the descriptions are too abstract. This book presents simple concepts in a light manner, as if you were sitting at poolside with beverage in hand speaking directly to the author.

Second, this book is based on the graphical user interface—specifically, the Windows interface, which should make some concepts easy for you to grasp. Concepts are presented in the order in which they will be useful to you, which is not necessarily the traditional teaching order. If you've already worked your way through such traditional methods, give this book a chance; you may be pleasantly surprised.

Each chapter ends with beginner-, intermediate-, and advanced-level review questions based on the material you studied in that chapter. The answers usually come directly from the text or are deducible from the text, but occasionally you might need to experiment a little. Try to answer the questions at all difficulty levels. If you get stuck, turn to the answers provided in Appendix B. Also, look at the review sections after reading each chapter and return to them frequently. After you've gone through several chapters, you'll begin to understand more often the reason why a concept was illustrated or a question was asked. Returning to questions that frustrated you earlier and realizing that now you know the answers can be a big confidence builder.

The key words of the title are *By Example*. Throughout the book, you're directed to follow steps or take certain actions, and you should follow every step and take every action. Most of what you gain from this book will come from what you do, not from what you read. The examples are presented at three levels of difficulty and you should read them all. You may want to go through the book once to get the basic concepts, and then go back and do the harder questions and exercises to cement what you've learned.

How Much Should I Know About Windows?

To understand this book, you should be able to identify common objects in the Windows operating environment, including windows, scroll bars, menu bars, title bars, icons, buttons, and system menus. These objects are explained from a programmer's perspective, but if you've never used them before, understanding how they work will be challenging. Also, you should have a feel for how Windows dialog boxes work and how to act within them. (If you've used Windows much at all, you probably know this stuff.)

If you're not familiar with Windows and how it works, you should read Que's *Easy Windows 3.1*. Also, if you need to brush up on your basic computer hardware knowledge, read Que's *Computers Illustrated*. *Delphi By Example* assumes that you know what the mouse and other common hardware devices are and how to use them; however, if you're not sure which end of a disk to stick in the floppy drive, you should read these two books first.

Mouse Operations

In this book, the following phrases tell you how to operate your mouse within Delphi:

- *Click on.* Move the mouse pointer so that it is in the area of the screen specified and press the left mouse button. (If you've reversed these buttons, as many left-handed people like to do, whenever the instructions say to press the left button, press the right button instead.) Sometimes the buttons are referred to as primary and secondary mouse buttons, which would be the left and right buttons, respectively, unless you have reversed them.
- *Double-click on.* Press the left mouse button twice rapidly.
- *Drag.* Press and hold down the left mouse button while you're moving the mouse pointer.
- *Drop.* Release the mouse button after a drag operation.

A drag-and-drop operation usually looks as though you actually pick something up, drag it across the screen to a different location, and then drop it.

Conventions

The following conventions are used in this book:

- Code lines, functions, variable names, and any text you see on-screen appear in a special `monospace` typeface.
- Placeholders within code are in `italic monospace`.
- User input following a prompt is in **`bold monospace`**.
- File names are in regular text font, usually all uppercase.
- New terms are in *italic*.
- Special-purpose keys are referred to by the text that actually appears on them on a standard 101-key keyboard. For example, press "Esc" or press "F1" or press "Enter."
- The Backspace key, which is labeled with a left arrow, usually is located directly above the Enter key. The Tab key usually is labeled with two arrows pointing to lines, with one arrow pointing right and the other pointing left.
- The cursor keys, labeled on most keyboards with arrows pointing up, down, right, and left, are called the up-arrow key, down-arrow key, right-arrow key, and left-arrow key.

- Key combinations that you must press simultaneously are separated by plus signs. For example, "Press Ctrl+Alt+D" means that you press and hold down the Ctrl key, then press and hold down the Alt key, then press and release the D key. Always press and release, rather than hold, the last key in a key combination.
- Case is not important unless explicitly stated. So "Press A" or "Press a" means the same thing.
- If you're required to type text, the text you must type will appear in **boldface**. For example, "Type **The quick brown fox jumped over the lazy dog**." Usually, however, the line is set off by itself in a monospace typeface, as shown in the following example:

```
This is how text typed outside a paragraph will look
```

Icons Used in This Book

The following icons are used to indicate examples at a certain level of difficulty:

Level 1   Level 2   Level 3

The following additional icons are used to identify material shown in a box:

Tip   Caution   Note

Pseudocode is a special way of explaining a section of code with an understandable, English language description. You often see pseudocode before a code example. The following icon represents pseudocode:

Pseudocode

Overview

The first four chapters of this book cover a lot of material on how to work with Delphi, and contain background material that helps familiarize you with the world of visual programming.

The next 11 chapters discuss the fundamentals of Delphi. By way of example, traditional elements of Delphi are related to the visual elements of Delphi.

Chapters 16 to 21 show more-advanced Delphi elements. The last chapter is devoted to design—how to program *well*. In a sense, reading this book is like taking a course on building a house, where you first learn about hammers, nails, and lumber, and then how they go together, and then how to build the house.

When you're done with this book, you should be able to accomplish quite a bit with the product. While anyone can design a window with Delphi, you'll be able to write code that makes that window act in a way that serves your particular needs. You'll be able to write a simple game, or a program for managing your time or your address book. But that just scratches the surface: This book should open your mind to the underlying power of Delphi, where all things are possible.

Delphi is a rich environment, capable of a lot more than could possibly be crammed into one book. Future study should take you to Que's Special Edition *Using Delphi*, which takes off where this book ends.

Part I

Programming in the Age of Graphics

CHAPTER 1

The Modern Computer and the Programmer

"The Modern Computer" is something of an oxymoron: By the time you've described it, it's obsolete. Today's computers are not like the homogenous PCs of the past, all of which had a system unit, a floppy disk drive, and a separate monitor. Today, some computers are desk size, some come in notebook size, and still others are small enough to fit in the palm of your hand. Most computers have floppy disk drives (and many now also have CD-ROM drives), although some portable computers do not. Virtually all have some kind of fixed disk drive—today's programs demand one—and all have screens. Screens vary from CGA and monochrome (in their death throes) to standard VGA to super high-resolution monitors available on high-end machines. And most computers have a keyboard, although some use an electronic pen.

Regardless of their individual configurations, computers of all eras have had one thing in common: the requirement for technically skilled human beings—programmers—to make them act in productive and useful ways. Because you've picked up this book, you probably have some interest in becoming a programmer. Take heart. Learning to program has never been easier. Some people might say that mastering programming has never been harder, but mastering programming isn't a concern here. *Delphi By Example* sets you on the road to getting the most from your computer.

Looking at Hardware

Before you go any further in this book, you must determine what kind of computer you plan to program and under what conditions. This book places few restrictions on the type of hardware you may run: Your computer should have a monitor, a keyboard, some kind of pointing device (such as a mouse), and a hard drive. Some of the examples allow you to work with a printer, too, although it's not a requirement for you to have one to use this book.

You may see on-screen references to colors from time to time, but these references are limited primarily to how they relate to programming issues. You're not asked to find anything on-screen based on its color, so a color monitor isn't a requirement.

You don't learn about hardware in any detail in this book. The whole point of Windows is to isolate the programmer from the hardware. You will be programming for Windows, and you will let Windows figure out how to get done what you want. The only hardware you really need to consider are the central processing unit and random-access memory, described in the following sections.

The Central Processing Unit

You command the computer by using the keyboard and mouse. You tell it what programs to run, as well as when and where to save data on your disk drives. The computer responds to you through the monitor and perhaps through the system speaker or sound card.

But what part of the computer receives the key and mouse commands? What part translates mouse motions into pointer movement? For that matter, what part draws the pointer and all the other images that appear on-screen?

The answers to these questions have many parts, but for now concern yourself with only one facet of the answers. Often, if you ask people who have desktop systems about their computers, they point to the case and say "That's the computer." The case, of course, doesn't do the computing, but the computer is in there.

A small piece of plastic and silicon residing in that case, larger than a postage stamp but considerably smaller than a 3 1/2-inch disk, is what you can call, with some satisfaction, the computer. (Being flat and small, it is also called a *chip*.) The chip actually does compute. Given instructions such as *multiply two times four*, it counts two plus two plus two plus two, and comes up with the correct answer.

Technically, this chip is called the *CPU*, or the *central processing unit*, because almost all commands go through this piece of hardware. Nearly everything that happens on your computer is controlled through the CPU.

CPUs are measured in a number of ways, the primary way being *speed*. How fast can it multiply two by four? If you're running Windows, the odds are good that you have a CPU made by Intel Corporation. Intel has made five generations of chips that have been used in making personal computers like the one you're using. These generations are named the 8086, the 80286, the 80386, the 80486, and the Pentium. Each one is faster than its predecessor, and yet each one is compatible with the previous generations.

The only reason to know what kind of CPU you have is that the *older* CPUs are not compatible with the *newer* ones. While an 80386 can do anything an 80286 or 8086 can, it can't do everything that an 80486 or a Pentium can. If you buy a software package that carries a warning that it requires an 80386 or higher and your machine has an 80286, then you cannot use that software.

> **Eeny, Meeny, Miny, and Steve**
>
> Knowing that Intel made the 8086, 80286, 80386, and 80486 CPUs, you might wonder why the company didn't call the next generation *80586* instead of *Pentium*. The decision was a marketing one. In the United States of America, you cannot trademark a number. You cannot create a product called *9*, for example, and then say that no one else can use the number *9* to describe one of his or her products.
>
> Intel has had increasing competition from other CPU manufacturers, such as Cyrix and AMD. (One of their chips may be in your system unit.) These other manufacturers also make 8086, 80286, 80386, and 80486 chips, and also call them by those names, even though Intel invented the chips. By calling the "80586" the Pentium (the prefix *pent* meaning *five*), Intel has ended that imitation. No manufacturer can use that name, and Intel doubtlessly hopes that the name *Pentium* distinguishes its product from competitors' products.
>
> On the other hand, given Intel's recent troubles with the Pentium chip, competitors may come to appreciate the help in distancing their products from the flawed chip.

If the CPU does the computing, and the disk drives provide the "permanent" memory for a computer, this doesn't explain how the computer can "remember" anything that hasn't been saved to disk or why the computer "forgets" when you turn off the machine.

Random-Access Memory

If the computer's hard drive, floppy disks, and CD-ROMs are its long-term memory, its short-term memory is *random-access memory* (RAM). As an analogy for RAM, look at the guitar in figure 1.1.

Chapter 1 ◆ The Modern Computer and the Programmer

Figure 1.1
An analogy for RAM.

On a guitar you can play each string individually. If you want to play the second string from the bottom, for example, you don't have to play the four strings above it, or the one string below it. The strings are randomly accessible.

You can change the string's sound by pressing down between two of the frets on the guitar neck. This pressure does not change the other strings. And, no matter what you do, the string can have only one sound at any given point in time.

If you carry this analogy to the computer, RAM has many more strings than a guitar and many more possibilities than the 15 or so playable notes to which a guitar string is usually confined. The essential points, however, are the same. Any location in RAM can have only one value, and that value does not affect any other location.

Now, when you talk about a location in RAM, you really mean a physical place or *address* just as real as the frets on a guitar. RAM comes on chips smaller than the CPU, but each chip is divided into hundreds of thousands (or millions) of addresses. Each location is discrete—not influenced by the others—and can hold one of 256 values.

Delphi *By*
EXAMPLE

Why 256?

The smallest unit in RAM is stored as an electrical charge or as no charge, making a sort of electric switch that can be either one (charge) or zero (no charge). For this reason, modern computers are called *digital*. There's no in-between ground; the switch is either on or off. Eight of these switches make up a single address in RAM. This is the reason for the 256 range, as explained in the next section.

> **Note:** The zero/one switch is the basis for digital computers. All information on a digital computer system is created from combinations of this smallest of possibilities: zero or one. This zero/one possibility is called a *bit*. Eight bits is called a *byte*.
>
> Because each address has eight of these digital switches, the byte is the smallest amount of memory you can actually address.

Digital vs. Analog

Digital clocks are ubiquitous today, but despite many people's fears of 20 years ago, they have not replaced the analog clock. A digital clock shows the exact time—if it's 3:24, the clock shows the numbers 3:24. Analog clocks, of course, use hands on a dial to show the time. Reading an analog clock, you're as likely to say "a quarter to four" as "3:45."

If the computer were not digital but analog, working with it might be much easier. Instead of eight switches, a location in RAM could be more like a dial, with 10 levels of electrical charge. If a location in RAM were made of one of these dials, it could hold a number from 0 to 9. If you had two or three dials, the RAM location could hold numbers as high as 99 and 999, respectively. With eight locations, you have eight 9's, or 99,999,999. One RAM location could hold any of 100 million different values.

Put another way, one dial in this imaginary analog computer could hold 10^1 (ten to the first power). Two dials could hold 10^2; three dials, 10^3. A power indicates how many of the number you multiply together to get your answer. For example:

$10^1 = 10$ = 10 values (0–9)

$10^2 = 10 \times 10$ = 100 values (0–99)

$10^3 = 10 \times 10 \times 10$ = 1,000 values (0–999)

Unfortunately, computers are digital, which means that one switch can hold one of only two values, zero or one. With two and three switches, your computer can hold as many as four and eight values, respectively. For example:

$2^1 = 2$ = 2 values (0–1)

$2^2 = 2 \times 2$ = 4 values (0–3)

$2^3 = 2 \times 2 \times 2$ = 8 values (0–7)

13

Chapter 1 ◆ The Modern Computer and the Programmer

If you keep going, you finally have the answer to the question, "Why 256?"

$2^8 = 2 \times 2 \times 2 \times 2 \times 2 \times 2 \times 2 \times 2$ = 256 values (0–255)

Eight bits (2 to the eighth power) is called a *byte*. It is one location in RAM and is the fundamental unit of measurement in computers.

This series of numbers (2, 4, 8, 16, 32, etc.) is called *the powers of two*. As you program computers more, you'll get to know these numbers well. Because computers are based on zeros and ones—because they are digital—the powers of two come up often!

Measuring RAM

If you've ever wondered why when you turn off your machine it forgets everything you haven't saved to disk, now you know. RAM requires a constant flow of energy to maintain the electrical charge that represents all those zeros and ones.

You've learned that the fundamental unit of measurement in computers is the byte. Early on, computers evolved a greater storage capacity than could be measured in mere bytes. The first IBM PC measured its RAM in *kilobytes* (or *K*).

If you know your metric system at all, you know that a *kilo* is one thousand, and you probably figure that a kilobyte is 1,000 bytes. Almost. A kilobyte actually is 1,024 bytes. Why 1,024? Because it's close to 1,000 and it's a power of two.

$2^{10} = 1,024$

You may, therefore, hear someone say that 64K is 65,536 bytes. It's not 64 x 1,000—it's 64 x 1,024. The same is true of the original PCs that held up to 640K of memory. They actually held 655,360 bytes.

Computers grew faster than anyone expected them to, and kilobytes quickly became too small an amount to use as a measurement. The next level up from kilobytes is *megabytes* (or *M*).

Even though the prefix *mega* usually means one million, in computerese a megabyte is 1,048,576 bytes.

1,024 x 1,024

> **Note:** Just to confuse matters further, a megabyte is also sometimes considered to be 1,000 x 1,024 bytes. Sometimes it is even considered to be 1,000,000 bytes. Fortunately, the exact amount is seldom important.

In the early days of the PC, 640K of RAM was a power user's dream. Now you need 2M of RAM just to start Windows, and generally 8M to effectively run most Windows programs.

> This discussion of kilobytes and megabytes also applies to hard disk drives, although the smallest hard drive to be used on IBM PC-compatible machines was 10M. Currently, most hard drives these days have hundreds of megabytes.
>
> Some hard drives, however, have thousands of megabytes. The *gigabyte* (around 1,000M) drives are already becoming common, and are available for around $500.
>
> The next level up is *terabytes*, around 1,000G. Why would anyone need this much storage? One example is a good virtual reality system, which might require that much storage capacity for fluid three-dimensional animation.

Looking at Software

In the preceding section, you looked briefly at the CPU but you didn't really learn *how* the CPU knows what to do. *How* does it know what to draw on-screen? *How* does it know what to do with the mouse clicks? *How* does it give the computer the appearance of life?

> **Note:** "The appearance of life" is a good phrase to keep in mind. No matter what your computer does, someone somewhere has told it to do that. It is no more alive than a hammer or, perhaps a closer analogy, an automated assembly line. Like the assembly line, the computer moves and responds to things in its environment but only because someone has told it to do so.
>
> Because computers do things that have been programmed into them in the past, people tend to attribute intelligence or life to them. This tendency will only get worse as computers begin to understand the spoken word and speak back to users. Keep in mind that these capabilities must be programmed by a human being.

The answer is *software*. Software is a detailed list of instructions that the CPU must follow. If you've ever used a computer, you've worked with software. Windows, for example, is a piece of software.

Program vs. Data

Software that instructs the computer what to do is called a *program*. The Write word processor that comes with Windows is one example of a program. A program contains a list of instructions to the computer:

Chapter 1 ♦ The Modern Computer and the Programmer

*If the user types a letter, put that letter in RAM,
and show that letter on the screen.
If the user issues a command to save the current file,
write that file to the disk.*

Instructions written for the computer to understand are called *code*. The preceding example is an English-language description of code, sometimes called *pseudocode*, and is much easier to understand than actual code, unfortunately.

Also included in the category of software is *data*. Data does not instruct the computer to do anything; instead, it provides information to the software and the software user (you). If you write a letter by using Write, for example, the letter is data. Your letter does not tell the computer what to do; Write does.

Operating Systems

The biggest, most complicated program running on most computers is the *operating system* (OS). The OS is the first program to appear on any computer and it stays active until the machine is turned off.

One of the main purposes of the OS is to handle the hardware. For example, if Write wants to put a letter you typed on a disk, it gives the operating system the text of that letter and a name for that letter, and the operating system actually puts that file on the disk.

Without the operating system, every program in your computer would have to contain special instructions for writing to the hard disk. And every program would have to contain special instructions for writing to floppy disk drives. And, sometimes, different brands of drives require different instructions. A small word processing program such as Write would quickly become huge if it had to know all these details.

Operating systems handle the disk drives, monitor, printer, keyboard and mouse. The more capabilities an operating system has, the less work each program has to do.

DOS and Windows

You probably use Windows most of the time, but you also might use an operating system called DOS from time to time. DOS stands for *Disk Operating System*, although it handles more than just disks. DOS draws no pictures on-screen and doesn't respond to the mouse at all. If your computer runs on DOS, the first thing you see on-screen is the DOS command prompt, which looks like figure 1.2. DOS waits for the user to type a command and then responds to it—frequently with an error message because the user has typed the command wrong.

Figure 1.2
A command prompt under the Disk Operating System.

```
C:\
```

Compare this system with Windows, which is considerably easier to use. You don't need to memorize commands, you can use the mouse, and Windows is a lot nicer to look at than DOS. So why even mention DOS here? Because Windows is a program that runs under DOS!

That's right. It isn't fair to say that Windows is not an OS, because it does all the same things that an OS does. However, it cannot run without DOS running first. When you start your computer, you probably get a glimpse of something that looks like figure 1.2. Windows was added to DOS to make DOS easier to use. Some day, according to Microsoft (the company that makes Windows), Windows and DOS will be fused together into one OS.

Files and File Names

At this point, you might want to look at one of the most crucial functions performed by the operating system: file management.

Data saved to a disk is called a *file*, and every file must have a name. If your operating system didn't allow you to name your files, every time you wrote a letter in Write and then saved it, you would have a difficult time getting it back. You might have to go through every file on your disk to find it. Fortunately, Windows lets you name your files.

Windows imposes restrictions on what you can name a file, however. You can't, for example, name a file "Letter to my grandmother on her 80th birthday." The name can be no longer than eight characters—a character is a letter, number, or symbol and only some symbols are allowed. You can call your file LETTER80, for example, or GRAMMA80. The name may be followed by a *dot* (that is, a period) and up to three more letters, which are called the file's *extension*. The file extension often indicates what kind of file it is. Write data files, for example, usually end in WRI, so the letter might be named GRAMMA80.WRI.

A program typically has EXE as its extension, which is short for *executable*. If you see a file with the EXE extension, you know that it is a program and that you can execute it.

You can override extensions, but doing so is not generally a good idea. You can, for example, call the letter to your grandmother GRAMMA80.EXE, but you cannot execute it, and you might have difficulty remembering that it is a Write file. As a general rule, most programs add the appropriate extensions to file names for files used by that program, and you should not override them.

> You read earlier that an operating system reduces the work that individual programs must do. The restriction on the length of file names is one area where Windows is stuck right back with DOS. (For years, Novell's DOS has allowed file names to be much longer, but Microsoft—the leading seller of DOS—has never added that capability.) To make up for this deficiency, some programs allow you to add information about a file beyond the eight characters for the name that the program can subsequently read back to you when you look at it.
>
> If you save a file called GRAMMA80.WRI, for instance, your word processor might allow you to attach the following text: "A letter to my grandmother in honor of her 80th birthday." Then, when showing you a list of files, that program places the attached text next to the file name.
>
> What's wrong with this approach? First, each program has to attach the text on its own. Second, each program is essentially blind to the data that another one wrote. If you use a different word processor, for example, your letter is back to being GRAMMA80.WRI without any explanatory text. After enough time has passed, you may not remember whether this file is a letter to your grandmother or a grammar lesson.

In this book, you occasionally are referred to specific files; the name of the file, usually without the extension, appears in uppercase. (Delphi assigns file extensions automatically.)

Directories

Key to the concept of file management is the *directory*. If you compare an electronic file to a real-world file, the directory is like a file cabinet or a folder. A directory can contain many separate files and is an indispensable tool for organization. And, unlike a real-world file cabinet, a directory can contain any number of other directories that, in turn, can contain any number of directories of their own.

Understanding the importance of directories is not hard. Say your hard disk drive holds 130M of information, which makes it relatively small by today's standards. But it has over 1,000 files on it. If you had to look for one file by picking through all 1,000 files, your ability to cope would be greatly reduced, not to mention your efficiency and productivity.

The OS provides directories for you and the programs you use. From the hard disk's standpoint, the disk contains just a bunch of data—it doesn't even distinguish between one file and the next. And without the operating system directories and your clever file names, files would be completely unmanageable on a large system.

Directories have the same name limitations that files have—eight characters followed optionally by a three-character extension. (Directory names appear in full and in uppercase throughout this book.)

Directories can contain sub-directories. To describe a file within a specific directory and sub-directory in this book, names will be shown together, separated by a backslash. For example, if you read "Load \DELPHI\EXAMPLES\LISTBOX\LISTBOX.PRJ," that would mean to load the file LISTBOX.PRJ located in the LISTBOX sub-directory of the EXAMPLES sub-directory of the DELPHI directory.

Example: The Windows File Manager

To help you understand directories, open the Windows Main icon. (You open an icon by double-clicking on it.) Open the File Manager icon, which is located in the Main program group.

File Manager presents you with a view of your disk drive. The hard disk that you are currently using is at the top, probably called C, or possibly D or E, or even some other letter. Underneath that is a tree showing all the other directories on your disk—if you have many directories, you might not be able to see them all at once.

The topmost directory is called the *root* directory. If programs (and you) never created any directories, everything would go in the root directory, and you would never be able to find anything.

Notice that the directories are represented by icons that look like file folders. Using File Manager, you can look at files within a directory merely by selecting the folder. You select a folder by clicking on it or using the cursor keys to move up and down. To the right of the directory tree is a list of the files and directories that are in the selected directory. (The directories within a directory are called *sub-directories*.) As a general rule, it's a good idea to keep as few things in the root directory as possible because it's hard to find them there. If you put your letters to grandma and your checkbook statements all in the root directory, you aren't really taking advantage of the whole directory concept.

Look through the various directories on your disk. You may recognize some of them as having been created by specific programs. Word for Windows, for example, creates a directory called WINWORD. Windows itself creates a directory called WINDOWS.

If you have a directory named DELPHI, you've already installed Delphi. You can see that Delphi set up several subdirectories when you installed it. (If you haven't installed it, don't worry—Chapter 3, "Introducing Delphi," covers installing and running Delphi.)

You need a place to work on the examples in the upcoming chapters, so create a directory now that you can use later. Make sure you are in the root directory. Select File from the menu bar above the directory tree, and from the menu that appears, select Create Directory. Type **BOOKPAS** and press Enter. BOOKPAS appears as a new directory under the root. If you open this directory, you see that it doesn't contain any files.

Summary

Software is any detailed set of instructions (called code) that tell the computer what to do. A program is one particular piece of software. Data is the information from which the program operates. DOS, Windows, and other operating systems are just extremely complex programs that simplify tasks for other programs. File and directory names under DOS and Windows can be as long as eight characters and can also have a three-character extension. Files usually have specific extensions that describe what kind of files they are. And directories are places to put files.

Review Questions

1. What is the true computer inside the computer called?
2. How does the computer remember things?
3. What is a byte? What is the range of values that can be expressed with one byte?
4. What animates the computer?
5. Give an example of a file name.
6. How do directories help make it possible to find files? Which is the root directory?
7. Name an operating system. Is Windows an operating system?
8. What are the instructions to the computer called?
9. Does a data file contain instructions to the computer?
10. What are file extensions? How are they used?
11. How many bytes are in a megabyte?

CHAPTER 2

Traditional Programming

In the preceding chapter, you learned that programs are lists of instructions to the computer. As you might have guessed, these instructions can be quite involved. For example, the number of instructions in a piece of software such as Windows, can be a dizzying thought indeed—particularly when you consider that an instruction like the following can't be written in English:

```
If the user double-clicks, open the object under the mouse pointer
```

Instructions like this require thousands of explicit instructions to the computer and are written by programmers. In the preceding chapter, you learned that as operating systems get more complex and do more of the work, programmers are required to do less. As a result, you'll do things in this book just to *learn* about programming that would have been considered spectacular a few years ago.

Before you look at modern programming, however, it's important to look briefly at how programming was done yesterday. Along the way, you'll explore some concepts that will be important to you later.

The Machine's Language

The CPU, as you know, is the part of the computer that actually computes. The instructions on which the CPU operates are microscopic. For example, look at the following:

```
Put the number 4 in Box A
Put the number 3 in Box B
Add Box B and Box A together
Store the Result in Location C
```

Believe it or not, all the operations the CPU performs are this small. Because `Location C` can be a place on-screen or a file on disk or output to a printer, you can see how you might be able to build a program this way. Doing so is a lot of work, however, and is made even more difficult because you can't actually use English phrases like `Put the number 4 in Box A`. A command like `Put a number into someplace` would have a number value, such as 40. Using numbers for commands is called *machine language*. This same program written in machine language might look like the following:

```
40 04 01 40 03 02 62 01 02 41 02 03
```

This program isn't real, but a simulation of what a program in machine language might look like. People actually used to program this way.

The Assembler

Some relief came for programmers in the form of assemblers. An *assembler* is a program that enables you to deal with machine language through a set of more easily remembered names. The previous program, for example, might become the following:

```
LDA 4
LDB 3
ADD A, B
MOV B, C
```

An assembler takes those commands and turns them into machine language. Still, you're talking about doing very small things. When you consider the sheer number of instructions it takes to set up a simple message box that says "Hello," you can see that even with an assembler, it is a tremendous undertaking.

> Many people still program in assembler because with assembler it is possible to produce the fastest, most efficient code possible. Delphi, in fact, comes with a built-in assembler for advanced programmers who want to streamline their code.
>
> 99 percent of all programming tasks are best done in a more comprehensible language such as Delphi, of course; but, for high-performance programs like games, that 1 percent can make all the difference in the world.

Compilers

The computer can use nothing else but machine language. People quickly realized, however, that the dozens of instructions used to display a little bit of text on-screen could be encapsulated and given an English or near-English name. In fact, you could save tremendous work by building a *programming language* where each word in the language represented a number of machine language instructions.

Programming languages are a result of this kind of thinking and therefore are different from each other. Everyone has an opinion about what is the best way to work, and many of these people decide to make up a language that reflects their opinions. Here are just some of the words used in various languages to display something to the user:

```
Write
Print
Display
Say
sprintf
Put
```

You may think that these differences are dumb or that they make computer languages hard to learn. In fact, once you understand the basic concepts of programming, you begin to look for the similarities in languages. This book teaches Delphi, which uses the word Write to display something. After learning Delphi, you then could easily apply what you learned to BASIC. One of the first things you would learn is how similar the languages are. BASIC uses the word Print to display something. You might be surprised how easily you can learn other languages after you learn Delphi, but the truth is, most computer languages are more similar to each other than dissimilar.

The CPU itself doesn't understand the command Write, and Write must somehow be turned into machine language. The program that turns the easily understood commands such as Write into machine language is called a *compiler*. This book deals with the specific compiler that works with Delphi.

In this book you won't learn much more detail about the compiler than to be appropriately grateful that it exists and that it removes much of the tedium of programming. Modern compilers do more than turn typewritten words into machine language, however. Consider writing a program to display a dialog box like any of the ones you've used in Windows—say, the Control Panel's font dialog box. If you were to write the program in English, it might look something like the following:

```
Draw a box that is 5 inches across and 4 inches down.
Draw a box about 2 inches across and half an inch down
  about a quarter of an inch from the right-hand border
  and mark it "OK."
Draw a box about an inch below that, the same size,
  and mark it "Cancel."
```

After you type these instructions, you must *compile* the program—that is, run the instructions through the compiler, which turns them into machine language—and then run the program to see whether you got it right. You want to talk tedium? Getting all these measurements right and positioning everything right on-screen can take hours or days of work.

Delphi, however, enables you to put things on-screen by using the mouse. With Delphi you design visually, by actually seeing what the final product will look like as you progress. Using Delphi saves enormous amounts of time, and can even simplify the task of learning Delphi.

The World's Shortest Pascal Program (Almost)

The following code is the world's shortest Delphi program. Well, almost.

```
program First;
begin
   end.
```

The first line is not strictly necessary with Delphi. That line is more of an indication to you, the programmer, that what follows is a program. You should always begin a program with the word `program` followed by the program name.

Your computer has certain requirements about how programs should start and stop. By putting `begin` and `end.` in a file, you tell the compiler that these instructions are a program. The compiler then turns them into the necessary machine language instructions. This process is similar to an airplane taxiing for takeoff: The airport's requirements must be met before the plane can actually use the runway.

The concepts of `begin` and `end` are important. Every computer program starts, and every computer program stops. (As you learn later, sometimes programs get lost on their way to the `end` and cannot be stopped except by turning off the computer or by asking Windows to stop them for you.) What happens in between, however, has changed radically since the beginning of computer programming.

A Brief History of the User Interface

When computers were first invented, they weren't much like the tool you use now. They were as big as houses and as expensive as a hundred houses. The mouse did not exist, and no programmer expected someone to be sitting at the computer typing something in response to what the computer did. As a result, what went between the beginning and the end of a computer program was almost always something like the following:

```
Read a file in
Do something with that file
Write the new file out
```

This original user *interface*—the original way that computers interacted with their users—was used for decades. Everything was set up in advance. The user basically started the program with some values—such as the location of the file—and then had to wait for it to stop.

Many DOS programs still work on this principle. Although it may seem odd to you that this system persists even today, consider this situation: What if your Aunt Veronica gives you a list of names and addresses from her old word processor, and she wants you (the only computer genius she knows) to put these names and addresses in order. You can use a program that forces you to retype the information and put it in order as each name is typed—the interactive method—or you can use a program that runs just like the preceding program:

```
Read in the address file
Sort the address file
Write the address file out
```

Sometimes a little bit of user interface goes a long way.

By the time the Delphi language was invented, direct keyboard communication was more common. Computer monitors were less common (than they are now) and those that existed were nothing like the ones on which you run Windows today. Printers also were less capable, being little more than mechanical typewriters. In fact, monitors and printers were essentially interchangeable. A computer program in that era prompted users for information and allowed them to make choices while the program was running. Here's what such a program might look like, with the user's typing appearing in bold monospace type:

```
Please Enter Your Name?
Blake
Hello, Captain BLAKE.
There are three enemy vessels present.
Please make a selection:
1) Move your starship.
2) Fire your weapons.
3) Flee this sector.
Your choice?
Q
Error on input. Re-enter.
3
Fleeing like the cowards we are.
Would you like to see a map of the Galaxy , Captain BLAKE (Yes or No)?
Y
Please answer with a 'Yes' or a 'No'
```

Don't laugh. The preceding isn't output from an actual program, but many programs were far less sophisticated than this one. Giving the user a choice after the program had started was quite a leap forward. But, as you might imagine, the programs were written the same as always. The preceding program might begin as follows:

```
begin
Write "Please enter your name?" on the screen.
Read the user's name from the keyboard
Write "Hello, Captain" the user's name here
Write "There are three enemy vessels present."
Write "Please make a selection:"
Write "1) Move your starship"
```

At some point, the program ran out of instructions and stopped. Users had little control over how the program moved. If, for example, they were prompted for a 1, 2, or 3, but wanted a map of the galaxy, they were out of luck; they had to wait to be asked by the program. Granted, this example is just a game, but similar problems occurred in serious programs.

This sort of user interface was used for years by, well, computer nerds. However, as computers got into the hands of the common man, it became clear that the interface was inadequate. Users wanted to be in control of the program, not the other way around.

User-Controlled Programs

The concept of the user being in control, although perhaps obvious to you, required a considerable amount of technology. The truth is, programmers found it easier to write programs that didn't interact with the user. Even DOS barely interacted with the user, and not very nicely at that. After you started a program in DOS, for example, the OS was virtually lost to you. You had to leave that program before you could look at a directory or do anything that DOS let you do. You were at that program's mercy.

Now, under Windows, you can almost always get away from a program—you can hide a program in the background and come back to it later. From this comparison, you can see that even operating systems have evolved along the same standard as other programs. The operating systems used to be hard to use and control, and now they're relatively easy. What was it that made this shift possible?

The concept behind the shift in computer use is *events*. What's an event? In computer terms, an event is something that happens—anything, really. Pressing a key is an event. Moving the mouse is an event. The computer has an internal clock that "ticks" about 18 times per second; a tick of that clock also is an event. If your printer runs out of paper, that's an event.

What do events mean to programmers? In the past, programmers wrote programs that looked like the following:

```
begin
    Do something;
    Do something else
    Get some input from the user
    Do another thing
    end.
```

There was an inexorable path through the program. The computer demanded user input at a certain time and acted on that. Any events that occurred when the program was not checking for them were ignored (or possibly saved for a later time when the program did check for them)! The process is almost barbaric when you think about it. Following this path certainly made it difficult for you to tell the program whether you had changed your mind about something.

Now programs look something like the following:

```
begin
   If an event has occurred, then handle that event appropriately;
     otherwise, continue with any current activities.
   If the user has not ordered the program to end, then go back and check
     for the next event.
end.
```

What isn't expressed in the preceding program is that if there are no current activities, the program does nothing except leave users free to do whatever they want to do next. No single part of the program hogs the computer, and the user is in complete control.

> **Caution:** Keep in mind that badly behaving programs do exist. These programs do monopolize the machine and do not leave the user in charge. In such cases, the user actually might have to turn off the machine to get the offending program to release Windows. Obviously, you are not taught to write programs like that in this book. As operating systems increase in power, they are more able to remove these offending programs from their systems or just ignore them. More advanced operating systems are superior to Windows in this regard, but Windows is light-years ahead of DOS, which actually *expects* to be monopolized by a single program.

Introducing the Object

One of the things that has made this revolution in programming possible is the *object*. Computers are more or less simulations of the real world. A word processor is a simulation of a typewriter. An accounting program is a simulation of a ledger. A flight simulator is a simulation of an airplane. People eventually realized that instead of writing programs around actions, such as "do this" or "do that," they could write programs around things. The computer instructions became commands to the things—the objects—and programs started to change. The following example shows how events come into the program and are handled by an object:

Chapter 2 ◆ Traditional Programming

```
begin
    if an event has occurred, then send it to the appropriate object
end
```

The events are consequently handled by the appropriate object:

```
Airplane: If the user has pulled back the throttle, go up.
Airplane: If the user has pushed the throttle forward, go down.
Airplane: If the user has pressed eject, open the cockpit.
```

You do everything in Delphi by using objects. Throughout this book, you deal with all the same objects that you've used in Windows every day. A window, for example, "knows" how to close itself and does so when you double-click on the system menu icon. When you click on a button, it "knows" how to draw itself as if it were being pressed physically.

What does it mean that the object "knows" something? It simply means that, in the past, programmers wrote instructions like the following:

```
If the user has clicked the mouse
    on the system icon, open the System menu
    on the maximize icon, make the window large
    on the TrueType button, put up the TrueType dialog
```

The programmers put all the instructions to handle all the events in one place. This list might be huge; the program had to know and explicitly state all the possibilities for a mouse click.

With objects, the event goes to the button itself (or the system icon or the maximize button), and the object contains the necessary instructions:

```
button: If the mouse is clicked, redraw myself as depressed.
system icon: If double-clicked, then close the window.
maximize icon: If clicked, grow the window to full size.
```

The button doesn't know anything about the system menu icon or the system icon, and, in fact, doesn't need to know or care about anything but itself and the user. And the main part of the program, which used to have to list all the possibilities now for all events that might occur at any time in the future, does not have to include any deatils on what happens when the user clicks a button.

Although it may seem obvious, even natural, that instructions be associated with an object, to computer programmers used to writing programs like the following, this concept was as foreign a notion as they could imagine.

```
begin
    Do this;
    Do something else;
    Do one last thing;
end.
```

In fact, some programmers still insist that objects are a fad—but then, some people thought automobiles were a fad, too.

Real-World Objects

How do you describe objects in the real world? If someone points to this book and says "What is that object?," what would you say? You might respond by saying, "It's a book." If the person doesn't know what a book is, you then might list the things that distinguish books from other objects: cover, pages, binding, and so on. But if the person then sees a magazine, he or she might get confused. Is it a book, too? Well, no, but the two are similar.

Human beings often take for granted the ability to distinguish between objects. We can tell the difference between a book and a magazine, between a hardcover and a softcover book, between a large book and a small book, and even (usually) between a fiction book and a nonfiction book. We also can distinguish the similarities: they all have pages, they all have writing on them or are meant to be written on, and so on.

Object Classes

The computer has no capability to understand objects. The Delphi compiler, however, enables you to describe objects in ways that are useful to you and that make programming easier.

Some zoologists do nothing else but classify animals as "members of the dog family" or "members of the ape family." As a programmer, you classify objects as belonging together and thereby reduce the work needed to describe similar objects.

If you were to describe a book in terms of pages, a cover, and a binding, for example, you could later describe a magazine to the compiler as "like a book, only with these differences." You might consider the magazine to be part of the book family, or you might more correctly classify both in the family of "printed materials."

Example: Windows Objects

You use computer objects all the time if you use Windows. The icons that appear in the Program Manager are objects (see fig. 2.1). Notice how they open a window when you double-click on them? These objects are related.

Chapter 2 ♦ Traditional Programming

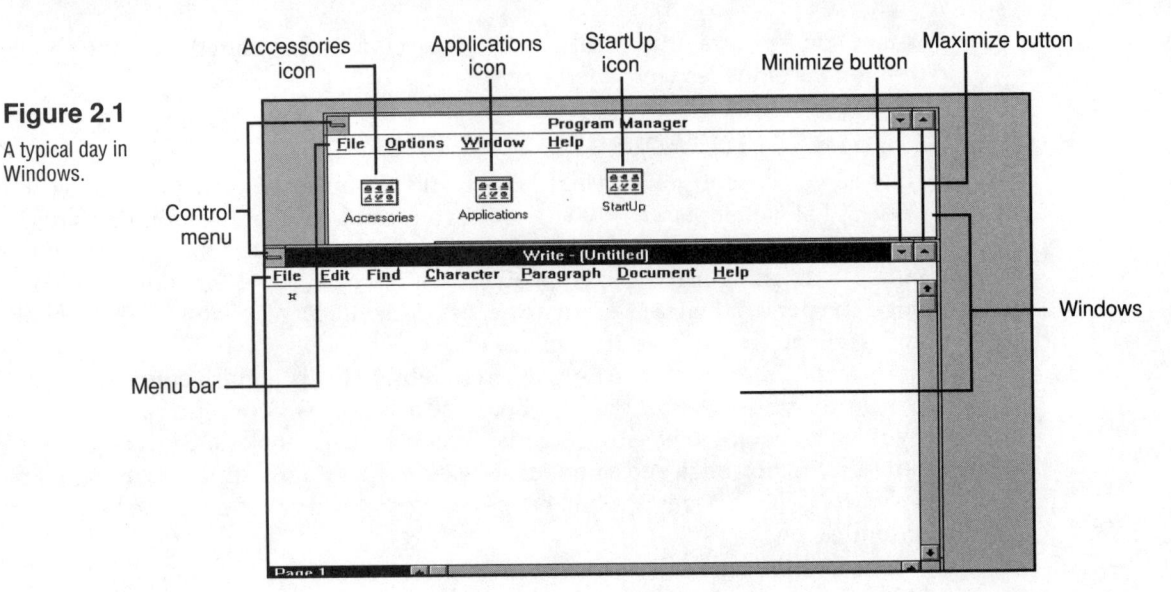

Figure 2.1
A typical day in Windows.

[Figure shows Program Manager window with callouts: Accessories icon, Applications icon, StartUp icon, Minimize button, Maximize button, Control menu, Menu bar, Windows]

What about the windows themselves? You can resize them or zoom them or move them around the screen. These objects are related, too, even though they may have different things inside them.

What about the things inside windows? The system menu icon, the maximize button, the minimize button, and the menu bar seem to be present in just about every window you open—and act the same regardless of whether you're running Write or working out of the Program Manager. These things all seem to be objects as well. And you can guess that a menu bar in Write is probably related to the menu bar in Program Manager.

These objects are in the same *class*—the class of menu bars, the class of windows, or whatever. In computer terms, objects are grouped together under classes and are distinguished from one another by their *properties*.

Object Properties

You belong to the class of human beings. You have a brain, a heart, and a myriad of other things in common with other human beings. You also have a host of properties that distinguish you from other humans.

You may have more or less hair than someone else has, a different eye color, more fillings in your teeth, less facial hair, shorter body length, a different gender, and so on. You have a different name than others, different initials, a different family and background, and a different job. Yet, even if all these properties were identical between you and other humans, you would still be different because you and other humans occupy a different physical space.

If you're asked to describe the properties of an object in real life, you'll probably miss the most obvious one. For example, if you have two copies of this book (please feel free to buy a second copy for this experiment) how do you distinguish one from the other? By where they are physically.

No two objects in the real world are identical because they must at least be in different places. The same is true in Windows. You can open two Write windows, load the same document in them, and maximize them both, but you can't see them both at once because one is on top of the other. Not physically, of course, but from Windows's standpoint one has to be drawn over the other. To keep objects from being drawn in the same space, Windows creates the illusion that your screen is like a desk with papers on it. You can stack and rearrange them, you can even put them side by side, but they can't both appear in the same space.

> **Tip:** Location is a property.

You might distinguish two otherwise identical copies of this book in one other way. Have you ever had this dialogue with someone?

"Have you seen my book?"

"Which book?"

"The one I'm reading."

You see here another way that you distinguish between objects—whether or not they are the focus of your attention. You may have no idea what book your friend is talking about—you don't know where her attention is focused. As a programmer, you use the concept of which window is currently on top or where the mouse is clicked to figure out where the user's attention is currently focused.

Example: Focus in Write

For this example, open two copies of Write. Place them side by side. Now type **Hello**. The text appears in one of the windows on-screen. It is the *focused* window—the one on which you're currently focused.

Now click on the other window and pay attention to the band across the top (the title bar) that reads Write - (Untitled). Notice that the color of the title bar changes. Windows makes the window that you are focused on more prominent than others. Type **Hello** again. The text then appears in the newly focused window.

Example: Focus in the Fonts Dialog

For this example, go to the Program Manager, double-click on Main, and then double-click on the Control Panel. (The Control Panel contains all the options that you can set for Windows.) Now double-click on the icon marked Fonts. The Fonts dialog box appears, as shown in figure 2.2.

Figure 2.2

The Fonts dialog box.

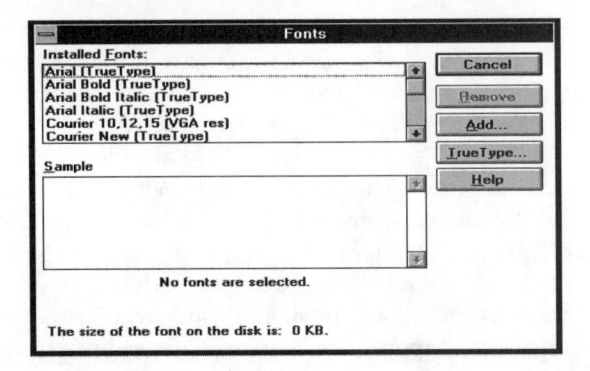

Of the two boxes in this dialog box, one contains a list of installed fonts and the other shows a sample of the currently selected font. (Press the spacebar and use the cursor keys to select a font.) Press Tab repeatedly. Notice how the buttons on the right surround their text with a dotted-line box? This dotted line indicates the current focus—Windows' impression of where you're focusing your attention.

No matter where you've tabbed to, you can always change the focus instantly to some other area by using the mouse. For example, tab to the installed fonts box and then click on the TrueType button. The TrueType dialog box appears; Windows responds to your direction immediately.

Windows and Delphi take care of all this work for you, so why should I even bring it up? Because it underscores how far the user interface has come. For example, in the past, programmers wrote programs that were virtually unaware of the user; today, programmers write programs that are concerned with where the user's attention is focused. In the future, focus may be controlled not just by the mouse but also by a device that actually tracks the movement of the user's eye.

Anything that distinguishes one object from another is a property. This includes location, size, color, and whether or not the user is focused on it. In programming, you take the same standard objects, such as those used in the Program Manager and Write, and alter the properties of those objects to make new programs.

Object Behavior

Besides properties, one other aspect of an object distinguishes it from others: its *behavior*. Behavior can be divided into two areas. The first area is *cosmetic*: A button, when clicked, draws itself as though it were actually being pressed. This behavior is cosmetic—most buttons in any program will act this way—and really has no effect on the program.

The second area is *functional*: A button, when clicked, can call up a new window, print a document, play a tune, or whatever. This behavior is *intrinsic* to the program. It is part of the program's functionality.

Generally, you don't change the cosmetic behavior of objects. You usually want your buttons to react outwardly the same as other buttons in other programs. The functional behavior of the button, however, is where you do most of your programming. The changes you make here actually define what your programs are and what they do.

Summary

Programs are detailed lists of instructions to the computer. These instructions are written by programmers, usually in a language that resembles English. A compiler turns the English-like language into a series of numbers that represent instructions the computer can understand. These numbers are called machine language.

The world's shortest Delphi program is

```
begin
    end.
```

These two lines tell the compiler that you're going to write a program, and the compiler then generates the necessary machine language instructions for you to prepare for the program to follow.

Programs have gone from being virtually oblivious to their users to allowing users some control over them to allowing users nearly complete control over them almost all the time. The way the computer interacts with the user is called the user interface.

Programs allow the user this control through the recognition of events. An event is anything done by the user or the computer that a program should respond to. Programs have been further simplified by allowing instructions to be packaged into objects, which are computer simulations of real-world things. Objects have properties, such as where they are and what they look like, and they have behaviors, such as what they do when the user clicks on them. You program in Delphi by creating and changing objects.

Review Questions

1. What are programs? Who writes them? Is Windows a program?
2. Are programs written in English?
3. What's an event? Name some common events in Windows.
4. What's an object? Name some common objects in Windows.
5. What are object properties?
6. What are object behaviors?

Chapter 2 ◆ Traditional Programming

7. What is the world's shortest Delphi program?
8. What is the word program used for in Delphi?
9. What converts an English-like language into instructions the computer understands?
10. What language does the computer understand? What does it look like?
11. In the past, how did computers display their output?
12. What is an assembler?
13. What is a class?
14. Explain the concept of focus.

Part II

Working in the Delphi Environment

CHAPTER 3

Introducing Delphi

Delphi is the tool you use to learn the Object Pascal language. This chapter shows you how to install, start, and stop Delphi, and also how to go about setting up Delphi so that you can begin to do some useful programming.

Installing and Running Delphi

Installing Delphi is straightforward. Insert the disk labelled "Install" into the appropriate disk drive, open the File Manager, and click on the icon for the appropriate drive. From the list of files presented, double-click on INSTALL.EXE.

> **Note:** According to the documentation, Delphi will run on any machine that runs Windows 3.1. You will need about 35 megabytes of free disk space for the basic version and about 30 megabytes more for the Client/Server Edition of Delphi. You should have a computer with at least 8M of RAM and a CPU no slower than an 80386 33 Mhz. With anything smaller, you may become frustrated with Delphi's speed and performance.
>
> Programmers usually require more memory and disk space than other users, as well as faster machines, so you should keep that in mind when buying or upgrading your computer.

For example, if your A Drive is a 5 1/4-inch disk drive—the larger of the two common formats—then you would put the disk in the A drive, click on the A icon in the File Manager and then double-click on INSTALL.EXE.

The Delphi install program (like other Borland products) shows a picture of an automobile dashboard and a road stretching out to infinity. On the dashboard is a "speedometer" that tells you how far in the installation process you have gotten.

Before you actually go through the process of installing, however, you must answer a few questions. Life is easiest if you take the defaults provided.

After you answer the vital questions, the install program will begin installing Delphi on your hard drive. It will periodically tell you to remove and insert disks, and the installation process could take a while, so bring a book.

> **Tip:** If you have a CD-ROM drive, and purchased Delphi on CD-ROM, the installation process is the same—except you don't have to do any disk swapping and you can leave the room or take a nap while the installation is running!

Delphi puts *hundreds* of files on your hard disk. Some of these files are programs—additional tools that will allow you to make your code better—while others are sample programs showing you how to do certain things.

The only files that are likely to be of interest to you immediately after finishing the book are the files found in the C:\DELPHI\EXAMPLES directory. These files are programs that, in themselves, are mini-educational documents.

After you gain the basic understanding of Delphi that this book will provide, you'll be able to learn from at least some of these programs. (Others are bound to be quite complex.) A good approach to take is to run these programs and see whether any of them do things that you would like to know how to do. Then look at the code (provided by Borland) to learn *how* they were done.

This kind of informal education has served programmers from the beginning of computer time, and once you finish this book it will be open to you as well.

If installation and setup went well, you should discover a new program group in Program Manager. The Delphi group contains a number of tools for writing your own programs, but the one with which you'll spend most of your time in this book is called Delphi, appropriately enough.

Elements of a Delphi Program

In the old days of programming, getting started was really easy—you typed code into a text editor, saved it, and had the compiler compile it. But those steps were a long way from getting something as fancy as a Windows program.

When you start Delphi by double-clicking on the Delphi icon, you are greeted by a complex, cluttered screen (see fig. 3.1) that can be overwhelming at first, especially if you try to take it in all at once. In the following sections, you look at each of the on-screen objects broadly, in terms of how they relate to a Delphi program. In the next chapter, you get your hands dirty working with the tools, and then you start programming.

Figure 3.1
The Delphi environment.

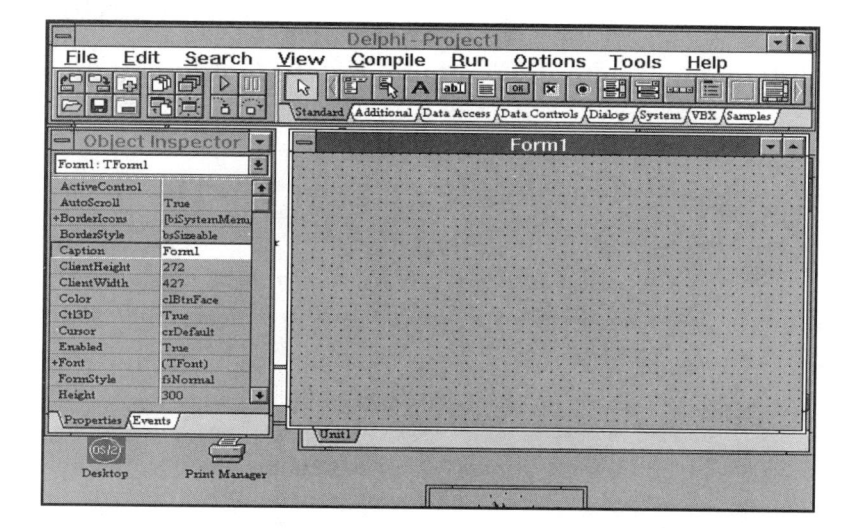

> **Note:** Screen shots provided with this book may look different from your screen for a number of reasons. However, these differences should be superficial and shouldn't prevent you from getting the point of the figures.

The Form

The most prominent item on the Delphi screen is a window filled with tiny dots (see fig. 3.2). This window is the *form designer*, or just *form* for short. A form is really just a window, like all the other windows you've learned about. It's an object and has properties and behavior that you can change.

Chapter 3 ◆ Introducing Delphi

Figure 3.2
The form.

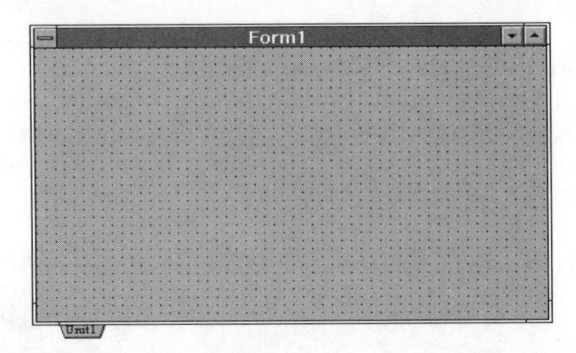

Mostly, however, the form is where you put all your other objects—all the buttons and scroll bars and icons go here. Using Delphi, you also can add a menu bar to your window.

Delphi always starts you off with a blank form named Form1. You can change this name, as you learn later in this chapter. With the form, you control how your program looks.

The Code Editor

A program, of course, is more than just a screen design. You must add code to give the program functionality. Underneath the form, mostly obscured, is the Code Editor.

If you click on the Code Editor to bring it to the foreground, you notice that it already has code in it (see fig. 3.3). Delphi eases the challenge of programming by adding certain necessary code to every program. Do not read this code! By the end of the book, you'll have learned what all of this code means. For now, ignore it.

> **Note:** If you're coming from Visual BASIC or a similar tool, you may notice that Delphi doesn't restrict how much of the code you can see. In Delphi's Code Editor, you can see your entire program at any time!

Figure 3.3
The code window.

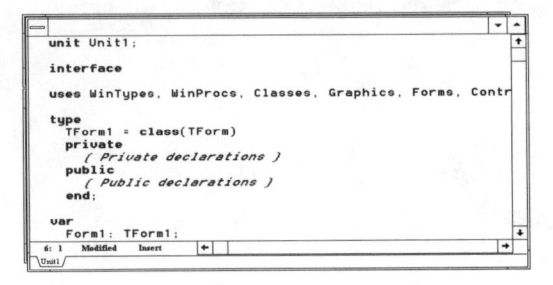

Units and Forms

At the bottom of the Code Editor, notice the tab. The Code Editor is capable of "holding" many files. That is, you can use the Code Editor to edit more than one file at a time. Each file is represented as a tab along the bottom of the window so that you can easily switch back and forth by using the mouse or by pressing Ctrl+Tab.

When you start Delphi, or when you select New Project from the File menu, Delphi gives you a project that is composed of exactly one window (or *form*), called Form1, and one unit, called Unit1. Unit1 will describe the behavior that Form1 has that is new to it (and not simply carried over from a standard window).

To begin with, Form1 starts out with the same behavior found in other windows. As a programmer, you may want to change that behavior, and Unit1 is where you will write the code that describes how Form1 is different from other windows.

Unit1 and Form1 are saved as two separate files on disk. The code in Unit1 would be saved as UNIT1.PAS ("PAS" as in "**Pas**cal"). The Form1 file, which contains a description of the form that you paint on-screen, would be called UNIT1.DFM ("DFM" for "**D**elphi **F**or**M**"). Of course, you can change the name from UNIT1.

Sometimes code units have no associated forms. You can have a unit, for example, that sorts things or accesses a database such as Paradox or dBASE. This kind of code unit doesn't need to draw anything on-screen. Delphi allows for code units that have no associated forms.

The Project

Delphi uses a third type of file, called a *project file*. A project file is just another file containing Pascal code, with one important distinction: Every program you write in Pascal will have *exactly one* project file. Your programs may have many units, but the project file is what is traditionally called the *main program file.* (You'll look at one below and see that it very much resembles the World's Shortest Delphi program shown in the last chapter.)

Delphi does not start out showing the project's code window for your program. Why? Because Delphi automatically generates this file for you, and you generally won't want to change it. Nonetheless, for your earliest examples, you'll want to get to know this file.

A *project* in Delphi is code that unifies all the code units and forms that ultimately make up the program. In the upcoming pages, you design forms and write code and, if you're a good programmer, you will often design forms and write code that can be used in more than one program. Suppose, for example, that you write a program to play Poker and design a form to simulate a card table—maybe with an icon representing the dealer. You might want to use this same card table later to create a program to play Blackjack.

Chapter 3 ♦ Introducing Delphi

Working with the Project Manager

Projects enable you to use multiple forms and units in your code, but they also give you a way to keep track of your programs. When you start Delphi, it gives you a new project, complete with a blank form and matching unit code file. However, for reasons explained in the previous section, it doesn't automatically show you the project code.

One way to open the project code is through *Project Manager*. The Project Manager is a special window that you can activate by selecting View from the menu bar and Project Manager from the pull-down menu.

Figure 3.4
The Project Manager.

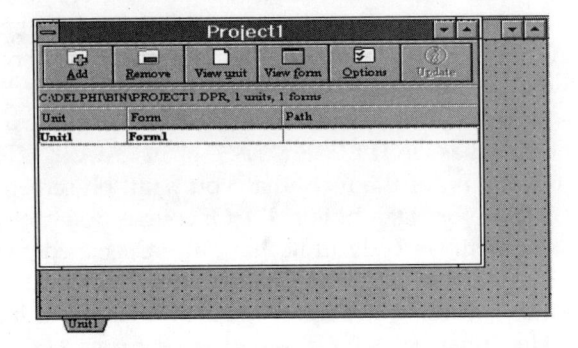

Click the right mouse button on the Project Manager and a pop-up (or *context*) menu appears. From this menu, select View project. This action brings the code window to the foreground, showing something that should look suspiciously like the World's Shortest Delphi program. (Don't try to figure what the code means just yet.)

> **Tip:** You can also see the project code by selecting from the View menu, "Project Source."

> **Note:** Notice that after "Unit1" the code window gets a new tab that reads "Project1."

The Project Manager has its own toolbar at the top and its own popup menu, as you have seen, which allows it to manipulate the units and forms of a project. About the only thing you can't do with the Project Manager is load an existing project or start a new one. Of course, you might realize that you could just shut Delphi down and start it again if you wanted a new project, but that is cumbersome, and you will often want to work on an existing project.

Example: Loading a Project

To open a project you've worked on before, pull down the File menu and choose Open Project. A standard Windows File dialog box appears, enabling you to pick a project from existing projects on disk. For now, select DELPHI\DEMOS\DRAGDROP\DRAGDROP.DPR.

> **Tip:** The DPR extension stands for **D**elphi **PR**oject.

A new form and also a code window with a fair amount of code in it is loaded. Delphi keeps track of what you do within a project. If you change anything about this project—say, add some text to the code window—Delphi keeps track of your changes. If you then try to load DRAGDROP.DPR again, Delphi warns you and asks you whether you want to save the current project.

This request is important for two reasons. First, it means that you'll always have a warning if you try to open a project when you haven't saved the current one—Delphi lets you work on only one project at a time. Second, it means that if you ever accidentally make a damaging mistake to your project that you can't undo, then you can reload the project from the disk to restore it.

Example: Creating a New Project

To create a new project, you can choose New Project from the File menu. If you made changes to the current project, Delphi asks you whether you want to save them. If not, it opens a code window and a blank form for you to work with, just as when you first started it.

You can also choose Open Project and type in a name that doesn't already exist. Follow these steps:

1. From the File menu, choose Open Project.

2. Open the directory that you created in Chapter 1—BOOKPAS. It's still empty, but you're about to remedy that situation.

3. Type **First** under File Name and press Enter. Delphi adds the DPR extension to your project file.

These steps produce a simpler screen than the one you've been working with. No form or code window appears at all, and instead you get the Project Manager. Using the Project Manager, you can add forms and units, as you'll learn in the following sections.

Chapter 3 ◆ Introducing Delphi

Example: Saving Projects

To save the current project, choose Save Project from the File menu. If you have a name for your project, as you do here with First, Delphi saves the project without prompting. If your project name is still Project1, Delphi prompts for a different file name. Also, if you have a unit open as Unit1, Delphi asks for a name for the unit.

You can also rename a project by using the Save Project As option. If you have saved the project under one name (for example, FIRST) and then save it under another (for example, SECOND), Save Project As will not delete the FIRST project. (You must delete it yourself with File Manager or whatever tool you use.) This approach enables you to copy a project file effectively.

> **Note:** Delphi automatically determines the correct extensions for projects and units. Although you are not required to maintain the project extension (DPR) or the unit extension (PAS), changing the extensions does make working in the environment more difficult. In this book, all examples use the default extensions.

Example: Adding Forms to Projects

As stated previously, if you are a *good* programmer, you will reuse forms and code from one project to another. A form can be a part of many projects. For example, you could add the form used in the DRAGDROP project to the FIRST project. Using the Project Manager, select the plus sign on the toolbar or the Add File option from the pop-up menu. From the File menu, choose Add to Project. The standard Windows File dialog box appears again, but this time files with the extension PAS are shown.

Go back into the DELPHI\DEMOS\DRAGDROP directory, where you'll see a single file called DROPFONT. If you double-click on that file, your project will have that new form and Delphi will open up the code window for that form. This change has no effect on the DRAGDROP project you opened a moment ago.

> **Caution:** You can change either the form or the code unit associated with the form and save either one back into the DELPHI\DEMOS\DRAGDROP directory. If you do, the changes you make *will* affect the DRAGDROP project. This is actually part of the point of having reusable code and forms: You can make changes that affect all your programs. If you want to make a change for a specific program, you can change the form and save it under a different name. To do so, from the File menu, choose Save File As.
>
> You might do this if, for example, you had a number of programs that used the DROPFONT form but you wanted to have one program that added an extra button to that form.

You can also add a new (blank) form to your project by choosing New Form from the File menu or by clicking on the SpeedBar icon that depicts a "shiny" window. ("Shiny" is depicted as it might be in a comic strip— with lines radiating from the object.) When you add a new form to a project, Delphi shows you the "Browse Gallery," which allows you to select from a number of forms that can give you a head start on programming your own forms. For the examples in this book, however, you'll always start with blank forms.

Example: Removing Forms from Projects

In the Project Manager, a unit and its associated form (if it has one) are shown on the same line. If you click on the DROPFONT line of the Project Manager, you can remove this form by clicking on the minus sign on the Project Manager's toolbar. If you select Remove from the File menu, Delphi pops up a dialog box that allows you to remove any of the forms in the project. The DROPFONT form disappears. If you made any changes to this form or code, Delphi allows you to save them before removing them.

Example: Adding and Removing Units

When you add a form to a project, a code unit is added as well. Every form has an associated code unit. When you remove that form, the unit goes away, too. You can watch this process as it happens—the code window adds a tab for every unit added.

You can also add a plain unit, with no form attached, to your project. From the File menu, choose New Unit. A code window pops to the foreground, and a new tab is added. Delphi assigns default file names to new units (like Unit1, Unit2, Unit3, and so on) when they are first created but which you can, of course, change. The tabs in the code editor will match the file names, so that you can click on "Unit1" to select Unit1, for example, or "First" to get the main project code.

You remove units the same way you remove forms. Click on the line that shows the name of the unit—there will be no form associated with a plain code unit—and press the minus button. Again, if you've made changes to the unit, Delphi asks whether you want to save your changes.

Example: Closing Projects

To close a project, you can select Close Project from the File menu, or you can start a new project, open an existing project, or just exit Delphi. Any of these things will close the current project.

Delphi always asks whether you want to save a project if you have made changes since the last time you saved. In fact, if you are about to do anything that might cause you to lose work, Delphi asks you whether you want to save first.

Example: Deleting Projects, Forms, and Units from Your Disk

You cannot delete projects, forms, or units by using Delphi. If you want to remove any work that you have done, you must use the File Manager or (if you know how) delete it from a DOS prompt.

To delete the FIRST.DPR file by using the File Manager, follow these steps:

1. Open the BOOKPAS directory.

2. Select FIRST.DPR and press Del. The File Manager asks whether you're sure you want to delete the project.

3. Choose OK, and the file is gone.

No special locks are put on any Delphi files—you can delete them freely. Deleting the project destroys whatever work was done in the actual project file; it doesn't destroy any of the associated forms or units. Delphi deliberately makes it difficult for you to destroy a lot of work accidentally. You must delete each form, unit, and project separately to remove it from your hard drive.

> **Note:** Sometimes when experimenting, you might want to make a particular project easily removable. The secret of easy removal is to keep all the projects and units in a single separate folder (a folder containing no other projects) and then delete the entire folder when done.

By the way, just because you've deleted the project file, you haven't really lost much. Because all the form information is stored separately, you can recreate *any* project file simply by starting a new project and adding to it all the forms and units that were in the project you want to recreate. Provided you can remember what they were, it will be a very simple task.

Ending Delphi

You can end Delphi as you do any Windows program—by clicking twice on the system menu icon, or by pressing Alt+F4 when the main menu bar is active. Under the File menu is an Exit option, which enables you to exit from Delphi by using menus.

Summary

Delphi installs from the "Installation Disk" by using the INSTALL.EXE program. Delphi requires as much as 65M of disk space, and you should have at least 8M RAM.

Delphi consists of numerous useful tools for programmers, but the program you use most is called Delphi. A Delphi program consists of a project file, form files and their associated code units, and code units that are not associated with forms. Forms and code units can be used in more than one program. A project can have many forms and many code units. Delphi provides no easy way to delete a project or its associated forms and units.

Review Questions

1. What is a code unit?
2. What is a project?
3. Can a project have multiple forms and code units?
4. Can the same form or unit be used in more than one project?
5. When you make a change to a form or unit that is used by more than one project, which projects are affected?
6. Why can't you delete a project and all of its associated forms and units using Delphi?
7. Can you work on a unit or file that *isn't* part of the current project?

Review Exercises

1. Start a new project and save it under the name "Test."
2. Start a new project with the name "Test2" without saving it.
3. Add an existing form to Test2.
4. Add a new form to Test2.
5. Add a code unit with no attached form to Test2.
6. Save Test2.
7. Delete Test and Test2, remembering to delete all associated form and unit files.

CHAPTER 4

What's On-Screen?

To prepare for this chapter, start up Delphi again. The various items that appear on-screen are called, in total, the Delphi *environment*. You work within this environment for the rest of the book. Look at figure 4.1 and refer to it as the various aspects of Delphi are described.

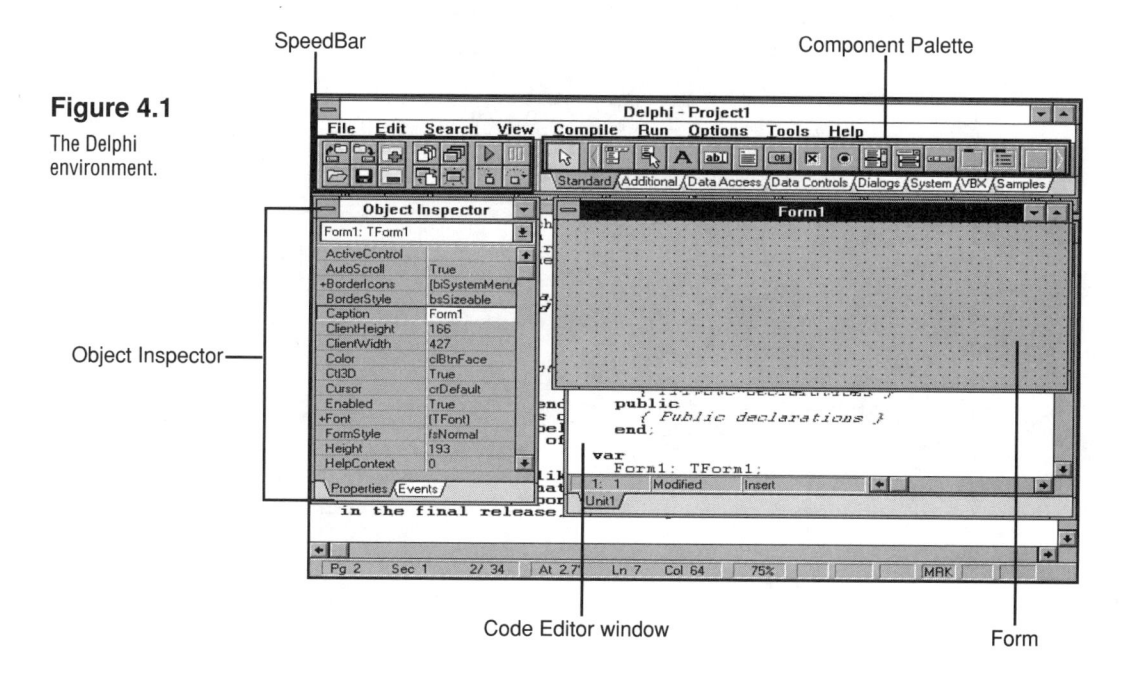

Figure 4.1
The Delphi environment.

Chapter 4 ◆ What's On-Screen?

The Standard Objects

Because Delphi is a Windows program, it has all the usual capabilities of such a program. You can move, resize, and minimize most of the windows in Delphi.

You've already used the menu bar, and because it's really no different from any other menu bar in any other Windows program, it's not covered here.

> **Tip:** When you focus on a particular part of the program, press Alt+F10 and the program will often pop up a local menu with appropriate options for that object.

The SpeedBar

The SpeedBar allows you quick mouse access to a number of common functions, all of which are available through the regular menu items (see fig. 4.2).

Figure 4.2
The SpeedBar.

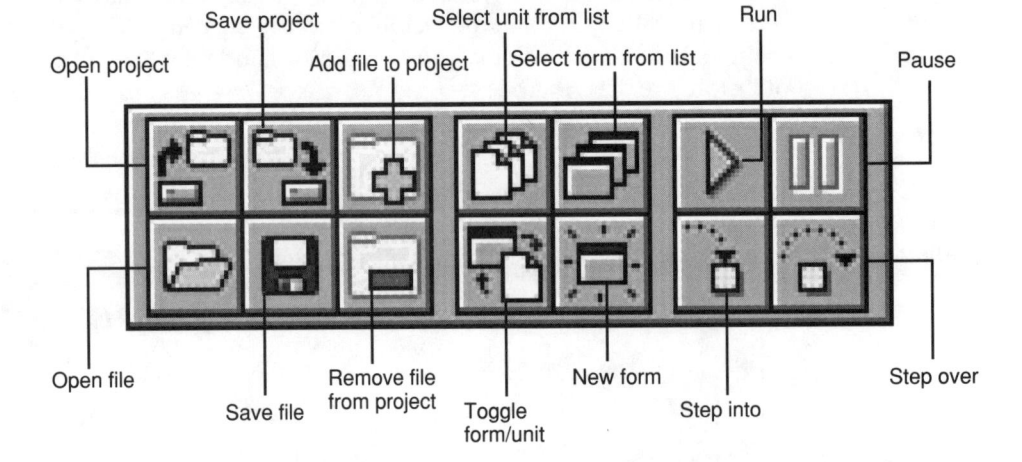

Labels on SpeedBar: Open project, Save project, Add file to project, Select unit from list, Select form from list, Run, Pause, Open file, Save file, Remove file from project, Toggle form/unit, New form, Step into, Step over

> **Tip:** Moving the mouse over the SpeedBar or Component Palette provides you with information about what the button does or represents.

Tip: You can hide the SpeedBar by clicking the right mouse-button on it and selecting "Hide" from the pop-up menu.

Here's what most of the SpeedBar buttons do:

The button that shows an arrow connection from a hard drive to a folder allows you to open a project. (This button is identical to the File menu selection Open Project.)

The button that shows an arrow connection from a folder to a hard drive allows you to save a project. (This button is identical to the File menu selection Save Project.)

The button that shows a folder with a plus sign over it allows you to add a file to the current project. (This button is identical to the Project Manager button with the same appearance.)

The button that shows a folder with a minus sign over it allows you to remove a file from the current project. (This button is identical to the Project Manager button with the same appearance.) Adding and removing a code unit will also add or remove the associated form unit if there is one.

The button that looks like an open file folder enables you to load a unit. Clicking on this button will also automatically load the associated form, if there is one. (The button is identical to the File menu selection Open File.)

To the right of the Open File button is a button that looks like a disk. Clicking on this button saves the current code window. (This button is the equivalent of the File menu selection Save File.)

On the right-most clump of buttons, at the upper left-hand corner, is a picture of many documents stacked one on the other. This icon is the "select unit from list" icon (or simply "select unit" for short). This button allows you to select a unit from a list of all the units in the current project.

To the right of the select unit is a picture of many forms, stacked similarly. This button is the "select form from list" icon (or simply "select form") and it allows you to select a form from a list of all the forms in the current project.

Chapter 4 ◆ What's On-Screen?

Underneath the select form icon is a "shiny" form, which allows you to create a new form (and associated code unit). This button is equivalent to the similar button in the Project Manager. Forms added in this manner are added to the project (and not just opened as with the File menu's Add File selection).

To the left of the shiny form button is a picture of a document and a form on the same button with arrows connecting them. This is the toggle form/unit button, which allows you to switch between the current form and its associated code unit. This button is functionally the same as the View menu's Toggle Form/Unit selection.

Most of the functions provided by these buttons you worked with in the last chapter. You'll look at and use the far right-most clump of speed buttons later on. Right now, though, look at the two buttons at the top of the middle clump.

> **Tip:** You can customize the SpeedBar. To change or add functions, right-click on the SpeedBar and select Configure from the pop-up menu.

The Form and Unit Selectors

To bring a specific form or unit to the foreground, use the form or unit selectors—the top two buttons on the middle clump of the SpeedBar. These buttons correspond to selections in the View menu.

Frequently, you'll have so many windows on-screen that you'll have a difficult time finding exactly what you're looking for. These buttons—one looks like a stack of slightly offset documents, the other like a stack of forms—will pop up a dialog box that allows you to choose from any of the forms and units in your current project. Click on them now and you'll see that they display only one unit or one form, because that's all that you have in your current project.

Double-clicking on a name in the dialog box will pop that unit or form to the foreground and automatically select it. This feature is especially handy if you closed or minimized a form or code unit.

> **Tip:** These two buttons correspond to the View menu Units and Forms items respectively, and can be accessed by using the shortcut keys Ctrl+F12 for the Units item and Shift+F12 for the Forms item.

The Toggle form/unit button, on the other hand, brings to the foreground the code unit associated with the current form or the form associated with the current code unit. This feature can be handy for flipping back and forth between a form and its associated unit. This button corresponds to the View menu's Toggle Form/Unit.

The Form and the Component Palette

As you learned in Chapter 3, the form is a window your program displays when it starts. Using Delphi, you can design dialog boxes just by arranging objects on the form. The form is much like a regular window in Windows. In other words, if you want to change the size of the form, you can resize it by clicking on one of the borders and dragging it to a smaller or larger size.

The objects that you put on the form come from the *Component Palette*. The Component Palette is covered with buttons, each one representing a specific object (see fig. 4.3). For example, click on the button that shows the word OK in a rectangle. Notice that it appears to sink as if it were a real button. Now click anywhere on the form.

Figure 4.3
A form and the Component Palette.

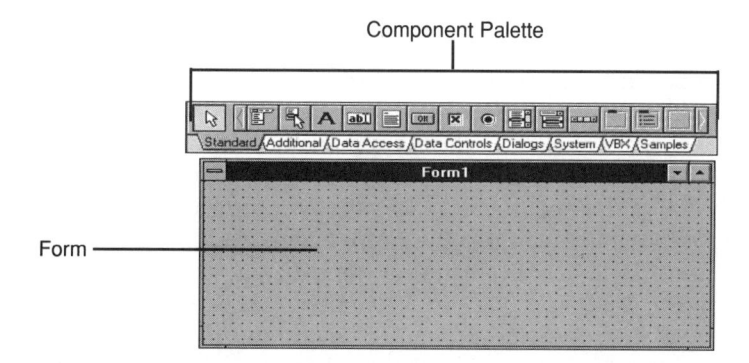

Note: The objects that you use to build your applications are *components* of your application, hence the Delphi term *Component Palette*. Like an artist's palette, which holds the colors the painter will use in the painting, the Component Palette determines what objects will go into the making of your application.

Components on a form that are visible to the user are called *controls*, presumably because they allow the user to control the application in some way.

Components and controls are both classes of objects.

Chapter 4 ◆ What's On-Screen?

A push button, labeled Button1, appears on the form where you clicked, and its button pops up on the Component Palette.

That's just one way to place a component on a form. Go back to the Component Palette and this time *double-click* on the button component. A button appears in the center of your form. Double-click it again, and then once more. Notice that the buttons appear slightly offset from one another on the form so that they are at least partially visible. When you double-click to place a component on the form, the button on the Component Palette never depresses.

> **Note:** If you hold down the Shift key while clicking a button on the Component Palette, you can place objects on the form by repeatedly clicking the mouse. This shortcut saves you from having to move from bar to form, bar to form, but allows you to place your controls more exactly than you can with a simple double-click.
>
> To stop placing a control, you must click the pointer button that is always on the left side of the Component Palette.

There's another way to place a component on a form, and size it at the same time. Click on the button component of the Component Bar and then click and drag the mouse from one corner of the form to the other. An outline of the button appears as you drag. Release the mouse and the button appears on the form.

Still *another* way to place a component on a form is to call up the Component List. From the View menu, select Component List and you'll get a dialog box that shows you an alphabetic list of all the components available to your form. You can search the List and select a control to put in your form by pressing enter.

Why would you use the Component List? Well, if you had your form well planned out in your head (or on paper) you might use the Component List as a speedy way to add all the components you needed *through the keyboard!* Then, when they were all on your form you could arrange and size them with the mouse. (This would probably result in less overall work.) But if you're designing the form as you go, the mouse gives better instantaneous feedback.

Notice that the last push button you placed is surrounded by black squares. The squares, called "sizing handles," tell you that the component is currently *selected*. You can resize the object—make it bigger or smaller—by clicking and dragging on one of the squares. Experiment with resizing now. (Notice that when you position the mouse cursor over one of these sizing handles, the cursor changes to a double-ended cursor, just as it would if you wanted to resize a window.) You also can move the component by clicking directly on the component and dragging. Try moving the push buttons around a little.

> **Customizing the Grid**
>
> The dots that appear on the form are a grid that determines what sizes any given component can be. By default, the sides of a component placed on the grid will fall on one of those dots, which are 8 pixels apart. Forcing the components to fit into fixed sizes, called "snapping to the grid," makes it easier to create an even, professional-looking design.
>
> You can hide the grid, you can turn off the "snap to grid" feature, and you can even change the distance between the dots, from the Preferences page of the Environment notebook. (Select Environment from the Options menu.)
>
> All of the programs in this book were designed by using the standard sized grid with the "snap to grid" feature active.

Selecting Multiple Components

If you click on a push button other than the currently selected one, it becomes the selected component, which is made apparent by the sizing handles. You can select multiple components by clicking on them while holding down the Shift key. This shortcut is handy for moving a group of objects as a unit. If you move one component, all the other selected components move with it. Click on a blank space on the form, to deselect all the components.

Now click and drag your mouse on an empty spot on the form. As you drag the mouse, a rectangle appears and grows. Any components that this rectangle surrounds become selected. If you select multiple push buttons this way, you can verify that this method is no different from the preceding method of selecting multiple objects. Now click on a blank spot to deselect them both.

Selected components can be cut or copied to the clipboard, as well as pasted from the clipboard.

Sizing Multiple Components

You cannot directly resize two objects at once, but you can make them the same size through a special dialog box. Start by selecting the objects you want to change; then, from the Edit menu, choose Size. A dialog box pops up, requesting you to choose how you want the objects sized. As you can see, you can make a group of objects match the smallest in the group or the largest, and either horizontally, vertically, or both. Experiment with how these settings work by changing the sizes of the push buttons and then seeing how they are affected by the Size dialog box.

Chapter 4 ◆ What's On-Screen?

Example: Sizing Controls

Start a blank form and place three buttons on it by using the click-and-drag method so that they are all different sizes. Call up the Size dialog box and use the "shrink to smallest" options for both height and width. Observe what happens.

Now call up the Size dialog box again, and enter 60 and 60 for the width and height. This step creates square buttons, like you might find on the SpeedBar or the Component Palette.

Now stretch one of the buttons very wide and another very tall, and call up the Size dialog box and select "grow to largest" options for both height and width.

As you can see, Delphi gives you a tremendous amount of flexibility in sizing your controls.

Aligning Components with Each Other

You also can make a group of components align themselves to each other or the form. From the Edit menu, choose Align. Align has several options, which you can better understand if you have at least three push buttons on the form (all selected, of course). Because alignment is more difficult to get used to, several possibilities are illustrated in figures 4.4 and 4.5.

Figure 4.4
Three columns of push buttons showing vertical alignment.

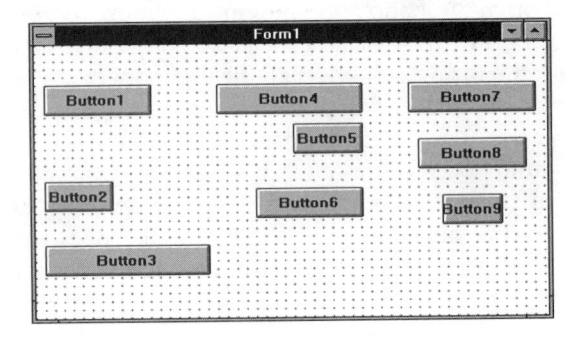

Figure 4.5
Three rows of push buttons showing horizontal alignment.

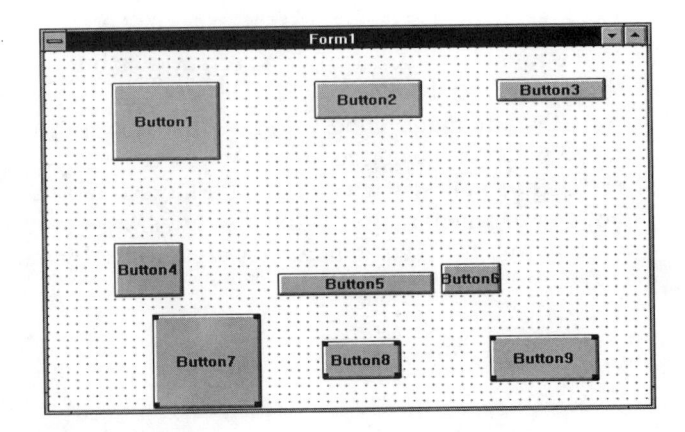

In figure 4.4, nine push buttons are grouped together in three columns. Button1, Button2, and Button3 are one group; Button4, Button5, and Button6 are another; and Button7, Button8, and Button9 are the third. Buttons 1, 2, and 3 are (vertically) aligned on the left side. Buttons 4, 5, and 6 are aligned on the right. Buttons 7, 8, and 9 are aligned down the middle, meaning that their centers are in one straight line. Buttons 7, 8, and 9 also are evenly spaced vertically. That is, there is the same amount of room between Button7 and Button8 as there is between Button8 and Button9.

In figure 4.5, nine push buttons are grouped together in three rows. Button1, Button2, and Button3 are aligned (horizontally) along their top borders. Button4, Button5, and Button6 are aligned on the bottom. Button7, Button8, and Button9 are aligned so that their centers are in a straight line across the form.

Centering a group vertically on a form means that the distance between the top border of the highest object and the top of the form is equal to the distance between the bottom border of the lowest object and the bottom of the form. In figure 4.4, Button4, Button5, and Button6 show this concept.

Centering a group horizontally on a form means that the distance between the left border of the leftmost object and the left side of the form is equal to the distance between the right border of the rightmost object and the right of the form. In figure 4.5, Button7, Button8, and Button9 show this concept.

> **Caution:** Be careful which options you use when aligning objects. If you align a column of objects vertically or a row of objects horizontally, you end up mushing them all together. Figure 4.6 shows what happens when a row of push buttons is left-aligned.

Figure 4.6

The same rows of push buttons: the top row is left-aligned; the middle row is aligned vertically on the form; and the bottom row is aligned horizontally on the form.

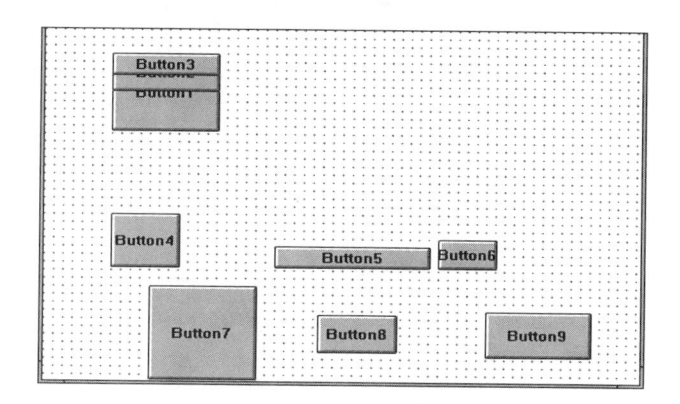

The Alignment Palette

Although the Alignment Palette is not visible by default, you can call it up. This feature not only gives you fast access to Delphi's aligning power, but also provides a visual cue to what happens when you select a certain option.

From the View menu, select the Alignment Palette option. This small dialog box appears in the upper left corner of your form (provided you haven't moved the form from the default location) and graphically shows what happens to your controls if you select a certain option.

Example: Aligning Components on the Form

Randomly place three buttons on the form and select them all. Now align them (vertically) along the top. What happens if you now align them to the left?

Spread them out again and try aligning them so that they are vertically centered. What happens if you now align them to the bottom?

Keep moving the buttons around at random and repeat this experiment with the Alignment Palette as well as with the Alignment dialog box until you are comfortable with the effects of the various options.

Removing Components from the Form

You can remove the currently selected component on a form by pressing Del. You also can remove a selected group in this fashion.

> **Caution:** Be careful when using the Del key. Delphi deletes any object or any group of objects you ask it to, regardless of the kind of work you've done with them. Before deleting a lot of work, save your project to the disk. That way if you make a mistake, you can always restore your original.
>
> You can undo one deletion by using the Edit menu option Undo, but *only* if you haven't added anything new to the form since you made the deletion.

Other Objects

Many more objects are available than just those visible on the Component Palette. Underneath the buttons on the Component Palette are small tabs with names on them. Right now, the Standard tab is selected and prominent. If you click on the tab marked Additional, you see a new set of buttons. These buttons also represent objects that you can use in your program.

Another tab is Dialogs. That tab enables you to use the standard Windows dialog boxes, such as the File dialog box that Delphi uses, and others that you may have seen in Windows.

Another tab is VBX. VBX is the extension used by Visual Basic—a program similar to Delphi—which works with the BASIC language. Because it's been around for a while, many VBX controls are available and Borland has cleverly made it possible for you to use some Visual Basic controls in your Delphi programs. (You do use them, too, in the upcoming chapters.) In this way, you can build upon the work of others.

> **Note:** If you purchased and installed the Visual Solutions Pack, you'll have many more controls on the VBX page than you may see in figures used in this book.
>
> Occasionally, some mention will be made of components from the Visual Solutions Pack, which will be signalled by this icon.

Delphi even enables you to create your own objects and put them on the bar—an advanced topic you can explore after learning the basics from this book.

The Object Inspector

The Object Inspector, located to the left of the form, gives details about the currently selected object or objects (see fig. 4.7). To look more closely at the Object Inspector, close your current project (without saving) and select from the File menu, New Project. Then add one push button to the blank form.

Figure 4.7

The Object Inspector.

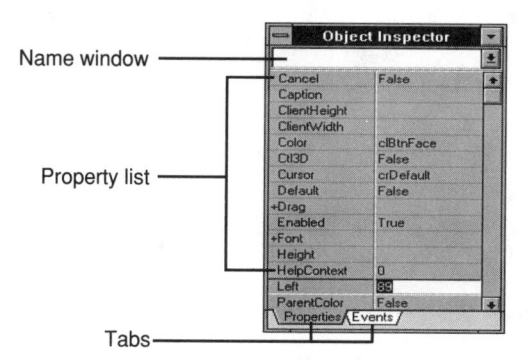

Select Button1 now. The Object Inspector changes to show you Button1's properties. Underneath the Object Inspector title bar, the name Button1 should appear. This *Component List* combo box tells you that Button1 is the currently selected object.

You can select any of the available objects through the Object Inspector itself. The Object Inspector's Component List is a standard combo box. If you click on the down arrow to the right of the Button1 text, you get a list of objects for the current project. Notice that Form1 is one of the objects that you can look at, as is Button1. If you select Form1, the Object Inspector changes to show the properties of that form.

Properties

Underneath the Component List in the Object Inspector is a list of the properties for the currently selected object. Select Button1 to see those properties.

Notice the scroll bar on the right side of the Object Inspector. The thumbnail (that's the small square that moves along the scrollbar) indicates that more properties for the object are available than can fit on-screen at a time. You can see how many properties a push button has by using the mouse to scroll down.

Although a push button has a lot of properties, the button has even more properties than is immediately apparent. For example, find the Font property; it has a + sign to the left of it, which indicates that more properties related to fonts are available than the one shown. Double-click on Font. Another series of properties appears, and some of them are marked with a +. Double-click on Font again, and the properties hide themselves.

What Does It All Mean?

Remember, the more work the operating system does the less work the programs written for that OS must do. Windows reduces the amount of work that programs must do by providing a number of objects such as push buttons as part of the OS. These buttons are basically part of Windows, not Delphi!

The unfortunate side effect is this: Windows wants to leave you as free as possible to change the appearance of objects. As a result, the objects often have a large number of properties, all of which must be specified in order for Windows to draw a push button.

Fortunately, Delphi simplifies things by providing *defaults*. Defaults are properties that are set to the usual or expected value. You never have to worry about any property unless you want to change it. As big as this book is, you'll cover only a small fraction of the properties that the objects have.

You learned a great deal about properties in Chapter 2, "Traditional Programming." Using the Object Inspector, you finally can see how properties really work in programs. Next, you're going to use the Object Inspector to change some object properties.

Button1 is really not much of a caption to put on a push button. Usually, push buttons say something like "OK" or "Cancel" or something meaningful. In the next section, you're going to change the caption for Button1.

Using the Object Inspector Editor

To change the caption for Button1, you start by selecting it, if it's not already selected. Then you find the property called Caption in the Object Inspector. This property reads Button1. You can edit the caption by clicking on that line of the Object Inspector.

Editing text in the Object Inspector is like editing in any other Windows program—you type in letters and they appear on-screen at the location of the *cursor*, a blinking vertical line.

You can move the cursor by using the cursor keys. Note that in the Object Inspector, if you move the cursor down, you move to a new property. If you are editing text with multiple words, you can move from word to word by holding down the Ctrl key and repeatedly pressing the right-arrow key or the left-arrow key.

Pressing the Home key moves you to the beginning of the line. Pressing the End key takes you to the end of the line. You can delete the character to the right of the cursor by pressing the Del key. You can delete the character to the left of the cursor by pressing the Backspace key. (The Ins key doesn't do anything in the Object Inspector.)

If the text is selected, it is replaced by whatever you type. You can identify selected text because it appears in *reverse video*—light characters on a dark background.

You can select text by clicking the mouse over the first letter you want selected and dragging it from there to the last letter you want selected. You can also hold down the Shift key and move the cursor over the letters you want selected.

Example: Changing Properties

To change the property by using the Object Inspector, delete the text Button1 and then type **Hello**. The push button's text changes as you type. This method is the most common way of changing a property. When possible, Delphi makes it even easier by providing you with a list of valid choices.

For example, scroll down the Object Inspector until you find the button's Visible property. Notice that this property has a combo box of its own. (If you're using the keyboard, you can press Alt+down arrow to drop down the combo box, otherwise click the mouse on the down arrow.) Delphi allows you to select True or False—the only possible values for Visible—without forcing you to type those words.

> **Note:** Even if you set the Visible property to False, the control will still be visible until you actually run your program. (It would be difficult to work with an invisible component!)

61

In the following sections, you look at some of the more obvious properties of the push button to get a better grasp of what you can do with the Object Inspector.

Example: Changing the Size Property

Underneath the Caption property in the property list of the Object Inspector are two properties called Height and Width. These properties control the size of the object. Just as you can resize the object by dragging on the border, you can change an object's size more precisely by directly editing the properties.

Try this exercise. Change the values of Height and Width to 50 and 50 to create a square push button. Now change one or both of the values to 1,000 and watch the push button's edge extend off-screen. How big can you make it? At some point, a message will appear, warning you that you typed an invalid size.

The screen boundaries for a control ends inside the window in which it is being drawn. In other words, no matter how big you make Button1, it never extends outside the window. This feature is called *cropping* or *clipping*, which is a feature of Windows.

> **Tip:** If you modify the Height and Width properties directly with the object inspector, you are circumventing the Snap to Grid option.

Other Properties

The properties Top and Left determine the distance from the top of the form and the distance that a control is from the left of the form. You can change the position of the push button by using the mouse or by directly editing the Left and Top properties. By editing the Left and Top properties, you can place a control very precisely.

One property that's fun to play with is the Cursor property. This property determines what the mouse pointer looks like when you move the pointer over the object. Click on Cursor now, and you'll see a list of options. Click on an option in the list to change from crDefault to one of the other cursors. When you run the program, the mouse pointer will change when you pass it over the push button.

Another fun property is the Font property. With it, you can change the look of the push button's caption. If you click on Font, you see three dashes to the right of the line. If you click on the dashes, you get a standard Windows Font dialog box. For fun, try some of the different fonts.

Different objects have different properties, of course, but most have the properties you've worked with in this section. You'll explore properties further later in the book.

Group Properties

Notice that when you select both of the push buttons on the form, the Object Inspector shows a subtle change. The change appears at the top of the Inspector—where the object name usually appears, is just a blank. But the properties listed are all the same.

If you change properties in the Object Inspector when multiple objects are selected, you change those properties for all the objects selected. This shortcut is actually quite handy.

If you change the Left property, for example, you align the push buttons on the left side. If you change the Height or Width properties, you force all the objects to have the same height or width. This rule applies to all the properties shown in the Object Inspector.

Some alignment tricks can't be done with the Object Inspector. For example, you can't align objects on their right side or space them evenly. However, you can change objects or groups of objects in a precise and uniform way.

Behavior

As you learned in Chapter 2, an object is defined in terms of its properties and behavior. By using the Object Inspector, you also can control the behavior of an object.

Underneath the properties listed in the Object Inspector are two tabs. The tab in the foreground is labelled "Properties" and you can always click on that to see the properties for any object on your form. Next to that is a tab labelled "Events." Remember that part of making an application is making components respond to specific events. Click on the Events tab to see what events a push button responds to.

You discover that the push button responds to many different events, including things like being clicked (OnClick), being double-clicked (OnDblClick), and so on.

If you want the push button to do something when the user presses it (as you normally would), you create code for the OnClick event. If you want the push button to react a certain way when the user presses a key, you can create code for OnKeyPress.

You can modify the behavior for an event by double-clicking on the edit line that appears to the right of that event name, or by pressing Ctrl+Enter when that edit line in the Object Inspector is focussed. You'll be doing this later on in the book.

Using the Code Editor

In Delphi, the window where you actually type in code, the Code Editor, is typically hidden under the forms (see fig. 4.8). The significance of this—that it is "hidden"—

Chapter 4 ◆ What's On-Screen?

is hard to appreciate unless you realize that all programming used to be done by typing in code, and that Delphi represents a shift in the way programming is done.

Figure 4.8
The code window.

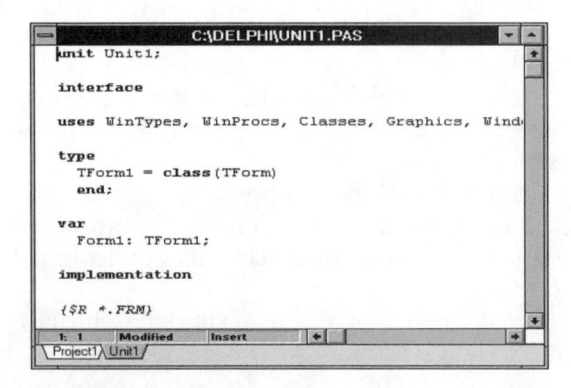

```
                    C:\DELPHI\UNIT1.PAS
unit Unit1;

interface

uses WinTypes, WinProcs, Classes, Graphics, Wind

type
  TForm1 = class(TForm)
  end;

var
  Form1: TForm1;

implementation

{$R *.FRM}

1: 1    Modified    Insert
Project1 \ Unit1 /
```

You can get to the Code Editor by clicking on it. If you can't see it around the form window, you can minimize the form window or move the form window until you can see it. You first looked at the Code Editor in Chapter 3. Now you can actually experiment with it.

The Delphi Code Editor is a text editor. Text editors are similar to word processors such as WordPerfect or Write, but generally less elaborate. If you've ever worked with a word processor, you shouldn't have any difficulty working with the Delphi Code Editor. The rest of this section will walk you through the Code Editor's functionality.

First, select from the View menu the Project Source item. Now, go to the top of the document by pressing Ctrl+Page Up. Then select all the text in the document by pressing Shift+Ctrl+Page Down. Next, press Del. These steps should empty the code window—something you wouldn't normally do—and leave you free to concentrate on the editor.

As with the Object Inspector's line editor, the code window has a cursor. Type some text and you'll see that the letters appear on-screen at the location of the cursor, and that the cursor moves forward. Keep typing until you reach the edge of the screen. Unlike a word processor, Delphi's text editors do not wrap words around. You are not creating a document that has to look good on paper, and the compiler doesn't care whether your text fits neatly across one page.

The editor will help you out a bit. If you keep typing without pressing Enter, you'll see a thin gray line approach from the right. This line tells you where the edge of the paper would be if you were to print out the program. It's generally not a good idea to go past this point. You can, though. In fact, the editor doesn't stop you from typing a line over 200 characters long. The compiler, however, flags as an error any line over 128 characters. Borland has never really seen fit to stop you from typing something just because it doesn't compile. (This capability may seem odd, but programmers who use Borland editors often use them for other things besides programming, and Borland knows that. Hence, Borland tends to allow you to do things that don't necessarily make sense in the context of Delphi programming.)

> **Note:** As you type, you may notice that certain words appear darker than others. You'll learn why in the next chapter. Don't worry about it now.

In the code windows, you can edit your text the same way you do in the Object Inspector, with several embellishments:

- All the cursor control keys work, so you can move up and down lines of code. Press Enter to start a new line or break an existing line.

- The Ins key toggles the editor between *insert* and *overwrite* mode. Insert mode is the most common these days: whatever you type goes into the text at the cursor position, and everything to the right is moved over. In overwrite mode, what you type still goes into the text at the cursor position, but characters to the right are overwritten by the characters you type. Toggle back and forth to get a feel for the difference. (Sometimes overwrite mode is much handier.) At the bottom of the editor is an indicator that tells you when you're in Insert or Overwrite.

- When you type so much that the text can't fit on one screen, the text window scrolls. You can click on the scroll bars to adjust the current view of the text. The screen scrolls with the cursor, too, so you can use the left-, right-, up-, and down-arrow keys to view your text.

- The Home key moves the cursor to the beginning of the line; End moves it to the end of the line. Page Up moves the cursor up one screen; Page Down moves it down one screen. Ctrl+Home takes you to the top of the screen; Ctrl+End takes you to the bottom of the screen. Ctrl+Page Up takes you to the beginning of the document; Ctrl+Page Down takes you to the end of the document. You can use the Shift key in conjunction with any of these keys or the cursor keys to select text.

- Use standard Windows commands to cut and paste the selected text to and from the Clipboard. Ctrl+Ins copies the text to the Clipboard; Shift+Del copies the text to the Clipboard and removes it from the current document (called *cutting*); Shift+Ins copies the text from the Clipboard at the current cursor position (called *pasting*); Delete deletes the selected text without copying it to the Clipboard.

Chapter 4 ♦ What's On-Screen?

> **Note:** When you copy text to the Clipboard, you destroy whatever text is currently in the Clipboard.

- ♦ You can place *bookmarks* in your code by typing Ctrl+K and then a number from 0 to 9. This keystroke actually appears in the code as a box with the number in it. You then can go to that bookmark by pressing Ctrl+Q followed by the same number.

This information is all you need to get started and comfortable using the text editors. Table 4.1 shows all the editing key combinations in use in the Delphi program.

Table 4.1. The Delphi editing keys. A comma indicates a key that should be pressed after previous keys are released.

Description/Cursor Movement	Keystroke
Character left	Left arrow
Character right	Right arrow
To one word left	Ctrl+Left arrow
To one word right	Ctrl+Right arrow
One line up	Up arrow
One line down	Down arrow
Beginning of line	Home
Start of next line	Enter
End of line	End
Top of window	Ctrl+Home
Bottom of window	Ctrl+End
Top of document	Ctrl+PgUp
Bottom of document	Ctrl+PgDn
Beginning of block	Ctrl+Q, B
End of block	Ctrl+Q, K
Last cursor position	Ctrl+Q, P
Insert and overstrike	Insert

Text+Scrolling Keys	Keystroke
One line up	Up arrow
One line down	Down arrow
One page up	Page Up
One page down	Page Down

Text+Selection Keys	Keystroke
Character left	Shift+Left arrow
Character right	Shift+Right arrow
Word left	Shift+Ctrl+Left arrow
Word right	Shift+Ctrl+Right arrow
Current line	Shift+Down arrow
Line above	Shift+Up arrow
Begin text block	Ctrl+KB
End text block	Ctrl+K K
Read block from disk	Ctrl+K, R
Write block to disk	Ctrl+K,W
Print block	Ctrl+K, P
Indent block	Ctrl+K, I
Unindent block	Ctrl+K,U

To Insert, Copy, and Delete	Keystroke
Copy selected text without clipboard	Ctrl+K,C
Move selected text without clipboard	Ctrl+K,V
Delete selected text and copy it to the Clipboard	Ctrl+Ins
Paste the contents of the Clipboard	Shift+Ins
Insert a blank line before the cursor position	Home,Ctrl+N

continues

Table 4.1. Continued

To Insert, Copy, and Delete	Keystroke
Delete one character to the left of the cursor Backspace	Ctrl+H
Delete one character at the cursor	Del
Delete the rest of the word the cursor is on	Ctrl+T
Delete selected text	Ctrl+Delete

Bookmark Keys	Keystroke
Set up to 10 bookmarks	Ctrl+K,0+9
Go to a specific bookmark	Ctrl+Q,0+9

Miscellaneous	Keystroke
Pair matching	Ctrl+Q,[
	Ctrl+Q,]
Repeat last command	F3
Restore error message	Alt+S, C
Undo	Alt+Backspace
Search	Ctrl+F
Search and Replace	Ctrl+R

Example: Finding Text

Sometimes programs get very long, and finding a particular place in them can be difficult. You can go to any spot you choose in a program, no matter the length, by marking that spot with a bookmark.

If you forget to use a bookmark, you can find the spot you want by using the program's Search capabilities. To get the Search dialog box, press Ctrl+F, or by selecting from the Edit menu, the **F**ind item (see fig. 4.9).

Figure 4.9

The Search dialog box.

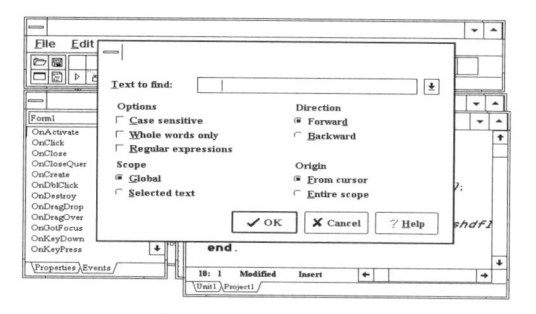

To get used to the searching capability, try this example. First, type the following text into the code window—the one that you emptied out in the previous section:

```
Borland's Delphi
has evolved greatly
until it has become as
powerful as any tool available.
```

Next, open the Search dialog box, type **IT** (all uppercase), and press Enter. The editor responds with Search string 'IT' not found. By default, the text editor searches from the current cursor position.

Press Ctrl+Page Up to go to the top of the document. Then press F3, which is a shortcut to repeat the last search command. Now the cursor moves to the it, which is the selected text. If you now type DELPHI (all uppercase), that text replaces the it. (Make sure you're in Insert mode.)

Now take a look at the Search dialog box again. Press Ctrl+Page Up to go to the top of the document. Then open the Search dialog box (Ctrl+Q, then F). Its options are separated into four sections: Options, Direction, Scope, and Origin.

In the Options section, you can choose whether to search for whole words and whether case should matter. If you had checked the Case sensitive box earlier, your uppercase IT never would have matched the lowercase it in the text.

If you now search for as in your text, you find five occurrences: the text contains has two times, Delphi one time, and as two times. The search finds all these words unless you check the Whole words only box. Checking this box eliminates two of the occurrences because the as found in them are not whole words.

The text editors consider text to be a whole word if it is delimited (surrounded by) spaces or punctuation. To get a feel for this capability, add the following text to the preceding example and search for as, non-case sensitive, whole words only.

```
as
        as
as.
"as"
{as}
```

The text editor locates all of these occurrences.

The Direction options are self-explanatory. (Do you want to search forward from the current position—the usual—or back?) The scope is less obvious: You can select a block of text and search for something within the selected block. Normally, you want to search the entire document. Delphi automatically sets the scope to "selected" if you have selected any text in your document.

When you did the example search earlier in this section, you first pressed Ctrl+Page Up to go to the beginning of the document. You can, however, choose Entire Scope from the Origin options, and the editor searches from the top of the document (or from the selected block) rather than from the current cursor position.

Example: Replacing Text

You also can replace found text by typing in new text, as you did in the preceding section, or by having the editor replace found text with different text, as you'll do now.

Call up the Search and Replace dialog box by pressing Ctrl+Q, and then A, or by selecting Replace from the Search menu. Here you have two lines to enter text: In the first, you enter the text you're searching for; in the second, you enter the text to replace it with.

Type **as** in the first line and **(as)** in the second; then press Enter. The editor positions over the first as and asks `Replace this occurrence of 'as'`? Choose No. Press F3 to repeat the command, and the cursor moves forward and again displays a dialog box asking if you want to replace the text. Again, choose No.

Most of the options in the Search and Replace dialog box are the same as they are in the Search dialog box. With the Search and Replace Dialog box, though, you get the additional Prompt on Replace option. Call up the Search and Replace dialog box and click off that option. Because you're in the middle of the document, click the Entire Scope option as well.

The Search and Replace dialog box has a Replace All push button, which isn't present in the Search dialog box. With it, you can replace every occurrence of some text in the current file with some other. Click on that push button now. The results should give you a taste for why you should use Search and Replace with discretion. Every occurrence of as, even those in the middle of words, is replaced with (as). This Search and Replace creates a mess that would not be easy to get out of except for one thing: The Undo command.

Example: Undo

To undo the most recent changes to your code, you can press Alt+Backspace. Do that now to get rid of the (as)'s in your document. You can even undo your undo, through the text editor's Redo capability. Despite this capability, you should follow two basic rules when using Search and Replace.

The first is to save your file (from the File menu, select Save File) before making drastic changes to it. This rule applies to Search and Replace or any other changes you might make.

The second is don't do a Search and Replace unless you're sure you know what will happen. When you need to do a global replace, try it first without the prompt but not using the Replace All push button. Then use F3 to repeat the replace a few times to be sure you'll like the results. Then go back to the Search and Replace dialog and select Replace All.

Summary

Delphi has all the usual Windows objects in it, including a menu bar, system icons, and so on. It also offers a SpeedBar, which enables you to make certain choices by using the mouse more quickly than by pulling down a menu. You can bring any unit or form in your project to the foreground by clicking on its name in either the form selector or unit selector.

The key elements of the Delphi environment, however, are the Component Palette and form window, which enable you to design forms for use in your projects; the Object Inspector, which enables you to examine and change object properties and behavior; and the Code Editor, which enables you to enter Pascal code.

Review Questions

1. The functions covered so far are "Save project," "Open project," "Open file," "Save file," "Add to project," "Remove from project," "Select form," "Toggle form/unit," and "New form."
2. Locate and describe the function of the Component Palette.
3. Where do you put objects from the Component Palette? What is another name for these objects?
4. Where does the code for a program go?
5. What does the Object Inspector list?

Chapter 4 ◆ What's On-Screen?

6. Can you change the properties and behaviors of an object from the Object Inspector?

7. If you copy some text to the Clipboard, what happens to any text that might already be in there?

8. What is a "Whole word" search?

9. How do you add more than one of the same kind of object to a form without constantly going back to the Component Palette?

Review Exercises

1. Create a form that has five columns of three identical buttons (for a total of 15 identical buttons).

2. Make the buttons perfectly square.

3. Delete one of the buttons. What operations can you do on the form and *still* use the Undo feature?

Part III

Approaching Delphi

CHAPTER 5

Working with Pascal

In this chapter, you warm up with some traditional Pascal and basic programming concepts. You also become familiar with using the editor in conjunction with some of the tools available and the actual programming process. At the end of this chapter, you examine the elements of Pascal that you need in your Delphi program.

The World's Shortest Pascal Program, Revisited

To begin your journey into Pascal, you need to start with a cleaner slate than Pascal usually provides. To do so, follow these steps:

1. Start up Pascal, if it is not already started.
2. Close the current project by choosing Close Project from the File menu.
3. Open a new project by choosing Open Project from the File menu.
4. When the file dialog appears, select the BOOKPAS directory and type **short**. Pascal shows you an Open File dialog box.

> **Tip:** This is a good way to start a project "clean"—that is, with a specific name and without any forms.

Chapter 5 ♦ Working with Pascal

5. For this experiment, delete *all* the code in the Code Editor by pressing Ctrl+Home, then Ctrl+Shift+End, then Delete.

Now type the world's (almost) shortest Pascal program in the editor. Here it is, one more time:

```
program AlmostShortest;

begin
   end.
```

Note: Remember to clear all existing code before you type this program into the Code Editor. If you type the program in a unit window or in a window that has other code in it, the program won't work.

Notice that in the Project code window, the words `program`, `begin`, and `end` are darker than `AlmostShortest`. `program`, `begin`, and `end` have special meanings in Pascal, so Pascal presents them more prominently.

Tip: "Syntax highlighting" means anything that Pascal recognizes as an integral part of the Pascal language—its *syntax*—becomes prominently displayed or *highlighted*.

Run this program by pressing F9, which causes Pascal to compile your program and run it. (It does so very quickly—something you may not appreciate until you program in another language or environment.) You can also compile and run a Pascal program by pressing the Play button, which is the top-left button on the right-most SpeedBar cluster, or by choosing Run from the Run menu.

How Fast Is It?

If you're used to working with just about any other visual product (like Visual BASIC, PowerBuilder, or VX-REXX) you may discover that in some cases, particularly with very large programs, Pascal takes somewhat longer to start running a program. This is because most other visual products are "interpreted."

In Chapter 2, you learned that the program that turns English-like words into machine code is called a *compiler*. However, another program that can turn words into machine code is an *interpreter*.

> The difference between the two is this: When you compile a program, all of your source code is turned into machine code, and from this the compiler creates a new file that is directly executable. Roughly speaking, an interpreter compiles a program line-by-line—it waits until a particular line of code is being run before converting it to machine code, and reconverts that code every time it runs it. Anybody who wants to run the code must also have the interpreter with them. (In Visual Basic, this is the infamous VBRUNnnn.DLL).
>
> The result is that an interpreter is usually able to start running a program faster than a compiler, since it doesn't have to convert the whole file; however, a compiler usually produces much faster code. Also, a compiled program doesn't require an interpreter to run. (Pascal programs can run without any additional DLLs.) Some compilers, notably C and C++ compilers, are so slow that many programmers settle for a slow-running program (such as one produced by Visual BASIC) rather than work with them.
>
> Compilers for any language are generally very slow compared to interpreters, but Borland's Pascal compilers have always been an exception—they generate code as fast as many interpreters. With Pascal, you can program with near-instant feedback (as in Visual BASIC or any interpreted language), but create programs that are blazingly fast (as with C/C++ or any compiled language).

If you typed this program correctly, the screen flickers for a moment and you return to Pascal. As you learned in Chapter 2, all you've done is tell the compiler that you're going to program something—you haven't actually programmed anything yet. (If you made any errors, Pascal gives you some idea what they are and places you over the problem point. This code is so simple that any errors are probably simple typos.)

If you typed everything correctly, now deliberately introduce an error into the program. Type **g** after `begin` so that it reads `beging`. Notice that `beging` lightens. Syntax highlighting is more than a cute trick—it can actually alert you to an error before you try to run your program.

Now run the program again by pressing F9 and note what happens. Pascal signals that you made an error and says `begin expected`. That's pretty smart. Pascal is not so smart that it actually corrects what is an obvious mistake to you, but it does place you exactly where the error is.

The compiler's ability to place the programmer at the exact point where the error occurs is the feature (along with low prices and speedy compiles) that built Borland. Before Borland's Pascal, no popular compiler did that. At this point, correct the error and move on.

Chapter 5 ◆ Working with Pascal

Your First Pascal Lesson

One of the crucial lessons in learning any programming language is to increase clarity. You can write the greatest code in the world, but if nobody else can read it, you'll be a hunted person. Pascal is superior to many other languages because the code is often readable by people who don't understand computer languages. If you see

```
Write('Hello, world!');
```

you probably expect the computer to display the text Hello, World somewhere.

Code is often not so obvious, however. Sometimes you may find a clever way to do something, so that even though *what* is happening is obvious, *why* it is happening is not. When you create a piece of code like that, common courtesy dictates that you add *comments* to explain it. Comments are ignored by the compiler. They are strictly for human beings. In Pascal, you write a comment by enclosing text in curly braces ({ }). For example, change the preceding program to the following:

```
program AlmostShortest;

begin
  {This code does not do anything.}
  end.
```

You can compile and run this program, but it isn't any different than before. As you can see, comments aren't ignored by the text editor—they appear italicized. Italics are also useful. For example, take the curly brace off the end of the comment:

```
program AlmostShortest;

begin
  {This code does not do anything.
  end.
```

Note that now end is italicized as well. Everything in your program after an opening curly brace is a comment until a corresponding closing curly brace appears. If you try to run this program, you get an Unexpected End of File error message. Pascal requires that every program end with an end. The end is now considered a comment by the compiler.

Example: Your First Real Pascal Program

You've seen the word "unit" several times without really learning what it is. Before getting started on your first real Pascal program, you must understand this concept. A *unit* is a file containing Pascal code that is not actually a program, but that is used by programs to obtain access to objects or capabilities that the programs don't otherwise have.

> **Note:** Units are covered in detail in Chapter 21, "Objects."

Units come into play often in Pascal. All the controls on the Component Palette are stored in units, for example. Normally, you don't have to worry about them because Pascal makes sure that all the right units are available. But for your first program, you're going to regress somewhat.

In Chapter 1, you learned that programs and operating systems used to act more like typewriters. That behavior is so ingrained into the way some programmers think that Borland included a special unit that enables you to create a program in Windows that mimics a typewriter.

You just need to add two lines to the short program to make it do something:

```
program AlmostShortest;

uses WinCrt;      {Add this line}

begin
   {This code does not do anything.}
   Writeln('Hello, World!');      {Add this line too}
   end.
```

(Ignore all the puncuation marks here for now. You'll learn about those in the next section.)

Actually, quite a bit is going on here. The Pascal word that indicates a requirement for a unit is uses. WinCrt contains the special commands that enable you to create a window that is like a typewriter.

The second line that you add here is a Writeln statement. Writeln means "display the text and start a new line." To get a feel for the overall effect, run this program now.

A window named Project1 appears, and inside the window is the text Hello, World!. (Less than spectacular, I know, but everyone starts this way.) Now add the following line after the first Writeln statement:

```
Writeln('Don''t laugh, at least it doesn''t have any bugs.');
```

Then compile and run the program again.

The Don't laugh... text appears directly beneath the Hello, World! text, as if you were printing it out on a printer. If you keep adding lines, eventually the Hello, World! text scrolls out of the window. Unlike most Windows programs, however, in this program the text is gone forever. There's no way the user can get it back.

Chapter 5 ◆ Working with Pascal

Punctuation

Why should you waste your time with this simple program? Partly because you should learn how a traditional program works, and partly because it illustrates some simple aspects of Pascal punctuation. Pascal's method of punctuation is logical, but it is not at all intuitive.

Pascal uses a semicolon (;) after every statement. For example, the following line is a statement, so it ends with a semicolon:

```
program AlmostShortest;
```

The next line is also a statement, so it ends with a semicolon:

```
uses WinCrt;        {Add this line}
```

But what about the following line:

```
begin
```

Why isn't there a semicolon after `begin`?

In Pascal, `begin` is not really a statement. It tells the compiler, "treat this next sequence of instructions as one statement until you get to the end." This sequence of instructions is called a *block* of code. (This punctuation isn't exactly intuitive, and many people like to just put a semicolon after a begin and let it go at that.) Because begin starts a block of code, you'll be programming a lot of code that looks like the following:

```
begin
   {some instruction;}
   {some instruction;}
   {some instruction;}
   end;
```

where the comments would be replaced by genuine Pascal code.

`begin` and `end;` signal that a series of instructions are to be treated as a block. (You'll discover more uses for blocks later.)

Return to your program. The following are both statements, so naturally they both end with semicolons:

```
Writeln('Hello, World!');      {Add this line too}
Writeln('Don''t laugh, at least it doesn''t have any bugs.');
```

Finally, you have

```
end.
```

Once again, Pascal seems to defy nature and logic by putting a period after the `end` instead of a semicolon. This `end` statement ends the block started by the earlier `begin`—the one without the semicolon. Normally, you put semicolons after `end` statements. This instance is the one exception because it doesn't just end a block, it ends the program.

80

Now you're ready for the remaining punctuation in the program. The `Writeln` statements seem to require a punctuation all their own. First is the text that appears on-screen, which is surrounded by single quotation marks:

```
'Hello, World'
'Don''t laugh, at least it doesn''t have any bugs.'
```

Text in Pascal programs is always surrounded by single quotation marks.

> **Note:** If you actually need to use single quotation marks (or apostrophes) within your text, you must place two single quotation marks in a row.

The text itself is surrounded by parentheses, as in the following:

```
Writeln(. . .);
Writeln(. . .);
```

I use ellipses (…) throughout this book to indicate that I've left something out of the code—in this case, the part you've already looked at. An ellipsis never appears in real program code.

`Writeln` takes the information in parentheses and sends it to the screen. The information within the parentheses is called a *parameter*. A parameter supplies `Writeln` with the necessary information to do what you want. You learn more about parameters later on in this chapter and in Chapter 8.

Why, you might wonder, doesn't punctuation just work like the following, more minimal example:

```
Writeln 'Hello, World'
```

The answer is: Because it just doesn't. All kidding aside, it actually could have worked this way, but the designer of Pascal decided that parameters should be enclosed in parentheses and the semi-colon should be used to end statements—a common custom in many computer languages. The parentheses and semi-colons can make the code easier to read, however.

Punctuation Errors

Don't worry too much about punctuation in Pascal. You can't accidentally do something terrible because you forgot the correct punctuation (unlike some other computer languages). Remembering when and where to put semicolons can be frustrating sometimes, but Pascal shines with regard to catching punctuation errors when they matter.

> **Tip:** You can quickly check the punctuation of your program by selecting the **C**ompile menu's **S**yntax Check option.

To understand this point, take the opening parenthesis out of the first `Writeln` statement and try to run the program. The compiler stops directly over the missing parenthesis. All right—Pascal thinks a semicolon is missing, but you know better. You usually will.

Put the parenthesis back in and add a semicolon after `begin`. If you run the program again, you'll discover that it works this time. You can use a semicolon all by itself in a Pascal program. The semicolon is called a *null statement*—it does nothing—and it exists because sometimes you'll forget where the semicolons are supposed to go.

> **Tip:** When in doubt, you can usually add a semicolon without any effect on your program.

You explore punctuation issues further in this book as they arise.

Getting Help

Delphi can teach you a lot about itself and Pascal through its help system. You can get help through the Help menu by choosing either Contents or Topic Search from that submenu. Contents provides an overview of the entire Delphi product, and Topic Search enables you to search the Help index for specific topics. For right now, stick with using the Topic Search; otherwise you will run into many advanced concepts if you just browse the Contents section.

> **Tip:** Delphi also has Computer-Based Tutors, which guide you through the process of learning how to use Pascal.

Even better than the help menu selections is Delphi's context-sensitive help. Context-sensitive means that the program offers help based on what part of the program currently is the focus of your attention. (Previous chapters covered the concept of focus and how focus is used in programming: Delphi's help system is an excellent example of that concept put to use.)

For example, click on Delphi's main title bar and press F1. A help screen appears that details all the help available. That makes sense: You weren't focused on anything in particular.

Now click on **File** on the menu bar. The pull-down menu appears with the New Project option highlighted. Press F1 again. This time, Delphi gives you information about what New Project will do if you select it. The help screen also has links to information about what projects and forms are. That's pretty handy.

Perhaps the most useful aspect of context-sensitive help is found in the editor. Click on the word `begin` in your small program and press F1. A help screen describing `begin` appears. Look at the following description:

```
The begin and end reserved words group a series of statements together
into a compound statement.
The compound statement is then treated as a single statement.
```

This rather technical description is a succinct restatement of what you learned earlier about blocks of code. Here, a block of code is called a *compound statement*, and `begin` and `end` are called *reserved words*.

> **Caution:** The preceding example illustrates an important point about the Help system. Don't go poking around in it just yet. Things are described in a very technical manner, and even a simple help screen like the one just described can contain words and concepts you won't understand. For example, what is a *reserved word*?
>
> If a word is reserved, you cannot use it for any purpose other than the one predetermined by the Pascal language. Therefore, `begin` in a Delphi program always signifies the beginning of a code block. It can never mean anything else. The catch here is that you haven't learned yet about other uses for words in Delphi.
>
> By the end of this book, you should be comfortable enough with Delphi and Pascal so that you can use the help system freely. Even then, however, you should keep a computer dictionary and the Delphi printed manuals handy so that you can find out about concepts and words you don't understand.
>
> There's also a graph at the top of the Help screen, which "explains" the Delphi syntax for a word. You may look at that and understand it just intuitively. If not, ignore it. You'll be able to tackle those graphs after you've learned the basics of programming.

By the time you finish this book, you will find that the Help system is an indispensable tool, both for increasing your knowledge and for refreshing your memory.

Debugging

When a computer program has an error in it, it is called a *bug*. Removing the bugs from your program is called *debugging*. A large percentage of the time spent on computer programs is spent debugging.

Chapter 5 ◆ Working with Pascal

> **The Source of the Term *Bug***
>
> Early digital computers were large, noisy things. They used large relay switches, which flopped back and forth from one position to the other to represent zeros and ones.
>
> A popular legend has it that one day a program on one of these early machines malfunctioned. According to the legend, a woman named Grace Hopper looked into the problem and found that a moth had flown into the computer and lodged itself onto one of the relays. It caused the program to malfunction. Grace Hopper logged the incident, and henceforth all errors in programs are referred to as *bugs*.
>
> The late Grace Hopper, who is held in high regard in computer circles, wanted it known for the record that she only reported the bug, and the name of the technician who actually found it is lost to history.
>
> Although this story is true, it may not be the true source of the term *bug*. The author of this book speculates that the word predates computer usage, and perhaps is derived from the Welsh word *bugaboo*, meaning "a troublesome thing."

Generally, two categories of bugs exist. The first category contains all the missing semicolons, misspelled words, and other *syntax errors*. These errors in grammar are quickly caught by Pascal, as you saw when you removed the closing curly brace of your comment earlier. Pascal, unlike some languages, has rigid rules of grammar that prevent programmers from making many of the most obvious and stupid mistakes. As a matter of course, you'll make dozens of syntax errors every time you sit down to program, and you'll spend very little time correcting them because Pascal is so fast at pointing them out.

The second category of bugs contains *logic errors*. Often, programmers describe things to their compilers, and the compilers create functioning programs from the instructions—yet these programs don't actually do what the programmers intended.

Remember how you took out the parenthesis from the statement, and the compiler gave you the message `Semicolon expected` even though you were clearly missing a parenthesis? Well, what is obvious to humans is not necessarily obvious to the programs that humans write. Consequently, you can write a program about bananas and then accidentally put in something that refers to oranges, and no computer in the world will catch the error.

Delphi provides you with considerable tools to help determine whether you've made a logic error. You look briefly at two of these tools in the following sections and return to them later when you have more serious programs to debug.

The Worst Kind Of Bug

Logic errors are the most pernicious. As I was writing this chapter, a pre-release version of Delphi was up on my machine and it crashed. (Pre-release software—made available to authors of books before it's made available to the general public—tends to have a lot more bugs.) The crash not only ended Delphi, but also Word for Windows and even brought Windows itself to an untimely close.

Example: Tracing

Caution: To follow along with the debugging examples in this chapter, call up the Environment notebook by selecting the **O**ptions menu and the **E**nvironment item. On the first page of the notebook (Preferences) there is a group of checkboxes labelled debugging. Make sure that "Step program block" is checked or Delphi will not behave as described in the following examples.

Delphi makes it possible for you to watch your code as it actually executes through an *integrated debugger*. This process is called *tracing*. Underneath the Play button on the SpeedBar are two other buttons featuring a dotted line with an arrow at the end and a box. The first button shows the arrow going into the box. The second button shows the arrow going over the box. These buttons are the Trace Into and Step Over buttons, which for now can serve the same purpose.

Click on one of the buttons. The screen flickers for a moment, and your code window appears. This window is slightly different than it was before; this time, the first line of the program (begin) is highlighted. In this state, the Code Editor is sometimes referred to as the "integrated debugger" or the "debugging window."

Tip: You also can start the integrated debugger by pressing either F7 or F8, or selecting either Trace into or Step over from the Debug menu.

You can still edit code in the Code Editor even though the program is running; but, if you do so, Pascal will ask you if you want to recompile the code so that the changes will take effect. If you answer "Yes," Pascal will recompile and restart the integrated debugger so that you are now back at the very beginning of the program.

If you answer "No," on the other hand, the program will continue to execute and any changes that you made will have no effect until the next time you compile. This, while it has uses, is more difficult to manage because the Code Editor shows

Chapter 5 ◆ Working with Pascal

> the changed code (but the program that's running is based on the code from the last compile). This technique should be used sparingly, when you want to verify the effect of several lines of code in one debugging session.
>
> In general, if you make a change, it is better to recompile and use the Goto command (from the **D**ebug menu select **G**oto, or press F4), which will start a new debugging session and return you to the current cursor position—but with the altered code actually in effect.

The integrated debugger shows you which line of code is about to execute. Click the button again, and the highlight bar moves forward to the following line:

```
Writeln('Hello, World!');
```

When you click on the button with this line highlighted, your program's typewriter-like window opens up and `Hello, World!` appears in it.

Click on the button again, and the next line appears, highlighted, in the Code Editor. Click on the button once more, and the typewriter window, which is labeled `inactive`, comes to the foreground (see fig. 5.1).

Figure 5.1
The integrated debugger in action.

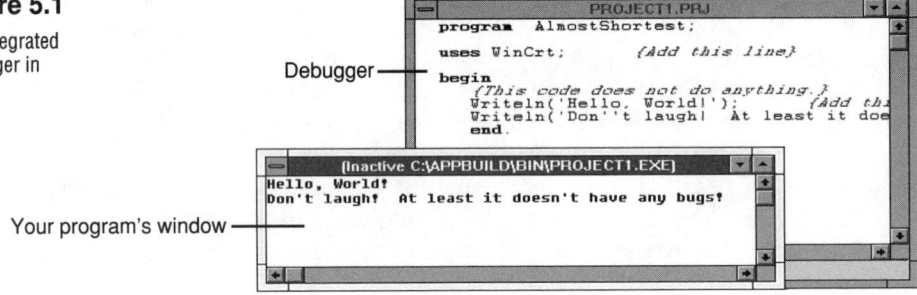

Debugger
Your program's window

The tracing features of Delphi can help you pinpoint exactly where your program has gone wrong.

Breakpoints

You often have a good idea of where your program is in error, or at least up to what point everything is all right. If you know at what point things start to go haywire, you can position the cursor in the edit window and press F4. The program then runs up to the cursor's location and stops. (You also can use this feature by choosing the **G**oto cursor from the **D**ebug menu.)

Sometimes your program will break down and you won't know where it occurred, so the Goto capability isn't always quite right. By using the integrated debugger, however, you can set *breakpoints*. Breakpoints are places in the code where Pascal pauses execution until you tell it to resume, whether by tracing or by using the Goto cursor feature. You can have many breakpoints at one time. By setting breakpoints at any point in your program about which you may have a question, you can track down a slippery logic bug.

To set a breakpoint, click the left mouse button in the margin to the left of the line of code on which you want to stop. To remove the breakpoint, click again. You can also set and remove breakpoints at the current cursor position by pressing F5.

Object Methods

As mentioned earlier, you don't dwell on traditional Pascal in this book. The subsequent chapters are devoted largely to working Delphi-style, which is more entertaining than the traditional environments in which you might learn Pascal.

You've worked with properties already, and you've even seen how the Object Inspector lists events that a component will respond to. Those responses are *object methods*. You'll find an in-depth explanation of object methods in Chapter 21, "Objects," but you can't do *anything* in Pascal without at least a basic grasp of what they are.

Objects in Pascal

Objects in Pascal are referred to by their names. (You can name objects freely, as you'll see in the next chapter.) If you have objects that you call MyWindow, MyScrollbar, and MyButton, for example, they appear in a Pascal program as follows:

```
MyWindow
MyScrollbar
MyButton
```

You refer to an object's properties by typing the name of the object, inserting a period, and then adding the name of the property. For example, look at the following line:

```
MyButton.Height
```

The name MyButton.Height refers to the height of the object MyButton.

Behaviors (usually called *methods*) also are referred to by the name of the behavior following the object name and a period. For example, examine the following:

```
MyButton.Click
```

This name refers to what MyButton does when clicked.

Sometimes an object can respond different ways in the same method. For example, look at the following:

```
MyWindow.ColorYourself
```

Sometimes it is most efficient to have the same object method act slightly differently in different circumstances. In this case, you might want `MyWindow` to color itself red or you might want it to color itself blue. To make this possible, methods sometimes take *parameters*, which alter the way a method behaves. Depending on whether you want to color the window red or blue, the preceding command to color the window becomes as follows:

```
MyWindow.ColorYourself(Red)
```

or

```
MyWindow.ColorYourself(Blue)
```

`Writeln`, you might realize now, is like a disembodied method—it has no object. It just sends whatever is described as its parameter to the typewriter-window regardless of anything else that is going on.

Automatically Generated Code

Pascal, as you have seen, automatically generates code for you when you start a new project. In fact, Pascal generates a great deal of code for you, which is good on one hand, because you don't have to write that code, but bad on the other, because if you're just learning Pascal, you don't necessarily understand the code—and you should understand *all* the code in a program you call your own. Pascal automatically generated code is called a *code frame*. Think of code frames like the frame of a house you're going to build: Pascal takes care of the busy work, leaving you free to decide on the important aspects of your program.

The thing to remember about code frames is that you don't have to understand them right away. By the time you get to the end of this book, you'll know just what all the code does. Until then, you should concentrate on the code you enter here.

You can already understand some of the automatically generated code, which you'll look at next. To examine this code, start a new project. (You can save the "almost shortest" program if you want. You can store all the code that you enter from this book in the BOOKPAS directory you created in Chapter 1.)

Use the Project Manager to view the new project code, by following these steps:

1. Start a new project (Select from the File menu, New Project)

2. From the View menu, select Project source.

The code should look like this:

```
program Project1;

uses
  Apps,
  Unit1 in 'UNIT1.PAS' {Form1};

begin
  Application.Run(Form1);
end.
```

You get a program statement, with the default name of `Project1`. (You can change it by selecting Save Project As from the File menu.) After that is the `uses` statement, which has two units specified in it. Just as the `WinCrt` unit enabled you to create a program that mimicked a typewriter, the `Apps` unit contains the object that allows the program to act like a Windows program.

Then the program uses `Unit1 in 'UNIT1.PAS'`, followed by the comment `{Form1}`. From Chapter 3, "Introducing Delphi," you may recall that each form has an associated unit and that when you open a new form, it is called Form1, so it only makes sense that the code unit is called Unit1. (You can change the form name using the Object Inspector by changing the `Name` property of the form.) Unit1 is the name by which Delphi knows the form unit, and this is followed by the word `in` and the DOS/Windows filename in single quotes. (You can and should change both the name of the unit and the file that the unit is stored in by choosing Save File As from the File menu.)

> **Note:** The reason for the separation of the Delphi name and the DOS/Windows file name is so that you can use longer than eight-character names for units in your program. The following is allowed, for example:
>
>   uses AllOfYourEggs in '1BASKET.PAS';
>
> In this book, however, all unit names will match their file names.

Next, you have the main block of code, `begin` and `end.`. But you still have one unexplained line of code:

```
Application.Run(Form1);
```

The `Apps` unit contains the object that allows the program to act like a real Windows program. The object is called `Application`, and it has only one method you care about, `Run`.

Remember `WriteLn`? It knew that it was going to put text on a screen, but you had to supply the text as a parameter to it. `Application.Run` handles all the events that the user generates, but it has to know exactly *where* to send those events. By using `Form1` as a parameter to `Run`, you're telling the `Application` object just where the events in your program have to go.

Chapter 5 ◆ Working with Pascal

The Run method code, translated into English, looks something like the following pseudocode:

begin
 if an event has occurred, then send it to the appropriate object
end

In upcoming chapters, you write the code to handle events that Application.Run sends to your form.

You're still not quite ready to look at the code in the unit window. Unfortunately, Delphi puts several advanced items into that window, where most of your code also has to go.

Altering Object Behavior

Delphi provides an easy way for you to modify the most common event that occurs for any object. Try the following steps:

1. Open a new project.

2. On a blank form, place a single button.

3. Double-click on the button.

Delphi takes you into the unit window and into a code block that looks suspiciously like the World's Shortest Pascal program:

```
procedure TForm1.Button1Click(Sender: TObject);
begin

end;
```

You have a begin and end, as before, but this time the end has a semicolon after it. The semicolon makes sense—the only time end has a period after it is when it is used to end the entire program. Therefore, you're left with only the following line to explain:

```
procedure TForm1.Button1Click(Sender: TObject);
```

Right now, you can understand this line in only the loosest terms. In a few more chapters, you should be ready to look at it more technically, but you need to understand it somewhat before you go on.

Remember this English-language code?

```
Airplane: If the user has pulled back the throttle, go up.
Airplane: If the user has pushed the throttle forward, go down.
Airplane: If the user has pressed eject, open the cockpit.
```

You learned in Chapter 2, "Traditional Programming," that events are sent to the appropriate object, where instructions exist to handle those events. These instructions are like miniprograms. They identify the object to which they belong and they have a name. In your main program, you have the following:

```
program AlmostShortest;
```

The instructions in an object to handle an event, therefore, look like this:

```
procedure AnObject.AnEventMethod;
```

The word `procedure` in the second example is analogous to the word `program` in the first, except that Pascal *requires* the word `procedure`—it's not optional, like `program`. The name of the object is `AnObject` and the name of the event to which the object is going to respond is `AnEvent`. Look at the following line:

```
procedure TForm1.Button1Click
```

This line describes what the `TForm1` object does when `Button1` is clicked. (Pascal adds a `T` to the name of all objects in your project for reasons you learn later.)

Between the parentheses are the parameters on which this procedure is going to operate. Ignore them for now. All you need now is to know that when you double-click an object on a form, Delphi creates a code frame in which you can describe how the form reacts to that event.

Summary

Delphi highlights words that have special meaning in Pascal. After you enter a program, you can compile and run the program in one step. Delphi also has an integrated debugger that enables you to step through the code line by line. You can get help from Delphi on the following subjects: how the editors work, how the debuggers work, what the objects available are, and even basic Pascal concepts. Delphi generates code frames that you can modify to describe how objects respond to certain events.

Pascal has a logical, if not entirely intuitive, way of handling punctuation. Statements end with semicolons. `Begin` and `end` denote blocks of code that are treated as one statement. Comments are enclosed in curly braces. Text is enclosed in single quotation marks. Parameters are enclosed within parentheses.

You refer to objects by name. An object name can be followed by a period and a property name or a method name. Methods can have parameters. The word `procedure` denotes a Delphi "mini-program."

Review Questions

1. Name two ways to get help from Delphi.
2. How do you compile and run a program in Delphi?
3. What are comments? When do you use them? How are they delimited in a Delphi program?
4. How do you refer to objects in Delphi? What about their methods? Their properties?
5. What is debugging?
6. What is syntax highlighting? What is it good for?
7. How would Delphi respond to this program?

   ```
   program ReviewQuestion;
   uses WinCrt;
           Writeln('By Example");
           end.
   ```

8. Is `begin` a statement?
9. How do you get an apostrophe or single quotation mark into Pascal text?
10. How do you step through a program?
11. What does `WinCrt` do? Do you use `WinCrt` in a typical Windows program?
12. How do you set a breakpoint?

Review Exercises

1. Type a letter to the author in a code editor. (Say lots of nice things.) Observe that some words are presented differently than others.
2. Start a new project in Delphi, remove any forms from it, and write a Delphi program that does nothing. Add a couple of lines to print out some text.
3. Using the File menu's Open Project selection, open a project that does not exist. Add a form that does not yet exist by selecting Open File from the File menu.

4. Get help on your programs by using the context-sensitive Help feature of Delphi.

5. Use any of the editing features described in the chapter to create a program that prints out the same line of text 30 times.

6. Deliberately introduce bugs into a working program. Observe how accurate (or not) Delphi is at identifying the bugs.

7. Using the program from line 5, set up breakpoints and watch how the IDE stops on those lines. Compare restarting the code by stepping through it or by selecting Run from the Run menu.

8. Open a new project and change Form1's Name property to "MyForm". Find out what happens to the automatically generated line in the project file:

```
Application.Run(Form1);
```

CHAPTER 6

Variables

You've explored how objects have *properties* and *methods*. But, as you learned earlier, the whole concept of objects is a relatively new one. You may have wondered what was done before. Before object-oriented programming, properties and methods were separate and properties were stored as *variables*.

As a programmer, you may think of a variable as a place to hold a single piece of information. A variable can hold your age, your birthdate, your name, but it can hold only one of these things at a time. If you use a variable to hold your name and then later use it to hold your address, your name is gone. That variable now stores your address.

Technically, a variable is an area of RAM to which you give a name. This definition explains a lot if you think about it. Just as a string on a guitar can play only one note at a time, a variable (an area of RAM) can hold only one item—or value—at a time.

If you were working in machine language, you would actually have to specify which area—or address—in RAM you want to use, but fortunately, the Delphi compiler does all that for you. All you have to do is *declare* the variable. A variable declaration has two parts, a *name* and a *type*. The following sections discuss these parts.

Deciding on Variable Names

Older computer languages limited the names you could give variables. Like DOS and Windows file names, variable names in these older languages might have been restricted to eight characters, or something similar. In Pascal, variable names can be up to 63 characters long, so you can (and should) give your variables descriptive names.

Chapter 6 ◆ Variables

If you want to keep track of the current balance in a checkbook program, for example, you can create a variable called

```
CheckbookBalance
```

or perhaps just

```
Balance
```

> **Note:** Pascal variable names actually can be longer than 63 characters, but everything after the 63rd character is ignored. For example,
>
> ```
> AVeryVeryVeryVeryLongAndInvolvedVariableNameSixtyFourCharacters
> ```
>
> is equivalent to
>
> ```
> AVeryVeryVeryVeryLongAndInvolvedVariableNameSixtyFourCharactersPlusABunchMore
> ```

> **Tip:** In truth, long variable names are a chore to type, and very long names actually make your program harder to read. Try to limit your variable names to 15 or 20 characters.

Restrictions on Variable Names

A variable name cannot have spaces. For example, you cannot have a variable name like the following:

```
Checkbook Balance
```

Instead, that variable name should look like the following:

```
CheckbookBalance
```

Alternatively, you can use the underscore character (_) to connect words:

```
Checkbook_Balance
```

The underscore character can even start a variable name:

```
_The_Long_And_Winding_Road____
```

As this example shows, you can use several underscores together, though this example clearly overdoes it.

If you don't want to use underscores, you can make the words in a variable clear by capitalizing them, as in the following name:

```
TheLongAndWindingRoad
```

Keep in mind that Pascal is not sensitive to letter casing. For example, these two variable names are equivalent:

```
x
X
```

And these three also are equivalent:

```
TheLongAndWindingRoad
thelongandwindingroad
thelOngandWindIngROAD
```

Some languages (notably C++ and Smalltalk) treat all three of the preceding names as different variables. Because Pascal does not, you can use capitalization to clarify variable names but not worry if you miss an occasional capital letter. (You'll occasionally be inconsistent with the capitalization when you type the same variable name frequently.)

Using Numbers in Variable Names

You can use letters and underscores anywhere within a variable name. You also can use numbers anywhere in a variable name except as the first character. The following names are acceptable to the Pascal compiler:

```
Beverly_Hills_90210
DeepSpace9
```

These names, however, are not acceptable:

```
1600PennsylvaniaAvenue
8December1989
```

Example: Object Names vs. Variable Names

The rules you have just learned apply to any name used in Pascal, including object names. Try the following steps:

1. Open any project (even a new one) in Pascal.

2. In the Object Inspector, locate the Name property of any object. (In a new project, the form will be the only object.)

3. Try several combinations of names using underscores, numbers, and letters.

Notice that Pascal warns you if you put in an illegal name.

> **Note:** A name (for anything) in Pascal is called an *identifier*. In much of the documentation for Pascal, you see terms such as *object identifier* or *variable identifier*, which mean the name of an object or a variable.

97

Forbidden Identifiers

Pascal has certain key words that are basic to the compiler's functions. You cannot use these *reserved words* (or sometimes called just *keywords*) as variable names. For example, you cannot use the following as variable names:

```
begin
end
program
```

The Variable Type

After you decide on a name for a variable, you also must decide on the variable's *type*. A type describes how the variable is used and what kind of information it can store (as well as how much). One Pascal type, for example, is called *char*, which is short for *character*. As you might imagine, a char variable holds one character of information.

In Pascal, you must enclose characters in single quotation marks, as in the following examples:

```
'a'
'A'
'%'
'@'
' '
```

A character is always exactly one byte long, even if that character is blank.

What Really Goes On

As you may recall from an earlier discussion, machine language requires the actual address of a place in RAM. What happens when you declare a variable is that you call a certain place in RAM by that name. If you tell the Pascal compiler (in Pascal code, of course) to

```
Declare a variable called "ALetterOfTheAlphabet" as a char
```

the Pascal compiler then translates every occasion where you use the variable `"ALetterOfTheAlphabet"` into an actual RAM address. (A RAM address might be something like 14556, which would refer to the 14,556th byte of memory.)

All this means is that you never have to care what address `ALetterOfTheAlphabet` really occupies, and you can refer to it by a meaningful name rather than 14556.

When to Declare a Variable

In the preceding chapter, you worked with the basic outline of Pascal code:

```
begin
   . . .
      end.
```

Later, you looked at how Pascal generated object methods:

```
procedure ObjectName.ObjectMethod(parameters);
begin
   . . .
      end;
```

You may have wondered why Pascal even bothers with `begin` and `end`. After all, can't the compiler figure out that the first instruction is the beginning and the last is the end? What could come before `begin`?

In fact, while statements between `begin` and `end` are to be translated into machine instructions—things for the CPU to do—the instructions before `begin` are the ones that really make *your* life easier. Here, you declare variables, and this keeps you from having to access RAM directly.

Now take that idea back a few steps and look at it more closely. You've seen code using English:

If the user clicks on the button marked "Print" then print out the Bank Balance

You've also learned that you can't actually use English as a programming language because it isn't exact enough and that computers need to be told exactly how to do everything. So, what is "The Bank Balance" exactly? Well, somewhere in your program, you had to have written an instruction like the following to the compiler:

Declare "The Bank Balance" to be a variable capable of holding the User's Bank Balance.

Your English-language program therefore looks something like the following:

Declare "The Bank Balance" to be a variable capable of holding the User's Bank Balance.
begin

  . . .
  If the user clicks on the button marked "Print"
  then Print Out the Bank Balance
  . . .
  end.

All variable declarations must come before the code in which they are used.

Chapter 6 ◆ Variables

> **Note:** Some languages do not have variable declarations, or they make declarations optional. The first time the compiler sees a variable used, it determines either based on context or on the first letter of the variable what type the variable is and, in rare cases, what the value of the variable should be when first used.
>
> As a result, Delphi may look to you like it requires "extra" work than these other languages. The downside of "automatic" declaration is that if you misspell a variable name, the compiler of one of these other languages doesn't tell you!
>
> For example, assume that you have a variable called "Dog" that you're using to hold the name of your dog. If you type **Dof**, the compiler never catches it, and instead just assumes you wanted a *new* variable called "Dof"!

How to Declare a Variable

Declaring a variable is fairly easy. You first have to tell the compiler that you are going to declare variables by using the keyword var. You then type the name of your variable, followed by a colon, and then followed by the variable's type. For example, look at the following:

```
var
    AChar: Char;
begin
. . .
    end;
```

You now can use the variable AChar in your code.

You can declare multiple variables under one var:

```
var
    char1 : Char;
    char2 : Char;
```

You can list multiple variables before the colon and type part of the declaration:

```
var char1, char2: Char;
```

And, you can have as many var statements as you want, as long as they precede the begin:

```
var char1: Char;
var
    char2: Char;
    char3: Char;
var char4, char5: Char;
begin
```

The String Type

The type char is of limited use because it can hold only one character. Most of the time, you need a bunch of characters together—or more technically, a *string*—to do anything useful.

Like a string of pearls, a string of characters is a series of characters one after the other. In Pascal, the character string type is simply called `string`. In fact, any series of characters is called a string, including this text from the preceding chapter:

```
'Hello, World'
'Don''t laugh, at least it doesn''t have any bugs'
```

Text like this is called a *literal* string.

As you may have guessed, strings use the same single quotation mark punctuation scheme that you learned about in Chapter 5 in conjunction with `WriteLn`. A Pascal string can hold up to 255 characters.

The space taken by a string, however, is 256 bytes. There is one space for each character the string can store, but the first byte tells how long the string really is. For example, look at the following string:

```
'Hello, World'
```

The *length byte*, as it is called, has a value of 12. In the following example, the length byte has a value of 47.

```
'Don''t laugh, at least it doesn''t have any bugs'
```

Pascal also allows *null strings*. A null string is expressed as

```
''
```

and its length byte has a value of 0. The important thing to realize about a null string is that it is not a series of blanks or spaces, like the following:

```
'        '
```

A null string contains nothing—not even blanks.

Declaring Strings

Declaring a string is not much different from declaring a character. You can use any valid identifier (name), and where you used `char` before, you now use `string`:

```
var
   AString: String;
begin
...
   end;
```

Chapter 6 ◆ Variables

As mentioned earlier, once you put var into your code, everything after that and before the begin is treated as a variable declaration block. You therefore can define multiple strings:

```
var
    AString: String;
    AnotherString: String;
    AndAnotherString: String;
begin
. . .
```

And again, if you have a number of variables (as in the preceding example) all the same type, you can save some typing by declaring them all at once, separating each name with a comma, and ending the series with the colon and the string keyword. The following is identical to the preceding example:

```
var
    AString, AnotherString, AndAnotherString: String;
begin
. . .
```

> **Tip:** You can also declare variables of other types (like chars) within the same variable block.

Declaring Shorter Strings

You now know that a string takes up 256 bytes of space. If you don't need all that space, you can shorten the string. Shortening a string involves more Pascal punctuation, as shown in the following example:

```
var
    AString: String[30];
```

The following strings take 11 bytes, 16 bytes, and 184 bytes of RAM, respectively:

```
AString       : String[10];
AnotherString : String[15];
AThirdString  : String[183];
```

> **RAM Shortages**
>
> You might rightly wonder why you should care about whether a string occupies 31 bytes of RAM or 256 bytes of RAM. Your computer (and the computer of someone using your programs) has to have at least 2M of RAM to run Windows, right? That's more than 2,000,000 bytes. So who cares about 200 bytes more or less?
>
> It's true that you shorten a string to save memory and that you shouldn't worry how long your strings are in small programs. However, suppose that you were writing a word processing program, and you saved every string as 256 bytes. If most were fewer than 80 bytes (a difference of more than 170) and you had 10,000 strings in a document, you would be wasting more than 1,700,000 bytes.
>
> Also keep in mind that your program isn't the only one running. The user may have many other programs up alongside of yours, and Windows itself uses almost 2M of RAM by itself. It's *polite* to use resources wisely.

Assigning Values to a String

Now that you have a string, what do you do with it? The first thing you do with a string (or any variable) is assign some value to it. What the value is depends on how you are going to use it in your program, as you'll see in the following paragraphs. But first, take a look at how you make an assignment in Pascal.

A Pascal program is made up of *statements*. You've seen a number of statements already, such as

```
Writeln('Hello, World!');
```

and even touched on the fact that `begin` and `end` tell the compiler to treat a series of Pascal statements as a unit (or block).

The most basic of statements is the assignment statement, indicated with a colon followed by an equal sign, as shown in the following line:

```
:=
```

This colon-equal symbol means "assign the value on the right to the variable on the left." With the string example, the assignment

```
AString := 'Hello, World';
```

in English means

> *Assign the value 'Hello, World' to AString.*

Chapter 6 ◆ Variables

If you were still working with WinCrt, you could use Writeln and AString together, as shown in the following line:

```
Writeln(AString);
```

This feature has the same effect as the first Writeln of the Pascal program from the preceding chapter, and will cause "Hello, World" to appear on-screen.

> **Note:** Values such as 'Hello, World' that appear in the program code are called *literals*. The 'Hello, World' string and 'Don''t laugh!' strings would be called literal strings. This distinguishes them from variable strings, such as AString.

Characters and Strings

Characters variables can also be assigned values, except that unlike strings the text assigned to a character can be only one character long, as shown here:

```
var AChar: Char
begin
   AChar := 'C';
   AChar := 'Some long text'; {No! This won't work!}
   end;
```

Characters and strings have an odd relationship to each other. You can assign a character to a string, but you can't assign a string to a character. For example:

```
var
   AChar: Char;
   AString: String;
begin
   AString := AChar;   {This works.}
   AChar := AString;   {This will not compile}
   end;
```

This concept isn't too hard to understand: A string can hold all the information in a character, but a character cannot hold all the information in a string. Pascal calls this a *type mismatch error*. You explore type mismatch errors a great deal in the upcoming chapters.

Example: The Label and Button Objects

For this example, you take a look at the string data type in a Pascal program. First, create a new project and then add a button and a label object (see fig. 6.1). The label control is indicated on the Component Palette by a large letter *A*. The label object is a component that describes something to the user. Here you use it to display a message.

104

Figure 6.1
A form with a label object and a button.

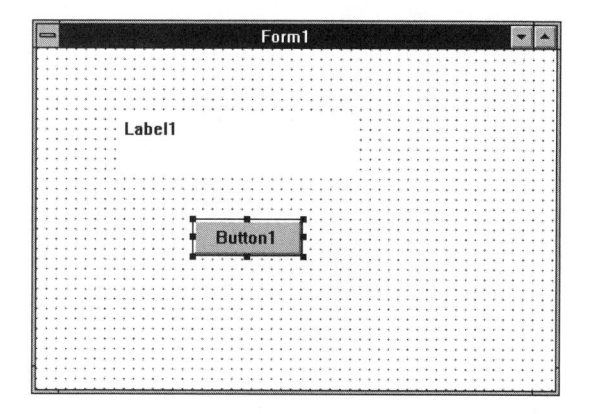

Now double-click on Button1. Pascal generates the code frame for how the form should react when Button1 is clicked. Modify the code frame as follows (the lines not marked as "Add this line" will be generated by Delphi):

```
procedure TForm1.Button1Click(Sender: TObject);
var NewCaption: String;   {Add this line}
begin
   NewCaption := 'Hello, World!'; {Add this line}
   Label1.Caption := NewCaption;   {Add this line}
   end;
```

(You don't need to put in the comments. They just show you what code to add.)

Here you can see object properties and variables working together: You declare a string; you assign a value to the string; and you assign the string's value to the caption of the label. Give it a try. When you click the button in the running program, the label caption changes from Label1 to Hello, World!.

Wait a minute. You just changed an object's property by assigning it a new value! How can that be? If the preceding code works, then would the following have worked just as well?

```
begin
   Label1.Caption := 'Hello, World!';  {Add this line and remove existing
line.}
   end;
```

Yes. This method has the same effect as the previous code.

As in variables, object properties have types. And, like variables, an object property can have just one value at time, which you changed in the preceding example. The logical conclusion to this discussion is that Label1.Caption is a variable of the type string, or at least can be treated as such.

It's only logical to assume that the captions of buttons are *also* strings. Maybe you can do something with that assumption, as the next experiment shows.

Chapter 6 ♦ Variables

Continuing on with this form, see if you can't influence the button from the label object. Double-click on the label object. Pascal presents you with a code frame. From the name of the method

```
procedure TForm1.Label1Click. . .
```

you can see that, functionally, a label can be used in much the same way as a button.

> **Note:** One helpful thing to remember about Pascal is that it is as consistent as possible concerning names and events. The Caption property works for buttons and labels and for most objects with a text value that is displayed to (but not editable by) the user of your program.
>
> Click on is always the term used to describe what happens when the user clicks the mouse on an object.

Sure enough, you can use this method to allow the label to "return the favor" by changing the button's caption.

```
procedure TForm1.Label1Click(Sender: TObject);
begin
   Button1.Caption := 'Touché';
   end;
```

> **Note:** You can enter a character into a Pascal program that isn't on your keyboard by finding out its ASCII value (see Appendix A) and then pressing and holding Alt and using the numeric keypad to enter its value. Then release Alt and it should appear.
>
> For example, to get an é, place the cursor after the "Touch" text and press and hold Alt while typing **130**. Then release Alt.

String Concatenation

Pascal, like all computer languages, has operators. An operator acts on one or more variables and results in a new value based on the values of those variables. You can tack one string onto the end of another string through the use of the Delphi string concatenation operator. The string concatenation operator is probably one of the most illogical aspects of Pascal: It is the + sign. If you have the following:

```
AString := 'Cats';
AnotherString := ' and Dogs';
```

then this line

```
AThirdString := AString + AnotherString;
```

sets AThirdString to have the value Cats and Dogs. The string concatenation *operator* results in a value of the string on the right appended to the string on the left. (Many languages use a special symbol for string concatenation so that it can't be confused with addition.)

Example: String Concatenation and Autosizing

Now try out string concatenation by changing the button-click procedure from the previous example. (You can get to it by double-clicking on the button object again.) Make it switch the button caption to Press me again! and change the label caption to match the following:

```
Label1.Caption := Label1.Caption + 'Hello ';
```

Now change the starting caption of the label by using the Object Inspector. Just delete the text there and don't put anything in its place. Can you guess what happens when you run this program?

After running it, locate the AutoSize property of Label1 and change it to False. Make the label considerably larger than is necessary to hold the initial Caption. What do you think will happen now? End the problem (Alt+F4) and find the Label's Word Wrap property in the object Inspector. Set this to true. What kind of result do you think *this* will produce? Check out figure 6.2.

Figure 6.2
String concatenation and the label object.

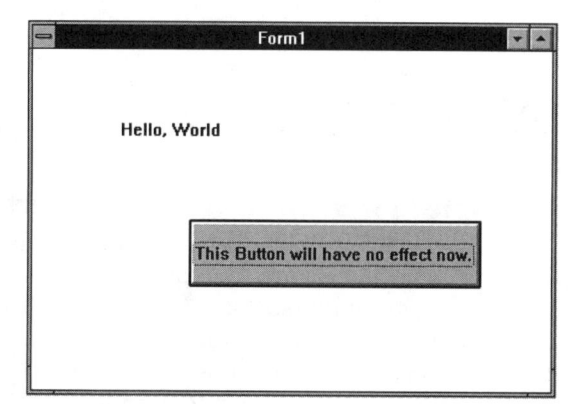

You started with a string—called a *null* string—that had no characters in it. Every time you pressed the button, 'Hello' was added to the text. This example is probably as clear an example of how string concatenation works as you'll ever see.

Labels and Word Wrap

Word Wrap has nothing to do with strings but is a function of the label component. If a label's caption is too long to fit within the label's specified boundaries, the label breaks the caption at the word and starts on the next line.

Chapter 6 ♦ Variables

If the label doesn't have enough height, all or part of the subsequent lines of the caption are cut off. (Notice in figure 6.3 that the bottom of the last Hello line is cut off.)

Figure 6.3
A label that doesn't have enough height.

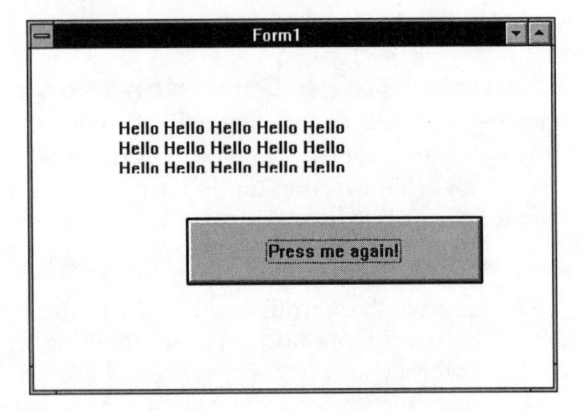

[Figure: Form1 window showing "Hello Hello Hello Hello Hello" repeated on three lines (third line cut off) and a "Press me again!" button]

This feature comes into play only if the AutoSize property is False. With Autosize on, the label never wordwraps because it is constantly resizing itself so that the entire Caption fits on one line.

> **Caution:** Buttons do not have the Word **W**rap feature. Text for a button always appears on one line. If the text doesn't fit on one line, it is cut off. Buttons have no AutoSize property.

Example: Maximum String Lengths

One thing you should know is what happens when you try to add data to a string already 255 characters long. The easiest way to find out is to stretch the label object in the previous example so that it takes up a lot of room, and then run the program.

What happens? At some point you get just a portion of the word "Hello." The effect is like being cut off in mid-sentence on the phone: "Hello, Hello, Hello, He." That's the indication that you tried to add more data than the string could hold. The string takes as much of the data as it can hold and discards the rest.

Summary

Variables are storage places with specific names that can hold data for a program. They are much like object properties. In Pascal, an identifier can have up to 63 significant characters; it can include underscores and (after the first character) numbers. Identifiers that are the same as Pascal keywords are forbidden. Variables have a name and a type.

The char type holds one character of data and takes up one byte. The more useful string type takes up as much as 256 bytes and holds as much as 255 characters of data. The first byte of a string is the length byte, which describes the length of the string.

You can assign values to a string with an assignment statement; an assignment statement in Pascal uses the colon-equal symbol; you can concatenate two strings together with the + sign; and you can treat some object properties, such as the caption of a label or a button, as a string variable.

Review Questions

1. Can a variable hold two values at once?
2. What is the keyword used to tell the compiler you are going to declare a variable?
3. What punctuation mark separates a variable name or names from the variable type?
4. How long can a variable name be? Can it begin with an underscore? A number? Can it have spaces?
5. What is a variable type? Name a type.
6. How do you concatenate two strings together?
7. How do you assign a value to a string? A char?
8. Can begin be the name of a variable?
9. What is a variable, in terms of RAM?
10. Give an example of how you declare multiple variables of the same type.
11. What happens in this code?

    ```
    var
        S: String[6];
    begin
        S := 'Hello, World';
        end;
    ```

Chapter 6 ◆ Variables

Review Exercises

1. Write a program with a button and a label where the button's caption constantly gets longer. Note the absence of **W**ord **W**rap with the button object.

2. Write a program with a button and a label where the label object is big enough to hold more than 255 characters. Write the program so that pressing the button makes the label caption longer and longer. Note that trying to add characters to a string already 255 characters long has no effect on the string.

3. Create a simple program that has a label and a button where pressing the button switches the captions of the label and the button. (If the label reads "Hello" and the button reads "World," for example, pressing the button should make the label read "World" and the button read "Hello.") You need to declare a string variable in the Button1Click procedure to hold the caption of the first control you change.

4. Using the WinCRT unit covered in Chapter 5, declare several char variables and several string variables of varying lengths, assign them values, and use them with the Writeln procedure. Note that Writeln treats all kinds of strings and chars the same.

CHAPTER 7

Using Numbers

In the preceding chapter, you learned what a variable is, how variables are declared, legal variable names, and two of the basic Pascal variable types—characters and strings. You learned how to assign values to variables, and what operators are. You also looked at the + operator, so now you should be able to determine the value of C in the following code:

```
   var
     A, B, C: String;
begin
   A := '11';
   B := '11';
   C := A + B;
end;
```

If you think C is '22', then you need to go back and look over the last few sections of Chapter 6. C is '1111'.

It may seem odd that Pascal doesn't add the two numbers together. But they really aren't numbers. They are character strings with numerals in them. A numeral represents a number. It is the symbol '1' or '2', not the quantity. You make this distinction all the time in real life, believe it or not. Every day you deal with numerals without ever considering them to be mathematical figures. For example, when was the last time you did math with your ZIP code or added up the numbers on your Social Security card? Phone numbers, credit card numbers, and license plates are all examples of everyday numerals that, unless you are a numerologist, you will never plug into a math equation.

Pascal therefore uses the plus sign (+) to concatenate two strings. Because you can't add two strings together, you really have little chance of confusion.

Numbers in Delphi

Delphi, of course, allows you to use numbers. Delphi has several data types with which you can do math. These data types are divided into two main groups, *integer* and *real*. Integer types represent what are commonly called *whole* numbers. Numbers such as 1, 2, 10,000, or 10,000,000 are all integers. Integers can be negative numbers as well, such as –1, –2, –10,000 or –10,000,000. An integer is a number with no fractional or decimal part. (The real types can have a decimal part and are covered in Chapter 13, "Pascal Math.")

Expressing Integers

Integers are expressed in a Pascal program more or less as you write them in real life, with the exception that thousands are never separated with commas. Here are some valid examples:

```
1
-1234
1066      {No comma between the 1 and the zero}
1281989   {No commas here either}
```

Commas are not just unnecessary but are not allowed. You also cannot break a number with spaces. The compiler considers such numbers in error:

```
1,066
1 234 567
1,281,989
```

The only punctuation you can use with an integer is a minus sign, which must go at the beginning of a negative number.

```
-1234     {This will work.}
- 1234    {This, too.  You can put spaces between the minus and the
number.}
1234-     {This doesn't mean -1234}
```

You can lead a number with as many zeros as you want, keeping in mind that the zeros have no effect on the value. So 1 and 000000001 are the same number in Pascal. You cannot have a decimal point with an integer, even if the numbers following the decimal point are all zeros. Although the numbers 1.0 and 1 may mean the same thing to you, they are not the same thing in Pascal.

Numeric Types

You've learned how every variable has a type and read about the `string` and `char` types. In Pascal, there are specific types for holding numbers as well. As a child, you may have played the "I can count higher than you can" game. Whatever number your opponent came up with, you could go higher by adding one to it. (If your opponent knew the trick, too, of course, the game rapidly became boring.)

Your computer (and by extension Delphi) is drastically limited by comparison. To store a number takes RAM, and the bigger the number, the more RAM it takes. To understand how numbers are stored, backtrack and look at the char type briefly.

The char variables take exactly one byte of space and represent one of up to 256 possible characters. (This fact makes sense—a byte can hold one of 256 values.) What's actually in the location of RAM labelled by the char variable is a number from 0 through 255. Somewhere in your computer is a table that equates the numbers from 0 through 255 to characters. (Also, see Appendix A.) This table of characters is called the *ASCII character set*, or sometimes the IBM extended ASCII character set.

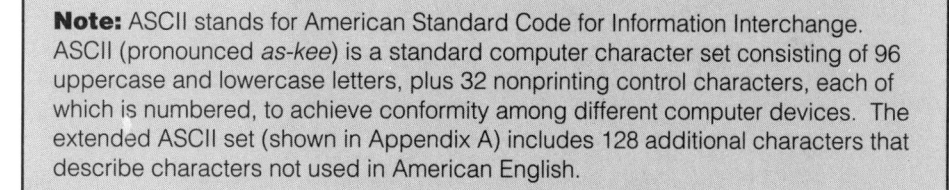

> **Note:** ASCII stands for American Standard Code for Information Interchange. ASCII (pronounced *as-kee*) is a standard computer character set consisting of 96 uppercase and lowercase letters, plus 32 nonprinting control characters, each of which is numbered, to achieve conformity among different computer devices. The extended ASCII set (shown in Appendix A) includes 128 additional characters that describe characters not used in American English.

If you were going to store a number in the computer, you might use the characters '0' through '9'. One byte then stores a single decimal digit, which is something of a waste of space. After all, a byte can hold up to 256 values, and you're going to use only 10 of them? The other problem with this approach is that the CPU itself does math based on the values in the byte, not based on the numerals '0' through '9'. So, Pascal would have to translate the decimal numerals into their byte equivalents before doing math on them, anyway.

Instead, Pascal integers are based on the actual numbers used by the CPU. Table 7.1 shows these types.

Table 7.1. Pascal integer variable types.

Name	Size	Examples	Minimum	Maximum
Shortint	1 byte	-100, 4, 24	-128	127
Integer	2 bytes	-10000, 444, 6	-32768	32767
Longint	4 bytes	-100000, 12, 324567	-2147483648	2147483647

Chapter 7 ◆ Using Numbers

The Longint is the largest integer type in Pascal and, in most cases, is the largest type the basic Intel CPU can work directly with. Special code has to be written to allow you to work with numbers that can have a value over 2 billion.

These capacities may look random, but they aren't. The Shortint can hold 256 values (128 negative + 127 positive + zero), or one byte. The integer can hold 65,536 values, or 256 * 256. The Longint can hold 256 * 256 * 256 * 256, or about 4.3 billion. If Delphi stored the data as characters, as you learned earlier, these same four bytes could hold only four decimal digits, or 10,000 values total (10 * 10 * 10 * 10).

In Pascal, you can look at the one- and two-byte sizes differently, as shown in table 7.2.

Table 7.2. Pascal unsigned integer variable types.

Name	Size	Examples	Minimum	Maximum
Byte	1 byte	100, 4, 24	0	255
Word	2 bytes	10000, 12, 40000	0	65535

You use the Byte and Word variable types to represent values that should never be negative. Because they can never be negative, they are referred to as "unsigned."

Working with Integers

You declare integer variables in the same fashion that you declare string and character variables: with a name (or comma-separated names), followed by a colon, followed by a type. You must make declarations after the var statement and before the begin statement. For example,

```
var
    B: Byte;
    I, J, K : Integer;
    L: Longint;
    PenniesIMakePerHour: byte;
    PenniesIMakePerWeek: Word;
    DollarsPerYearIdLikeToMake: Longint;
begin
    ...
```

Note: A tradition in programming has been to declare variables used for many different purposes in the same code with one-letter names. The traditional integer variable name is I. If you need more, you declare the next integer variable J, the one after that K, and so on. (Some languages even automatically assume that I is an integer variable and don't require it to be declared as such.) As with all variables, you can, of course, use longer names.

The plus operator and assignment statement you looked at in the preceding chapter also work with integers. You therefore can follow the declarations from the preceding example with code like the following:

```
B := 10;
I := 1;
J := 2;
K := I + J;
L := K + B;
```

Here, the + really is a plus sign. In this case, 1 + 1 equals 2, and so on.

```
K := I + J;
```

This code adds the value in I (1) and the value in J (2) and assigns it to K. As a result, K has a value of 3.

This last line may give you pause, and rightly so. L is a Longint, K is an Integer, and B is a Byte. Can you add an Integer and a Byte together and assign the result to a Longint? To find the answer, read the following section.

Example: Experimenting with Data Types

Start a new project called NUMEXAM, call the new form NumberForm (change the Name property to NumberForm), and call its unit NUMBER (save the file as NUMBER). Start by putting a button on the form and changing its Name and Caption properties to "Retreat." Double-click on the button to enter the code window.

Tip: If you change the Name property *first*, the Caption property will automatically change to match it.

Using a code frame for a button clicking (like you did for the examples in the preceding chapter), try out the code from the preceding section. It should look like this all together:

Chapter 7 ◆ Using Numbers

```
procedure TNumberForm.RetreatClick(Sender: TObject);
{The above line is generated when you double-click on Retreat.}
var
   B: Byte;
   I, J, K : Integer;
   L: Longint;
begin
   B := 10;
   I := 1;
   J := 2;
   K := I + J;
   L := K + B;
   K := I + J;
end.
```

It doesn't have any effect on-screen, of course, but right now you're just thinking about what will actually compile. (You can use Ctrl+F9 to compile without running.) Notice that

```
L := K + B;
```

actually does work. What about these lines?

```
K := L + B;
B := K + L;
```

Did you expect them to work? They do, even though L and K might be considerably larger than 255, the highest value that B can hold. In practice, you wouldn't use code like this unless you had taken steps to ensure that the sum of K and L was not over 255.

All of the integer types are highly *compatible*. Compatibility refers to which types may be used interchangeably. Previously, you saw that char and string types were somewhat compatible—you can assign a char value to a string variable but not the other way around. In most circumstances, you can use integer types interchangeably. (You'll look at the exceptions later.)

While you're adding code, add these declarations:

```
var
...
   C: Char;
   S: String;
```

Then follow up with this code:

```
begin
...
   B := -1;
   B := 10 - 11;
   B := 0;
   B := B - 1;
```

```
C := '1';
B := C;
S := C;
C := S;
. . .
```

Notice a new operator, the - or the *minus* sign, in the preceding code. This operator works just as you might expect (4 – 3 equals 1). The line

```
B := B - 1;
```

tells the computer to take the current value in B, which is 0, subtract 1 from that value, and assign the result, –1, back to B.

Basically, then, the first four lines are an attempt to get an invalid value into B. As you try to compile the code, remove the lines that the compiler stops on. You should end up with just the following lines from the last block:

```
B := 0;
B := B - 1;
C := '1';
S := C;
```

You can't directly assign an illegal value to a variable. Therefore, the assignment of –1 and 10 – 11 to B both fail; –1 is out of the byte range, and 10 – 11 just gets translated into –1. You can assign 0 to B, however, and then subtract 1 from it. The compiler is apparently not smart enough to figure that one out.

You probably knew the other statements wouldn't work. You can't assign a string or a character to an integer and, as you learned before, you can't assign a string to a character.

Example: Range Errors

Wait a minute. You have a line of code that assigns an invalid value to a byte. If you click on that button, B is assigned a value of –1. Does the program fail when you run it and click on the button? (Try it!)

No matter how often you click on the button, the program does not fail. This observation may be rather alarming. Imagine writing a full-fledged program and assigning a bad value to a variable. You would want to know before you let other people use it only to discover that they were getting strange answers from your program.

Pascal can help you catch these errors, if you tell it to. Stop the program by using Alt+F4 and from Pascal's Options menu, choose Project. The Project - Compiler options dialog box shown in figure 7.1 appears. (If you have the project manager visible, go to the toolbar and click on the button that reads "Options" in it to bring up the project options dialog.) Don't worry about what all the options are. The only

Chapter 7 ♦ Using Numbers

one you're interested in right now is in the middle group, first in the list on the left—the check box labelled Range checking. Check this box and—so that the new option will take effect—select from the **Compile** menu the **B**uild All option.

> **Compiling vs. Building**
>
> When you compile your program, Pascal only compiles those units (and the project file) that have *changed* since the last compile. Changing an option doesn't count as changing the file, so if you want a compile option to take effect, you have to do a *build*.
>
> Building is recompiling every unit and the project file regardless of whether any changes have taken place since the last compile.
>
> Normally, of course, you will want to use the Compile option, because that will be much faster.

Figure 7.1
The Project - Compiler options dialog box.

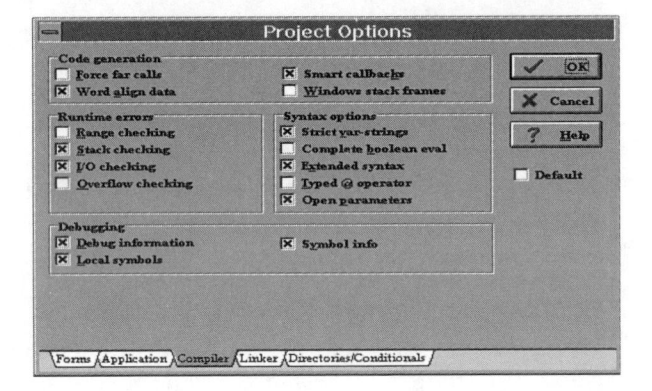

Now, if you click the button, your program will stop with an error. Continue on from there (press F9) and you'll see the Range check error message that would appear to the user, as shown in figure 7.2. This message comes from your program! By enabling range checking, you tell Pascal to add code to your program that tests whether or not an illegal assignment has been made and calls that error message when such an assignment occurs. Because this feature slows down the program and makes it bigger, programmers often work with it enabled until their code is bug-free. At that point, they disable range checking and give the smaller, faster code to their customers. (It's always safer to have the range checking on, though, so if you're writing an application that is fast enough with range checking on, you might just leave it on to be conservative.)

> **Note:** Pascal stops your program as a convenience for you, the programmer. A user of your program would only see the message shown in figure 7.2, not your code with the error. But you can keep Pascal from stopping your program by turning off the Break on Exception option. From the **O**ptions menu, select **E**nvironment. The Environment Options notebook will appear. On the first page (preferences) of the notebook is a group of checkboxes labelled *Debugging*. Deselect "Break on Exception" to keep Delphi from stopping your program. I don't recommend you do this as it can make bugs harder to find.

Figure 7.2

You can make your program alert you automatically to range errors.

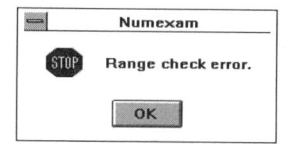

> **Caution:** When you get a range check error, your program is *suspended* but not actually *stopped*. In other words, the running program will appear in Windows' task list, and you really won't be able to do much until you reset the program.
>
> To reset the program, select the Program Reset item from the Debug menu.

This error message does not end the program, however. What happens to B, anyway? Does Pascal have some value that means "undetermined" or "I don't know"?

Example: Exceeding Boundaries

Knowing what happens to B is important for a number of reasons. It helps you get to know Delphi better, for one thing. Perhaps more important is that range errors account for a large number of bugs (extremely large, more than you want to know). Finally, the more things that happen in your program that you are unclear about, the less likely you are to be able to locate and remove bugs that occur.

Now, embellish this form a little bit with a *gauge*, which is a simple control that does nothing but measure the progress of some process. The gauge is on the Samples page of the object bar. Add one to the right of the button so that NumberForm now looks like figure 7.3.

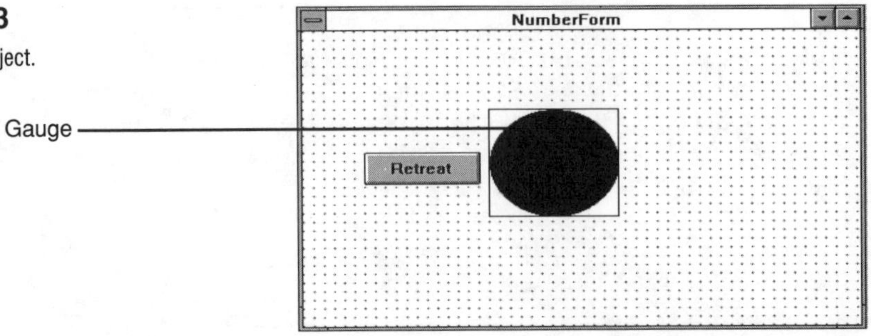

Chapter 7 ◆ Using Numbers

Figure 7.3
The Gauge object.

Change the name of Gauge1 to Gauge. Then change the `Progress` property of Gauge to 100. (It's not really important, but for this example, I also changed the `Kind` property to `Pie`.) Gauge measures progress in percentage points from 0 to 100 and shades itself according to how high progress is. As a result, when you change the `Progress` property to 100, it blacks itself out.

Now double-click on the button again and change the code and declarations to the following:

```
procedure TNumberForm.RetreatClick(Sender: TObject);
var
   B, C : Byte;
begin
   C := Gauge.Progress;
   B := C - 10;
   Gauge.Progress := B;
   {This code would reset Gauge to 100.}
   If B = 0 then Gauge.Progess := 100;
end;
```

The last line, `If B = 0 then Gauge.Progress := 100` does exactly what it says: If the variable B hits zero, set `Gauge.Progress` to 100. This step would prevent the variable from ever going below zero. (You'll cover the "If ... then" statement in detail in Chapter 10, "On One Condition.")

Now run the code. With each click on the button, `Progress` counts down toward zero. When it gets to zero, if you click again, you get a range check error just as before. And the gauge stays at zero. But say you want the gauge to go to 100, to repeat the cycle. You now have another mystery—and you still don't know what happened to B.

Range Checking

In the old days, a Turbo Pascal program that violated a variable's range with range checking turned on just ended. Or, in less generous terms, it *crashed*. It stopped, presented the user with a cryptic message, and that was that. Anything the user was doing at the time was interrupted and lost forever. As peculiar as it sounds, this result was preferable to many compilers that offered no range checking and let you work on a program that was constantly violating a variable's range and perhaps giving wildly wrong answers—or worse, giving subtly wrong ones.

With Windows, programs don't just end. (Well, they aren't *supposed* to just end.) If you have a bug, you want users to have an opportunity to save their work and get out of the program so they can report it to you later.

Pascal offers you a hand by enabling you to use its range checking, which doesn't crash the program but still alerts the user to the error. But Pascal has to more or less assume that the remaining part of the code is no longer valid. Therefore, when the range error is created as follows:

```
B := C - 10;
```

Pascal jumps to the error message and never jumps back. This process prevents any code that might be based on the false assumption that B is actually equal to the value of C minus 10 from being executed.

Example: So What in the Sam Hill Happens to *B*?

To find out what actually happens to B, you must turn off range checking. Do that now. Also, add another button called Advance to the right of the gauge. Change the code for RetreatClick as follows (see fig. 7.4):

```
var
    B : Byte;
begin
    B := Gauge.Progress - 10;
    Gauge.Progress := B;
end;
```

Then mark this block and copy it to the Clipboard. Now double-click on the Advance button to get to the code window and paste the code back from the Clipboard. Change the - 10 to + 10 so that the line in AdvanceClick looks like the following:

```
B := Gauge.Progress + 10;
```

Figure 7.4
The Gauge object with two buttons.

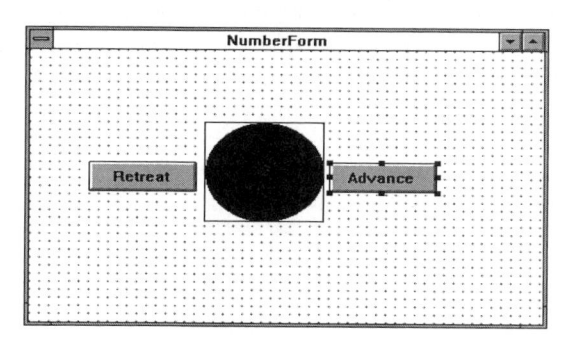

You're finally ready to find out what happens to B. Run the code and click on Retreat continually to reach zero. Now click on Retreat once more. The Gauge goes from 0 percent to 246 percent. If you click on Advance now, you find that the Gauge goes from 246 percent back to 0 percent. What if you keep clicking on Advance all the way to 250 percent and then click once more? The Gauge goes from 250 percent to 4 percent. Again, if you click on Retreat, it goes back to 250 percent.

Wrapping Around

Earlier in the chapter, you read about the possibility of a value that means "Undetermined" or "I don't know." Pascal has no such value. And, although some languages allow for variables to be unknown, the CPU and Delphi do not. You may have wondered what value a variable has before you assign a value to it. In other words, what value does C have in the following?

```
var B, C: Byte;
begin
   B := C + 1;
end;
```

For that matter, what value does B have? Before you assign a value to a variable, the variable is *undefined*. Being undefined means that the variable might have any value, and you cannot count on it being anything.

This description doesn't really seem to fit what happened to B. The gauge's progress property—which represented B—changed very consistently. If B refers to a single location in memory, and that location is at its highest value, what happens when you add 1 to it? Well, what would happen if B were two bytes (a word or integer) instead of one? The low byte would be set to zero, and the high byte would be incremented by one. This example is easy to visualize decimally. For example, if you have

```
09
```

and add 1, you get

```
10
```

and if you have only the right decimal place or ignore the left, you get a pattern that looks like '01234567890123456789 0' when you repeatedly add 1. The number wraps around. In math, this concept is called a *modulus*, and you use it every day.

Consider the following example: If it is 11:00 p.m., and you're thinking ahead two hours, you're thinking about 1:00 a.m. You "wrapped around" because the clock does not have a 13. The modulus is 12. If it's 7:50, 20 minutes from now will be 8:10. The modulus for minutes is 60.

In Byte and Word variables, the modulus is the maximum number the data type can hold. So, 250 + 10 becomes 4, and 0 – 10 becomes 246. The gauge illustrates this principle beautifully, and not just in the numbers. The amount of shading done on the gauge is on a modulus of 100. So if the progress property is 150 percent, only 50 percent is covered. If the progress property is 250 percent, again only 50 percent is actually covered.

Example: Wraparound with Signed Types

What happens if you declare B as follows:

```
B: Shortint;
```

Can you guess? Change the declaration of B in both procedures and give it a try.

The number goes back into the negatives—the gauge blanks out on negative numbers—and then what? It wraps around again. This time, the boundaries are –128 and +127, as shown in table 7.1. Negatives are more difficult to think of—128 + 1 equals –127, for example, and –127 – 1 equals 128—but the same wraparound is going on.

Some programmers actually take advantage of this capability in their code. They know that the number wraps around, so they disable range checking and write their programs with this capability in mind. I discourage you from following their example, however, because writing programs this way makes the programs harder to understand and also makes it harder to take advantage of the range checking features of Pascal.

Summary

In Pascal, as in most computer languages, a distinction is made between numerals (the character representation of quantities) and numbers (actual quantities). Pascal has two main groups of numeric types, real and integer. Integers in Pascal are whole numbers and must be expressed without punctuation, except for a leading minus sign for negative numbers.

There are five different integer types: Shortint, Integer, Longint, Byte, and Word, each of which is a different size and contains a different range of values. Integer types are highly compatible, however, and different types may be assigned, added, or subtracted in the same statement. The compiler can detect, while compiling, the direct assignment of an illegal value to an integer variable. If code is written that would exceed the allowed range for a type, Pascal can be set to generate an error message that interrupts the program without ending it. Range errors can also be totally ignored; in this case, the value for the variable wraps around so that it is within the acceptable range.

Chapter 7 ◆ Using Numbers

Review Questions

1. What is a numeral?

2. Can you directly add two `strings` or `chars` that contain numerals together in Pascal? In other words, can you do something like the following?

   ```
   var
       I   : Integer;
       S, T: String;
   begin
       S := '2';
       T := '2';
       I := S + T;   {Can this come out to be '4'?}
       S := S + T;   {Can this?}
   end;
   ```

3. What place do commas, decimal points, spaces, and minus signs have in Delphi integers?

4. What are the five integer types? What are their ranges? How big are they? (You may be approximate with the largest type.)

5. Are character and integer types compatible? Are character types compatible with each other? Are integer types compatible with each other?

6. If B is a `Byte`, W is a `Word`, and L is a `Longint`, which of these three lines of code will not compile?

   ```
   B := -1;
   W := -1;
   L := -1;
   ```

7. What happens in the following code when range checking is on? When it is off?

   ```
   begin
       B := 0;
       B := B - 10;
   end;
   ```

8. What value does C have in the following? What about B?

   ```
   var B, C: Byte;
   begin
       B := C + 1;
   end;
   ```

9. What does it mean when you say a variable has an undefined value?

10. Does Pascal have any way to express "I don't know"?

11. Can you directly add two character types together in other languages? What about integers and character types?

12. What does the variable I traditionally stand for?

Review Exercises

1. Write a program with a gauge and a button where pressing the button changes the gauge's value by adding one to it. By adding a larger number. By subtracting a number.

2. Write a program with a gauge and a button where pressing the button assigns the gauge the value of an undefined variable. It is possible that an undefined variable could always be zero (or some other value) on your machine, and then be different on a different machine. What does this say about using a variable without first assigning it a value?

3. Write a program with just a button where pressing the button declares and assigns values to variables of each of the five integer types. Compare what kind of value assignments will not compile to those which cause run-time range errors.

4. Write a program that doesn't have a form but uses WinCRT and `WriteLn` to display values. Declare variables of the five integer types and assign them values. Then display them with `WriteLn`. Note that `WriteLn` will accept a variable that is a string, character, or integer as a parameter.

5. Write a program that assigns a negative number to the Value property of a gauge object. What happens?

CHAPTER 8

Subroutines

Computers excel at repeating. Their entire value stems from their capability to do the same thing, repeatedly, quickly, and without getting bored or tired. Computers don't know how long or hard they're working. Human beings, on the other hand, are acutely aware of these circumstances.

Nowhere is this awareness more acute than in computer programming. Computer programmers are creative people who always have the nagging feeling that "the computer could be doing more of my work for me." Getting the computer to do more of the work, and freeing the programmers to work on the more interesting parts of a program, is the subject of subroutines.

What Are Subroutines?

In the old days, computer programmers might find themselvs writing code like the following:

Write "Would you like to continue?"
  Get User's Response
  If the response shifted to uppercase is "YES" or "Y" then Continue
  Otherwise if the response shifted to uppercase is "NO" or "N"
    then end the program
  otherwise write "I didn't get that." and go back four lines.
  ... {Code to do things would go here.}

Then, a few lines down, the programmers would come to another place where they wanted to prompt the user:

Chapter 8 ♦ Subroutines

> Write "This will replace the existing file. Is this O.K.?"
> Get User's Response
> If the response shifted to uppercase is "YES" or "Y" then Continue
> Otherwise if the response shifted to uppercase is "NO" or "N"
>   then skip the following code
> otherwise write "I didn't get that." and go back four lines.
> ... {Code to replace existing file would go here.}

And then, a few lines down, the programmers would come up with yet another place where they would write almost exactly the same code to prompt the user. This redundancy would gnaw at them. Why should they have to put in the same code over and over again?

There is more here than just simple laziness. Every time you write a line of code, you risk introducing new bugs into your code. Also, if you're copying the code over and over again, what happens if you find out that the first block you copied was wrong? You have to find all the places where you duplicated the wrong code and correct them.

To avoid constantly retyping the same code and all the problems associated with retyping it, programmers invented *subroutines* (sometimes just called *routines*). For the preceding situation, the programmer might write a subroutine called PromptTheUser, which looks something like the following:

> Write The Message Passed
> Get User's Response
> If the response shifted to uppercase is "YES" or "Y" then Return a YES
> Otherwise if the response shifted to uppercase is "NO" or "N"
>   then return a NO
> otherwise write "I didn't get that," and go back four lines.

The programmer could then invoke this code from the rest of the code:

> {Program code here.}
> If PromptTheUser "Do you want to continue?" returns yes, then continue
> otherwise end the program.
> {More code here}
> If PromptTheUser "This will replace the existing file. Is that O.K.?"
>   returns yes then continue,
> otherwise skip the code to replace the existing file.
> {More code}

Invoking the code is called *calling a subroutine*.

You can see how using subroutines can save work. It's like extending the language. You have a need for some function that wasn't made part of the language, so you create a subroutine to perform that function. Even if you could use English as a programming language, the ability to create new words like PromptTheUser would be a necessity. If a language has no way to concatenate two strings together, you can write a special routine to do that. If a language has no way to display a string on-screen, you can write a routine to do that. And so on.

Millions of subroutines have been written for Pascal. Most of them, written by programmers like you or me, will be used only by you and possibly by others you work with. You can buy packages that contain hundreds of subroutines to do much of your work for you, however. Pascal, itself, contains a massive collection of subroutines through which you can directly access Windows.

You have already encountered subroutines in this book. Even though discussions of subroutines don't appear until late in most language tutorials, certain subroutines are immediately introduced to the student. Without these subroutines, it is difficult or impossible for students to get a feel for how they are progressing. In the old typewriter-like days of Pascal, those routines were invariably Writeln and its complement, Readln.

Writeln is a standard Pascal routine to display a string on a typewriter-like device. You used it in Chapter 5, "Working with Pascal," to get a feel for the barest essentials of Pascal programming. In the following section, you go back to it briefly to get an idea of how subroutines work.

Simple Subroutines

To begin your work with subroutines, choose Open Project from the File menu to open a project called SUB. Use the Project Manager's pop-up menu (click the right mouse button or press Alt+F10) and select View Project to view the project file. You get a single code window with the standard Pascal code frame. Delete everything but the first line, the begin, and the end. Right after the program statement, add uses WinCRT. Your code window should now look like the following:

```
program Sub;
uses WinCRT;
begin
end.
```

First, you need to declare some variables. Just as before, you need to use the var keyword; it goes before the begin and after the uses. Declare a string variable S.

```
...
uses WinCRT;
var S: String;
begin
...
```

Now use the Writeln subroutine to display a simple message and follow it up with Readln:

Chapter 8 ◆ Subroutines

```
begin
   Writeln('Hello, World!   Type your name and press Enter.');
   Readln(S);
end.
```

Before the use of buttons, menu boxes, windows, and dialog boxes, the programmer got input from the user by using Readln. Readln instructs the computer to let the user type in a string and press Enter. The string that the user types goes into the variable S. Then, until the user presses Enter, the program is frozen.

You look at Readln and Writeln in detail later because they still have a place in programming. Right now, though, you're just going to use them to explore some simple subroutines. The first subroutine you're going to look at is called ClrScr.

Add the following lines after the Readln statement and try out the code:

```
ClrScr;
S := 'Hello, '+S;
Writeln(s);
```

The "Hello, World" message appears, and you have to press Enter to move the program along. Type in your name and press Enter. The screen clears and displays a customized greeting message. In my case, it displays the following:

```
Hello, Blake
```

Example: The Refresh Procedure

ClrScr clears the screen. The command works only if you're using WinCRT and writing a typewriter-style program. What it shows, however, is how a simple subroutine works. You enter the name of the routine, and the code is executed:

```
ClrScr;
```

Now, what if you want to add class to your simple greeting program? Say you want to write a title at the top of the screen, telling the user about the program. Add this line right after the begin:

```
Writeln('A Greetings Program from the book "Delphi By Example."');
```

Now the message appears at the top. When the user presses Enter, however, the message goes away. What if you want to have that line appear at the top of every page?

You write a subroutine. Call it Refresh, and it should go before the var statement, as shown in the following:

```
procedure  Refresh;
begin
   ClrScr;
   Writeln('A Greetings Program from the book "Delphi By Example."');
end;
```

(Notice that you can call a procedure, such as ClrScr, from within another procedure, such as Refresh.)

The preceding code should look familiar. You've seen the keyword procedure many times, starting in Chapter 5. At the time, you learned that it was analogous to the word *program*, and it began a sort of mini-program where you could change the behavior of an object.

That's all true. The word procedure tells the compiler that you are about to write a subroutine—and what is a subroutine but a miniature program? Procedure is followed by the name of the procedure. The name of the procedure must follow all the rules you learned in Chapter 6, "Variables." The name can be up to 63 characters long, consisting of letters and underscores, and numbers after the first character.

The whole program should now look like the following:

```
program Sub;

uses WinCRT;

procedure  Refresh;
begin
   ClrScr;
   Writeln('A Greetings Program from the book "Delphi By Example."');
end;

var S: String;

begin
   Refresh;
   Writeln('Hello, World! (Type your name and press Enter.)');
   Readln(S);
   Refresh;
   S := 'Hello, ' + S;
   Writeln(S);
end.
```

Pascal makes programming easier by enabling you to build your own commands that look like English words. If you want, you can build even more routines so that your program looks like the following:

```
begin
   Refresh;
   Prompt_The_User_To_Type_In_Name_And_Get_Name;
   Refresh;
   Display_a_Greeting_To_The_User;
end.
```

Chapter 8 ◆ Subroutines

Or you can be cryptic and mush everything together:

```
begin
    Go;
end.
```

where `Go` contains all the code you wrote previously.

This last example is extreme, but you will see code written this way. Part of the point of writing a subroutine, however, is to write code that you can use over and over again. If you have a routine called `Go`, which runs the whole program, what are the odds that you can use it again?

Subroutine Parameters

Part of making subroutines more useful and flexible involves using *parameters*. You encountered parameters in Chapter 5, too. Remember the following lines?

```
MyWindow.ColorYourself(Red);
MyWindow.ColorYourself(Blue);
```

The idea behind these lines is that the code the window uses to color itself is basically the same whether the color is red or blue. By passing a different parameter, you determine which color is used. You've already used two examples of procedures this way: `Writeln` and `Readln`.

`Writeln` has a basic purpose: to write a string to a typewriter-style device. It doesn't matter what the string is; `Writeln` always has to do more or less the same thing. The parameter to `Writeln` tells it what string to write. `Readln`, too, always gets keyboard input from the user. Its parameter tells it where to put that input; as before, you tell it to put the input into the string variable `s`.

Example: Revamping *Refresh*

You already have the `Refresh` procedure. But what if, in addition to clearing the screen and writing your standard message at the top, you also want to display some additional message? You can do that by changing `Refresh` to accept a parameter. Now take a look at how you revamp `Refresh`.

First, you need to let the compiler know that the `Refresh` procedure will take a parameter and that the parameter will be a string. You do so by adding the name of the parameter, followed by a colon, and followed by the type of the parameter:

```
procedure Refresh(AMessage: String);
```

Looks like a regular declaration, doesn't it? This parameter "declaration" tells the compiler that `Refresh` takes a string parameter and that `Refresh` calls that parameter `AMessage`. You can now access the `AMessage` variable just as if you had declared it in the normal fashion. The whole procedure now looks like this:

```
procedure  Refresh(AMessage: String);
begin
  ClrScr;
  Writeln('A Greetings Program from the book "Delphi By Example."');
  Writeln(AMessage);
end;
```

You can call the `Refresh` procedure from within the main body of the program, and you can use a variable or a literal string, as shown in the following:

```
begin
  Refresh('Hello, World! (Type your name and press Enter.)');
  Readln(S);
  S := 'Hello, ' + S;
  Refresh(S);
end.
```

The important thing to observe here is that `'Hello, World! (Type your name and press Enter.)'` and the variable `S` are both used as parameters and that their values ('Hello, World!' and the current value of S) will be transferred to the Refresh procedure's `AMessage` parameter. Also notice that the main body of the program is considerably shorter than before.

Watching What Happens Inside a Procedure

Now you're ready to use the debugging facilities of Delphi to take a look at what happens to the variables in your program as you run it. To look at variables while your program is running, you need to open a *watch window*. From the Views menu, choose Watch. (You may have to move the window around to arrange it so that you can see everything.)

Now add a "watch" by pressing Ctrl+F5 or choosing Add Watch from the Debug menu. A dialog box, titled "Watch properties," appears (see fig. 8.1).

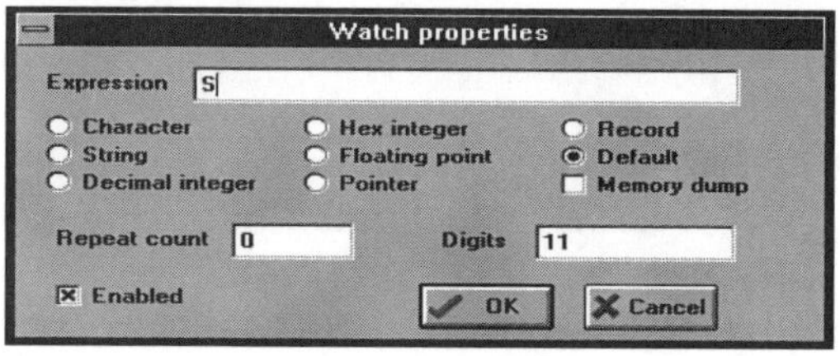

Figure 8.1

The Delphi Watch properties dialog box.

Type **S** in the edit line and press Enter. (Ignore the options for now.) Behind the Watch Properties dialog is the Watch window. The text S: [Process not accessible] appears there. Add another watch by pressing Ctrl+F5 and typing AMessage, and it, too, will appear in the watch window followed by : [Process not accessible]. (The "process" that's "not accessible" is your program— you haven't started running your program yet.)

Press F8; from the Debug menu, choose Step Over; or click on the SpeedBar button showing the arrow going over the box—called the Step Over button— not the one showing the arrow going into the box. If you've made changes to your program, Pascal re-compiles it, and then highlights the first line of code:

```
begin
```

This process of watching the code execute line by line is called *stepping*.

Now the watch window should look something like this:

```
S: ''
AMessage: Unknown identifier
```

The value of s can be anything at this point, not necessarily the null string shown here. It can be any random arrangement of characters. s is still undefined, a condition described in Chapter 7.

Step again (click on the Step Over Button or choose from the **Run** menu, **Step Over**), and the next line of code is highlighted. The watch window doesn't change. You should be on the Readln statement now. Step again, and the program's window comes to the foreground, asking you to type in a value. Type **Joe** and press Enter. The watch window now should look like the following:

```
S: 'Joe'
AMessage: Unknown identifier
```

Step again, and s changes value again:

```
S: 'Hello, Joe'
```

Now step to the end of the program and close the program's window to get back to Pascal. As you stepped through the program, s changed its value twice, but the watch window insisted that AMessage was an unknown identifier.

Scope

AMessage is unknown to the main body of the program. It is declared as a parameter in the Refresh procedure, and that procedure is the only code that knows about it. As a matter of fact, AMessage doesn't even exist outside of Refresh. The places where a variable is known is called its *scope*. The scope of AMessage is the Refresh procedure.

To get a feel for this concept, go through the program again. This time, however, use the *trace* feature of Pascal. Start tracing by pressing F7, by selecting **T**race Into from the **R**un menu, or by clicking on the SpeedBar button that shows the arrow going into the box (the Trace Into button). Again, the first line of code is highlighted, and just as before, S has some undefined value and AMessage is unknown.

Trace again (F7), and the highlight bar is over the call to Refresh. Trace again, and the debugger takes you into the Refresh routine. Now the begin of Refresh is highlighted, and the watch window no longer says that AMessage is unknown. (It's undefined, however, until after the begin statement, so it may have any value.) Trace again, and the watch window should reveal its value as 'Hello, World! (Type your name and press Enter.)'.

Further tracing takes you out of Refresh and back to the main body of the program where AMessage is once again an unknown identifier. A variable declared in a subroutine is created and destroyed within that subroutine. It doesn't exist anywhere else, and it exists only when Refresh is actually being called.

To illustrate this point, continue tracing. S is assigned a value, and then Refresh is called again. Trace until you get back to the begin statement of Refresh. What value does AMessage have? It may have any value, including the 'Hello, World' message it had previously. However, it is still undefined. Any value it has is coincidental. Trace again, and AMessage is assigned the value of S.

Every time you call a procedure, the variables that the procedure uses are created. Every time you leave a procedure, the variables that it created are destroyed. Again, this concept is called scope. AMessage's scope is the Refresh procedure.

Example: Procedures and Variables

The concept of scope is an important one, so now you're going to look at it from a different perspective. Save the SUB project and reopen the NUMEXAM project you created in Chapter 7. Everything you've learned about procedures also applies to object methods. If you open the code window, you can see that Pascal set up procedure statements for you when you double-clicked the Advance and Retreat buttons. Here are the two headers created:

```
procedure TNumberForm.RetreatClick(Sender: TObject);
procedure TNumberForm.AdvanceClick(Sender: TObject);
```

Object methods are mini-programs that describe the behavior of an object. *Procedures* are miniprograms that perform some action. Finally, you can understand the code frame generated when you double-click on an object in Pascal. It is

```
procedure FormName.EventName(. . . );
```

Chapter 8 ◆ Subroutines

where `procedure` tells the compiler that you're beginning a subroutine, `FormName` is the name of the form object, and `EventName` is the event that has occurred, such as the Advance button being clicked (`AdvanceClick`). (You look at the parameters for these object methods in Chapter 21.)

Right now, you're really concerned with the `B` variables declared in both methods. Look at the code for the `RetreatClick` method:

```
procedure TNumberForm.RetreatClick(Sender: TObject);
var
   B : Shortint;
begin
   B := Gauge.Progress - 10;
   Gauge.Progress := B;
end;
```

Position the cursor on `begin`, as if you were going to add some text there, and press F4. F4 tells the debugger to run the program, go to that line of code, and then stop. (You also can choose the Run to **C**ursor item from the **R**un menu. Make sure you position the cursor where you want it *first*, though.) When the form appears, click the Retreat button, and the debugger returns you to the code window.

What value does `B` show in the watch window? For whatever reason, when I tried this example, it came up 63 all the time. You may come up with zero, or any number between 0 and 255. If you step through the code, you see that `B` gets assigned the value of Gauge's `Progress` property minus 10, which should be 90. Now reposition the cursor on `begin` and go to that line again. Click the Retreat button again. Now what value does `B` show?

When I followed these steps, `B` came up 63 again. You may get 0 or 150 or even 90. The value is undefined. `B` is created for `RetreatClick`, then destroyed, and then created again when `RetreatClick` is called again. Can you keep track of the number of times the user clicks the Retreat button by adding the following code to `RetreatClick`?

```
var
   . . .
   TimesClicked: Longint;
begin
   . . .
   TimesClicked := TimesClicked + 1;
end;
```

The answer is no, because `TimesClicked` is undefined every time you call `RetreatClick`. (You can verify this answer by watching `TimesClicked` in the watch window while repeatedly using the Go to cursor command in the `RetreatClick` procedure.)

More Elaborate Procedures

You are not restricted to a single parameter when building a procedure, and many Pascal procedures have three or four (or more) parameters. Open up the SUB project again and take another look at the code:

```
program Sub;

uses WinCRT;

procedure  Refresh(AMessage: String);
begin
   ClrScr;
   Writeln('A Greetings Program from the book "Delphi By Example."');
   Writeln(AMessage);
end;

var S: String;
    L: Longint;

begin
   Refresh('Hello, World! (Type your name Enter.)');
   Readln(S);
   S := 'Hello, ' + S;
   Refresh(S);
end.
```

Suppose you expand the program to ask another question and get another response from the user:

```
S := 'Hello, ' + S ;
Refresh(S);
Writeln('What is your favorite color?');
Readln(S);
```

You can see a discernible pattern here: say something to the user, ask the user a question, and then get the user's response. When you find yourself writing the same or similar sequences of instructions, that's an indication that you might want to bundle those instructions as a procedure. You might want, for example, to have a procedure named RefreshAndPrompt that looks like the following:

```
begin
   ClrScr;
   Writeln('A Greetings Program from the book "Delphi By Example."');
   Writeln(AMessage);
   Writeln(APrompt);
end;
```

To tell the compiler that this procedure takes more than one parameter, you declare both parameters in the header, as follows:

```
procedure RefreshAndPrompt(AMessage: String; APrompt: String);
```

In essence, you can see that the parentheses are sort of an enclosed var statement. You can list many parameters and these parameters can have any type. The following line, for example, is a valid procedure declaration:

```
procedure AComplexProc(S: String; I,J,K: Integer; B: Byte; W,X,Y,Z:
➥Word);
```

You can see from the preceding line that you also can put two variables of the same type together, separated by commas. You therefore can declare your RefreshAndPrompt procedure like this:

```
procedure RefreshAndPrompt(AMessage, APrompt: String);
```

Now you *could* copy the code from Refresh and add this line:

```
    Writeln(APrompt);
```

so that RefreshAndPrompt is just like Refresh—with a few extra lines.

```
procedure RefreshAndPrompt(AMessage, APrompt: String);
begin
    ClrScr;
    Writeln('A Greetings Program from the book "Delphi By Example."');
    Writeln(AMessage);
    Writeln(APrompt);
end;
```

But what if you copied the code wrong? Or what if you found a bug in Refresh? You then have to fix the error there and in RefreshAndPrompt and any place else that you copied the text.

The whole point of having subroutines is to use them over and over again. By using a routine repeatedly, you gain confidence in it; it is less likely to have bugs because you will have had more chances to debug it. Also, if a bug does turn up, you can fix it in that one place.

Here you can take advantage of the fact that subroutines can call other subroutines and write RefreshAndPrompt, as follows:

```
procedure  RefreshAndPrompt(AMessage, APrompt: String);
begin
    Refresh(AMessage);
    Writeln(APrompt);
end;
```

Also, drop the S variable from the main body of the program and create more meaningful names, as in the following code:

```
var Name, Color: String;

begin
   RefreshAndPrompt('Hello, World!',
                    'Type your name and press Enter.');
   Readln(Name);
   RefreshAndPrompt('Hello, '+Name+'.',
                    'What is your favorite color?');
   Readln(Color);
end.
```

Long Lines

Notice the changes to the code in the preceding section. First, a single instruction was placed on two separate lines. This style is acceptable. Pascal pays no attention to lines. It looks for the semicolon to indicate the end of the statement. You can write a program like this:

```
program OneLine;uses WinCRT;var B:Byte;begin;B:=0;Writeln('2B or not' );
↪end.
```

You can compile and run this line. You also can write the same program as follows:

```
program
   OneLine;
uses
   WinCRT;
var
B
:
Byte;
begin
B :=
0
```

. . .and so on. The only restriction is that you cannot split a literal string over two lines. The compiler will stop on the following:

```
Writeln('This
   will not work.');
```

How can it know how many spaces are between 'This and will not work.'? If you do need to split up a long string, you can use the concatenation operator (+) to add two shorter strings together, as in the following:

```
Writeln('This '+
   'will work!');
```

In the preceding section, I took the two parameters to `RefreshAndPrompt` and put each on its own line:

```
RefreshAndPrompt('Hello, World!',
                 'Type your name and press Enter.');
```

Because the parameters are lengthy, splitting them can make the program easier to read. If you have shorter prompts, however, splitting the parameters is unnecessary. For example:

```
RefreshAndPrompt('Hello!', 'How are you?');
```

Deciding when to split up lines is personal preference, and you'll discover soon enough what works best for you.

I used the string concatenation operator to remove this line altogether:

```
S := 'Hello, '+S;
```

which became

```
RefreshAndPrompt('Hello, '+Name+'.',
                 'What is your favorite color?');
```

Now your program has two variables, `Name` and `Color`, that contain input from the user. Can you improve on the `RefreshAndPrompt` routine further?

Routines That Change Variables

As long as you know that you're prompting the user, why not just put the `Readln` in the `RefreshAndPrompt` routine? How do you define the procedure to have a third string parameter, one that contains the answer to the prompt?

```
RefreshAndPrompt(AMessage, APrompt, AnAnswer: String);
```

The code for this line can be as follows:

```
begin
   Refresh(AMessage);
   Writeln(APrompt);
   Readln(AnAnswer);
end;
```

Now the main body of your code is looking really good. Professional, even.

```
begin
   RefreshAndPrompt('Hello, World!',
                    'Type your name and press Enter.',
                    Name);
   RefreshAndPrompt('Hello, '+Name+'.',
                    'What is your favorite color?',
                    Color);
end.
```

Now you're ready to try out the code to see what happens.

Debugging Your Program

When you try to run the code from the preceding section, you'll find that it doesn't work. Why it doesn't work is not at all obvious, but the cure is simple, as you'll see.

Start by setting up a watch window with the Name and Color variables in it. Then step through the whole program. A good first choice; you're going to look at the effect that each line of the code has on the variables.

Note the values of Name and Color (some kind of garbage because they're undefined) and then step over the begin and the first RefreshAndPrompt. Next, type a name into the window. When you come back, Name hasn't changed! Repeat this operation with Color. The same thing happens—nothing!

When a step-through of the program doesn't reveal the problem, it's time to trace into the subroutines in question. First, close the program's window to get back to Pascal and restart the program. This time, trace into the RefreshAndPrompt procedure. Next, step over the lines in the procedure. (After all, you don't need to trace into Refresh, do you? It seems to be working fine.)

Step through the routine until you come to the following line:

```
Readln(Answer);
```

Then set up a watch for AnAnswer. Maybe the Readln procedure isn't setting AnAnswer to what you type in. Next, type in your name and press Enter. If you follow this procedure, you discover that Readln is setting AnAnswer to what you type.

> **Tip:** Borland tests its code rigorously before letting you use it in your programs. Does that mean there are no errors in Borland's code? No. However, you should look at your own code first before suspecting Borland.

What happens when you leave the procedure? AnAnswer is destroyed—just as all your other procedure variables were, and it becomes an *unknown identifier*. And the Name variable hasn't been changed! To understand why Pascal doesn't change Name requires some history, presented in the following section.

The *var* Parameter

Subroutines predate Pascal by many years and, although they helped programmers make bigger and more complex programs easier to understand, they also created some interesting problems. Suppose that someone had a routine that added two to any number that you passed as a parameter. If you wanted to use that routine, you put the following in your code:

```
AddTwoTo(X, Y);
```

Chapter 8 ♦ Subroutines

AddTwoTo was supposed to add two to X and put the answer in Y. And it did that. But it did it in this way:

```
begin
    X := X + 1;
    X := X + 1;
    Y := X;
end;
```

Your program knew that Y was the answer, but it also assumed that X was unchanged. In other words, you didn't know that the AddTwoTo procedure was going to change X, and you wrote your programs thinking that Y was two greater than X.

In many pre-Pascal languages, you could not be sure that any subroutine you called would change any or all of the parameters passed to it. The subroutine had the right to change them all, and if you didn't like it, that was your tough luck.

Pascal takes the reverse approach. A subroutine cannot change a parameter unless that parameter is specified as variable. You specify a parameter as variable by preceding the name with the keyword var. Your RefreshAndPrompt procedure declaration might look like the following:

```
procedure RefreshAndPrompt(var AMessage, APrompt, Answer: String);
```

But now, wait a minute. You've just given RefreshAndPrompt authority to change all of the parameters, which is not only unnecessary, it doesn't work. Add the var keyword and try it out. The compiler stops on the first text ('Hello, World!') and says Variable Identifier Expected.

The message is a literal string, but RefreshAndPrompt has asked for permission to change it. Well, that's not possible. You can only change a variable. You can use the following code, however:

```
var S, T: String;
   . . .
begin
    S := 'Hello, World!';
    T := 'Enter your name and press Enter.':
```

And you can call RefreshAndPrompt like this:

```
RefreshAndPrompt(S, T, Name);
```

Taking this approach, however, defeats the purpose of using the var parameter. Part of the reason for the existence of var in Pascal procedures is to make you consciously decide which parameters should be variables and which shouldn't. There's no reason for RefreshAndPrompt to change the message or the prompt, only the variable that's supposed to hold the information the user types. You can correct the problem by separating Answer from the declaration of the other parameters, as follows:

```
procedure RefreshAndPrompt(AMessage, APrompt: String; var Answer:
➥String);
```

Now, if you run the program, it should work just fine.

How this concept works is actually fairly simple. You've learned that a variable describes an area of RAM. When you have a var parameter, the routine gets the actual variable passed, describing the exact same area of RAM. When the parameter is not a var, Pascal makes a copy of it! In other words, the procedure can do whatever it wants with the copy of the variable because the copy is discarded as soon as the procedure ends, and the changes never affect the original variable.

What happens if you have an AddTwoTo procedure in Pascal like the one you read about earlier in this section? If, for example, you write it the same way but give the procedure permission to change Y only, as follows:

```
procedure AddTwoTo(X: Integer; var Y: Integer);
begin
   X := X + 2;
   Y := X;
end;
```

Y is changed, as is the copy of X. When the procedure ends, however, the copy of X is destroyed, whereas the changes to Y persist.

Const

What may not have occurred to you is that the procedure header parameters are like a "var" section, which is a handy programming convenience. In other words, using the admittedly simplistic AddTwoTo procedure as an example, this header

```
procedure AddTwoTo(X: Integer; var Y: Integer);
```

gives you the freedom to change X without worrying about the side-effects. Even though you have a line,

```
X := X + 2;
```

this won't have any effect on the calling code. If every variable in the header was alterable and you *didn't* want to alter X, you'd have to do something like:

```
procedure AddTwoTo(X: Integer; var Y: Integer);
var Z: Integer;
begin
   Z := X;
   Z := Z + 2;
   Y := X;
end;
```

(Ignore for the moment the fact that this procedure could consist of just the line "Y := X + 2".)

But there's a penalty for this convenience: The program copies X every time AddTwoTo gets called. Now, this routine coded more intelligently,

```
procedure AddTwoTo(X: Integer; var Y: Integer);
begin
   Y := X + 2;
end;
```

doesn't change X, but still the program copies X. This can, in some cases, result in a significant speed decrease believe it or not, when a routine is called maybe millions of time in one program and the parameters involved are much larger than integers (like strings, which force the compiler to copy as much as 256 bytes).

To avoid this overhead, programmers would often use var parameters even though they weren't going to change the variables. But this created the possibility that the parameters would be altered by mistake. Pascal resolved this dilemma by allowing you to label a parameter as constant, through the const keyword.

```
procedure AddTwoTo(const X: Integer; var Y: Integer);
begin
   Y := X + 2;
end;
```

A const parameter *cannot* be modified. You could not code AddTwoTo in this manner:

```
procedure AddTwoTo(const X: Integer; var Y: Integer);
begin
   X := X + 2;   {No!  Compiler will stop here!}
   Y := X;
end;
```

You'll see the keyword const appear quite frequently in the code examples later on in this book, but not for speed reasons. As a general rule, I declare all parameters as const unless I specifically want to change them—in which case they will be var parameters. In other words, I seldom use a non-labeled parameter—just const and var. The reason for this is simply that I like to keep strict track of what I'm changing and not changing in a procedure.

The Global Variable

You may not find the var solution entirely satisfactory. After all, you can still end up with a routine like the fictitious AddTwoTo(var X,Y: Integer), which changes both variables when it needs to change only one. Unfortunately, Pascal doesn't provide a way for you as a caller of a subroutine to not allow that routine to change your variables. You can design your own routines so that they don't change the parameters passed to them (a good idea), but you can't do anything about anyone else's routines you might use.

Say that, based on this principle, you decide that you don't want the RefreshAndPrompt procedure to change any of its parameters. How else could you still use the RefreshAndPrompt procedure to get what the user answered? One way is to define a variable for the *entire program* to hold those answers. Before both procedures in SUB, add this line:

```
var AnAnswer: String;
```

Then change the procedure definition of RefreshAndPrompt to

```
procedure  RefreshAndPrompt(AMessage, APrompt: string);
```

You don't need to change anything else in RefreshAndPrompt. The following line reads the user's input into the Answer variable, which you just declared:

```
Readln(AnAnswer);
```

Now you need to change the calls to RefreshAndPrompt to reflect the most recent changes and add code to assign the value in AnAnswer to Name and Color. Your code now should look like the following:

```
program Sub;

uses WinCRT;

var AnAnswer: String;

procedure  Refresh(AMessage: String);
begin
   ClrScr;
   Writeln('A Greetings Program from the book "Delphi By Example."');
   Writeln(AMessage);
end;

procedure  RefreshAndPrompt(AMessage, APrompt: string);
begin
   Refresh(AMessage);
   Writeln(APrompt);
   Readln(AnAnswer);
end;

var Name, Color: String;

begin
   RefreshAndPrompt('Hello, World!',
                    'Type your name and press Enter.');
   Name := AnAnswer;
   RefreshAndPrompt('Hello, '+Name+'.',
                    'What is your favorite color?');
   Color := AnAnswer;
end.
```

Observe once again that you can have a var statement in more than one place. You can have as many as you like, as long as they don't fall within a begin and an end statement. Do keep in mind that it is considered bad form to have a bunch of vars scattered throughout your program because they can make the program hard to read.

The main thing this program illustrates, however, is that when you declare a variable in a program, everything underneath that declaration can use that variable. Therefore, both Refresh and RefreshAndPrompt can use and change the AnAnswer variable. In fact, that's the premise on which this example is based.

A variable that can be used in this way is called a *global* variable. A variable declared within a procedure, such as the B byte variable you used in NUMEXAM, is called a *local* variable. Only the procedure can see and use a local variable.

The Function

Using global variables is considered bad form. Why? Because you never know what routine is going to change the variable. You knew (in this case) that only RefreshAndPrompt would change Answer, but the usual reason to have a global variable is to make it possible for many routines to have access to the same variable.

At the very least, the global variable is an inelegant solution to your problem. Using the RefreshAndPrompt procedure with the var parameter would be a better solution in most cases. However, you have one other alternative. Pascal enables you to write a routine that itself returns a value. Such a routine is called a *function*.

Declaring a function is like a cross between declaring a procedure and declaring a variable. You use the keyword function where before you used procedure. The function keyword is followed by the name of the function and the parameters (if any). A function also has a type, just like a variable. The following are all valid function declarations:

```
function GetAString: String;
function HighestOfTwoNumbers(I, J: Integer): Integer;
function LengthOfString(S: String); Byte;
```

To change the RefreshAndPrompt procedure into a function, you only need to replace the word procedure with function and give it a type. Because you want it to return what the user entered, the function should be a string type, as follows:

```
function   RefreshAndPrompt(AMessage, APrompt: string): String;
```

The code for the function itself should begin like this:

```
var Answer: String;
begin
   Refresh(AMessage);
   Writeln(APrompt);
   Readln(Answer);
. . .
```

at which point you have the result that you want to return in the variable Answer. Now you just have to assign that value to the result of the function, which is done as if the name of the function were the name of a variable of that type. Here's the rest of the routine:

```
   RefreshAndPrompt := Answer;
end;
```

If you don't assign a value to RefreshAndPrompt, Pascal considers the result to be *undefined*, just as if you had used an uninitialized variable.

You can now treat the RefreshAndPrompt routine as you might a string variable. Here is the complete code:

```
program Sub;

uses WinCRT;

procedure   Refresh(AMessage: String);
begin
   ClrScr;
   Writeln('A Greetings Program from the book "Delphi By Example."');
   Writeln(AMessage);
end;

function    RefreshAndPrompt(AMessage, APrompt: string): String;
var AnAnswer: String;
begin
   Refresh(AMessage);
   Writeln(APrompt);
   Readln(AnAnswer);
   RefreshAndPrompt := Answer;
end;

var Name, Color: String;


begin
   Name := RefreshAndPrompt('Hello, World!',
                  'Type your name and press Enter.');
   Color := RefreshAndPrompt('Hello, '+Name+'.',
                  'What is your favorite color?');
end.
```

Chapter 8 ◆ Subroutines

> **Note:** Did you remove the `AnAnswer` global variable? I did, but it wasn't strictly necessary. You can use the global `AnAnswer` variable or define a new one for the `RefreshAndPrompt` function. If you have both, it's important to be aware that a subroutine's local variables take precedence over a program's global variables. The `AnAnswer` variable that the `RefreshAndPrompt` routine uses is the local one.

Finally, you have a pretty decent solution. Your subroutines don't have any side effects, and your `RefreshAndPrompt` function returns whatever the user typed, after displaying a couple of messages. It isn't always convenient to avoid using global variables and `var` parameters, but it's usually a good idea.

> **Note:** Everything you've discussed so far regarding procedures and functions applies also to object methods. Although the object methods you've used so far have all been procedures, an object method can also be a function.

A convenience offered by Pascal (and some other languages) is the ability to access the result of a function as though it were a variable. Consider this possibility:

```
function SomeFunction(X: Integer): Integer;
...
begin
   SomeFunction := SomeValue;
   ...
   SomeFunction := SomeFunction + 10;    {<—No!  Not allowed!}
   ...
```

The compiler would spit out the errant line `SomeFunction := SomeFunction + 10;` as an error. This happens because the second appearance of `SomeFunction` is assumed to be *another call* to the `SomeFunction` routine. Pascal allows you not only to call a different routine from within a subroutine, but also to call a routine from within itself. (This is called *recursion* and is quite useful for some advanced programming techniques.)

Traditionally, Pascal forced you to declare a variable to hold the result of the function if you wanted to do any math on it:

```
function SomeFunction(X: Integer): Integer;
var SomeValue, Temporary: Integer;
begin
   Temporary := SomeValue;
   ...
   Temporary := Temporary + 10;
   SomeFunction := Temporary;   {You need this extra line.}
   ...
```

You were then forced to assign the temporary variable to the function. Pascal's Object Pascal introduces the concept of the Result variable. Result is a variable that can hold the result of the function without being confused with the function's name.

```
function SomeFunction(X: Integer): Integer;
...
begin
   Result := SomeValue;
   . . .
   Result := Result + 10;
. . .
```

Notice that you don't need to declare Result—it is always the type of the function—and that you don't need to assign Result to the function. It's as if Pascal adds for you the following code:

```
function SomeFunction(X: Integer): Integer;
var Result: Integer;   {Not really here.}
...
begin
   Result := SomeValue;
   . . .
   Result := Result + 10;
   . . .
   SomeFunction := Result; {Not really here}
```

You'll see Result from time to time in the code in this book.

The Pascal Library

A large part of the reason you have been introduced to the concept of procedures and functions now is that they are an important part of Delphi in general and Pascal in particular. In the old days, you could learn all about a language before going into the definition of a subroutine. But, except for your first WinCRT program in Chapter 5, everything you've done so far has been in a subroutine of one kind or another. It was important to take a long look at subroutines before moving on.

You write occasional subroutines in upcoming chapters. Throughout the rest of the book, however, you extensively use subroutines that Pascal provides for you. Related subroutines (and objects, for that matter) are grouped together in what are called *libraries*. Pascal comes, for example, with an extensive library of visual tools. You can buy libraries that contain tools for writing programs with complex graphics or that interface with sound cards.

Part of the key to successful programming is building on work that is already done. Libraries exist to make your job as a programmer easier.

Chapter 8 ◆ Subroutines

After finishing this book, one of the first things you might want to do is to read through the manuals provided with Pascal that describe the Pascal libraries. Not only will this give you a taste of the power of Pascal and Delphi, but also will be of help later on when you start to write your own programs. If you have some familiarity with what is in the libraries you have, you'll be much less likely to duplicate someone else's work.

Summary

Subroutines give you a way to package groups of instructions to make larger instructions and to extend and customize Pascal to your liking. They also reduce the likelihood of bugs and increase the readability of programs. A subroutine can be called from another subroutine. Pascal enables you to split statements into multiple lines, as long as you don't split a literal string.

Parameters allow subroutines to vary what they do to fit a given situation. A subroutine can have one, many, or no parameters. By default, Pascal does not allow parameters to be altered by a subroutine. Instead, the subroutine makes a copy of the parameter and allows the routine to change it. To allow a subroutine to change a parameter, you must declare that subroutine parameter as a var parameter. The const keyword prevents Pascal from making a copy of a parameter that isn't going to be changed by a routine.

Subroutines can return a value to the calling code. Subroutines that do not return any value are called procedures; subroutines that do are called functions. Within a function, Result is like an automatically defined variable that stands for the return value of the function.

Pascal comes with a considerable subroutine library that can reduce the amount of work you have to do when you program.

Before a variable or function is assigned a value, it is undefined and may contain anything. Variables declared in a subroutine exist only in that subroutine, and they are created when the routine is called and destroyed when it ends. Therefore, subroutine variables are always undefined when the subroutine is called. Subroutine variables are limited to the subroutines in which they are declared. The entire area in which a variable is known is called its scope. Global variables are declared outside of subroutines and can be known and used by any of the routines that follow their declarations. Subroutine variables can be used only locally; that is, by the routine that declares them.

Pascal enables you to watch how variables change with a watch window. You also can step through your program line by line, or trace into a subroutine.

Review Questions

1. What are subroutines and what is their purpose?
2. What are the two types of subroutines in Pascal?
3. Can a subroutine have no parameters? Can a subroutine have more than one parameter?
4. How long is any given variable in a procedure good for?
5. What is the purpose of a parameter?
6. What is the default value of a variable that hasn't been assigned a value?
7. What value does a function return if you don't assign it a value?
8. Can a subroutine call another subroutine?
9. How do you allow a subroutine to change a parameter for the calling code as well as itself?
10. Name two standard Pascal subroutines that you have used.
11. Can you split up a line in Pascal this way?

    ```
    B :=
    B      +
    1;
    ```

    How about like this?

    ```
    Writeln('Hello,
       World!');
    ```

12. How can you make the code in question 11 work while still keeping `'Hello,'` and `'World!'` on separate lines?
13. Open a watch window in Pascal and add a few variables to it. What does it mean when the window reports that a variable is an unknown identifier?
14. What is scope?
15. What is a global variable? What is a local variable? Which of the two takes precedence?
16. Technically, what does Pascal do with a var parameter as opposed to a regular parameter?

Chapter 8 ◆ Subroutines

Review Exercises

1. You know three subroutines already (`Writeln`, `Readln`, and `ClrScr`) that are part of the WinCRT unit. Write a program that engages in a "conversation" with the user. (The conversation will be extremely limited, of course, since the program will always respond in a similar fashion.) Make the program use the user's response in its "dialog." It might look something like this:

```
Hello (type a response)
```
> **Hi!**

```
What do you mean "Hi!"?
```
> **What?**

```
Do you often say "What?"?
```

Do a short program like this, without using any subroutines of your own.

2. Take the program from exercise 1 and expand and improve it by using subroutines to prompt the user. Use just one variable for the whole program to store the user's responses. (Hint: The variable will have to be *global*.)

3. Take the program from exercise 2 and now store the user's responses in different variables, so that the program retains certain information. For example:

```
What is your name?
```
> **Blake**

```
Hello, Blake. What is your favorite color?
```
> **Chartreuse**

```
People named Blake often like Chartreuse.
```

You can do this by using a `var` parameter or a function, whichever you prefer.

4. Write a program (using WinCRT again to keep it simple) that has a subroutine that calls another subroutine.

5. Trace through the program from one of the previous four exercises while watching *all* of the variables you declare in your program. Note the values when they are undefined, and the difference between local and global variables.

6. Write a program that has a global variable with the same name as a local variable in a subroutine. In this program, set the global variable to some value and then call the subroutine. Step through the program and watch the value of the variable. The program might look like this:

```
program Ch8Ex6;
var S: String;
procedure AProc;
var S: String;
begin
    S := 'XXX';
    end;
begin
    S := 'YYY';
    AProc;
end.
```

7. Write a program with a procedure that calls *itself*. What happens? (You'll look at this situation more in a later exercise.)

CHAPTER 9

Data Conversion

You may hear Pascal called "a strongly typed" language. Data types exist in all programming languages, although some circumvent typing by having only one data type. (The REXX language is an example of this: everything is a string of potentially infinite length. All math—literally everything—is done by using strings.)

You've observed that you cannot do the following in Pascal:

```
var
   B: Byte;
   C: Char;
   S: String;
begin
   B := 1;
   C := '1';
   S := '1';
   B := C;      {This will not compile}
   C := S;      {This will not compile}
   S := B;      {This will not compile}
end;
```

You cannot assign a char or a string to an integer type variable. You cannot assign any of the integer types to either of the character types. You can't even assign a string to a char. You may find this restriction annoying, or you may be grateful for it. This restriction prevents hard-to-find bugs from occurring in your code by preventing you at compile time from making illegal assignments. Thus, you're more likely to be annoyed than grateful, unless you've worked with another language and made one of these hard-to-detect mistakes.

Many languages allow one or more of these assignments to compile. What do these assignments do? Well, that depends on the language. A language called PL/I has literally pages of rules describing what happens when you assign one type of variable to another. (PL/I has many more basic data types than Pascal.)

Chapter 9 ♦ Data Conversion

I've programmed in PL/I for years, but I don't know the rules. To be sure what will happen, I have to get out the manual.

The idea behind PL/I was to make the desired conversion so that a string '11' became the number 11 when assigned from a character type to an integer type. This noble goal was designed to free the programmer from worrying about how to make a string into a number. The problem is, however, that programmers want different conversions at different times. Invariably, programmers end up assuming that the language compiler is doing one thing when in it is, in fact, doing something completely undesired.

In the C language, for example, you can do math by using characters. If you have a variable Ch that is a char type, you can add one to it. If you could increment character variables in Pascal, what do you think the effect of the following line would be?

```
Ch := Ch + 1;
```

Pascal could say that Ch has to contain a number, and adding one to it would raise it to the next number. Otherwise, the operation would be an error. In the C language, Ch can be any character, and the math is done as though Ch were an integer and the value of Ch + 1 were the next character higher in the ASCII table (see Appendix A). Therefore, the two lines

```
Ch := 'A';
Ch := Ch + 1;
```

would leave Ch with a value of 'B'—the next character after 'A' on the ASCII table. And these two lines

```
Ch := '9';
Ch := Ch + 1;
```

leave Ch with a value of ':' because the colon follows the numeral '9' on the ASCII table.

Some C programmers swear by this type of code, but because the code is not particularly legible or obvious, I would advise you against it, regardless of what language you use.

Why Is Data Conversion So Important?

As I mentioned in chapter two, in the early days of the user interface, computer nerds wrote programs for computer nerds. Basically, no one was expected to run a program who didn't have a fair degree of computer skill. As a result computer science classes and books could deal almost exclusively with the "meat" of programming: How to solve this problem, how to arrange data in this or that fashion, and so on.

Pascal's `Readln` and `Writeln` pretty much handled all the user interface needs that such a program had. But these routines didn't allow much editing, and they certainly aren't appropriate for a GUI like Windows. (You've seen `Readln` and `Writeln` in action already—do your WinCRT programs look like *Windows* programs? Do you think anyone would want to *use* them?)

Example: The Edit Line and Scrollbar Objects

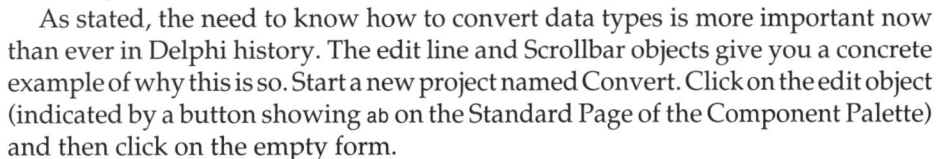

As stated, the need to know how to convert data types is more important now than ever in Delphi history. The edit line and Scrollbar objects give you a concrete example of why this is so. Start a new project named Convert. Click on the edit object (indicated by a button showing ab on the Standard Page of the Component Palette) and then click on the empty form.

For starters, just run the form and try out the edit line. This control should be familiar to you; it's the same input line all Windows programs use. Using the edit line, you can move the cursor, mark text, and so on, much like the editor in the Object Inspector. End your test run now and take a look at the edit line's properties.

First, change the object's name from `Edit1` to `Edit`. Now notice that the object has some familiar properties, including height and width. The property you're most interested in, however, is `Text`.

Almost every control has a property that represents some kind of user input. In the Gauge object that you looked at in the preceding chapter, for example, the value was `Progress`. In the edit object, it's `Text`. `Text` contains whatever the user typed. Often this property is called `Value`. It is the single-most important property of the control because it tells you what the user has specified. (Buttons are an exception; they don't contain user input, but they do execute code based on the user's choice.)

With `Edit`, that property is `Text`, and because the user can type anything into an edit object, `Text` is a `string` type. (Properties, like variables, have types too, as you saw in Chapter 6 with the labels examples.)

Underneath the edit object, place a *Scrollbar* object. The Scrollbar is on the tools' Standard page tab and indicated by a picture of a Scrollbar.

> **Note:** If you have the Visual Solutions Pack, you can also adapt this example to work with the *slider* control, which is represented on the VBX page by a playground slide. The slider property that contains the user input is called *value*. The other properties that you use here have the same names in the scrollbar objects as in the slider object.

Chapter 9 ◆ Data Conversion

Change the Scrollbar's Name from the default Scrollbar1 to Scrollbar. Scrollbar has a range of possible values, the lowest one usually being 0 and the default high range being 100. These values are reflected in the Min and Max properties. Change Max to 255, and before going any further, run the form again. You still can type stuff into the edit box, and now you can move the Scrollbar left and right. The Scrollbar property that tells the current position of the Scrollbar indicator—the little square that moves back and forth—is *Position*.

Example: The *Str* Procedure

What if you want the current position of Scrollbar to appear in Edit? You just have to set the Text property of Edit to be equal to Scrollbar's Value property. Double-click on the Scrollbar. Pascal opens up a new procedure—TConvertForm.ScrollbarChange (the form name will be whatever you have set it to, of course). At this point, you can't do the following:

```
procedure  TConvertForm.ScrollbarChange(Sender: TObject);
begin
   Edit.Text := Scrollbar.Position;
end;
```

Try it, and you see that Pascal stops at the offending line with the message Type Mismatch. Now you can see what I've been talking about all along. Edit.Text is a string. Scrollbar.Position is a number—specifically, an integer. You can't assign an integer to a string.

As you might imagine, of course, you aren't stuck here. If you can figure out how to do it, you can probably write a procedure that turns a number into a string. Fortunately, you don't have to because Pascal comes with a built-in procedure named Str. If you were to write the Str procedure yourself, you might declare it as follows:

```
procedure Str(ANumber: Longint; var AString: String);
```

Str translates ANumber into a string. You can use this procedure to take the Value of Scrollbar and convert it into the Text of Edit. Here's what the code looks like:

```
procedure  TConvertForm.ScrollbarChange(Sender: TObject);
var S: String;
begin
   Str(Scrollbar.Position, S);
   Edit.Text := S;
end;
```

First, you convert Value to S and then assign S to Text. Try out this code, and you discover that, as you move the Scrollbar, the text in Edit changes from '0' when the indicator is at the left side to '255' when it is at the right.

Converting a number into a string is a relatively simple task because any number in Pascal can be expressed as numerals in a string.

Example: The *Val* Procedure

After reading the preceding section, you may realize that there would also have to be a procedure to turn strings with numerals into numbers. If you were going to have the Scrollbar's value reflected in the edit line's text, for example, shouldn't the user be able to change the text in the edit line and have that change reflected in the Scrollbar?

For this example, you're going to add a button to the form. Call the button Convert, and place it right next to the input line. Your form should now resemble figure 9.1. (You needn't worry about the exact size or position of the controls in this example.)

Figure 9.1
The form for the Convert example.

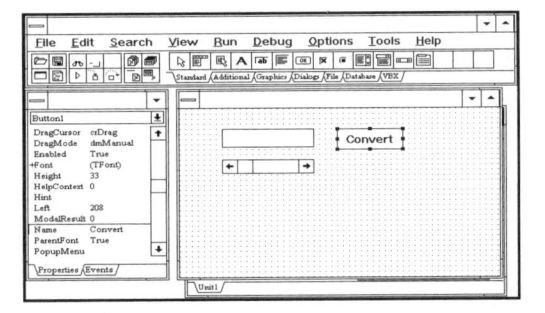

You can just connect the edit line directly to the Scrollbar, but doing so might be a bad idea because as the user is inserting and deleting characters, the Scrollbar indicator will bounce around rather oddly. Instead, you'll set the code to translate the contents of `Edit` into `Scrollbar`'s Position property to activate when the Convert button is clicked.

Double-click on the Convert button, and Pascal opens the code window for you. The procedure header appears, along with the `begin` and `end` statements:

```
procedure TConvertForm.ConvertClick(Sender: TObject);
begin
end;
```

Of course, you can't assign `Edit.Text` to `Scrollbar.Position` any more than you could assign `Position` to `Text`. You need a procedure to convert the string to an integer. Fortunately, Pascal comes with such a built-in procedure, which is called `Val`. `Val` takes three parameters: the string to be converted, the number variable in which to place converted contents, and an integer parameter that can be used in case of error. If you were to write `Val`, you might declare it as follows:

```
procedure Val(AString: String; var AnInteger: Longint; var Error: Integer);
```

Chapter 9 ♦ Data Conversion

The `Error` parameter is set to zero if the string can be converted to a number; otherwise, it contains the position of the first invalid character in `AString`. The validity of the string is something that must be considered when converting to a number. Where every number can be represented as a string, not every string can be represented as a number. (`'Hello'`, for example, has no numeric value.)

In `ConvertClick`, add the following code:

```
procedure TConvertForm.ConvertClick(Sender: TObject);
var B, Error: Byte;
begin
   Val(Edit.Text, B, Error);
   Scrollbar.Position := B;
end;
```

If you try to compile this code, however, you discover that it doesn't work. The compiler stops at `Error` in the `Val` statement and says `Integer expected`.

Incompatible Integers

In the preceding section, I had you add the code deliberately to show you that integer types are *not* compatible under all circumstances. Basically, you can use them interchangeably except when the variable is to be a `var` parameter to a procedure. So, if you have the procedure

```
procedure DoSomething(B: Byte; L: Longint);
```

you can call it with the statements

```
DoSomething(L, B);
DoSomething(W, I);
DoSomething(S, S);
```

where L is declared a `longint`, B is a `byte`, W is a `word`, I is an `integer`, and S is a `shortint`. All these examples will work. In fact, you can use L, B, W, S, and I interchangeably. Similarly, if you have the functions

```
function DoSomethingElse: Longint;
function DoAnotherThing: Byte;
```

you can use those same variables to receive the values returned by the functions

```
L := DoSomethingElse;
B := DoSomethingElse;
W := DoSomethingElse;
L := DoAnotherThing;
I := DoAnotherThing;
S := DoAnotherThing;
```

The only danger in the preceding example is the possibility of a range check error, in case `DoSomethingElse` or `DoAnotherThing` returns a value that is too large for the target variable. In any case, all of these examples will definitely compile.

If, however, you declare procedure `DoSomething` like

```
procedure DoSomething(var B: Byte; var L: Longint);
```

the only combination that works is the following:

```
DoSomething(B, L);
```

This example makes sense, if you think about it. In the first two cases, you are dealing with copies of the variable. Just as you can assign a `byte` to a `longint` or a `word` to a `shortint`, the compiler happily copies the values from and to your various integers. With `var` parameters, however, you are dealing with the *actual* variable (as covered extensively in the last chapter). If you have a `longint var` parameter, your procedure expects the address to a 4-byte variable. Nothing else works. Fortunately, the compiler catches this potential mistake.

Now you can go back to the example, which is easy to fix. Simply declare `Error` separately from the `B` variable:

```
procedure TConvertForm.ConvertClick(Sender: TObject);
var B: Byte;
    Error: Integer;
begin
   Val(Edit.Text, B, Error);
   Scrollbar.Position := B;
end;
```

And, to smooth the example out a bit, find the `Default` property of the `Convert` component and set it to `True`. Any form can have a default button. The default button acts as though it has been clicked when the user presses Enter.

Now test the program. The Scrollbar still alters the contents of the edit line. This time, however, if you type a value into the edit line and press Enter (or click the Convert button), the Scrollbar moves to match whatever value you typed.

Well, almost. You can type in a negative number or a number greater than 255, and you'll find that the modulus feature you saw earlier (in Chapter 7, "Using Numbers") with the gauge object is in effect. The `B` variable can be only from 0 through 255. Other values are wrapped around to become an acceptable value.

> **Note:** If you have range checking on, the values don't wrap around. Instead, you get a range check error. In Chapter 10, "On One Condition," you'll examine a way to avoid this error.

Chapter 9 ♦ Data Conversion

Example: The Label Object

You may have tried to type a nonnumeric value into the edit line. What happens? If Val encounters an invalid character in a string it is trying to convert, it puts zero in the target variable. (And, as mentioned before, it sets Error to the location of the bad character.)

To get a feel for how Val works, add another object—a label object—to the form directly under the Convert button. The purpose of the label object is to describe some other object on the screen or some event that is taking place internally in the program. For example, you can put a label such as *Volume* over the Scrollbar control or *Enter a number* over the edit line. Or you could have a label reflect some internal activity to give feedback to the user.

That's what you're going to do here: use the label object to report on the result of the conversion. First, change the Name of the label from Label1 to ErrorText. Now, change the Caption property, which contains the text that the label displays, to Error. Caption is the property of the label object that contains the text displayed. Can you make the ErrorText object display the contents of the Error variable used by Val? Give it a try. Then come back and follow along.

First, decide where to put the new code. You should put it somewhere in the ConvertClick procedure because that's where the Error variable exists. Logically, it must be after the Val statement because before that point Error is undefined.

Next you have to figure out how to put Error (an integer) into ErrorText.Caption (a string). Here's what the code looks like:

```
procedure TConvertForm.ConvertClick(Sender: TObject);
var B: Byte;
    Error: Integer;
    S: String;
begin
   Val(Edit.Text, B, Error);
   Scrollbar.Position := B;
   Str(Error, S);
   ErrorText.Caption := 'Error: '+S;
end;
```

Note: The last two lines of the preceding code could just as well have gone before the assignment to Scrollbar.Position, instead of after.

Now, just to get a feel for how Val works, run the code again and type invalid values into the edit line. Can you have leading spaces? What about a number that is really large—say 12 or 13 digits? Can you have spaces in between the numbers—that is, will the procedure pick up "1 2" as "12"? Can you have a plus sign? Often, the best way to understand how a standard Pascal procedure works is to write a piece of code to test it out.

Example: The *Copy* Function

You can be even more specific about what the Val procedure doesn't like by using the Pascal Copy function. Copy returns a portion of a string variable, starting from a position that you specify and going for a length that you specify. If you were to declare Copy, it would look something like the following:

```
function Copy(AString: String;   AStartingPlace: Byte;
➥HowMuch: Byte): String;
```

It would return HowMuch characters from AString starting at AStartingPlace.

Add another label to the form, call it InvalidChar, and change the caption to "Invalid: ". Now, in ConvertClick, follow up the change in ErrorText label's Caption property with a call to Copy. The code should now look like the following:

```
procedure TConvertForm.ConvertClick(Sender: TObject);
var B: Byte;
    L: Longint;
    Error: Integer;
    S: String;
begin
   Val(Edit.Text, B, Error);
   Scrollbar.Position := B;
   Str(Error, S);
   ErrorText.Caption := 'Error: '+S;
   S := '"'+Copy(Edit.Text, Error, 1)+'"';
   InvalidChar.Caption := 'Invalid: '+S;
end;
```

You set S to the offending character, which you surround with quotation marks so that a blank is visible. You then set the caption of InvalidChar to S. The only problem with this example is that InvalidChar always has a value, even when there is no error. If the AStartingPlace parameter of the Copy procedure is 0, instead of returning nothing or an error, Copy works as though it were a 1, returning the first character of the string. (This can be remedied through a conditional statement, described in the next chapter.)

Of course, you've only touched on a few of the data types in this chapter, so you can't examine all the data conversion possibilities yet. Later in this book, as you learn other data types, you look at how they convert into numbers and strings.

Summary

Pascal is called a strongly typed language because it does not automatically convert data types back and forth. This restriction forces you to think about converting the data but also keeps you from having to memorize rules about how the conversions are done. The programmer must specifically code conversions; for example, you call the Str and Val procedures, which convert a number to a string and a string to a number, respectively. In case of error, the Val procedure returns the position of the first invalid character in the string. The Copy function returns a substring of a string.

The edit object enables the user to type in data and to use the cursor keys to edit and mark text. The Scrollbar object enables the user to move an indicator along a track to select a value within a certain range. The button object has a Default property that causes it to be clicked when the user presses Enter. You use the label object to describe something.

Review Questions

1. What is the point of data typing? Why doesn't Pascal allow you to assign an integer to a string and vice versa?

2. What does the Str procedure do? Can it fail?

3. What does the Val procedure do? Can it fail? How can you tell where?

4. What does the Copy function do?

5. Can any integer type be substituted for any other integer type at any time?

6. If function DoSomething returns a LongInt, and variable B is a byte, is this dangerous? Why?

    ```
    B := DoSomething;
    ```

7. Can you cut text from an edit object to the Clipboard? Can you paste text from the Clipboard into an edit object?

8. What will the Copy function return in the following line?

    ```
    Copy('12345678', 0, 1);
    ```

Review Exercises

1. Rather than having an edit line object that reflects the position of a Scrollbar, write a program that has a *label* showing the position of a Scrollbar. (You'll use this skill in the next chapter.)

2. Try incorporating into the program for Exercise 1 a *gauge* that reflects the position of the scrollbar.

3. On the VBX page of the tool bar, there is a control called BiGauge which can be used similarly to the gauge object you've looked at already. Try incorporating this object into the program built in the previous two exercises.

4. Rewrite the conversion program from this chapter *without* the Convert button. In other words, make the Scrollbar move with each character the user types, and make the error and invalid labels instantly reflect any problems (like the user typing a character) that may occur. (Hint: Use the OnChange event.)

5. There is a Pascal function called Delete that removes characters from a string. The Delete procedure is declared like this:

```
procedure Delete(var S: String; Index, Count:Integer);
```

Where S is the text, Index is the first position to delete, and Count is the number of characters to delete. Modify the Convert program built in this chapter so that it eliminates the first offending character from the Edit object, if the user enters an invalid string. (You'll look at a way to eliminate characters if more than one is wrong in a later exercise.)

Part IV

Taking Charge of Delphi

CHAPTER 10

On One Condition

Have you ever said to someone, "I'll do it on one condition"? Implicit in that statement is the threat that you will do something else (or nothing at all) if the condition is not met. Almost all computer programs have *conditional code*—code executed only under certain conditions—and lots of it. Before you look at how to add conditional code to your programs, you must first look at a special data type.

The Boolean Type

"Relax. It's just zeros and ones" is an ironic computer saying, best used on someone who is tearing out his hair trying to find a bug in his program or who has just lost his data for the umpteenth time. Computer data and code is all zeros and ones, arranged in many different combinations so as to give those zeros and ones significance.

It should come as no surprise, then, that computer logic is based on just two possibilities. To the computer, the answer to any question is either *yes* or *no*, *true* or *false*—*zero* or *one*. The Delphi data type that reflects this concept is called *Boolean*. A Boolean variable can be either True or False.

> George Boole, an English mathematician who lived in the nineteenth century, invented the system of logic on which most digital computer programming is based. The *Boolean* data type is named in his honor.

Working with Boolean Variables

Boolean variables are declared in the `var` block of a program, as are strings and integers. Boolean variables are subject to the same name restrictions applied to other variables. The assignment operator works with them, but the + does not. The only values that can be assigned to a Boolean variable are `True` and `False`. Here are some examples of Boolean variables:

```
var
    WasInvalid: Boolean;
    B: Boolean;
    TestFailed, UnderAge, TruthOrDare: Boolean
```

Here are some examples as used in code:

```
WasInvalid := False;
B := True;
TestFailed := FALSE;
```

Pascal is not case sensitive, as mentioned previously, so `false`, `False`, and `FALSE` are all identical. `True` and `False` are Delphi keywords, so you cannot use them as variable names.

> **Note:** Deep down, `True and False` are just one and zero, respectively. In fact, most computer languages have no False and True keywords, but use zero and one—or zero and any other value—to represent False and True. These languages use actual integers as Booleans. Pascal, on the other hand, does not let you assign an integer to a Boolean, or vice versa.

Comparisons

Although you occasionally assign `True` or `False` directly to a Boolean variable, you are more likely to assign a value indirectly, to reflect the value of some test. Pascal has many operators that you haven't read about yet, and among these are the *comparison operators*.

You use comparison operators to test differences between variables. In Pascal, you can test whether a variable is equal to, not equal to, less than, or greater than another variable. Pascal uses the common mathematical symbols for these operators, as shown in table 10.1.

Table 10.1. The Pascal comparison operators.

Symbol	Description
=	Equal to
<>	Not equal to
>	Greater than
<	Less than
>=	Greater than or equal to
<=	Less than or equal to

You can use these operators with strings or numbers. With numbers, the result of any comparison is usually obvious. If Bool is a Boolean variable, for example, the following code shows how it would be set after certain tests:

```
Bool := 1 > 3;  {Bool is now false.}
Bool := 3 > 1;  {true}
A := 2; B := 2; {A and B are integer types.}
Bool := A >= B; {true}
Bool := A <> B; {false}
Bool := A = B;  {true}
Bool := A <= B; {still true}
```

Simple enough math. You can do the same comparisons by using strings, although the results are not necessarily as obvious:

```
Bool := '1' > '3'; {Bool is now false}
Bool := '10' > '3' {still false}
Bool := 'cat' = 'cat';   {true}
Bool := 'cat' = 'CAT';   {false}
Bool := 'CAT' < 'CATE';  {true}
Bool := 'a' > 'A' {Still true}
```

String comparisons are done on a character-by-character basis, where a character is "less" or "more" depending on its position in the ASCII table (see Appendix A). So '1' is less than '3', but '10' is also less than '3', because of what's being compared: not the numeric quantity the string represents, but the characters being used to represent it. (If you want to compare quantities, you must convert the strings to numbers first as discussed in the last chapter.)

Looking at the letter comparisons, you can see that although Pascal in general is not case sensitive, comparisons of one string to another are. The lowercase 'cat' is not equal to the uppercase 'CAT'. Also, 'CAT' is lower than 'CAT' plus anything else; 'CATE', 'CATA', 'CATZ' are all greater than 'CAT'. Another thing that may be surprising is that the lowercase `'cat'` is greater than the uppercase `'CAT'`. Again, these comparisons all fall back on the character's position in the ASCII table (see Appendix A). The uppercase letters all come first and are therefore lower in value.

You also can do string comparisons by using nonalphabetic, nonnumeric characters: for example, `'@'` is greater than `'!'` but less than `'['`. You won't have many occasions to care about this kind of comparison, fortunately.

Logical Operators

Boolean variables have a special set of operators that apply only to them. They are called the *logical operators*, and they consist of mostly English words with very specific meanings. (When I use them in this book, I spell them in all capitals to distinguish them from the English words.) These operators are AND, OR, XOR, and NOT. Table 10.2 shows how AND, OR, and XOR work.

Table 10.2. The logical operators.

Value	*Operator*	*Value*	*Result*
True	AND	True	True
True	AND	False	False
False	AND	True	False
False	AND	False	False
True	OR	True	True
True	OR	False	True
False	OR	True	True
False	OR	False	False
True	XOR	True	False
True	XOR	False	True
False	XOR	True	True
False	XOR	False	False

NOT negates a value, resulting in the rather obvious table 10.3.

Table 10.3. The *NOT* operator.

Operator	Value	Result
NOT	True	False
NOT	False	True

Some people find that thinking about the logical operators in English terms makes them easier to understand. For example, if you say, "This and that," you mean both statements must be true. If either is false—or if both are false—the entire statement, "This and that," is false. By comparison, "This or that" implies that either statement can be true. As long as both statements aren't false, the entire "This or that" statement can be considered true.

In English, however, an ambiguity exists. If you say, "This or that," you might mean that either may be true but not both. In contests, the announcement of the prize often says that you may have won "$10,000 or a new car." It doesn't mean you've won both. This example is called the *exclusive or*, which is shortened in computerese to XOR. If you say, "This or that but not both" (the more precise English language version of XOR) then as long as exactly one statement is true, the whole "This or that but not both" statement is true.

Example: Logic

Before you go on to use Boolean logic to control your programs, take a look at a control that more or less embodies the Boolean concept. This object is the *switch*. It is on the VBX page of the object bar. (Its actual name is "BiSwitch" but I'll just call it "switch" here.) In this example, you're going to see how to use Pascal to design complex forms. You're going to use the switch control to demonstrate what happens with the logical operators. You start by creating a form that looks like the one shown in figure 10.1. Follow these steps:

Figure 10.1
The beginning of LOGIC.

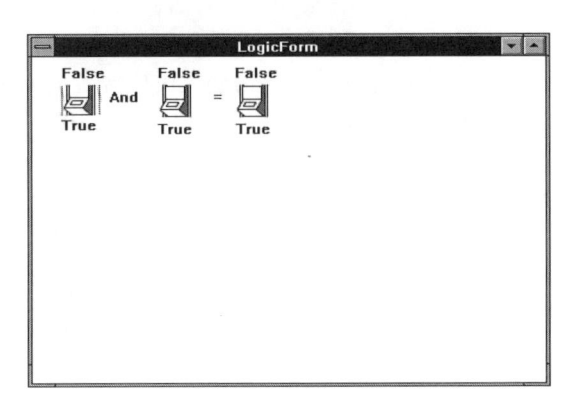

Chapter 10 ◆ On One Condition

1. Open a new project. Choose Save Project from the File menu to give the project file and unit file a name. (Pascal will ask you for a name for any unnamed units before saving the project.) Call the unit LogFrm and the project LOGIC. Change the Name property of the form to "LogicForm".

2. In figure 10.1, you can see that you need three switches and eight labels: three False, three True, an And, and an =. The quickest approach is to hold down the shift key and then click on the switch icon. You can now click on the form to repeatedly place switches on it. (To stop placing switches, you need to click on the cursor selection tool— the arrow that's always at the far left of the Component Bar.)

3. Group select all the switches and use the Object Inspector to delete the Caption property of the switch. Then adjust the width property so that the sizes of the objects are just big enough to accommodate the actual graphic of the switch. Adjusting the switches now reduces the clutter for the next step.

4. Place the switches where they should go on the form, aligning them vertically and spacing them evenly horizontally. Leave enough space at the top and bottom for the True and False labels and leave enough space between them to allow for the And label and the = label.

5. Change the name of the first switch to And1, the name of the second switch to And2, and the name of the third switch to AndResult.

6. Now go back to the Standard control page on the object bar and click on the Label icon. Place eight of these objects on the form, roughly where they should go.

7. Arrange the top three objects so that they are directly over the three switches and group select them. Use the Object Inspector to change all their captions to False. Repeat this step with the bottom three objects, changing their captions to True. If necessary, size the labels so that the words True and False are completely visible.

8. Place one of the remaining labels in between the first two switches and change its caption to And. Place the remaining label in between the second and third switch and change its caption to =.

9. Notice that you are not changing all the names of the labels. The only time it is really important to change a component's name from the default Pascal assigns is when you're going to refer to that object in your program. Now that you've set up your eight labels, you aren't going to change them or do anything else with them—so it doesn't matter whether they're called Label1 or Label8 or whatever.

Now it's time to change the objects' behavior. The property you are interested in is the switches' pOn property. This Boolean property is True when a switch is on and False when a switch is off. Whenever the And1 or And2 switch is clicked, you want the AndResult switch to reflect the logical AND result of their POn properties. To do so, you use a simple line of code:

```
AndResult.pOn := And1.pOn AND And2.pOn;
```

But where should you put this line? Select And1 and flip to the event page in the Object Inspector. Amazingly, there is no Clicked event for a switch. There's an OnOn event and an OnOff event, though.

Sometimes an object isn't set up the way you think it should be. When this happens, it's important to be able to work around the difficulty (or, when you get more experience, to write your own component that works the way you want it to). For this example, you work with the OnOn and OnOff events. To get Delphi to open a code window for OnOn, click on the edit side of the Object Inspector, directly to the right of OnOn. Pascal produces the following frame:

```
procedure TLogicForm.And1On(Sender: TObject);
begin

end;
```

You can make the AndResult switch respond to the user by clicking And1 on by adding this line of code:

```
AndResult.pOn := And1.pOn AND And2.pOn;
```

Swell. Does that mean you have to follow this procedure for And1's OnOff event and then do the whole thing over again for the OnOn and OnOff events of And2? Fortunately, no.

If you go back to the Object Inspector now and click once on the OnOff event, you'll notice that, besides the edit line being active, a down-pointing arrow appears at the far right. Click on it, and you discover that the Object Inspector opens a drop-down list of all the event routines you have written for the current form that can be called from this event. You can select And1On from the list. And you can do the same for the OnOn and OnOff events of the And2 switch.

Try this example. You'll find that the AndResult switch turns on when both And1 and And2 are switched on, and it turns off as soon as either is switched off. There's only one flaw. Users can change AndResult themselves and thereby make it incorrect. Now end the test and go back to the Object Inspector.

Most controls have a property called Enabled. When it is set to True, as it usually is by default, the user can directly use that control. In this case, you don't want AndResult changed directly—only through And1 and And2—so you would want to find that property and change it to False. (Note that Enabled would be a Boolean property.) Then, when you ran the program, you would not be able to directly change the AndResult switch.

175

Unfortunately, as with many VBX controls, the BiSwitch is lacking certain niceties, among them an `Enabled` property. Does this mean that you are stuck? Fortunately, no. The solution is as simple as having AndResult's pOn and pOff events *also* call And1On, just as And1 and And2's on and off events call it.

Now, when you run it and try to click on the AndResult switch, there is a slight flicker as the switch flips one way, then flips back to the correct setting because of the And1On event. (On many machines this will be too fast to see.)

To complete this example, follow the preceding steps to create two new rows of switches, one to illustrate the effects of the logical OR; the other, the logical XOR. Figure 10.2 shows these switches.

Figure 10.2
The complete LOGIC example.

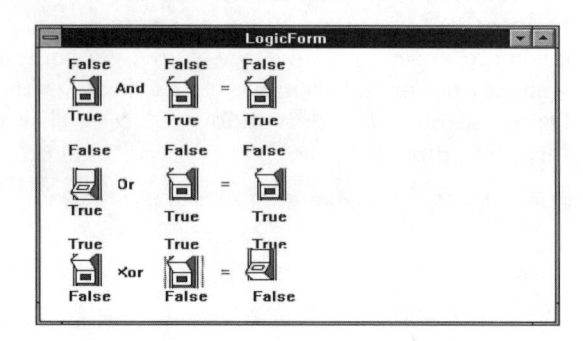

Remember: if you want your object to respond the same way to several events, have Pascal generate the code frame for one event and then use the Object Inspector to select that procedure for the other events. The code for the OR and XOR switches is as follows:

```
OrResult.POn := Or1.POn OR Or2.POn;
XorResult.POn := Xor1.POn XOR Xor2.POn;
```

You must put each line in the appropriate procedure, of course.

The *If-Then* Statement

If you think about it, you make conditional statements all the time. Even in the preceding chapters, when examples were written by using English, some of the examples looked like the following:

If the user has clicked here, do some action.

The idea here is that, if some condition is met, then something else happens. Otherwise, nothing else happens. In English, you use the words *if* and *then* (or sometimes just a comma in place of *then*) to express something conditional. The Pascal keywords used to express a condition are If and Then. For example,

```
If Bool then Writeln('Hello, World!');
```

Given that `Bool` is declared as a Boolean variable, the `Writeln` occurs only if `Bool` contains `True`.

You don't need a Boolean variable to use `If` and `Then`, however. The result of any comparison is either `True` or `False`, so just as before you had

```
B := 1 > 3;
```

you could also have

```
If 1>3 then Writeln('Hello, World');
```

Because 1 is always lower than 3 and the comparison 1 > 3 is always false, this code is never executed.

You're most likely to use `If` with at least one variable so that the code might execute some times and not others. For example,

```
If A>B then Writeln('Hello, World');
```

When A is greater than B, the message `Hello, World` appears. When A is not greater than B, no message appears.

Complex Logic

Sometimes a test is not as simple as just determining whether this Boolean variable is `True` or this integer is greater than that integer. You often may have more than one condition that needs to be met in order for some code to be executed. You can string these conditions out into multiple `If-Then` statements, as follows:

```
If Age<17 then if AccompaniedByAnAdult then YouMayBeAdmitted := true;
```

But what if you want to say that either of two situations may be true in order for some code to be executed? You can do that this way:

```
If Age>17 then YouMayBeAdmitted := true;
if AccompaniedByAnAdult then YouMayBeAdmitted := true;
```

Neither of these solutions is very elegant, however. What you really need is some way to link them together. Of course, you have such a way with the logical operators. You can use the logical operators freely with Boolean variables:

```
If Red AND Blue then TheColorPurple;
If Over17 OR AccompaniedByAnAdult then YouMayBeAdmitted;
```

When you're dealing with comparisons, however, Pascal insists that you place the comparison within parentheses. The following example doesn't work:

Chapter 10 ◆ On One Condition

```
If Age>17 OR AccompaniedByAnAdult then YouMayBeAdmitted; {Won't work!}
```

But this example does work:

```
If (Age>17) OR AccompaniedByAnAdult then YouMayBeAdmitted;
```

Enclosing Age>17 in parentheses forces the program to evaluate that portion first and turn it into a True or False value. You can string as many Booleans together with ANDs, ORs, NOTs, and XORs as you like. Remember that the only thing Pascal cares about is a final answer of True or False.

Example: Guess It!

The If-Then pair opens up a realm of new possibilities, which you now exploit in a simple guessing game.

1. Start a new project. Save the unit as GUESSFRM and the project as GUESSIT. You're going to set up a form to look like the one shown in figure 10.3. Change the form name to GuessForm.

Figure 10.3
The Guess It! form.

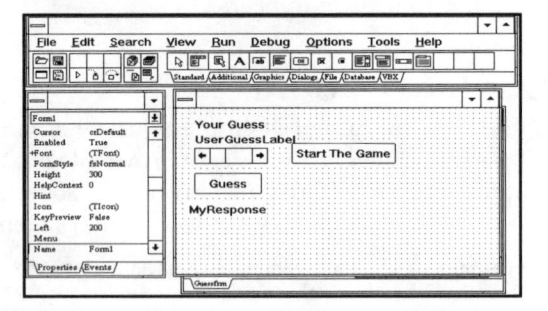

2. Place a label, Your Guess, at the top. Underneath that, place a SpinEdit control. The SpinEdit control can be found on the "Samples" page. The user is going to use the spin-edit to make a guess about a number from 1 to 100.

3. Call the spin-edit UserGuess and set its Enabled property to False. The guessing game will pick a number from 1 to 100 and the user must guess it by using the spin-edit, so set the spin-edit's MinValue property to 1, its MaxValue property to 100, and its Value property to 1. (You won't be able to see the Value property without scrolling down the Object Inspector.)

4. Underneath the spin-edit, put a button with the caption Guess, so that the user can, after adjusting the spin-edit to his liking, tell the program that the current spin-edit value is his guess. Give this button the name Guess. Disable this button by setting its Enabled property to False.

5. Underneath the Guess button, place another label. GUESSIT will use this space to give the user messages. Blank out the Caption property of this label and call it MyResponse.

6. To the right of all these buttons, place a button with the caption Start The Game.

> **Tip:** The button itself should be named StartTheGame. It's a good trick to make the name of the object equivalent to its Caption property minus any spaces.

The program should work as follows: When the user clicks StartTheGame, the program randomly selects a number between 1 and 100, clears out MyResponse.Caption (which will be showing the last message from the previous game), and enables the spin-edit and Guess push button so that the user can guess what that number is. StartTheGame will disable itself at this point and remain disabled until the game is over. Here's the code so far:

```
procedure TGuessForm.StartTheGameClick(Sender: TObject);
begin
   {Select Random Number}
   StartTheGame.Enabled := false;
   UserGuess.Enabled := true;
   Guess.Enabled := true;
   MyResponse.Caption := '';
end;
```

When playing, the user selects a number by using UserGuess and the Guess button, and GUESSIT tells him whether his guess was too high, too low, or correct, using the MyResponse label. The actual code to do this part is really easy using If-Then. Pretend you have a variable called MyNumber that contains GUESSIT's random number. See if you can write the code to tell the user where his guess falls. Put it in the subroutine for GuessClick. (Double-click on the Guess button to get there.)

Here's the code I used:

```
procedure TGuessForm.GuessClick(Sender: TObject);
var B: Byte;
    S: String;
begin
   B := UserGuess.Value;
   If B>MyNumber then S := 'Too High';
   If B<MyNumber then S := 'Too Low';
   If B = MyNumber then S := 'You Guessed It!';
   MyResponse.Caption := S;
end;
```

Your code may vary somewhat but should be essentially the same. Following is the code translated into English:

Compare the value from UserGuess to MyNumber and use the result of the comparison to set MyResponse.Caption.

You may not have used local variables such as the B and S above, so your If-Then statements may look like the following:

```
If UserSpin.Value > MyNumber then  MyResponse.Caption := 'Too High';
```

That's fine. I find my way a little easier to read, and it requires less typing.

You don't have a MyNumber variable yet, but you need one that you can access from all your subroutines. Therefore, you can't declare it within any particular subroutine. For now, the easiest approach to take is to declare MyNumber globally, by putting its declaration right before the UserGuessClick method itself. In other words, add the following var statement:

```
implementation

{$R *.DFM}

var MyNumber: Byte;   {ADD THIS LINE HERE!!!}

procedure TGuessForm.GuessClick(Sender: TObject);
var B: Byte;
, , ,
```

Now all you have to do is to have the computer pick a number and you're set. This process involves introducing two standard Delphi routines that can make programming a lot of fun.

Random

One of the things that makes computers fun is their capability to apparently do things at random. Because of this capability, they can simulate card and other gambling games. Pascal provides for this random feature through the Random function.

If you were to declare Random, it might look like the following:

```
function Random(Limit: Word): Word;
```

where Limit-1 is the highest number Random can return. (Zero is the lowest.) So the statement

```
W := Random(10);
```

can set W to 0, 1, 2, 3, 4, 5, 6, 7, 8, or 9. And the statement

```
W := Random(100);
```

can set W to any integer value from 0 to 99.

The number you want is from 1 to 100, however, so you need to call Random as follows:

```
MyNumber := Random(100)+1;
```

Now substitute this line for the comment you saw earlier in the StartTheGameClick method call:

```
{Select Random Number}
```

At this point, GUESSIT is ready!

Now, give GUESSIT a try. In fact, try it twice. Try it a third time. Notice something odd?

Randomize

The odd occurrence you find when playing Guess It! is this: No matter how many times you play the game, the computer always guesses the same number. Remember how I said that the computer generated apparently random numbers? Think about it for a second. How can a computer come up with a truly random number? It can't. (A truly random number would require original thought.) Pascal simulates randomness by calculating a series of numbers based on a *seed*. Unless you set the seed to some value other than the default, you get the same "random" numbers every time you run your program.

This fact is very useful to know. Imagine having a large program that works with random numbers, which seems to fail under some circumstances. Imagine trying to find a bug in this program when every time you run the program, the "random" numbers keep changing. The bug would be very difficult to track. Pascal, however, enables you to force the Random function to come up with the same "random" numbers every time.

Although this capability is useful in some circumstances, it's not what you want here. Pascal provides a procedure called Randomize, which puts a value into the seed. What value? To simulate randomness, the seed is set to a number based on the system clock—something like how many hundredths of a second after midnight it is. This setting ensures that the numbers that come out of Random are virtually random.

Now view the project source (from the View menu select Project Source) and add the following line of code after the begin:

```
begin
  Randomize;  {Add this line!!!!}
  Application.CreateForm(TGuessForm, GuessForm);
  Application.Run;
end.
```

Chapter 10 ◆ On One Condition

Or Else...

Implicit in any conditional statement is a threatened "or else." Your parents may have said to you, "If you take out the garbage, then I will give you your allowance." And you may have responded, "Or else what?" The answer to this question was probably a variety of unpleasant things.

The `Else` keyword is not nearly so unpleasant in Pascal. By using it, you tell the computer what to do when the condition of the `If` is not met. Look at the segment of the `UserGuessClick` that uses the `If-Then` pattern:

```
If B>MyNumber then S := 'Too High';
If B<MyNumber then S := 'Too Low';
If B = MyNumber then S := 'You Guessed It!';
```

Now if `B>MyNumber` is true, why should the computer then check to see if `B<MyNumber` or `B = MyNumber` is true? You know that they can't be. You can tell the computer not to check by using `Else`.

```
If B>MyNumber then S := 'Too High'
else if B < MyNumber then S := 'Too Low';
```

Notice that the semicolon after `'Too High'` is gone. `Else` is not a statement of its own, but a continuation of the preceding `If-Then` statement. Most people, when they start to program, want to put semicolons before their `Else`s; you should expect to do it from time to time, too. All that happens is that the compiler stops on the `Else` and complains `Error in statement`. (The `Error in statement` message usually means that you've stuck a keyword someplace it doesn't belong— like an `Else` at the beginning of a statement. Often it helps to check the preceding code to see that you've got the semicolons and other punctuation right.)

You can follow an `If-Then` with an `Else`. You can further improve the previous example by adding yet another `Else`:

```
If B>MyNumber then S := 'Too High'
else If B<MyNumber then S := 'Too Low'
else If B = MyNumber then S := 'You Guessed It!';
```

This point may not seem like a big deal, and in this case maybe it isn't. Sometimes `Else` can make a programming task easier or at least make the code more elegant. Even here, you can reduce the final `Else` to simply

```
else S := 'You Guessed It!';
```

Can you see why? If B is higher than MyNumber, then S is set at the line

```
If B>MyNumber then S := 'Too High'
```

and the subsequent `Else` is ignored. If B is lower than MyNumber, then S is set at the line

```
else If B<MyNumber then S := 'Too Low'
```

182

and the next Else is ignored. The only value of B remaining is the one that is equal to MyNumber. You don't need to test because you have eliminated all other possibilities.

If you try out the code, of course, it works just the same as before. But it is more efficient—the computer isn't doing any unnecessary work—and it's actually easier to read because you can see the connection between the three If-Then statements.

The Orphaned *Else*

One other interesting point touched on in the preceding section is, what happens if you have an If-Then statement like

```
If A then If B then DoC;
```

and you want to add an Else to make it into

```
If A then if B then DoC
else DoSomething;
```

When is DoSomething called? When B fails or when A fails?

The rule is that an Else belongs to the nearest If that doesn't have an Else already. So DoSomething is called when B fails. Then what if you want it to be called when A fails? You have to do the following:

```
If A then
    If B then DoC
  else
else DoSomething
```

To make this example work, you need to put two Elses in a row, the first one matching the If B and doing nothing, and the second one matching the If A and calling DoSomething. You learn how to avoid this situation altogether in the next section.

Blocks

Throughout this book, you've been using begin and end to denote the beginning and ending points of programs and subroutines. The code in between the keywords begin and end is called a *block*. A block of code in Pascal is treated sort of like a single statement—something that you read about early on in the book—and that is why begin is never followed by a semicolon. Semicolons end statements, whereas begin says to the compiler, "treat everything that comes after me as one big statement."

You can use begin and end anywhere in your routines or in the main body of a program. Anywhere. So you can do the following:

Chapter 10 ◆ On One Condition

```
begin
   Writeln('Hello, World!')
   begin
      Writeln('What is your name?');
      Readln(s);
   begin
      Writeln('Hello, ' + S);
```

As long as you match every `begin` with an `end`, your program should compile fine. In this case the program will run no differently than if you hadn't blocked the code using `begin` and `end`. One doesn't normally code this way.

However, `begin` and `end` are invaluable when used following an `If-Then` or `If-Then-Else` statement. Consider that, once the user guesses the number, you want to disable the `UserGuess` and `Guess` controls and reenable the `StartTheGame` button so that the user can play again. You can do it like this:

```
If B = MyNumber then UserGuess.Enabled := false;
If B = MyNumber then Guess.Enabled := false;
If B = MyNumber then StartTheGame.Enabled := true;
```

Or you can enlist `begin` and `end` to help out here:

```
If B>MyNumber then S := 'Too High'
else If B<MyNumber then S := 'Too Low'
else begin
   S := 'You Guessed It!';
   UserGuess.Enabled := false;
   Guess.Enabled := false;
   StartTheGame.Enabled := true;
   end;
```

This method is easier to code and easier to read. You're saying, "If `B` is equal to `MyNumber`, then execute this block of code." When `B` isn't equal to `MyNumber`, then this whole block of code is ignored. You don't have to check for equality on every statement.

With this last block replacing the old `If-Then` series the Guess It! game will now reset itself every time the user guesses the correct number.

The Orphaned *Else* Revisited

Remember this little beauty from a few pages ago?

```
If A then
   If B then DoC
   else
else DoSomething
```

Blocks are the key to making this code clearer. Rather than string a bunch of `If-Then` statements together, you have the first `If-Then` start its own block of code, as follows:

```
If A then
begin
   If B then DoC
   end
else DoSomething;
```

Although it may seem silly to have a one-line block of code, the `If B` is sheltered within its own block. The `Else` here now clearly applies to the `If A`. This blocked code is considerably easier to read than the `Else Else` code previously. This code is also easier to read should you add still another `Else`, this time to the `If B` code:

```
If A then
begin
   If B then DoC
   else DoD;
   end
else DoSomething;
```

The `If A` and `If B` statements are now discrete, with no danger of them being confused.

Elements of Style

You've learned about how liberal Pascal is when it comes to how statements are arranged. You can write an entire program on one line, as demonstrated earlier, or you can spread out your statements over many lines. Obviously, you will probably choose a *style* of coding that falls somewhere in between.

In programming, the term *style* not only encompasses what instructions you use or the approach you take in solving a problem, but also shows how you arrange those instructions on-screen. The same instructions placed sloppily on-screen will be harder to read than those placed with firm rules about where they should go.

You've seen quite a bit of my style of coding here, which is different from the style of code that Pascal generates. You will develop your own style as you program, and the most important thing about your style is that it be consistent. Being consistent doesn't mean that you should be a slave to your style, only that you shouldn't whimsically and drastically deviate from it.

I follow some simple rules when coding. In a `var` statement, I group variables together based on their function in the program. Within those groups, I put variables of the same type together. So, if I have a program that has a set of variables for calculating dates and another set of variables for holding user information, I group them together like this:

Chapter 10 ◆ On One Condition

```
var
   TheCurrentDate, TheCurrentYear : Word;
   DaysInAWeek, DaysInTheMonth    : Byte;

   UserName     : String;
   UserAge      : Byte;
   UserBirthdate: Word;
   UserMarried, UserHasChildren,
   UserHasHair  : Boolean;

var LoneVariable: Boolean;
```

This code fragment shows you a lot of my style: after the `var`, I indent everything three spaces; I like to line up the data types underneath each other; I'm not particular about where the data types actually go though (I have them near the middle of the page in one group and much further in for the next); I often start variable names with a word or a number of letters that identify them (such as `User`); if I have a single variable declared by itself, I often put it right after the `var` keyword. You'll also see me do this in procedures, where I started with a single variable but later added more:

```
var LoneVariable                         : Boolean;
    Oops, HereAreSomeMoreVariables       : String;
```

By comparison, the Pascal-generated code has one variable underneath the next, without lining up anything. Pascal also indents only two spaces.

When I have a `begin`, I indent everything after it three spaces, except `end`. To my eye, this indentation clearly delineates the whole block. For example,

```
begin
   DoSomething;
   DoMore;
   If SomethingIsNotTrue then
   begin
      If A>B then B := A;
      If B>C then B := C;
      if C<>D then begin
         DoStuff;
         DoMoreStuff;
      end;
   end;
end;
```

Commonly today, the `end` of a block is not indented with the rest of the code, so a block that Delphi generates looks like this:

```
begin
  CodeStuffHere;
end;
```

Keep in mind that Pascal doesn't care what you do. The only criteria for developing a style are whether you can read it easily, whether you like it, and whether somebody else can read it once they get used to your style.

Example: Guess It, Version 2.0

Now you're ready to put together everything you've learned and make the game a little more interesting.

1. Move StartTheGame over to the right and put in its place (from top to bottom) a label, another spin-edit, and three push buttons. (See figure 10.4.) What you're going to do now is make GUESSIT more competitive by having it try to guess a number in the player's head while the player is guessing the computer's number.

2. Change the caption—but not the Name property—of the first label to My Guess.

3. Change the Name of the spin-edit to MyGuess and set its Enable property to False.

4. Change the Names of the three buttons underneath to TooHigh, TooLow, and Correct. Put spaces after the Too in their captions for TooHigh and TooLow. You should have a form that looks like figure 10.4 now. Disable all the push buttons.

Figure 10.4
Form for the Guess It! game, version 2.0.

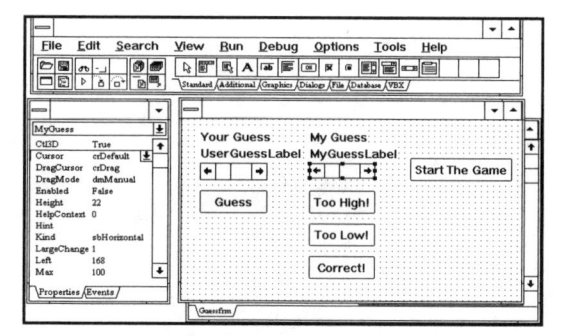

Again, the user must press StartTheGame to start the game. The guessing is done in turns, beginning with the user. But after the user makes a guess, GUESSIT makes a guess of its own. The user must then say if the number is too high or too low or if GUESSIT got the number right.

If GUESSIT didn't get the number right, it returns control to the user. Subsequent guesses that the program makes will be within the boundaries specified by the users when pressing Too High or Too Low.

How do you do this? You need the program to have the following features:

♦ It "thinks" of a new number at the start of each game. (Already got that.)

Chapter 10 ◆ On One Condition

- ◆ It lets the user guess what the number is and gives a hint as to whether the number was too high or too low, ending the game on a correct guess. (Already got that.)
- ◆ It makes a guess at the number in the user's mind and bases that guess on the user's previous hints of Too High or Too Low. This guess should appear on the spin button.
- ◆ If it guesses correctly, it ends the game.

You need two byte variables—call them GuessLow and GuessHigh. When the user clicks Too Low, the guess number goes into GuessLow. When the user clicks Too High, that number goes into GuessHigh. If the user clicks Correct, you end the game. You also need code to make the actual guess and set the value on the scroll bar and label.

First, set up the variables that you need. Add to the var statement where you globally declared MyNumber:

```
var
   MyNumber: Byte;
   GuessLow, GuessHigh,     {Add this line!}
   GuessIt: Byte;           {Add this line!}
```

StartTheGameClick doesn't change much except to reset GuessLow and GuessHigh, which might have a value from a previous game:

```
procedure TForm1.StartTheGameClick(Sender: TObject);
begin
   Randomize;
   MyNumber := Random(100)+1;
   MyResponse.Caption := '';
   StartTheGame.Enabled := False;
   UserSpin.Enabled := True;
   UserGuess.Enabled := True;
   GuessLow  := 1;   {Add this}
   GuessHigh := 100; {Add this, too}
end;
```

Notice that GuessLow represents the lowest value that the guess can be, and GuessHigh represents the highest.

Right now, UserGuessClick contains code to give a hint to the user and to end the game if the user guesses correctly:

```
procedure TForm1.UserGuessClick(Sender: TObject);
var B: Byte;
    S: String;
begin
   B := UserGuess.Position;
   If B>MyNumber then S := 'Too High'
```

```
else If B<MyNumber then S := 'Too Low'
else begin
   S := 'You Guessed It!';
   UserGuess.Enabled := false;
   Guess.Enabled := false;
   StartTheGame.Enabled := true;
end;
 MyResponse.Caption := S;
```

To this code, you are going to add the code that allows the computer to guess:

```
{code to make a guess here}
If B<>MyNumber then
begin
    UserGuess.Enabled := false;
    Guess.Enabled := false;
    TooHigh.Enabled := true;
    TooLow.Enabled := true;
    Correct.Enabled := true;
    B := GuessHigh - GuessLow;
    B := B + 1;
    GuessIt := Random(B) + GuessLow ;
    MyGuess.Value := GuessIt;
  end;
end;
```

Most of this code is just to disable the user's guessing controls and to enable the program's guessing controls. The following lines actually make the guess:

```
B := GuessHigh - GuessLow;
B := B + 1;
GuessIt := Random(B) + GuessLow;
```

The first two lines set B to the range of acceptable numbers. GuessHigh and GuessLow start at 100 and 1, respectively, so at first B has a value of 99. But, there are a hundred possible numbers to guess from, so you need to add one to it.

> **Note:** Frequently, in computer programming you don't need the *difference* between two numbers, but instead you need the *range* that two numbers represent, as is the case here. The difference between 100 and 1 is 99, but the range from 1 through 100 represents 100 possibilities. So you often find yourself adding 1 or subtracting 1 from the result of an equation, as you do here.

So Random(B) generates a number from 0 to 99, which you then add to GuessLow, giving you a number between 1 and 100.

Chapter 10 ♦ On One Condition

> **Note:** When I write code like this, I like to trace through it with my mind to see whether it will work the way I think it will for various numbers. For example, what if GuessHi were 80 and GuessLow 23? B would be set to 57+1, and Random would generate a number from 0 to 57, to which 23 would be added, giving a range from 23 to 80. I might try this system with several sets of numbers.
>
> This system is not meant to replace understanding what the code does, but to give me confidence that my understanding is correct.

The rest of the code is in the `TooHighClick`, `TooLowClick`, and `CorrectClick` routines. The first two are extremely similar; they just involve setting `GuessHigh` or `GuessLow` and enabling and disabling the appropriate controls.

```
procedure TForm1.TooHighClick(Sender: TObject);
begin
   GuessHigh := GuessIt;
   MyResponse.Caption := 'Darn!';
   TooHigh.Enabled := false;
   TooLow.Enabled := false;
   Correct.Enabled := false;
   UserGuess.Enabled := true;
   Guess.Enabled := true;
end;

procedure TForm1.TooLowClick(Sender: TObject);
begin
   GuessLow := GuessIt;
   MyResponse.Caption := 'Foo!';
   TooHigh.Enabled := false;
   TooLow.Enabled := false;
   Correct.Enabled := false;
   UserGuess.Enabled := true;
   Guess.Enabled := true;
end;
```

(I made the routines express different comments using `MyResponse.Caption`.)

You might suspect that you can create the code in a more elegant way—perhaps by combining the code from the two routines or something—and you'd be right. You look into ways to improve this in Chapter 21, "Objects."

Finally, you need to write code to handle the possibility that the program guesses correctly:

```
procedure TForm1.CorrectClick(Sender: TObject);
begin
   MyResponse.Caption := 'I win!';
   TooHigh.Enabled := false;
   TooLow.Enabled := false;
   Correct.Enabled := false;
   StartTheGame.Enabled := true;
end;
```

And there you have it—your first program that actually does something. Or the second version of it, anyway. It's not perfect. Some might even say it has bugs in it. For example, what happens if the user lies? You can change the program to catch those occasions where the user claims that the program's guess of 1 is too low or 100 is too high. Feel free to embellish the program, but retain this basic copy for later use.

Summary

A Boolean variable may be either `True` or `False`. `True` and `False` are Pascal keywords and may be assigned directly to a Boolean variable. A Boolean variable may also be assigned `True` or `False` based on the result of a comparison. You can compare two variables of similar types by using the following operators: >, <, =, <>, >=, <=. You can use logical operators with two Boolean values to create a new result. The logical operators are `AND`, `OR`, `XOR`, and `NOT`.

The `If-Then-Else` construction enables you to control the flow of your program so that some segments of code are executed only under certain circumstances. You can use logical operators to express more complex conditions. You also can use `begin` and `end` anywhere in your code to set off a block of code from the rest. Using `begin` and `end` is most usefully done after an `If-Then` or `If-Then-Else` to have a block of code executed only on certain conditions.

The `Random` function returns sequences of numbers that are apparently random. However, it returns the same sequence every time unless seeded using the `Randomize` procedure.

The switch object is a good representation of the Boolean variable. It may be either on or off. The scrollbar enables the user to select from a range of numbers by using the mouse or cursor keys. Pascal lets you assign the same routine to several different object events.

Review Questions

1. What is a conditional statement?
2. What is a Boolean variable?
3. What values does Pascal use to express true or false?
4. Name the six comparison operators.
5. In the following code, if the variable A has a value of 10 and variable B has a value of 10, which line is executed?

```
If A >= B then
        Writeln('A is greater or equal to B')
        else Writeln('A is less than B');
```

6. In nontechnical terms, explain what the Random function does.

7. What purpose do begin and end serve? How are all the statements in between a begin and an end treated?

8. What does Randomize do? Why is it necessary?

9. Is the following statement true?

```
'BAKERY' > 'BAKER'
```

10. What are the results of the following logical operations?

```
True AND False
True OR False
True XOR False
True AND NOT False
True XOR NOT False
```

11. If you are doing a comparison (A > B, for example) and you want a number of instructions to be executed if the comparison is true and just one instruction done if the comparison is false, how do you set up this comparison?

12. Can you have a semicolon before an Else?

13. What two numbers does Random(2) generate?

Review Exercises

1. Add two labels to the GUESSIT program that keep track of how many games have been won by the computer and by the player.

2. You should now be able to go back to Chapter 7 and see how the If-Then statement was used in the NUMEXAM project to attempt to reset the Gauge control. The line that reset the gauge was:

```
If B = 0 then Gauge.Progess := 100;
```

3. You should also now be able to produce a simple variation on the rather inane WinCRT "Hello, World!" program you worked on in Chapter 8. This time, use conditional logic to create a program that responds to user input. Something that might run like this:

```
Hello. What is your name?
```
Blake
```
Blake is one of my favorite names.
What is the title of your favorite book?
```
The Martian Chronicles.
```
Oh. That's an okay book.
My favorite is Delphi By Example.
```

But the same program might run like this, if someone else ran it:

```
Hello. What is your name?
```
Mike
```
Mike?!!?  What kind of name is Mike??
What is the title of your favorite book?
```
Delphi By Example.
```
I knew you were a Quality User.
```

And so on.

4. To get somewhat more sophisticated, take the program from exercise 3 and make it aware of more than one name, book, or whatever, so that it can respond differently in a number of different situations, as opposed to just two.

5. Write a program that uses a pair of If-Then-else statements like so:

```
If A then if B then DoC else DoD else DoE;
```

Trace the line to figure out what happens when A and B alternate being false. Then, rewrite the line using a begin-end block. Note any differences in readability.

6. Experiment with adding additional switches to the LOGIC program developed in this chapter. Can you add a switch to each of the three rows that represents a logical NOT?

7. Embellish the GUESSIT program to *catch* the user if he cheats—that is, if he says on one pass that 50 is too high, but on another that it is too low. In the event of cheating, make the program take a win by default.

8. In Chapter 9, you ran into a situation where you might want to convert a string to an integer, but the string might have a value that is too big for the integer. You can avoid many of those situations by using the If-Then construct. Load (or write) a program that does a conversion from string to any integer (smaller than a longint) and use If-Then prevent the value obtained from being assigned to an integer that is not capable of holding it. (Hint: Use a *longint* temporary variable in the Val procedure, then use If-Then to ensure that it doesn't exceed the capacity of the final variable.)

CHAPTER 11

A Special *Case*

With `If-Then-Else` you can handle any kind of conditional situation. But you can't always handle it gracefully. Consider offering the user a menu of choices:

```
A) Play Chess
B) Balance the Checkbook
C) Log on to Compuserve
```

The code that you might write to handle this might look like this:

```
If Command = 'A' then PlayChess
else if command = 'B' then BalanceCheckbook
else if command = 'C' then LogonToCompuServe;
```

And this works out all right as long as you don't have too many choices. When you get a large number of choices, the code starts to get ugly. Delphi has a particular construct that allows you to clean up code like this.

Start a new project and drop a label on it. Then go to the Samples page on the object bar and locate the *color grid* object, represented by a box with many colored squares in it. Drop the object onto the form next to the label.

The purpose of the color grid is to enable the user to select the foreground and background color of some object. (Allowing the user to customize colors is a common courtesy in modern programs.) If you click the primary mouse button on the object, it makes a foreground selection. If you click the secondary mouse button on the object, it makes a background selection. It identifies these selections by putting the letters FG and BG in the selected box. Now try out the form to get a feel for how it works.

Chapter 11 ◆ A Special *Case*

What you want to do now is to make the label reflect a change made in the grid. The color grid has a property `Selection` that refers to the selection made. If you double-click on the grid, Pascal generates a procedure that will be called whenever you change the foreground or background color that the grid indicates.

```
procedure TForm1.ColorGrid1Change(Sender: TObject);
begin
   end;
```

Because you don't want the label to just report a number from 1 to 16, which is what is in `Selection`, what do you do? You could code a bunch of `If-Then-Else` statements, like the following:

```
If ColorGrid1.Selection = 1 then Label1.Caption := 'Maroon'
else If ColorGrid1.Selection = 1 then Label1.Caption := 'Green'
else If ColorGrid1.Selection = 1 then Label1.Caption := 'Brown'
```

These statements certainly work, but you can handle this situation in a better way.

The *Case* Statement

When you have to write code to handle many possibilities for the same integer, char, or Boolean variable, you can use the Pascal `Case...of` structure. The `Case` statement is structured with the variable at the top and the choices underneath:

```
case AVariable of
   OneThing        : DoSomething;
   AnotherThing    : DoSomethingElse;
   YetAnotherThing: DoADifferentSomething;
   else GoOn;
   end;
```

`Case` statements *must* be terminated by an `End`. And, as you can see from this example, a case statement can also include an `Else` to catch all the choices not specifically handled.

For the color grid, you can code as follows:

```
case ColorGrid1.Selection of
   1: Label1.Caption := 'Maroon';
   2: Label1.Caption := 'Green';
   3: Label1.Caption := 'Brown';
   else Label1.Caption := 'Some other color';
   end;
```

If you need to have more than just one line of code, you can use a `Begin-End` block, as you learn later.

When Can I Use *Case*?

You can use Case with an integer, char, or Boolean variable, or any expression that resolves to an integer, char, or Boolean. For example, you can have a Case statement like the following:

```
Case Bool of
    True: DoThis;
    False: DoThat;
    end;
```

or

```
Case A>B of
    True: DoThis;
    False: DoThat;
    end;
```

If you have an integer variable such as ColorGrid1.Selection, you can test it in your Case statement, as follows:

```
Case Int of
    -1 : DoThis;
    1  : DoThat;
    end;
```

Notice that you can use negative numbers. If Int is neither -1 nor 1, then nothing happens. Just as with If-Then, an Else is not mandatory. You also can set up code to execute with a range of values by using the two periods (also called *double-dots*) between the low and high value, as follows:

```
case Int of
    1..10     : S := '1 to 10';
    10..20    : S := '10 to 20';
    0         : S := 'Zero';
    -1..-32768: S := 'A negative number.'
    else S := 'A number over 20.';
    end;
```

Note: You can see my style exerting itself here again. I like to line up the colons in a Case statement. Remember that Pascal doesn't care about extra spaces.

You can do all the same things with a char variable:

```
case Ch of
    'a', 'A': AWasSelected;
    'b', 'B': BWasSelected;
    else SomethingElseWasSelected;
    end;
```

Chapter 11 ◆ A Special *Case*

You also can use double-dots to express a range:

```
case Ch of
   'A'..'Z': S := 'An upper case letter';
   'a'..'z': S := 'A lower case letter';
   '0'..'9': S := 'A number.';
   end;
```

You can even express a nonrange group of numbers by using a comma. For example,

```
case Int of
   1, 3, 5, 7, 9: S := 'An odd number';
   2, 4, 6, 8, 0: S := 'An even number';
   end;
```

And you can mix and match the double-dots and commas to your heart's content:

```
case Ch of
   'A'..'Z', 'a'..'z': S := 'A letter';
   '0'..'9'          : S := 'A number';
   '!'..')'          : S := 'A shifted number';
   else S := 'An unknown  key';
   end;
```

The only danger with a range of code is forgetting that the first expression to which the `Case` applies is the only one to which it applies. A `Case` statement doesn't execute two separate blocks of code, even if the variable qualifies for two. If you have

```
Case I of
   1..10: DoStuff;
   5..15: DoMoreStuff;   {No!  5 through 10 will never make it here}
    . . .
```

and `I` is 5, only `DoStuff` is executed, not `DoMoreStuff`. Remember that the `Case` statement is just a cleaner way of expressing similar `If-Then-Else` statements:

```
If (I>=1) AND (I<=10) then DoStuff
else if (I>=5) and (I<=15) DoMoreStuff;
```

Coding this way doesn't make any sense either.

> **Note:** Traditionally, Pascal would allow you to overlap ranges, even when it didn't make any sense. However, Pascal catches overlapping parts of `Case` statements and will not, in fact, *compile* in such a case, presuming that you made a mistake.
>
> So, in actual fact, the previous examples won't even compile.

What Can I Do with a Matching Selection?

The consequence of any selection can be a single line of code, a block of code, or a null statement (a semicolon).

```
case I of
   1 : DoSomething;
   2 : begin
         DoStuff;
         DoMoreStuff;
       end;
   3 : ; {Does nothing}
   end;
```

You might use the null statement simply as a *placeholder*, which tells you where future code is to go. Also, because you know the variable can qualify for only one of the expressions, you might use a null statement purposefully to stop code from being executed for a specific value, as in the following:

```
Case I of
   3      ;  {Three is special, don't do anything.}
   else DoSomething;
```

So, there's no danger of you forgetting that the case of 3 is special and shouldn't be included with other numbers.

You can use any function that returns a char, integer, or Boolean in a `Case` statement. You can't use `Case` with every data type, however. In the old "Hello, world!" program that you created earlier in this book, you might be tempted to use the `Name` string in a `Case` statement to customize a message to the user. For example,

```
case Name of {This won't work!!!!}
   'Blake': Message := 'What will you program today?';
   'Jean' : Message := 'Hi, Mom!';
   'Sarah': Message := 'Get away from me with that glass of water!';
   end;
{Remember this doesn't work}
```

Ordinal Types

If you try to use `Case` with a string, you get the error message `Ordinal type expected`. *Ordinal* is one of those words you hear thrown around a lot without people explaining what it is. In English, *ordinal* means "to express an order"; words such as *first*, *second*, and *third* are ordinal.

Ordinal types in Pascal also express an order. For example, `0` is the first value that a byte can have, and `6` is the seventh value that a byte can have. The highest value is `255`, the 256th value that a byte can have.

Chapter 11 ♦ A Special *Case*

You can express the values of all the integers similarly. `False` is the first value that a Boolean can have, and `True` is the second. No value is in between the two, and no value can exceed the two.

With characters, `'A'` is the 66th value that a character can have, and `'B'` is the 67th. No value comes in between these two values. The value `'B'` expresses an order.

By contrast, consider the string. What is the first value that a string has? It doesn't really have one. A string value does not express an order. If you borrow from the character type and say that `'A'` is the 66th value a string can have and `'B'` is the 67th, what do you then do with `'AA'`?

Get the idea? There's little practical use in saying that some value is the first value that a string can have and some other value is the second, and that nothing can come in between them.

Although you haven't looked at them in detail yet, the same is true of *real* numbers. When you *aren't* dealing with integers, you can't say that `0` is the first value a number can have and `1` is the second. What about `0.1`, `0.5`, `0.9999`, and all the infinite numbers that come in between zero and one?

Although you probably have a good grasp of this concept, here's a rule of thumb: In Pascal, the ordinal types are the integer types and the variations on integer types. This list includes the char type, which is basically just like a byte filtered through the ASCII table, and the Boolean type, which is like a byte restricted to the values of zero and one (`False` and `True`).

As you encounter other data types in the later sections of this book, I'll let you know whether they are ordinal.

Case Limitations

`Case` is a rather limited feature. Just the fact that it doesn't work with nonordinal types is a severe limitation. In some situations, therefore, you must go back to using the `If-Then-Else`, as follows:

```
if name = 'Blake' then  Message := 'What will you program today?'
else if name = 'Jean' : Message := 'Hi, Mom!'
else if  name = 'Sarah': Message := 'Get away from me with that glass of water!';
```

`Case` has other limitations as well. The choices in a `Case` statement must all be literal values or things that can be turned into literal values at compile time. So you can do the following:

```
case I of
   1: ;
   2: ;
   3+1: ;
   end;
```

However, the following is not allowed:

```
case I of
  J: ;
  K: ;
  L: ;
  end;
```

You may be somewhat disappointed in the capability of the Case statement right now. (Frankly, I'm always a little disappointed when it doesn't do what I want it to.) However, Case should have a place in your programming. Whenever you're doing an If-Then-Else series on an ordinal type, keep in mind that

```
If I = 1 then DoThis
else If I = 2 then DoSomethingElse
else If I = 3 then DoMore
else If I = 4 then DoThat;
```

is usually harder to read and more work to type than the following:

```
case I of
  1: DoThis;
  2: DoSomethingElse;
  3: DoMore;
  4: DoThat;
  end;
```

Now it's time to use Case in an actual program. Say that you are going to Las Vegas for Comdex (the big computer industry convention) and you are thinking of playing some Craps while you are there. To warm up, you decide to write a program to simulate a Craps table.

1. Start a new project called DICE and call the form unit DICEFORM.

2. Add two label objects to the top left corner of the form. Name them Die1 and Die2.

> **Note:** The Visual Solutions Pack comes with a control that simulates a standard six-sided cube-shaped die, making this program that much easier. This control is on the VBX page, and it looks just like a die, with five pips (spots) forward and one on top. Use this control in place of the labels. The Value property tells how many pips are showing on top of the die.

3. Underneath the "dice," place a push button called Roll, and off to the right, place a label called Odds.

4. Start your program off by having the Roll button roll the dice and causing the Odds label to report on what the odds are of that particular number coming up. Double-click on Roll.

Chapter 11 ◆ A Special *Case*

5. Use two temporary variables to hold random values from one to six. Use the Str function to place the value for each die in the Text property. Then, based on the total of the two temporary variables, change Odds.Caption to reflect the odds of that value. Table 11.1 shows the odds of any number coming up on a pair of dice.

> **Note:** If you're using the Dice control in the Visual Solutions Pack, you can use the Value property, which is an integer, rather than the temporary variables described in step 5.

Table 11.1. Probabilities for certain sums appearing on two dice.

Sum	Odds
2	36 to 1 against
3	18 to 1 against
4	12 to 1 against
5	9 to 1 against
6	7.2 to 1 against
7	6 to 1 against
8	7.2 to 1 against
9	9 to 1 against
10	12 to 1 against
11	18 to 1 against
12	36 to 1 against

6. You can take advantage of the symmetry of these odds by lumping 2 and 12, 3 and 11, 4 and 10, 5 and 9, and 6 and 8 together in your Case statement. Here's what the completed procedure looks like:

```
procedure TForm1.RollClick(Sender: TObject);
var Msg, S : String;
    D1, D2: Byte;
begin
  Randomize;
     D1 := Random(6)+1;     {You would use Die1.Value and Die2.Value}
     D2 := Random(6)+1;     {If you were using the VSP Dice Control}

  Str(D1, S);
  Die1.Caption := S;
  Str(D2, S);
  Die2.Caption := S;

  case D1+D2 of
     2, 12  : Msg := '36 to 1';
     3, 11  : Msg := '18 to 1';
     4, 10  : Msg := '12 to 1';
     5, 9   : Msg := '9 to 1';
     6, 8   : Msg := '7.2 to 1';
     7      : Msg := '6 to 1';
  end;
  Odds.Caption := Msg;
end;
```

When you run it, the results should look something like figure 11.1 if you have the Visual Solutions Pack. If not, you'll have a text description of the dice.

Figure 11.1
The DICE program.

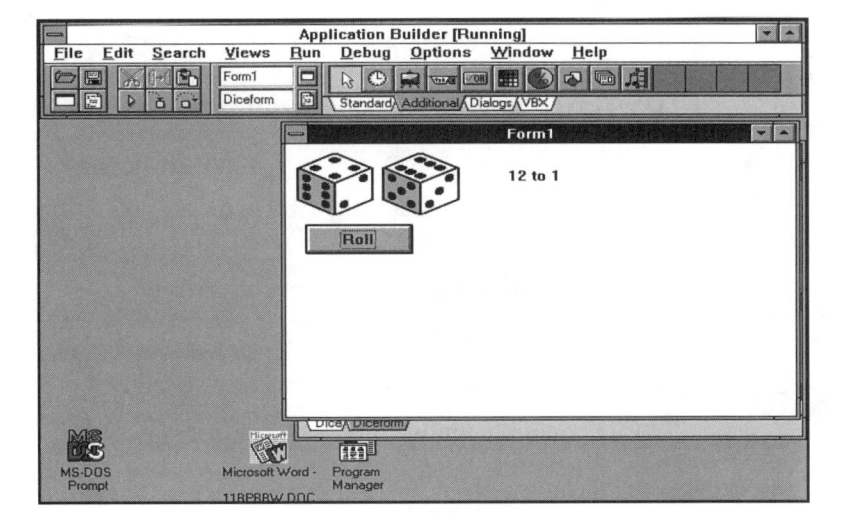

Chapter 11 ◆ A Special *Case*

You could go on and develop the game into a full-fledged version of Craps. You could do that—except that I've never really been clear on how the game works. Also, you have a lot more to cover before you embark on so large a project. So you won't continue with this now. Instead, you'll move on to other ways to control how a program flows.

Summary

The `Case` statement is a neater way to express a series of `If-Then-Else` statements. You can use it only with ordinal type variables, such as char, Boolean, and the five integer types. An ordinal type in Delphi can contain only values that express an order: 0 is the first value that a byte can have; 1 is the second, and so on. Strings are not ordinal. Char, Boolean, and any of the integer type variables are all ordinal. The expressions against which the variables are compared must be literals; variables are not allowed.

You can express a range within a case by using the double-dot (..). You can also use the comma to create a list of possibilities that may be satisfied. The consequence of a matched `Case` statement can be a single line of code, a block of code, or a null statement.

You also learned that the color grid object enables the user to select the foreground and background color for an object, and the die object emulates a six-sided die.

Review Questions

1. Explain how and why the `Case` statement is used.
2. Can you use the `Case` statement with a Boolean type variable? With a char? With a string?
3. Use a literal string as a basis for comparison.
4. Use a variable as a basis for comparison.
5. How do you express a range in a `Case` statement?
6. Can you use negative numbers in a `Case` statement?

7. Can you express a range of characters in a Case statement?

8. What is an ordinal type? Name two.

9. Is a Case statement ever absolutely necessary? That is, can you code anything with a Case statement that can't be coded with If-Then-Else.

Review Exercises

1. Using the WinCRT unit, set up a simple program to give a multiple-choice test. Use the Case construct to determine whether the right answer has been selected.

2. Looking at the program from question 1, consider the following procedure:

```
function  AskQuestionAndGetResponse(Question, Answer1, Answer2,
Answer3, Answer4: String; Correct: Byte): boolean;
var Answer: char;
    AnswerNumber: Byte;
begin
   Writeln(Question);
       Writeln('A> '+Answer1);
   Writeln('B> '+Answer2);
   Writeln('C> '+Answer3);
   Writeln('D> '+Answer4);
   Writeln; Writeln('Which do you choose?);
   Readln(Answer);
   case Answer of
      'A': AnswerNumber := 1;
      'B': AnswerNumber := 2;
      'C': AnswerNumber := 3;
      'D': AnswerNumber := 4;
      else begin
         Writeln('Invalid answer.   Wrong by default.');
            AnswerNumber := 0;
         end;
   end;
   AskQuestionAndGetResponse := AnswerNumber = Correct;
      end;
```

Would this procedure save you work? What limitations does using this procedure impose on your multiple-choice test?

3. Embellish the DICE program by adding a control for the user to guess which number will come up, and another control for the user to bet a certain amount that the number will come up.

CHAPTER 12

Repeating Yourself

In the original BASIC language, every line in a program was preceded by a line number. A simple BASIC program might look like the following:

```
10 Print "Hello, World!"
20 Print "What is your name?"
30 Input Name$
40 Print "Hello, "Name$
```

(`Print` and `Input` are the BASIC equivalents of `Writeln` and `Readln`.)

If you wanted to have the program go back and ask the user's name again, you would have used the `GoTo` statement with a line number. So, to make this program go on forever, you would add the following line:

```
50 GOTO 20
```

So, `GoTo` was used to change the flow of a program and to cause a segment of code to repeat. Instead of going to line 60 or 51 or whatever, it went back to line 20. The way it stands, this program contains an *endless loop.* No matter what the user does, the program always goes back to line 20. The programmer would then add a line to break the loop if the user had an acceptable name:

```
35 If Name$ = "Blake" then GOTO 1000
```

(If-Then has the same purpose in BASIC as Pascal. The '$' sign after `Name` indicates that `Name` is a string.)

The rub was that line 1000 might be anything. It might be:

```
1000 GOTO 500
```

and line 500 might be

```
500 GOTO 20
```

thus not actually getting you out of the loop at all.

Code that forces the reader to jump from place to place without apparent reason is called *spaghetti code*. When the flow of a program jumps back and forth gratuitously, the flow resembles a long strand of twisted pasta. The easiest programs to read are those that, unlike spaghetti code, go straight from top to bottom.

Delphi and the GoTo

I don't mean to pick on BASIC programmers here. Most languages have a GoTo, which has been abused by programmers of that language. Pascal itself has a GoTo statement but, because it has no line numbers, the GoTo must be done to a line of code that is labeled. If you had the statement

```
GoTo RollTheDice;
```

then elsewhere in your Pascal program you would have a piece of code that started with the *RollTheDice* label:

```
RollTheDice:
   Die1.Value := Random(6)+1;
   Die2.Value := Random(6)+1;
```

This code is much easier to read than GOTO 100. Also, if you use labels in your code, those labels must be *declared!* In this way, the reader of your code is alerted to all the possible destination points of a GoTo statement. The declaration requires the use of the keyword *label*.

```
label RollTheDice, MoveYourMice;
```

Immediately, the reader knows that you have two valid destinations for a GoTo. Label names follow the same rules as variable names.

Because GoTo has often resulted in spaghetti code, the GoTo statement has a bad reputation. Some people say, "Never use GoTos in your code." "*Never*" is a strong word. But in 10 years of Pascal programming, I've only used GoTo twice. Why? Because Pascal provides so many better alternatives to jumping around code at random. In the preceding situation, for example, why not just make RollTheDice a procedure?

```
. . .
RollTheDice;
. . .
procedure RollTheDice;
begin
   Die1.Value := Random(6)+1;
   Die2.Value := Random(6)+1;
end;
```

What you may recognize is that when you call a subroutine, the compiler is, in essence, doing a GoTo RollTheDice, and after that a "Go back to wherever you came from." No program of any complexity goes straight through from top to bottom.

The advantage of the subroutine over the GoTo is that the subroutine is less ambiguous and always returns to where it started. Also, procedures (like *WriteLn*) and functions (like *Random*) can be separated from the main body of a program and used by many programs.

The Loop Concept

Sometimes, however, you do want to loop back—to execute the same code repeatedly. What if you wanted to call *RollTheDice* six times? You could do the following:

```
RollTheDice;
RollTheDice;
RollTheDice;
RollTheDice;
RollTheDice;
RollTheDice;
```

But what if you want to do it *100* times? Typing in the code over and over again—well, that's doing more work than you have to.

What you need to do is establish a *loop*. A loop is a segment of code that repeats an operation a certain number of times. A loop often has a *counter* that indicates how many times the code has been repeated. This is important because the code usually is supposed to be repeated a certain number of times, and no more. To call *RollTheDice* six times, you might do the following:

```
    I := 0;
ReRoll:
    RollTheDice;
    I := I + 1;
    If I < 6 then GoTo ReRoll;
```

Tip: If you use a label, you might want to set it flush left so that it leaps out at the reader.

Example: Using the GoTo

Set up a new project—it doesn't matter what you call it, you're just going to use it as a temporary experiment—and on a form place a gauge and a push button. Double-click on the push button and add this code:

Chapter 12 ◆ Repeating Yourself

```
procedure TForm1.Button1Click(Sender: TObject);
label top;        {Need this to describe where the GoTo should go}
var I: Integer;   {This will count the number of repetitions}
begin
   I := 0;        {Start the counter at zero}
top:
   I := I + 1;
   Gauge1.Progress := I;
   Update;
   If I < 100 then Goto Top   {When you get to 100, fall through to the
   ↪end;}
end;
```

Note: The Form object has an `Update` method that forces every control on it to redraw itself. Normally, Pascal "freezes" the form so that it *won't* redraw itself until the method has ended. This makes the code go much faster, but it requires you to specifically ask for a redraw via the `Update` method.

Try this out. (You may want to change the *ForeColor* property of the gauge to something more pleasant than black.)

When you click on the button, the gauge counts up from 0 to 100. This is the loop in action. (Presumably, besides just incrementing the gauge's *Progress*, you would also be doing something useful.)

Now, add another gauge. Gauge1 does a process 100 times. What if you wanted to do the process represented by the *Top* loop 100 times? You could add another label, another counter, and when the *Top* loop finished its cycle, you could reset it and start again—doing this 100 times. The code would look like the following:

Caution: You may not want to run this code! It will tie up your machine for several minutes!

```
procedure TForm1.Button1Click(Sender: TObject);
label top, outer;
var I, J: Integer;
begin
   J := 0;
outer:
   I := 0;
top:
   I := I + 1;
   Gauge1.Progress := I;
   Update;
   If I < 100 then Goto Top
```

```
else J := J + 1;
Gauge2.Progress := J;
   Update;
   If J < 100 then GoTo Outer;
end;
```

This code is rapidly getting harder to read, isn't it? The process in the inner loop, *Top,* is going to be executed 10,000 times! For that reason, unless you have an extremely fast computer, or you aren't adverse to using Ctrl+Alt+Del to have Windows stop the program, you should change these two lines:

```
I := I + 1;
. . .
else J := J + 1;
```

to

```
I := I + 10;
. . .
J := J + 10;
```

That will bring the number of executions down to 100 (so it's safe to run now). Give this a try.

> **Note:** In truth, your computer can do tens of thousands of instructions in the blink of an eye, and Pascal can generate code that is that fast. However, although it looks like you're not doing much in your loop, every change of the gauges' *Progress* properties causes those gauges to be redrawn. This operation is very expensive in terms of time.
>
> That's why Pascal forces you to call Update in the first place—to keep things fast.

The *For* Loop

The code you just looked at works, even if it isn't pretty. However, it is completely unnecessary. With any luck at all, it will be the last GoTo you ever code. Pascal has no less than *three* other ways to do the same loop, which you'll look at in the upcoming pages.

The first approach you're going to look at applies especially well to situations like the preceding—when a counter variable controls the number of times the loop is executed. The approach involves the use of the keyword For.

```
for I := 1 to 100 do
```

You can put this in place of all the code you just wrote, and you can toss out the label declarations top and outer. (Don't remove the code to declare *I* and *J*, though.) This easy-to-read code says, "Give the counter (called the *control* variable) the first value (the *source* value) and increment it until it reaches the second value (the *destination* value), doing the following code for each pass." So, you start *I* at 1, change Progress, increment *I* by one, change *Progress* again, go back and increment *I* again, change *Progress* again, and repeat until *I* has reached 100.

The keyword Do can be followed by a Begin-End block of code, too.

```
. . ....for I := 1 to 100 do
begin
   Gauge1.Progress := I;

   Update;end
. . .
```

And, you can "nest" For loops inside each other, so your clunky block of GoTo code above can be reduced to the following:

```
for J := 1 to 100 do
begin
   Gauge2.Progress := J;
   Update;
   for I := 1 to 100 do
   begin
      Gauge1.Progress := I;
      Update;
      end;
end;
```

As mentioned earlier, if you want to run this and *not* tie up your computer for a while, you should reduce the number of executions from 10,000 to something more manageable, as in the following:

```
for J := 1 to 10 do
. . .
for I := 1 to 10 do
```

For Loop Variations

What happens if your source is lower than your destination? What would this code do?

```
For I := 10 to 1 do SomeFunction;
```

The answer is: nothing. *SomeFunction* would never be called because *I* starts out greater than its ending point. The loop is ignored.

If you do want to count down, however, you can use For-Downto, which decrements the control variable by one:

```
for J := 10 downto 1 do
. . .
for I := 10 downto 1 do
```

The For variable doesn't have to be an integer—it can be any ordinal type, including char.

```
For Ch := 'A' to 'Z' do
```

This code, for example, would run Ch through all the uppercase letters of the alphabet. There is, admittedly, limited use for this kind of code.

You can also use variables for the source and destination values. If you declare K and L as any of the five integer types, you could do something like the following:

```
K := 10; L := 1;
for J := K downto L do
```

Similarly, if *Char1* and *Char2* were character variables:

```
For Ch := Char1 to Char2 do
```

Just as with literal values, if the source is greater than or equal to the destination (when using To) or lower than or equal to the destination (when using DownTo), the loop is ignored. So in the code

```
K := 10; L := 1;
for J := K to L do SomeFunction;
```

SomeFunction is never called.

Save the current project—call the project GAUGER and the form GAUGEFRM—and reopen the GUESSIT project. With a For loop, you could use the GuessLo and GuessHi variables to create a traveling effect in the scrollbar so that the computer appeared to be "thinking" of its random number by replacing this line

```
        MyGuess.Value := GuessIt;
```

in the *GuessClick* method with this series of loops:

```
    For B := GuessLow to GuessHigh do
  begin
     MyGuess.Value:= B;
     Update;
     end;
  For B := GuessHigh downto GuessLow do
  begin
     MyGuess.Value := B;
     Update;
     end;
  For B := GuessLow to GuessIt do
  begin
     MyGuess.Value := B;
     Update;
     end;
```

Chapter 12 ♦ Repeating Yourself

The spin edit's numbers will appear to bounce back and forth before settling on the guess number.

You might naturally wonder what happens if you do something like this:

```
J := 1; K := 10;
for I := J to K do
begin
   Gauge1.Value := I;
   J := J + 1;
   K := K + 1;
   Update;
end;
```

What happens may surprise you.

Gauge1.Value is set 10 times—exactly as if you hadn't changed *J* and *K* at all within the loop. When you tell the compiler

```
For Variable := SourceVar to DestVar
```

you are telling it to use the values in *SourceVar* and *DestVar*—not the variables themselves. The compiler *copies* those values into its own private area where the programmer can't get to them to change them. Although some languages do allow you to alter the boundary variables (that is, the source and destination) in the midst of a loop, it is probably best that Pascal doesn't let you—the code would be very difficult to follow indeed.

For Loop Limitations

In your GoTo example, you reduced the number of times the loop was executed by incrementing your counter variables by 10. In that example, the gauges' *Progress* properties were set to 10, 20, 30 and so on. In the later For loop example, the gauges have been set from only 1 to 10, which doesn't look quite right.

You might be inclined to alter your For control variables directly to get the same effect, like the following:

```
procedure TForm1.Button1Click(Sender: TObject);
var I, J: Integer;
begin
   For J := 1 to 100 do
   begin
      Gauge2.Progress := J;
      J := J + 10;
      For I := 1 to 100 do Gauge1.Progress := I;
   end;
end;
```

Although Pascal *allows* this, I strongly advise you not to do it. Why? Because once a For loop starts, it doesn't stop until the control variable is *equal* to the destination value. *Equal* to. Not *greater than or equal to,* but *exactly equal to.* The preceding code will set *J* to 1, 22, and so on to 99 and 110. The code would merrily continue on seemingly forever. This state is called an *endless loop,* and is something you want to avoid.

> **Note:** While your program is in this loop, Windows is almost powerless. No other application can run. To stop it, you must press Ctrl+Alt+Del.

You can remedy this loop by changing the initial For statement

```
for J := 0 to 100 do
```

and the amount *J* is incremented

```
    J := J + 9;
```

so that *J* does exactly hit 100.

Remember, while you're only incrementing *J* by 9, the For loop itself increments the counter by one every pass. This is another place you can trip up when modifying the control variable.

Curiously, Pascal lacks the *step* or *by* keyword that most languages have, which allows the programmer to specify how much the control variable should be incremented. In BASIC, for example, you could write:

```
For I = 0 to 100 step 10
```

to increment by 10 each time through the loop, or

```
For I = 100 to 0 step -10
```

to decrement by 10 each time.

What do you do then, if you want to make your program look like it is counting to 100 by tens? Make a For loop that goes from 1 to 10, and set a temporary variable that increments itself by 10 for each pass. Going back to the gauge example:

```
    K := 0; L := 0;
    for J := 1 to 10 do
    begin
       K := K + 10;
       Gauge2.Progress := K;
       for I := 1 to 10 do
          begin
             L := L + 10;
             Gauge1.Progress := L;
          end;
end;
```

Chapter 12 ♦ Repeating Yourself

The Listbox and List Objects

A crucial skill every computer programmer needs is the ability to write what is called a *parser*. To parse means to "break down into parts." *To parse* is commonly used in English grammar to refer to the analyzing of a sentence. Computer programmers parse data or user input to figure out what the data means, or what the user wants done.

You're going to use *For* here to write a simple parser. Start a new project, and call the form unit "PARSEFRM" and the project itself "PARSE." Start with an edit line object at the top and make it wider, so that it goes across nearly the whole screen. Name it *UserInput*.

Underneath that, put a listbox object. (The listbox object is on the Standard page of the object bar, and looks like a box with some writing in it that has a scrollbar going up and down the right side.) Stretch the listbox object out so that it is as wide as *UserInput* and goes down the bottom of the form. Name it *Words*.

A listbox object presents a list of items from which the user makes a selection. The listbox has a property called *Columns* that determines how the list is displayed. If *Columns* is zero, as it is by default, the listbox shows the data as a single line going from top to bottom. If there are more items on-screen than it can show at once, it presents a vertical scrollbar so that the user can scroll to look at all the selections. If *Columns* is 1 or greater, the data will be displayed horizontally by using the number of columns specified. If there are more items in the listbox than can be shown at once, the listbox creates a *horizontal* scrollbar that moves the columns over so that the user can view all of the selections. You'll get a feel for how this works in a moment.

You need to add one more object, a push button named *Add*. When the user pushes *Add*, the program will take whatever has been typed into *UserInput*, break it down into words, and add those words to the listbox. Make the *Default* property of *Add* True. Figure 12.1 shows the form used.

Figure 12.1
The PARSE form.

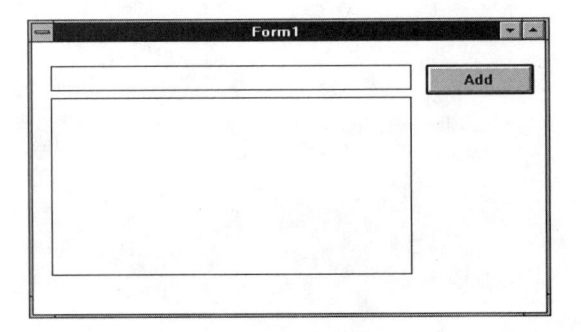

Before you get to the parsing, use the Object Inspector to look at one property of the listbox in particular. Find the *Items* property. To what value is this set?

It says "TStrings." An object may have, as a property, *another object.* Listbox isn't the first object you've come across that has another object as a property—but it is the first time you've cared. *Items* contains the selections for a listbox object. Click on the three dashes next to the *Items* property. Pascal puts up a dialog that allows you to add strings to the list. These strings would appear in the listbox object when the program started.

Close this dialog box and double-click on the *Add* button. Modify the frame to look like the following:

```
procedure TParseForm.AddClick(Sender: TObject);
var S: String;
begin
   S := UserInput.Text;
   Words.Items.Add(S);
end;
```

The *Items* object has a method, *Add,* that allows you to add items to the list while the program is running.

Run this code and type something into the edit line. Press Enter and the text appears in the listbox. You can press Enter repeatedly to fill the listbox with the same text over and over again. If you put enough text in the box, a scrollbar appears.

Now end the program and change the *Columns* property of *Words* to be five. Run the program again and fill up the listbox. What happens now? The data appears in five columns. If an item is too long to be seen in one column, it gets cut off. When you have too much data to fit on one screen, a horizontal scrollbar appears so that you can scroll through the columns.

Example: Parse

Now you need to code the actual parser. The idea behind the parser is that it should take a string of text and break out all of the words in that string.

Computer programs solve *problems*. The particular way in which a program solves a problem is called an *algorithm.* Algorithms are more precise than the general English language code you saw earlier,

```
If the User does something, have the appropriate object handle it.
```

but they can still be expressed in English (or any other language) and can be used by any computer programmer working in any language.

You need an algorithm to solve this problem. For the parser, your algorithm might be, in English:

Chapter 12 ♦ Repeating Yourself

*Set FirstChar to hold the position of the first word, assumed to be 1.
Increment Index from one to the number of characters in the string
Check to see if the character at Index is blank
If it is not a blank then extract the word from FirstChar to Index and
set FirstChar to be equal to index + 1.*

This is much easier to express in Delphi:

```
procedure TParseForm.AddClick(Sender: TObject);
var S, T: String;
    Index, FirstChar: Integer;
begin
   S := UserInput.Text;
   FirstChar := 1;
   for Index := 1 to Length(S) do
   if copy(S,Index,1) = ' ' then
   begin
      T := Copy(S, FirstChar, Index-FirstChar);
      Words.Items.Add(T);
      FirstChar := Index + 1;
   end;
end;
```

Note: The `Length` function returns the length of the string passed as a parameter. `Length(S)` returns the number of characters in S.

This has the additional code to actually add the word to *Items*. Try the code out. It *almost* works. If you type "Greetings from Helsinki," the words "Greetings" and "from" appear in the listbox. So what happened to "Helsinki"?

What you have here is a faulty algorithm. You detect the end of a word by checking for a space. But all text doesn't necessarily end with a space. You can remedy this easily by assigning S to be:

```
S := UserInput.Text + ' ';   {Space added to simplify algorithm}
```

Tip: This is a good place to add a comment to the program. Someone reading your code later may not know why you added the space.

If you don't add the space, you must check to see whether there is a space at the end of the string and then, if there isn't, add the word in a separate block of code.

```
If Copy(S, Length(S), 1) <> ' ' then
begin
   T := Copy(S, FirstChar, (Length(S)-FirstChar)+1);
   Words.Items.Add(T);
end;
```

218

This approach is considerably more complex. You might want to use the former approach and add a space.

Your code has another feature to it. If the user has entered two spaces in a row, as in "Hello World," your algorithm will assume that there is a word between the two spaces and insert a null string into the list. That's probably not what you want. You can handle this by detecting whether *T* is null before adding it to *List*.

```
If T<>'' then Words.Items.Add(T);
```

So, now the code doesn't add null strings to the *List* and it gets all the words in the string. Does that mean it's perfect? That depends on your point of view. Part of writing a good algorithm is knowing how the code is *supposed* to work. We were looking at the algorithm mostly as a way to use the For loop, so I didn't clearly define how the algorithm was supposed to work.

You'll often find while programming that you haven't clearly defined the problem that you want solved. You should establish as clear a definition of the problem as possible before starting your program. For example, what does your program do with punctuation marks? "Hello, World" yields "Hello," and "World." Should the comma be part of "Hello"? What about "Hello - World"? That yields "Hello" and "-" and "World."

You see how much you left to chance? Leaving things to chance is the genesis of many computer bugs. You'll come back to "PARSE" later to see whether you can improve on the algorithm.

> **Note:** Books on algorithms are available. These books describe the solutions to many common computer problems. A particularly good book on the subject is *Algorithms* by Martin Sedgewick. Sedgewick used Pascal in his book to describe the algorithms, because Pascal would be easy to understand and translate into other languages.
>
> A book on algorithms would be a good investment. Although you might find it great fun to figure things out for yourself, in sheer terms of getting things done it never hurts to work with known, tested solutions.

The *While* and *Repeat* Loops

Perhaps the reason that the For loop in Pascal is somewhat limited is because Pascal has two other types of loops that can accommodate most situations. These two loops are very similar, so you'll cover them together here.

The For loop is executed a fixed number of times. If you code

```
For I := 1 to 10 do Something;
```

Chapter 12 ◆ Repeating Yourself

you know that *Something* will be called 10 times exactly. Even if you use two variables for the source and destination, the For loop will be executed exactly *n* times, where *n* is equal to *(Source-Destination)+1*. You *can* shorten a For loop by changing the control variable, but this is a questionable practice (as it can result in endless loops).

What if you don't have a specific quantity in mind? What if you want a piece of code to be repeated as long as a certain condition is true?

```
Top:
    I := SomeFunction;
    J := AnotherFunction;
    If I+J<>0 then GoTo Top;
```

This example shows how you might code a loop like this by using a GoTo. As long as the sum of *I* and *J* is not zero, keep calling *SomeFunction* and *AnotherFunction*. In Pascal, this situation is commonly handled by using *While* or *Repeat*.

```
While I+J <> 0 do
begin
    I := SomeFunction;
    J := AnotherFunction;
end;
```

The While statement is followed by a Do, which can optionally be followed by Begin and End. You can have a one-line While statement:

```
While (I < 10) do I := I + 1;
```

> **Note:** Style: I like to put the expression that the While loop must evaluate in parentheses, as above in (I<10), but this is not required.

Note that if I<10 here:

```
While (I < 10) do I := I + 1;
```

or I+J equals zero here:

```
While I+J <> 0 do
```

the code following the Do is never executed.

Compare that to the Repeat statement:

```
repeat
    I := SomeFunction;
    J := AnotherFunction;
until (I+J=0);
```

> **Tip:** Style: I also like to put the expression that the repeat loop must evaluate in parentheses. This is not required either, however.

Repeat acts like its own Begin, as you can see here, with *Until* serving the same purpose as End. Regardless of what *I* and *J* are when the program comes to the Repeat, *SomeFunction* and *AnotherFunction* are called at least once.

Before Pascal, Pascal programmers would frequently code structures like this:

```
repeat
   Ch := GetCommand;
   Case Ch of
       'A': DoApples;
       'B': DoBananas;
       'C': DoCherries;
       end;
until (Ch = 'Q');
```

where *GetCommand* would wait for the user to press a key and the Case statement would process the keystroke. This cycle would be continued until the user selected 'Q' (for "Quit").

Repeat, While, and Case all used to be much more important to the Delphi programmer than they currently are in Pascal. Virtually *every* program that interacted with the user would have some kind of Repeat or While statement to get user input and a Case statement to process that input. As a matter of fact, the same or similar code is still there, but hidden from you. If you look at the project code window for any of the projects you've worked with you'll see:

```
begin
  Application.CreateForm(TForm1, Form1);
  Application.Run;
end.
```

You've looked at this before: *Application* is an object, *Run* is a method that puts *Form1* up on-screen when your program is executed. Buried within the Run method is code that looks something like the following:

```
repeat SendEventTo(TheCurrentWindow) until TheUserTerminatesTheProgram;
```

There isn't a Case statement—the program just keeps track of what object should get what events, and you handle those events as they arise.

Parse, Version 2

You're going to try to rephrase the algorithm in PARSE by using a Repeat or a While statement. Let's start by clarifying the algorithm in English:

Chapter 12 ◆ Repeating Yourself

InWord begins False.
Index begins 1.
FirstChar begins 1.
While Index is less than the length of the string
    See if the character at the current Index is a letter or number or underscore
      If it is, and InWord is not true, then
        set InWord to true and
        set FirstChar to Index
      If the character is not a letter then
        if InWord was previously true, you've come to the end of a word (extract it)
        Set InWord to false
      Increment Index

What you're going to do is go through the string, one character at a time, as before, but this time you're going to limit your definition of a "word" to a string of letters or numbers that may also include the underscore character—much like the Delphi definition of an identifier.

If the current character does not fall into those categories, then you are not currently in a word. Spaces, punctuation marks, and special symbols are all considered not to be part of the word.

> **Note:** Characters that separate words from each other are called *delimiters*. There are many delimiters in English, such as the space and the comma.
>
> All of the punctuation symbols you've seen and used in Pascal serve as a delimiter in addition to serving whatever other purposes they might have. For example, the assignment symbol and the "+" operator in
>
>   `I:=I+1;`
>
> not only say "add" or "assign," but also separate the two "I"s and the "1" in the statement.
>
> Pascal, as you might imagine, has a very sophisticated parser.

Revise the code to match your algorithm. You have one new variable, *InWord*.

```
var
    S, T            : String;
    InWord          : Boolean;
    Index, FirstChar: Integer;
begin
```

You're going to assign `UserInput.Text` to *S*, just as before, and set up (or *initialize*) all your variables.

```
S := UserInput.Text+' ';
InWord := False;
Index := 1;
FirstChar := 1;
```

You're going to go through each character of the string now:

```
while(Index <= Length(S)) do
begin
   T := Copy(S,Index,1);
```

First you're going to test to see whether it's a letter, a number, or an underscore:

```
If ((T >= '0') and (T <= '9')) or
   ((T >= 'A') and (T <= 'Z')) or
   ((T >= 'a') and (T <= 'z')) or
   (T = '_') then
begin
```

Well, that's kind of ugly—yet sometimes you have no choice but to make a long list of conditions that apply to a certain block of code. Notice the use of parentheses to force the compiler to evaluate these three comparisons properly:

```
((T >= '0') AND (T <= '9'))  or
```

So, T must be within '0' and '9' OR

```
((T >= 'A') and (T <= 'Z')) or
```

within 'A' to 'Z'—the upper case letters—OR

```
((T >= 'a') and (T <= 'z')) or
```

within 'a' to 'z'—the lower case letters—OR

```
(T = '_') then
```

an underscore. If these conditions are met and you're not already in a word, this must be the first character of a new word. In any event, you want to set *InWord* to True.

```
      If not InWord then FirstChar := Index;
      InWord := true;
   end
   else begin
```

Otherwise, you aren't in a word. If you were in a word previously, that means the word is complete, and you want to add it to the list.

```
      If InWord then begin
         T := Copy(S, FirstChar, Index-FirstChar);
         Words.Items.Add(T);
      end;
      InWord := False;
   end;
```

In any event, you're going to set *InWord* to false. The most important part comes now, and it's also the easiest to forget. You have to increment index, otherwise the routine will run forever.

```
      Index := Index + 1;
   end;
end;
```

You might wonder why this couldn't all have been done with a For loop. It *could* have. A While loop is virtually interchangeable with a For loop, but a While loop is considerably more flexible.

For example, you could put this:

```
while (Index <= Length(S)) and not Terminate do
```

What's Terminate? Some Boolean variable you set to True when you want to end the While loop *before* it gets to the end. So you can make the conditions of the loop more complex than you can with a For variable. You can also make them simpler.

```
while not Terminate do
```

Then, after incrementing *Index*:

```
      Index := Index + 1;
      Terminate := Index > Length(S);
   end;
```

Any number of other things could also cause you to set *Terminate*.

Example: Loading the Dice

Save this and go to the Dice project again. For this example, you'll fix it so that the user can't lose. In this case, you couldn't use a For loop very effectively. Could you use a While loop? (Double-click on the *Roll* button to get to the code that rolls the dice.)

```
. . .
   D1 := 0;  D2 := 0;
   While ((D1 + D2)<>7 ) AND ((D1 + D2)<>11) do
   begin
      D1 := Random(6)+1;
      D2 := Random(6)+1;
   end;
. . .
```

A Repeat statement here would actually be cleaner. Add a byte variable called *Value* to the procedure and set up the dice-rolling code like this:

```
...
   repeat
      D1 := Random(6)+1;
      D2 := Random(6)+1;
      Value := D1+D2;
   until (Value = 7) or (Value = 11);
, , ,
```

In this case you don't have to set D1 and D2 to zero because the Repeat statement is *always* executed at least once. So, there are enough differences between Repeat, For, and While to make having them all worthwhile.

Break and Continue

I confessed earlier that I *had* used GoTo on one or two occasions in the past. The reason I used them was because I found myself in a While, Repeat, or For loop, possibly in some block of code nested several layers deep—and I needed to get out! GoTo was the clearest way to express what I needed. Consider something like this:

```
While ThisIsTrue do
begin
   If SomethingIsTrue then
   begin
      DoThis;
      DoThat;
      If ThisIsOK then
      begin
         DoMore;
         If NotOk then InTrouble;
         {more code here}
      end;
      {Even more code}
   end;
   {Still more code}
end;
```

What happens if you get to InTrouble and find out that there's some kind of error? You just want to go back to the top of the loop and you don't want any other code executed. Or, you want to leave the While loop immediately—again without any of the other code executed. To work around an error that can occur that deep in a procedure can result in code as difficult to read as any spaghetti code. So, on the rare occasion this occurred, I used a GoTo.

Borland added two features to Pascal in recent years to handle this difficult situation. To immediately go to the top of any For, While, or Repeat loop, use the *Continue* procedure. To immediately exit any For, While, or Repeat loop, use the *Break* procedure.

Chapter 12 ◆ Repeating Yourself

Example: Parser, Version 2.5

Now, you shouldn't need to use *Continue* and *Break* very often. If things get so complicated that you begin to consider it, check to see whether what you're doing can't be done in some other, simpler fashion. However, take a look at how they might work within the "PARSE" project.

Double-click on the *Add* button to get to your parsing routine. Now, after the *Copy* command, but before *T* is checked to see whether it is a letter, number, or underscore, enter the following line:

```
If T = '*' then Break;
```

You'll say that an asterisk appearing in the input line is an error and that the routine can go no further. This is your made-up equivalent of running out of disk space or paper in the printer or some other error which, should it occur, requires that you stop everything and allow the user to handle the situation before proceeding.

Try this out. If you type "An asterisk is an * error," the listbox will look like figure 12.2. So, the loop is broken when the asterisk is encountered and the procedure never sees the word "error."

Figure 12.2
PARSE encounters an error.

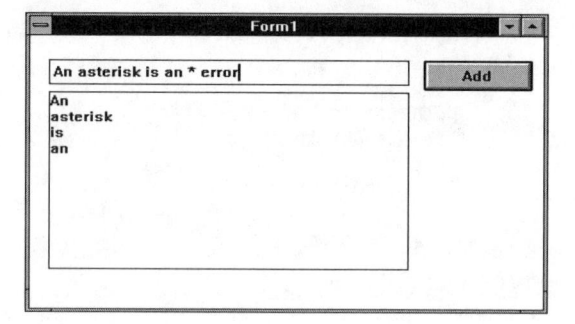

Trying out Continue will be a little more complex. You'll make your parser even more like the Delphi parser by saying that anything enclosed in curly braces is comment. "PARSE" should ignore it. To do this you'll take the following steps:

◆ Add a Boolean variable, *InComment*, which tells you whether you are currently in a comment. (Set it to False, initially.)

◆ Before checking to see whether T is a word character or the illegal asterisk character, check to see whether it is an opening curly brace, or if you're in a comment already.

- If you are in a comment, check to see whether the character is a closing curly brace. If so, set *InComment* to False.
- If it's not a closing curly brace, set *InComment* to True.
- Either way, if you're in a comment, delete the current character.
- Go back to the top to get the next character.

You know how to do all of this except delete the offending character. Pascal has a procedure named *Delete* that works much like the *Copy* procedure. If you declared it, the procedure would look something like this:

```
procedure Delete(var S: String; Index, Count: Integer);
```

Delete removes *Count* characters from string *S* starting at position *Index*. So,

```
Delete(S, 1, 1);
```

deletes the first character in string *S*, and

```
Delete(S, Length(S), 1);
```

deletes the last. In your case, you want to delete one character at the current index:

```
Delete(S, Index, 1);
```

You should now be able to code this segment. Altogether, this is the most sizable piece of code you've written so far.

```
procedure TParseForm.AddClick(Sender: TObject);
var
    S, T              : String;
    InWord, InComment: Boolean;
    Index, FirstChar : Integer;
begin
    S := UserInput.Text+' ';
    InWord := False;
    InComment := False;
    Index := 1;
    FirstChar := 1;

    while Index <= Length(S) do
    begin
        T := Copy(S,Index,1);
        If (T = '{') or InComment then {Delete commented out characters}
        begin
            If T = '}' then InComment := false
            else InComment := true;
            Delete(S, Index, 1);
            Continue;
        end;
```

```
        If T = '*' then Break;   {Error character}

        If ((T >= '0') and (T <= '9')) or
           ((T >= 'A') and (T <= 'Z')) or
           ((T >= 'a') and (T <= 'z')) or
           (T = '_') then
        begin
           If not InWord then FirstChar := Index;
           InWord := true;
     end
        else begin
           If InWord then begin
              T := Copy(S, FirstChar, Index-FirstChar);
              Words.List.Add(T);
           end;
           InWord := False;
        end;
        Inc(Index);
     end;
end;
```

Note that related blocks of code are separated with a single blank line. This action makes the code easier to digest by allowing the user to look at the related instructions as a group.

Now, if you run this and enter "Hello{This is a comment}World," the list box will get just one entry, "HelloWorld." The comment is completely ignored.

> **Caution:** One easy mistake to make when using Continue is to forget to increment your counter. If you use Continue from a For loop, you don't need to increment it—that's part of what the For loop does. But, if you're using Continue with a While loop or a Repeat loop, and you place the Continue statement *before* your code to increment the counter, that code is ignored just as all your other code is ignored.
>
> You got away with it here—can you see why? You didn't have to increment *Index* because you actually are shortening the string.

There's one other thing to notice here that harkens back to the subject of algorithms. As discussed earlier, an "*" would be an error. But the code to remove comments occurs *before* the code to stop on an asterisk. In other words, an asterisk within a curly brace counts as a comment, not an error.

This may be okay or may not be. The real issue here is that it was *undefined*, and a good algorithm should not have any undefined responses.

Summary

GoTo is a way that programmers used to get code to repeat or to jump over code they didn't want executed. Abuse of the GoTo led to spaghetti code and programmers searched for ways to avoid jumping around in code. Pascal provides three ways to set up loops without GoTo: For, While, and Repeat. The For loop allows the programmer to set up code to repeat a fixed number of times. The While and Repeat loops allow the programmer to repeat code based on one or more conditions. For loops are limited in the sense that they can only progress forward or backward by one. Adjusting the For control variable within the For loop itself is ill-advised, possibly leading to an endless loop. In a Repeat loop, the code segment is always done at least once; in a While loop the code is not necessarily done at all. These are the main differences between those two kinds of loops.

Break is a procedure that stops a loop altogether. *Continue* forces the code to go to the top of the loop. *Continue* will advance or regress the control variable in a For loop. *Delete* is a procedure that deletes characters from a string.

The listbox is an object that displays a list of choices and allows the user to select from them. The listbox has, as one of its properties, the list object. The list object contains the selections and has a method, *Add*, that allows you to add to the list while the program is running.

Parsing, or breaking data down into pieces, is a crucial skill. An algorithm is a particular way of solving a particular problem. Characters that serve as separators between groups of other characters are called delimiters.

Review Questions

1. What does GoTo do?
2. What does *Break* do?
3. What does *Continue* do?
4. What is the While loop? What is the Repeat loop? How are they different?
5. What is an *algorithm*?
6. What is the *control variable* of a For loop?
7. What are the *source* and *destination* values in a For loop?
8. What do you need to use a GoTo in Pascal?
9. What does the keyword *downto* do?
10. What does it mean to *parse* user input?

Chapter 12 ◆ Repeating Yourself

11. What happens if you alter the control variable of a For loop so that it exceeds its destination value?
12. What is a delimiter?
13. Should you ever use a GoTo?
14. Can you use a char type variable as a control variable in a For loop?

Review Exercises

1. Now that you know how to loop, go back to the multiple-choice exercise of the last chapter and correct the procedure shown so that it *insists* that the user give a response of either A, B, C, or D. Other answers should simply cause the procedure to redisplay the prompt "Which do you choose?".

2. In Chapter 9, "Data Conversion," you built a CONVERT program that converted the text from an edit line into a position on a scrollbar. Using Delete and a loop change the program so that it not only detects invalid characters but deletes *all* of them from the text.

3. Write a program with a gauge and three buttons where each of the three buttons fills the gauge from 1 to 100, but each using a different kind of loop.

4. Fix the GAUGE program built in this chapter so that it increments the gauges in steps of 50, 25, 10, 5, and if you have a very fast machine, 2. Do this without modifying the For loop control variable.

5. Repeat the exercise in step 4, but this time do it by modifying the control variable. This is a more dangerous exercise, so be careful.

6. Modify the PARSE program so that it has a second listbox. In this listbox put all the punctuation, but none of the spaces.

CHAPTER 13

Pascal Math

You've done a little math already with the plus and minus operators, '+' and '-'. Pascal has a wide array of operators that work with numbers, as well as many functions and procedures for performing specific math tasks. In this chapter, you'll look at these, and also at the other numeric data types—the *real* types.

Simple Math

Pascal's built-in operators handle addition, subtraction, multiplication, and division of integer types. Also, because integers (by definition) cannot have decimal points, Pascal has an operator that enables you to get the remainder of a division operation. Table 13.1 shows you examples of valid Pascal integer operations.

Table 13.1. The integer operators.

Operator	Operation	Example	
+	Addition	A := 5 + 3;	{A is 8}
-	Subtraction	A := 5 - 3;	{A is 2}
*	Multiplication	A := 5 * 3;	{A is 15}
div	Division	A := 5 div 3;	{A is 1}
mod	Remainder	A := 5 mod 3;	{A is 2}

Chapter 13 ◆ Pascal Math

> **Note:** In computer terms, code that is evaluated and reduced to a single value is called an *expression*. An expression consists of *operators* (like +, -, >, and so forth) and *operands*. Operands are the values that are operated on. In the expression "5 + 3," + is the operator, and 5 and 3 are the operands.
>
> In Pascal, a variable or a function can be an operand, too. In the line
>
> ```
> B := ValFn(S) + I;
> ```
>
> *ValFn* and *I* are both operands.

The only operators you haven't already encountered in this book are the asterisk for multiplication, the keyword *div* for division, and the keyword *mod* for remainder. Mod is an abbreviation for *modulus*. The modulus is the remainder after an integer division. For example,

```
uses WinCRT;

var A: Integer;
    B, C: Byte;

begin
    A := 1000;
    B := A;
    C := A mod 256;
    writeln(A:10, B:10, C:10);
end.
```

would result in C being equal to B.

Just as you learned in Chapter 7, "Using Numbers," an assignment that causes a variable to exceed its specified range will result in a range error (if range checking is on) or will cause the value to wrap around (if range checking is off). This is probably most important to keep in mind when multiplying—the value 20 is well within range for byte or shortint, for example, but 20*20 isn't.

On the subject of *overflows* (to overflow is to exceed the range of a variable type), you should know Pascal is a little sneaky with regard to math. What value would you expect C to end up with here?

```
var
    A, B: BYte;
    C   : Longint;
begin
    A := 200;
    B := 200;
    C := B*A;
end.
```

You can start a new project (from the File menu, select New Project), remove any forms (from the View menu select Project Manager, click Unit1/Form1 and press the minus icon), clear out the project window (click the secondary mouse button on the project manager, select View Project, select all the text in the code window and press Delete), and put this code in directly. Then step through the code until you get to the *End*. To find out what the value of *C* is select from the Debug menu, Evaluate/modify.... You should see figure 13.1.

Figure 13.1
The Evaluate/Modify dialog box.

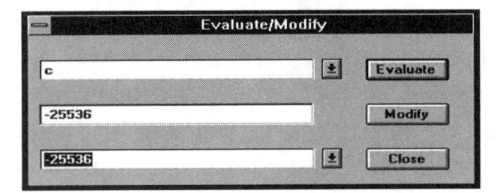

The Evaluate/Modify dialog box will give you the value of any variable available in the current scope or any expression it can calculate. You can enter 2 + 2 in the dialog, for example, and see that that expression is 4. (The dialog cannot generally give you the result of a function, however.)

Type **C** (or c) in the top line. (It is sometimes handy to be able to change a value while running a program, but right now, you're just interested in what the program came up with as a value for *C*.) It's not 40,000, is it? It's *-25,536*. Why -25,536? Well, what if you had an integer *I*, and code like this?

```
C := 40000;
I := C;
```

What would *I* be? If you run this and check it out in the Evaluate/Modify dialog, you'll see that I is *-25,536*. The value 40,000 is too large for an integer, which has a maximum positive value of 32,767. After that, it wraps around to the negative, so that 32,767 plus one is equal to -32,768! You saw how this worked in Chapter 7, "Using Numbers." What you haven't established is *why* the compiler did the math as though *C* were an integer.

The compiler takes the type of the first *operand* of any equation and does the math in that type—but it never does math with anything smaller than an integer. In other words, the math is done without regard to *C* at all. You can get around the integer problem by transferring *B*'s value to a longint before doing the math:

```
var
   A, B: Byte;
   C    : Longint;
begin
   A := 200;
   B := 200;
   C := B;
   C := C*A;
end.
```

thus forcing the compiler to do the math within a longint range.

Chapter 13 ◆ Pascal Math

Example: Integer Calculator

You can't implement a full calculator program yet because you haven't begun to look at real numbers, and a calculator that only does integers is of limited value. However, the experience of building a basic calculator will serve you later on when you want to incorporate real numbers into the design.

Also, as this is a complete, functioning program, longer than any others you've developed, it will introduce you to some new concepts, and also some new problems that you'll have to solve later on.

Start a new project named CALCINT and create a form (call the unit CALCINTF and name the form `CalcForm`) like the one pictured in figure 13.2. There are eighteen buttons, five in the first row, five in the second, and four in the third and fourth. All of the buttons are the same size except for the equal key, which was made to fill out the bottom of the calculator.

Figure 13.2
The CalcInt Program Form.

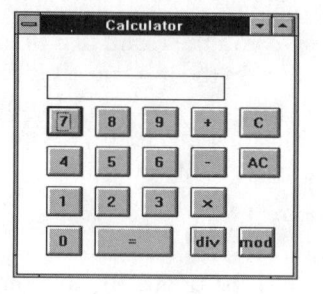

The buttons are numbered, have the five integer operators you've covered plus the equal sign, and also a *clear* and *all clear* button. These objects should be renamed after their caption: the 0 button should have the name "Zero," the 1 should be "One," the + should be "Plus," and so on. The div (shown with a [#246]) and mod buttons should be "divide" and "modulo" since Div and Mod are both reserved words and can't be used as identifiers. The C button should be named "Clear" and the AC button should be named "AllClear."

Tip: You can insert special characters directly into the *Caption* property by holding down the Alt key and then using the numeric keypad to type the ASCII value of the desired special character (for example, 246 for the division symbol), then releasing the Alt key. See Appendix A for a complete ASCII chart.

> **Note:** The fastest way to build this form is to press and hold the Shift key, then click the push button icon. Then, click the form 18 times. You don't have to count, just wait until the caption on one reads "Button18." (To stop placing push buttons, click the cursor select button on the Component Bar, the one shaped like an arrow.)
>
> Select all these buttons at once and use the object inspector to change their width from 89 (the default) to 40, which should make them square. Then, arrange the buttons in the manner shown in figure 13.2.
>
> If you change the properties of the 18 buttons by clicking a button, changing its *Name* and *Caption*, then clicking the next, changing its *Name* and *Caption*, you'll find yourself going back and forth a lot more than necessary.
>
> Instead, click the Object Inspector's object selection combo box and select the very first object. Then, select Name and give it the appropriate name. Now, press Enter. This will select the form and the object you just changed. Press Tab. This selects the next object. Press Enter again and you're back at the Object Inspector, where you can now change the name of the next object. Do this with every object on the form, and then repeat the process for the Caption field. Once you get the hang of it, this can be much faster than clicking the mouse back and forth.

You may notice when testing the form that the Tab and cursor keys don't work as expected. The order of controls on a form is not based in any way on their position. Instead, the first control you put on a form is first, the second is second, and so on. If you aren't careful, you'll end up with a Tab order that is confusing.

Pascal offers a better way to change the tab order. Click mouse button 2 on a blank space on the form and select Tab Order from the pop-up menu. The Tab Order selection dialog appears, showing a list box with all the controls that your form has on it. To re-order them, you can either click and drag the control to a new location, or you can select a single item and click either of the buttons showing the up or down arrows.

Before implementing the calculator program any further, it would help if you considered how a real-world calculator works: Enter a number, press an operator, enter another number, enter another operator or equal, and so on. There are two things that make this tricky: The first is that the operator doesn't apply until *after* the next number is entered, so you couldn't have the plus key do this, for example:

```
procedure TCalcIntF.PlusClick(Sender: TObject);
begin
   Total := Total + ValFn(Entry.Text);
end;
```

Chapter 13 ♦ Pascal Math

> **Note:** Assume that Total is a longint and ValFn is a function that you'll build to streamline conversion from text to numeric data:
>
> ```
> function ValFn(S: String): Longint;
> var Code: Integer;
>     L    : Longint;
> begin
>    Val(S, L, Code);
>    ValFn := L;
> end;
> ```
>
> Writing this one function will save you a fair amount of typing.

Now, consider if all the operator keys were set up this way: A user entering "30," pressing "+," entering "10," and pressing "-" would get an answer of "20." The user wanted "30 + 10 - " the next number, but got "+ 30 - 10." This approach applies the operation to *Total* and the current number, not the current number and the number not yet entered.

You'll be looking into how to design programs in the last chapter, but as you can see, even when writing an apparently simple program, some thought must be given to how things will be done.

> **Tip:** It's always a good idea to think about the object you're trying to simulate before sitting down to program.

Calculators follow three basic rules:

♦ Pressing a digit concatenates that digit to the current number in the entry field, unless the current number is complete.

♦ Pressing equal or an operator tells the calculator that the current number is complete, and the last operation selected should be performed on the current number and the total.

♦ Pressing an operator also sets up the next operation to be performed.

To take this from English to code, you first figure out the variables you'll need. The "current number" will be *Entry.Text*, so you won't need a special variable for it. *Complete* would be a boolean variable, indicating that the next digit pressed should clear *Entry.Text* before the digit is added. The last operation the user selected, call it *Operator*, could be a char variable set to "+", "-", "x", " ", or "m." Finally, you'll need *Total*, a longint to hold the result of the operations.

In the "CALCINTF" unit, find the var section generated by Delphi. It should look like this:

```
var
   CalcForm: TForm1;
```

Follow that with your three variables:

```
   Total     : Longint;
   Complete  : Boolean;
   Operator  : Char;
```

Now, define the behavior for one of the digit keys, say *Zero*. Double-click the *Zero* button and add the following to the code frame:

```
    If Complete then Entry.Text := '';
    Entry.Text := Entry.Text + '0';
```

Block this text and copy it to the clipboard. Now, go back to the form and double-click the *One* button. Copy the code back from the clipboard and make the appropriate change:

```
    If Complete then Entry.Text := '';
    Entry.Text := Entry.Text + '1';
```

Repeat this for each digit key. (Yes, there are better ways to do this, and you'll look at them later on in Chapter 21.) Now, right before the *ZeroClick* method, add the *ValFn* function and another function you'll call *StrFn*. *StrFn* will be the complement of *ValFn* and turn numbers to strings. (Any time you know you'll be converting from strings to numbers and back, these functions will come in handy.)

```
function ValFn(S: String): Longint;
var Code: Integer;
    L    : Longint;
begin
   Val(S, L, Code);
   ValFn := L;
end;

function StrFn(L: Longint): String;
var S: String;
begin
   Str(L, S);
   StrFn := S;
end;
```

Now it's time to create the code for the operator keys. The operator keys have to do several things:

♦ They must calculate based on the *previous* operation selected.

♦ They must set *Complete* to true.

Chapter 13 ◆ Pascal Math

♦ They must set *Entry.Text* to the total of the new number. (Good calculators give a running total every time the user presses a new operator.)

This definitely calls for a subroutine. For one thing, when pressed, an operator has to calculate a new total based on the *previous* operator. Since that could be any of the five operators, you'd end up putting all the code for all the operators in each of the operator's click procedures. Instead, make a procedure named *Calculate*, and put it after the *StrFn* procedure.

```
procedure Calculate(Number: Longint; NextOp: Char);
begin
   If not Complete or (Total=0) then
   case Operator of
      '+': Total := Total + Number;
      '-': Total := Total - Number;
      'x': Total := Total * Number;
      '[put a div sign here, ASCII #246]': Total := Total div Number;
      'm': Total := Total mod Number;
   end;
   Operator := NextOp;
   Complete := True;
end;
```

That takes care of everything except setting *Entry.Text* to the new total. Do that in the click routines. Starting by double-clicking the *Plus* button, and add this code:

```
Calculate(ValFn(Entry.Text),'+');
Entry.Text := StrFn(Total);
```

Repeat this code for *Minus*, *Multiply*, *Divide*, and *Modulo*. The parameters passed by *Multiply*, *Divide*, and *Modulo*, must be "x," "d," and "m" respectively in order for *Calculate* to work.

That leaves you with just the *Clear* and *AllClear* buttons. Double-click *Clear* and add these lines:

```
Entry.Text := '0';
Complete := true;
```

Pressing *Clear* puts a "0" in *Entry.Text* and sets *Complete* to true so that a zero appears in the entry field, but that is replaced by whatever the user types—just like a real calculator.

Pressing *AllClear* should do the same, but also should set *Total* to 0 and *Operator* to "+." Why set the operator to "+"? Because, if the user presses (for example) "x" and then presses *AllClear*, "x" is still the value in *Operator*. When the user subsequently enters a number, that number will be multiplied by *Total*, which is zero.

Putting it in other terms, setting *Total* to 0 and *Operator* to "+" is like starting the equation:

```
0 + . . ..
```

Otherwise, *Total* and *Operator* will be undefined.

In fact, you should start off *Total* and *Operator* with those values (that is, zero and plus), as well as setting *Complete* to True. Switch to the *CalcInt* project window, and add the necessary code to the program block before *TApplication.Run(Form1)*.

```
begin
   Total := 0;
   Operator := '+';
   Complete := True;
   Application.Run(Form1);
end.
```

Set *Entry.Text*'s *Caption* property to zero, and you have just one change left to make the "CALCINT" program work. Double-click *Entry*. The default event for an entry field is *Changed*. Add this line of code:

```
If Entry.Text = '' then Complete := False;
```

If *Entry.Text* is null then it has already been erased and *Complete* has fulfilled its purpose. So, you're using the fact that other events are going to erase *Entry.Text* to toggle the *Complete* variable, preventing *Entry.Text* from being cleared when it shouldn't be. You now can compile and run this program.

You'll come back to the "CALCINT" program as you touch upon ways to improve it.

Integer Subroutines

Borland provides you with a number of procedures and functions that you can use with integers, as table 13.2 shows. (The routines that Borland has written for you and included with Delphi are called *built-in* procedures and functions.) The table shows what the function's name is and what kind of parameter it takes. The next columns show the data type the routines operate on and an example of how they would be used. These routines are interesting in that they are all things that can be done with one line of code, and that one line equivalency is shown in the next column. Finally, the Returns column shows what the functions return.

Table 13.2. Standard integer procedures and functions. (Integer refers to any of the five integer types.)

Routine	Type	Example	Equivalent	Returns
Dec(O)	Ordinal	Dec(O);	O := O - 1;	
Dec(O,n)	Ordinal	Dec(O,3);	O := O - 3;	
Inc(O)	Ordinal	Inc(O);	O := O + 1;	
Inc(O,n)	Ordinal	Inc(O,3);	O := O + 3;	
Pred(O)	Ordinal	O := Pred(O);	O := O - 1;	same
Succ(O)	Ordinal	O := Succ(O);	I := I + 1;	same
Hi(W)	Word	B := Hi(W);	B := W div 256;	byte
Lo(W)	Word	B := Lo(W);	B := W mod 256;	byte
Odd(I)	Integer	Bool := Odd(I);	Bool := (I mod 2)=1;	Boolean

The Inc and Dec Procedures

Inc and *Dec* are procedures that enable you to add and subtract a value from a variable. The line

```
Inc(I);
```

is the same as the line

```
I := I + 1;
```

So why do *Inc* and *Dec* exist? Primarily because the compiler can generate more efficient code for *Inc* and *Dec* than it can with the more traditional "I := I + 1." As a result, you'll see *Inc* and *Dec* a lot in other people's code.

The other interesting thing to note about *Inc* and *Dec* is that they can have one *or* two parameters. You can code this:

```
Inc(I, 3);
```

"*Inc(I,3)*" means "Increment I by 3" or "I := I + 3." Some subroutines in Pascal, like *Inc* and *Dec*, have *optional* parameters. When subroutine headers with optional parameters are described in Pascal's help system, Borland surrounds the optional part with square brackets. The headers for `Inc` and Dec are shown as:

```
Dec(var X [ ; N: Longint])
Inc(var X [ ; N: Longint])
```

The *N* parameter is optional in both cases. In case you were thinking of declaring your own procedure headers using square brackets to indicate optional parameters, you should know that Object Pascal does not allow you to have optional parameters in your subroutines.

Another thing you cannot do in your subroutines that *Inc*, *Dec*, and other built-in routines do is have a parameter like *X* in the above definition. *X* can be any ordinal type—longint, char, or whatever, and *Inc* and *Dec* will work fine no matter which. (You'll see more of this later on.) This gives you another reason for *Inc* and *Dec*'s existence besides speed. If *C* is a char, you can't code this:

```
C := C + 1;
```

But you can code this:

```
Inc(C);
```

While I don't recommend incrementing and decrementing characters, in the next chapter you'll encounter another kind of ordinal data type that cannot be incremented through the plus sign where you might legitimately need Inc and Dec.

Pred and Succ

Pred and *Succ* (short for "predecessor" and "successor") comprise another set of functions that work with any ordinal type. They're basically the same as *Dec* and *Inc*, respectively. The only difference is that they return the value of the variable passed, minus or plus 1. In other words, they return a variable's successor or predecessor.

So, you could code this:

```
C := Succ('A');
```

to set a *char* variable *C* to the value 'B'. 'B' is the successor of 'A'.

In truth, you aren't that likely to use these functions frequently, but they do illustrate another feature that the built-in routines can have that yours cannot. *Pred* and *Succ* return results in the same type as the variable passed.

```
Succ('A');
```

returns a char.

```
Succ(1);
```

returns an integer type.

As with Inc and Dec, I don't generally recommend that Pred and Succ be used with characters. Pred and Succ are best used with *enumerated* data types, described in the next chapter.

Hi and Lo

Hi and *Lo* work only with word variables. A word variable, if you'll recall, is two bytes long.

```
B := Hi(W);
```

would set *B* to the most significant byte of word *W*, while

```
B := Lo(W);
```

would set *B* to the least significant byte. This has value on those occasions where some procedure or function you call uses a word-type variable to store two bytes. (Low-level Windows access requires things like this a lot.)

Odd

Odd simply returns True if the value passed is odd (in other words, not divisible evenly by 2).

Real Types

Real data types enable you to express much larger and much smaller numbers than possible with integers. The five real data types are shown in table 13.3, where the "Sz" column shows the size in bytes for each type, and the "Digits" column shows how many digits of the value are significant.

Table 13.3. Pascal real variable types.

Name	Sz	Example	Minimum	Maximum	Digits
Real	6	12345.678901	2.9×10^{-39}	1.7×10^{38}	11-12
Single	4	.0000001	1.5×10^{-45}	3.4×10^{38}	7-8
Double	8	8187038565555	5.0×10^{-324}	1.7×10^{308}	15-16
Extended	10	-45.0004096012	3.4×10^{-4932}	1.1×10^{4932}	19-20
Comp	8	102019660331	$-2^{63} + 1$	$2^{63} - 1$	19-20

As you can see, the ranges are so high that they must be expressed in powers of 10 just to fit on the page. Remember that "10^{38}" (ten to the thirty-eighth power) is a "1" followed by 38 zeroes. So the highest amount expressable with the real data type would be:

170,000,000,000,000,000,000,000,000,000,000,000,000

The other thing to note is that even though the number may be very large or very small, only a certain number of digits are *significant*. Basically that means that the data type can keep track of as few as seven and as many as twenty digits. In other words, if *R* is a real variable:

```
R := 1.0000000000001;
R := R + 1;
```

then *R* is equal to 2. The ".0000000000001" is discarded. If *R* were a double or extended type, the decimal portion would be preserved. At most, however, you can only count on 19 digits of any number being accurate.

The comp data type deserves special attention, only because it holds what you and I would call *integers*. A comp variable has no decimal portion, but is still treated as a real type, not an integer.

The reason for this is that the main CPUs of all DOS/Windows machines actually don't work off of anything but integers. The real data types are emulated by complex code built in to the Delphi compiler. The integer types that you've studied can all be handled directly by the CPU. And the largest integer that any CPU currently running DOS/Windows can handle is the four-byte *longint* you've used so often.

Because you might need a larger integer, Borland has provided the comp type. However, the comp type must be treated as a real number and is not considered an ordinal type.

The real operators, shown in table 13.4, are almost all the same as the integer operators, except that there is no Mod or Div operator. Instead, division is handled by the forward slash operator, '/'.

Table 13.4. The real operators.

Operator	Operation	Example	
+	Addition	A := 5 + 3;	{A is 8}
-	Subtraction	A := 5 - 3;	{A is 2}
*	Multiplication	A := 5 * 3;	{A is 15}
/	Division	A := 5 / 3;	{A is 1.66666667}

The exact value of a division with a repeating decimal depends on the precision of real type used. So, in the case of "5/3" the value will be one, followed by a decimal, followed by some number of sixes, and one seven. (Pascal rounds the last significant digit.)

Chapter 13 ◆ Pascal Math

Real Functions

Unlike the built-in integer procedures and functions, the subroutines used with real data types actually handle some very complex tasks. Table 13.5 lists the built-in Pascal real subroutines.

Table 13.5. The built-in Pascal real routines. (Real refers to any of the five real types.)

Name	Example	Returns
Round(R)	L := Round(R);	Longint
Trunc(R)	L := Trunc(R);	Longint
Frac(R)	R1 := Frac(R2);	Real
Int(R)	R1 := Int(R2);	Real
ArcTan(R)	R1 := ArcTan(R2)	Real
Cos(R)	R1 := Cos(R2);	Real
Exp(R)	R1 := Exp(R2);	Real
Ln(R)	R1 := Ln(R2);	Real
Pi	R1 := Pi;	Real
Sin(R)	R1 := Sin(R2);	Real
SqrRt(R)	R1 := SqrRt(R2);	Real

All routines that deal specifically with real numbers are functions, most of which return real type results.

Round and Trunc

Pascal provides two ways to get an integer value back from a real type. *Round* rounds the real number to the nearest whole number. *Trunc* merely drops the fraction. In either case, an error message (similar to the Range Check error you saw earlier) will appear if the value of the real exceeds the range of the longint.

Frac and Int

Pascal also provides two ways to break up a real number into its integer and fractional (or decimal) parts. *Frac* returns the decimal value of a real, while *Int* returns the integer value. In other words, if *R* is a real variable, this would be true:

```
R = Int(R) + Frac(R);
```

SqrRt

The *SqrRt* function returns the square root of the parameter. This is the number that, when multiplied by itself, gives the parameter.

```
R := SqrRt(4);          {This will give 2}
R := R * R;             {This will set R to 4}
```

When the result is not a whole number, as in

```
R := SqrRt(3);          {This will give 1.73205080756888}
```

then whether this works

```
R := R * R              {R is 3?}
```

depends on R. In this case, if *R* is a real it will end up as 2.99999999999636. If *R* is a single, double or extended, it will end up as 3. Real has less capacity to hold small numbers than the other types.

Of course, *R* could be a comp, in which case its final value would be 4. Remember that comp types can only hold integers. The square root of 3 (rounded) is 2. From this you might suspect that comp types holding small values shouldn't (in general) be used with any of the real math functions.

The Advanced Math Functions

The remaining six functions are invaluable in some circumstances. I've used them in only a handful of the thousands of programs I've written, but when they're necessary, they're indispensable.

However, to describe them in detail that would make sense would require me to either make assumptions about your math background, or to explain a great deal of math that is not directly on the subject of Delphi and Pascal.

If you understand what they are in math terms, the Pascal interpretations are obvious. If you don't understand what they are, don't worry.

Real vs. Integer

The question then arises—any time you need a numeric variable—whether to use real or integer data types. You could argue that you might as well always use the extended data type for every number, because it can hold any number you need. It would reduce the need for you to do range checking and so forth.

The drawbacks, however, are numerous. You cannot use a real type variable, for example, as the control variable in a *for* loop. Also, every numeric variable you use will take 10 bytes. If you're only holding a number from 1 to 100, you're wasting nine bytes of memory. (This may not seem like a big deal, but if you're using many thousands of these variables, the wasted space adds up tremendously.)

Real type variables are also generally slower than integers.

Example: Calculator, Version 0.1

There is a less obvious reason for not using real numbers that you can discover if you go back to the "CALCINT" program. Open that project now and save it as "CALCREAL." Save the unit as "CALCRF."

Now, find the line

```
Total : Longint;
```

and change it to

```
Total: Real;
```

Recompile. The compiler will stop on a number of things as errors, and you'll have to change these to make the program work again. The first line flagged will be:

```
÷: Total := Total div Number;
```

change the "div" to a "/":

```
÷ : Total := Total / Number;
```

The next problem line will be:

```
'm': Total := Total mod Number;
```

Take that line out. The next problem line will come in one of the digit click routines:

```
Entry.Text := StrFn(Total);
```

The problem here is that the *StrFn* function takes a longint and you're passing a real. Instead of changing this line, change the declaration of *StrFn* from

```
function StrFn(L: Longint): String;
```

to

```
function StrFn(L: Real): String;
```

You don't need to make any other changes. The built-in *Str* function can handle real or integer types.

Now, the program will compile, but you're still using *ValFn*, which returns a longint.

```
function ValFn(S: String): Longint;
```

when you need a real, so change this to

```
function ValFn(S: String): Real;
```

You've created one other problem here:

```
Calculate(ValFn(Entry.Text),'+');
```

Calculate takes a longint, but should take a real. Change

```
procedure Calculate(Number: Longint; NextOp: Char);
```

to

```
procedure Calculate(Number: Real; NextOp: Char);
```

Finally, the program should compile and run. Just to give it a try, do a simple equation, like adding 9 and 9. Figure 13.3 shows you what happens. (The next example section improves on the real-number calculator.)

Figure 13.3
Working with real numbers.

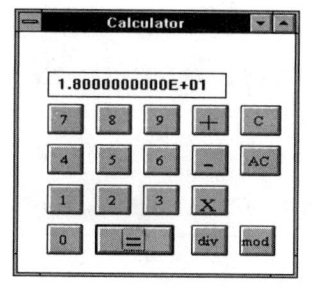

Scientific Notation

The number on the calculator is, in fact, accurate. It's simply expressed in scientific notation. Scientific notation makes it possible to express very large or very small numbers without using dozens (or hundreds) of zeroes.

The format for scientific notation is a number followed by an 'e' or 'E' followed by another number. For example:

```
1E1
```

Chapter 13 ♦ Pascal Math

The number to the right of the E tells you how many places to move the decimal. "1E1" is equal to a value of 10. (The decimal place is moved one to the right.) The number to the left of the E (the *significand*) may be positive or negative, and have several digits to the right of the decimal. (A plus sign may or may not be used to indicate a positive significand.)

```
-1E1         {-10}
+2.4E12      {same as 2.4E12 with no '+'.  2,400,000,000,000}
1.2E6        {1,200,000}
-40.3E2      {-4,030}
```

> **Note:** You may have a significand of any value within the ranges of any real type, but Pascal will always convert the significand to a number that is greater than or equal to 1, and less than 10.
>
> For example, -40.3E2 would become -4.03E3.

The number to the right of the E (the *exponent*) must be a whole number, but it may be negative, positive, or zero. If positive, it tells you how many places to the right to move the decimal. If negative, it tells you how many places to the left to move the decimal. (A plus sign is optional in indicating a positive exponent.)

```
1E+3         {Same as 1E3 with no '+'.  1,000}
4.3E-6       {.0000043}
3.145E0      {3.145}
-6.6102E3    {-6,610.2}
```

Generic Subroutines

There are three subroutines that can be used with both integer and real types. They are shown in Table 13.6.

Table 13.6. The built-in Delphi numeric routines.

Name	Example	Returns
Abs(N)	N1 := Abs(N2)	same
Random(W)	W1 := Random(W2)	integer
Random	R := Random	real
Sqr(N)	N1 := Sqr(N2)	same

Abs returns the absolute value of the number passed—that is, its unsigned value.

You've used *Random* with a word value parameter before to express range. If you don't pass it a parameter, however, it returns a real number that is less than 1 and greater than or equal to zero. This can be used to generate a range larger than 64K. For example:

```
R := Random * 1000000;
```

R can be anything from zero to 999,999 and can have a decimal portion.

The *Sqr* function returns the result of the value passed multiplied by itself.

```
R := Sqr(R);
```

is equivalent to:

```
R := R * R;
```

Example: Calculator, Version 1.0

The following shows you how to revamp the calculator to be a real decimal calculator, that doesn't show answer in scientific notation unless absolutely necessary.

To do this, you need to change only one routine. *StrFn* currently looks like this:

```
function StrFn(L: Real): String;
var S: String;
begin
   Str(L, S);
   StrFn := S;
end;
```

Str has some formatting capabilities. You can make it convert a real number into a string that isn't in scientific notation by specifying the length and number of decimals that you want the string to be. To specify a length for any number, simply add a colon after the number followed by the desired length:

```
Str(L:6, S);
```

S will come out at least six characters long. (*Str* never truncates a number to make it fit the length specified; it will only pad it out.) If the number doesn't require six spaces, *Str* will flush the value right. In other words, if L has a value of 1, s will be '   1', with five blanks followed by the '1'.

To specify that a real number should be displayed with three decimals, add another colon followed by the desired number of decimals:

```
Str(L:6:3, S);
```

S will come out to be at least six characters long again, flushed right as necessary, but with always three decimal places and a decimal point. If *L* is 1.2345, *S* will come out ' 1.235', with a single space at the left to pad the length to six and the decimal portion rounded to the third decimal point.

Instead of using the *Str* procedure, however, you're going to write your own code to translate reals into strings. This block of code will be the longest you have written to this point in this book, and will illustrate a number of important programming issues.

Here are the procedures you'll take:

- First, convert *L* using *Str* into a string *Scientific* with 10 digits after the decimal point. (10 digits is the default returned by *Str*.)

- *Str* will make the first character of *Scientific* negative if it is a negative number or blank if it is positive. If it *is* negative, note that in the Boolean *Negate*.

- Delete the first character of *Scientific*.

- The decimal point in *Scientific* will be followed with 10 digits, but zeroes immediately to the left of E are not significant (1.2030000000E10 is the same as 1.203E10—the zeroes in between '3' and 'E' are meaningless), so delete those.

- Read *Scientific* from left to right and put any digit into your conversion string *Converted*. Stop when you hit the 'E'.

- The number after the 'E' is the exponent. Convert that to an integer *Exponent*.

- *Str* puts the decimal at position two in the string. If you add 2 to *Exponent*, you have the location that the decimal place should actually go in *Converted*.

- If this location is greater than the length of *Converted*, that tells you your number is too small and you need to add zeroes on the end.

- If this location is less than 1, that tells you your number is too big, and you need to add zeroes on to the beginning.

- If the location of the decimal point is still past the end, don't insert it. (This prevents returns like "1000.".)

- If *Converted* is too big to fit in *Entry*, return *Scientific*; otherwise, return *Converted*.

That's a lot of steps. Go through the steps again, this time while coding the routine. Start by declaring your variables:

```
function StrFn(L: Real): String;
var
   Sc, Scientific, Converted, Digit : String;
   I, Exponent                      : Integer;
   Negate                           : Boolean;
```

First, you convert *L* using *Str*.

```
begin
   Str(L, Scientific);
   Sc := Scientific;
```

(Notice that I added a variable *Sc* here and following. You're going to be altering *Scientific* a bit, but there is some possibility you'll need the straight output of *Str*, so I stored the value in the variable *Sc*.)

Now, check to see if *L* is negative and save that, then delete the first character of *Scientific*.

```
   If Copy(Scientific,1,1) = '-' then Negate := true
   else Negate := false;
   Delete(Scientific, 1,1);
```

Now, you're going to get rid of trailing zeroes that *Str* puts in *Scientific* to the left of the E. The routine used to locate the letter 'E' is a built-in function called *Pos*.

```
   I := Pos('E', Scientific);
```

Pos returns the location of the first string ('E') in the second string (*Scientific*) if it's there, or zero if it isn't. It always will be there, of course, since *Str* will always put an 'E' into a string converted from a real. In fact, *Str* always puts the E in the same place, so you could just figure out where and set *I* to that number.

I prefer to use *Pos* because if you were to set *I* to 13 (knowing that that was where the "E" ends up), for example, and later found a bug in the function, you might change *Scientific* again and forget you were counting on the position of E being 13, thus introducing another bug into the code. The *Pos* function will always be right.

Next, check for zeroes to the left of the E and delete them.

```
   dec(I);
   while (Copy(Scientific,I,1)='0') do
   begin
      Delete(Scientific, I, 1);
      dec(I);
   end;
```

Now, you're going to read what remains in *Scientific* from left to right and take the digits out to form a new number. One of the easiest things to forget at this point is that *Converted* is undefined—it could be anything, because you haven't initialized it.

```
Converted := '';
```

Starting at position 1, move from left to right and put the digits found into *Converted*. Stop when you get to the E.

```
I := 1;
repeat
   Digit := Copy(Scientific, I, 1);
   If (Digit<>'.') and (Digit<>'E')
      then Converted := Converted + Digit;
   inc(I);
until (Digit = 'E');
```

I is now one position past the E, directly at the start of the exponent. Convert that to a number.

```
Val(Copy(Scientific, I, 5), Exponent, I); {Longest exponent is -4932}
```

Notice that the *Copy* routine takes the five characters after E. There usually won't *be* five characters after the E. Five is the maximum number. So what happens if you use *Copy* to take more characters than are there? The *Copy* routine just returns what is there. In other words, this line could just as well have been:

```
Val(Copy(Scientific, I, 255), Exponent, I);
```

because you know that the exponent is the last thing in the number.

Str places the decimal in the second position of the string, and the exponent tells you how far to the right or left to move the decimal. This is expressed easily.

```
I := Exponent + 2;
```

There's a chance that the number you have built in *Converted* is too small (like 43 when *L* is 4300) or too large (like 43 when *L* is .0043) so you can't just insert the decimal point. You need to add zeroes.

```
while I > Length(Converted)+1 do Converted := Converted + '0';
while I < 1 do
begin
   Inc(I);
   Converted := '0' + Converted;
end;
```

Finally, if the decimal place isn't at the end of the number, put it in.

```
If I <= Length(Converted) then Insert('.', Converted, I);
```

Insert is a built-in procedure that inserts the first string ('.') into the second string (*Converted*) at position *I*.

Finally, add back the negative sign if necessary. If *Converted* is too big, return *Sc* (the unchanged *Scientific*), otherwise return *Converted*.

```
    If Negate then Converted := '-' + Converted;
    If Length(Converted) > 17 then StrFn := Sc
       else StrFn := Converted;
end;
```

This, in miniature, is what it is like to design and implement programs. As mentioned earlier, you'll learn about this process in more detail in Chapter 22, "Better by Design," but as your programs get longer and more complex, you'll have to start thinking more before typing and mousing.

Part of the process of implementation, however, is finding out what has been done for you already. In the preceding example, I used two Pascal routines *Pos* and *Insert* that you had never used before, as well as *Str*, *Copy*, *Val*, *Delete*, and *Length*. If those routines didn't exist—or if you just didn't know about them—you would have to code them.

You'll get to know many of the standard routines quite well in the pages of this book, and touch on many more. But when programming on your own, you'll want to browse through the help files— particularly the help for "System Unit" which contains what I've been calling the "built-in" routines— to see which routines you can use.

Now finish up "CALCREAL" with some minor changes to make it even more useful. Delete the "mod" button—you can't use it with real data types anyway. Shrink the *Equal* key and move it to the right so that you can squeeze a decimal button next to the zero.

Your calculator now should look like figure 13.4.

Figure 13.4

The CALCREAL program, complete!

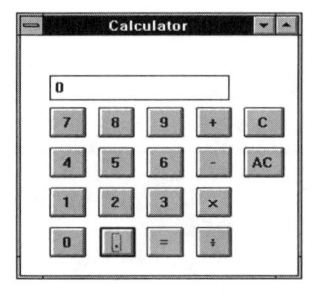

Now, add the code for the decimal point button (call it *Decimal*). It's pretty much like the code for any of the digit buttons, with one exception:

```
If Complete then Entry.Text := '';
If Pos('.', Entry.Text) = 0 then
   Entry.Text := Entry.Text + '.';
```

You first check to see if there is a decimal point already in *Entry.Text*. A number can have only one decimal point.

Chapter 13 ♦ Pascal Math

Operator Precedence

Although you've crafted a fairly complex program, you've actually only done very simple math up to this point. Before moving on to the next chapter, you need to look at the issue of *operator precedence*. To what values do you suppose the following steps will set the integer variables I, J, K, and L?

```
I := 1 + 2 - 3;
J := 1 - 2 + 3;
K := 1 * 2 + 3;
L := 1 + 2 * 3;
```

I is 0, *J* is 2, and *K* is 5. *L*, on the other hand, is 7! This may surprise you—it always surprises me. When I read an equation, I calculate from left to right. 1 plus 2 is 3. 3 times 3 is 9. So, where did 7 come from?

The answer lies in the fact that Pascal does not calculate from left to right, but according to rules of *operator precedence*. According to these rules, multiplication always is performed first. 2 times 3 is 6. 6 plus 1 is 7. Table 13.7 shows the order in which Pascal calculates expressions.

Table 13.7. Operator precedence—the order in which an expression is evaluated.

Operators	Precedence
not, + sign, - sign	1st (highest)
*, /, div, mod, and	2nd
+ (add), - (subtract), or, xor	3rd
=, <>, <, >, <=, >=	4th (lowest)

Notice that the plus and minus signs are different from the addition and subtraction operators.

To get a feel for this, open a new project and try out some of these operators. You can use `Writeln` and the WinCRT unit in a project to rig a simple test. Once you understand that expressions are not calculated from left to right, however, I don't recommend that you memorize the preceding table.

Instead, I encourage you to use parentheses to force the order of evaluation that you want. So, instead of wondering or trying to remember whether in

```
K := 1 + 2 * 3;
```

K is going to be 7 or 9, just separate off the part of the formula you want done first with parentheses:

```
K := (1 + 2) * 3;
```

so that you *know* that K equals 9.

You've been using parentheses since Chapter 10, "On One Condition," to help simplify complex logic statements. I recommend that you use them anytime there is a chance of ambiguity.

Summary

There are five operators that work with integers; they perform addition (+), subtraction (-), multiplication (*), division (div), and remainders (mod). An expression consists of an operator and one or more operands. Pascal evaluates expressions using the data type of the first operand, but never in a type smaller than integer.

Real types are capable of expressing much larger—and also much smaller—numbers than can be expressed with integers. The five real data types are real, single, double, extended, and comp. Comp is an oddity because it only deals with very large integers (positive and negative). The real types only consider a certain number of digits significant. The real operators are +, -, *, and /. Pascal usually expresses real numbers, regardless of their size, in scientific notation. Scientific notation consists of a significand (typically a number greater than or equal to zero and less than two) and an exponent.

The concept of *operator precedence* means that expressions in Pascal are not evaluated from left to right. Instead, some operations are done before others. Operator precedence can be essentially ignored through the liberal use of parentheses, which force evaluations to be done in a specific order.

Pascal provides a number of built-in routines to work with integer and real numbers. Built-in routines can have optional parameters and the same routine can work with completely different data types. A built-in function can return completely different data types depending on what is passed to it. Pascal does not allow you, however, to write new functions and procedures like this.

The *Pos* function locates a substring within a string, or returns zero if the substring isn't there. The *Insert* function inserts a string into another string at a specified location. The *Copy* function (which you've examined before) works even if you tell it to copy past the end of a string.

Pascal has an evaluate/modify dialog that allows viewing and changing variables. The Tab order of objects on a form can be changed through the *TabIndex* property.

Chapter 13 ♦ Pascal Math

Review Questions

1. What are the five integer operators?
2. Which operator do the integer types have that the real types don't?
3. What is the evaluate/modify dialog used for?
4. What does the *TabIndex* property do?
5. Name two of the integer routines, what they do, and how they could be expressed in Pascal code.
6. Name the five real types. Which one isn't really "real"?
7. Name a real function. What does it do?
8. What is scientific notation? What separates the two components of a number expressed in scientific notation?
9. What value does this number have?

    ```
    1.245E-10
    ```

10. Express this number in scientific notation:

    ```
    5,721,062,400,000
    ```

11. What does *Pos* do?
12. What does *Insert* do?
13. What is operator precedence and what impact does it have on programmers? How do you circumvent operator precedence?
14. What would S, a string variable, be set to by this:

    ```
    S := Copy('1234567890', 8, 255);
    ```

15. Name a subroutine that works with both real and integer data types. How is it called and what does it do?
16. What is an expression? What is it made up of?
17. Can a variable be an operand? What about a function? A procedure?
18. What value will C have at the end of the following code?

```
var
   A, B: Byte;
   C   : Longint;
begin
   A := 255;
   B := 255;
   C := B * A;
end.
```

What about this code?

```
var
   A, B: Byte;
   C   : Longint;
begin
   A := 100;
   B := 200;
   C := B - A;
end.
```

Why?

19. Can a built-in routine accept completely different types for the same parameters? Can a built-in function return different types depending on the parameters it is passed? Can you code routines in Pascal that do this?

20. What are the names of the two components of a number expressed in scientific notation? Why is the comp type not considered an integer?

21. What steps would you take to give a button a caption of [ASCII233], the greek letter *theta*?

Review Exercises

1. In the previous chapter's *"For* Loop Limitations" section, the Gauge controls were incremented through temporary variables this way:

```
    K := 0; L := 0;
    for J := 1 to 10 do
begin
    K := K + 10;
    Gauge2.Progress := K;
    for I := 1 to 10 do
        begin
            L := L + 10;
            Gauge1.Progress := L;
        end;
end;
```

Using the multiplication operator (*) you can set the two gauges' Progress properties without using K and L. Make the necessary changes for this to work. (Hint: Use the values of the control variables, multiplied by 10, to set the gauges.)

2. Make a simple program that allows the user to enter two whole numbers and shows the result of the division of those two numbers using the "/" operator *and* the "div" and "mod" operators. So, if the user entered 10 and 3, you would have one label showing "Answer: 3.333333" and another showing "Answer: 3 with a remainder of 1".

3. One thing not discussed in this chapter is division by zero. A number divided by zero has no result in modern math. In both the calculator programs and the previous two exercises, make sure that no code like this:

```
x div y
```

or this

```
x / y
```

is executed if Y is zero.

4. Redo the calculator program this way: Have two entry fields and a label lined up in a row, and have a row beneath that row with the real operators described as captions on push buttons. The program should let the user enter numbers into the entry fields, and then calculate the label's caption based on which push button the user presses.

5. Embellish the calculator program to do math functions like *ArcTan* and *Cos*. (Don't do this exercise if you don't know the meaning of those functions, or if you don't know how a regular calculator with those capabilities behaves.)

Part V

Additional Data Types

CHAPTER 14

User-Defined Types and Enumeration

So far you've looked at chars, strings, Booleans, the five integer types, and the five real types. Pascal has many more data types than these. In fact, Pascal has an infinite number of data types, which is possible because Pascal enables you to create your own data types to fit whatever programs you write.

Say that you are writing a program that plays cards. You might have some code that looks like the following:

```
case Rank of
   1          : {an ace}   Value := 11;
   11, 12, 13 : {Face card}Value := 10;
   . . .
```

This code would be considerably easier to read if you didn't have to use numbers to indicate card ranks:

```
case Rank of
   Ace              : Value := 1;
   Jack, Queen, King : Value := 10;
   . . .
```

Additionally, suppose you have a subroutine that works with the rank and suit (spade, heart, diamond, or club) of a card:

```
procedure CardProc(Rank, Suit: Integer);
```

Because you are mentally making the translation from an integer to the rank and suit values, the compiler doesn't know the difference, and it becomes possible to make a mistake such as calling CardProc with the rank and suit reversed:

```
CardProc(1,13);
```

There are only four suits, so 13 couldn't possibly be right. But if you're deep enough into the program, making this mistake would be easy. What if you could declare CardProc like

```
procedure CardProc(ARank: Rank; ASuit: Suit);
```

so that the compiler would catch

```
CardProc(Clubs, King);
```

as a type mismatch error?

In Pascal, you can do so through *user-defined data types*. User-defined data types are types that you create to fit a particular need.

Enumerated Types

The word *enumerate* means "to name one by one; to specify as in a list." Enumeration is one way to create a user-defined data type. Any time you have one or more variables that can have a set number of specific values (called *elements*), you can create an enumerated type.

In the card game example suggested in the preceding section, both rank and suit are good candidates for enumeration. Rank would have 13 elements, and suit would have four.

Other good candidates for enumeration might be months (12 elements), days of the week (7 elements), or even states of the United States of America (50 elements).

Declaring a User-Defined Data Type

A Pascal program consists of several parts: a program declaration (optional), a var section (also optional), and a main block of code (denoted with begin and end.). In addition, a Pascal program can have another section, devoted to declaring the user-defined data types for the program. You start this section with the keyword type.

In a traditional Pascal program, the type section is included only once, before the var section:

```
program Example;
type
   . . .
var
   . . .
begin
   . . .
end.
```

In a Pascal program, however, you can have the type section many times, before and after the var section:

```
program Example;
type
   . . .
var
   . . .
type
   . . .
begin
   . . .
end.
```

As with the variables, all types must be declared before use—that is, before the var block in which you declare variables of those types.

Type identifiers are subject to the same restrictions as all other identifiers. To denote a type, you begin with the name of that type followed by an equal sign:

```
MyType = . . .
```

What follows depends on what kind of type you want to declare. For enumerated types, the equal sign is followed by a list of the type's elements, separated by commas and enclosed in parentheses:

```
type
   Suit = (Spades, Hearts, Diamonds, Clubs);
   Rank = (Ace, Two, Three, Four, Five, Six, Seven, Eight, Nine, Ten,
   ↪Jack, Queen, King)
```

The elements of an enumerated type are also identifiers and are subject to the same restrictions as type and variable identifiers. For that reason, Rank cannot be written as follows:

```
Rank = (Ace, 2, 3, 4, 5, 6, 7, 8, 9, 10, Jack, Queen, King);
```

2, 3, 4, 5, 6, 7, 8, 9, and 10 are not valid identifiers. If you don't want to spell out the names, you can put an identifying initial in front of the number, as follows:

```
Rank = (Ace, R2, R3, R4, R5, R6, R7, R8, R9, R10, Jack, Queen, King);
```

Here are some other examples:

```
DayOfWeek = (Sunday, Monday, Tuesday, Wednesday, Thursday, Friday,
↪Saturday);
Month = (Jan, Feb, Mar, Apr, May, Jun, Jul, Aug, Sep, Oct, Nov, Dec);
Titles = (Mr, Mrs, Miss, Ms, Dr, Sir, Honorable);
```

Unfortunately, there is no way to get a string description of an enumerated data type. If S is a string, the following doesn't work:

```
Str(Spades, S);   {This won't work!}
```

Chapter 14 ♦ User-Defined Types and Enumeration

This line doesn't work because the enumerations are used to check types—so that you, the programmer, don't use the wrong type calling the wrong procedure—and as a way to make the code easier to read. Delphi drops the element names as soon as the program compiles.

You declare a variable of a user-defined data type just as you would declare a variable of a `string` or `integer` type. In the `var` section, you add the following:

```
var
    Card1Rank, Card2Rank : Rank;
    Card1Suit, Card2Suit : Suit;
    Day                  : DayOfWeek;
```

The Pascal compiler handles type checking. That's a big part of the reason to use enumerated types. If we had the above `type` and `var` declarations, the compiler wouldn't allow the following line:

```
Card1Rank := Card1Suit;
```

(It would allow this if both variables were integers.) The compiler does allow the following, of course:

```
Card1Rank := Card2Rank;
Card1Suit := Card2Suit;
```

Ordination

Enumerated types are ordinal. By putting elements into a list, you are expressing an order. You therefore can code something like this:

```
If Ace > King then . . .
```

This type of coding is often useless. In the definition of rank, `Ace` comes before `King` and is therefore less than `King`. In a real card game, the Ace may be lower or higher than the King, depending on the rules of the game being played.

Sometimes it can be handy, though. If you have an enumerated type called `Condition`,

```
Condition = (Trivial, Minor, SemiImportant, Important, Critical, Fatal);
```

and two variables, `Situation1` and `Situation2` of that type, you can code something like the following:

```
If Situation1 > Situation2 then HandleSituation1First
else HandleSitutation2First;
```

One of the advantages of using an enumerated type is that as long as you refer to the elements by name only, such as

```
case Card1Suit of
   Spades: . . .
   Hearts: . . .
   Clubs: . . .
   Diamonds: . . .
end;
```

it really doesn't matter whether `Suit` is declared

```
Suit = (Spades, Hearts, Diamonds, Clubs);
```

or

```
Suit = (Clubs, Diamonds, Hearts, Spades);
```

When you store everything as an integer and try to keep track in your head that "King is a 13" and "Ace is a 1," then if you decide later that you want Ace to be represented by 14 instead of 1, you have to change all the parts of your program that are based on Ace being 1. With enumerated types, you can rearrange elements or even add new elements without having to change other relevant code:

```
Suit = (Spades, Hearts, Diamonds, Clubs, Moons, Stars, Clovers, Horse
➥shoes);
```

Because enumerated types are ordinal, you can use them in `Case` statements, as you have seen. You can also use them in `for` loops. For example,

```
For ASuit := Spades to Horseshoes do SomeProcedure(ASuit);
```

This capability is sometimes very useful.

Ord

Several of the routines discussed in the preceding chapter dealt with ordinals, not just integers. Enumerated types are ordinals, so you can use `Dec`, `Inc`, `Pred`, and `Succ` with enumerated types. Given the previous declaration of `Rank`,

```
Succ(Jack)
```

returns `Queen`. If variable `R` has the value `King`,

```
Inc(R)
```

results in a range-check error because `King` is the highest value that `R` can hold. Here you see another advantage of the enumerated type. Using a regular integer to express rank can legally result in a card having a rank of -40 or 123.

Especially useful with enumerated types is the `Ord` function. The `Ord` function returns the ordinal value of any type. Using the previous declaration of `Rank`,

Chapter 14 ♦ User-Defined Types and Enumeration

```
Ord(Ace)
```

returns zero. The ordinal value of the first element in an enumerated type is always zero. The second element is one, the third is two, and so on. These ordinal values are, in fact, the ones used in the compiled program. In other words,

```
R := Ace;
```

is identical to coding

```
R := 0;
```

except that in the latter case you don't get the type checking, range checking, and improved readability. Enumerated types exist to make the programmer's life easier.

You might think that using Ord is a bad idea, and you are basically correct. After all, the whole point of enumerated types is to use descriptive identifiers rather than plain numbers—numbers that can mean anything. However, some programmers use Ord to shortcut certain tasks. Using Rank as an example again,

```
Rank = (Ace, Two, Three, Four, Five, Six, Seven, Eight, Nine, Ten, Jack,
↪Queen, King)
```

you might have code to convert these into numeric values:

```
case R of
   Ten, Jack, Queen, King     : Value : = 10;
   Ace                        : Value : =  1;
   Two                        : Value : =  2;
   Three                      : Value : =  3;
   Four                       : Value : =  4;
   Five                       : Value : =  5;
   Six                        : Value : =  6;
   Seven                      : Value : =  7;
   Eight                      : Value : =  8;
   Nine                       : Value : =  9;
end;
```

Instead of all this coding, you can use Ord to shortcut the process:

```
Case R of
   King, Queen, Jack, Ten    : Value := 10;
   Ace .. Nine               : Value := Ord(R) + 1;
end;
```

Note: The subrange punctuation (..) works with enumerated types the same as it does with integers and chars. (See "A Special *Case*," Chapter 11.)

Using Ord definitely saves some typing. However, if for some reason you change the order of the elements in Rank—say, putting Ace after King—you introduce a bug into your code that might be hard to find.

Subrange Types

After you declare an enumerated type, you can create another type that is a *subrange* of it. In other words, given the rather unconventional suits described here:

```
Type
    Suit = (Spades, Hearts, Diamonds, Clubs, Moons, Stars, Clovers,
    Horseshoes);
```

you can then make another type that consists of only the more conventional suits:

```
Type
    Suit = (Spades, Hearts, Diamonds, Clubs, Moons, Stars, Clovers,
    Horseshoes);
    StandardSuits = Spades..Clubs;
```

The .. punctuation indicates the boundaries of your new type. StandardSuits is a type that allows suits from Spades to Clubs only.

You can make a subrange from any ordinal type. In fact, they're probably most useful when used with the integer or char types.

```
type
    LegalRange = -100 .. 100;
    Letters    = 'A'..'Z';
    LowerCase  = 'a'..'z';
    Numerals   = '0'..'9';
```

Radio Buttons and the Group Box

The Pascal data types are interesting in that they can usually be illustrated very well with a specific kind of control. Edit controls, for example, illustrate the concept of strings. Gauges (and the spin buttons and sliders from the Visual Solutions Pack) illustrate how integers work. The switch illustrates the Boolean data type perfectly. Enumerated types are no exception. They are illustrated well through *radio buttons*.

You can find the radio button control on the Standard page of the Component Bar. When selected, this button looks like a circle with a black dot in the middle of it. An unselected radio button looks like an empty circle. When you select one radio button, the previously selected radio button deselects. You can select only one radio button at any time.

Chapter 14 ♦ User-Defined Types and Enumeration

Start a new project and place three of these radio buttons on the form. (This exercise is just to illustrate a point; don't worry about what to call anything.) Run the program, and you should have something that looks like figure 14.1.

Figure 14.1

Example radio buttons.

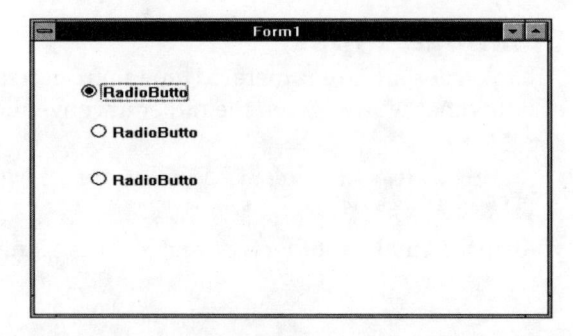

These buttons are called radio buttons because car radios used to work this way. You pushed a button for one channel; then, if you pushed another, the previous one popped up. Exactly one radio button is always selected. The analogy is somewhat lost in more modern cars where the buttons on the radio don't go down at all, but it still holds true that the radio is always tuned to exactly one station. The property that tells you whether a specific radio button is checked is a Boolean property called Checked.

What if you want to make another set of radio buttons? Drag three more radio buttons onto the form, directly to the right of the first three. Try running this modified form. Notice that these three buttons are lumped in with the previous three. In other words, instead of two groups of three, you have one group of six.

Delphi provides another control, the *group box*, that allows radio buttons to be treated as different sets. The group box is represented by a square with three horizontal lines in it and a shaded area at the top part of the box. You can use group boxes as a decorative or informative border around a group of controls, but you must use them to separate sets of radio buttons.

Remove the radio buttons from the form and place two group boxes down, side by side. Then put three radio buttons in each box, sizing as necessary.

> **Caution:** You must lay down the group box first, before the radio buttons, and you must place the radio buttons inside the group box. This order creates a special relationship between the group box and the radio buttons. To see if you've done this procedure correctly, try to move the radio button outside the group box. The radio button seems to vanish as you try to drag it over the group box border.
>
> To move controls from the form to a group box after you have laid them down, choose **Cut** or **Copy** from the Edit menu to remove or copy the current controls selected into the Clipboard. Then select the group box and choose **Paste** from the Edit menu to place them "in" the group box.
>
> If you do this, be aware that controls are positioned the same distance from the top and left borders of the group box as they were from the form. In other words, if the control was in the lower-right corner, you may not be able to see it without first adjusting its Left and Top properties. More on this later.

The group box is said to be the "parent" of the controls inside it. These controls are called the group box's "children" or "child controls." You cannot move the controls outside of the group box borders, nor can you cause a child to draw anything outside its parent's borders. If you move a group box, all the child controls move along with it. If you delete a group box, all the child controls are deleted.

Controls in a group box have `Left`, `Top`, and `TabIndex` properties, which refer to their relationship with the group box and not the form. In other words, if you put a radio button at the top-left edge of the group box so that it covers the group box's caption and part of the frame, you find that `Left` and `Top` are both zero. If you move the group box, you discover that although the group box's `Left` and `Top` properties change (in relationship to the form), the same properties in the child controls (which are in relationship to the group box) do not change.

Similarly, a control in a group box may have a `TabIndex` of zero; it is the first control in that group. The `TabIndex` property of the group box itself determines the order in which the controls of the group box are selected relative to the controls on the rest of the form. For example, say that you have a group box with the three controls, where the group box has a tab index of 7 and the three controls have tab indexes of 0, 1, and 2. You can think of the tab indexes for those controls as being 7.0, 7.1, and 7.2 relative to the form.

Now, if you try out this form, you find that you can make one selection from each of the two groups. You may also notice that you can't get from one group to the other by using the keyboard.

Chapter 14 ◆ User-Defined Types and Enumeration

You've already learned how the `TabIndex` property can change the tab order—the order in which the tab and the cursor keys select items. Another property called `TabStop` is set to `True` if the user can use the Tab key to get to that control. Buttons automatically have this property set to `True`, so you've never had to think about it before. Radio buttons, by default, have the `TabStop` property set to `False`.

By custom, the first element of a group should be a tab stop, whereas other elements of the group should simply be selectable by the arrow keys. Tab, in other words, should move the user from group to group, not from control to control. Select the topmost radio buttons of each group and change the `TabStop` property to `True`. The two groups should now work with the Tab and arrow keys.

> **Note:** Customs are not always clear-cut regarding which controls should be tab stops. Figure 14.2 shows a typical form containing an entry field, a list box, and several buttons. In some programs, pressing Tab when the cursor is on the OK button takes you back to the input line, and you must use the arrow keys to move from button to button. In other programs, pressing the Tab key moves the cursor from the OK button to the Yes button to the No button to the Cancel button and finally back to the entry field.
>
> Using the Tab key or the arrow keys may seem like a trivial point to you. But if you make the wrong choice here, you can affect the users' opinion of the entire program. So which should you use? Only your users can tell you that for sure.

Figure 14.2
A Tab stop dilemma.

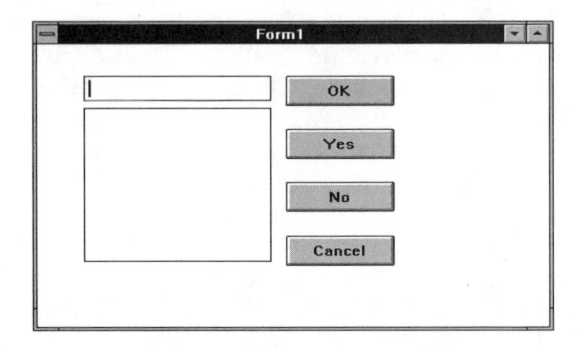

Save the project radio buttons project we've been playing with as RSP and save the form unit as RSPForm.

The Radio Group

Delphi comes with a component that eases creating a group of just radio buttons. (The preceding discussion of groups can be applied to a group box that contains *any* kind of component.) This component, the TRadioGroup object, has an Items property which you edit from the Object Inspector. Press on the "—" that appears directly to the right of the Items property when selected in the Object Inspector. Delphi will pop up a simple dialog box that allows you to enter a number of strings.

To create a list of items for your radio group, enter the strings that you want to appear, and from that list the radio group object creates and arranges the radio buttons evenly spaced within its own bounds. It won't automatically arrange them in multiple columns if they get too crowded vertically, but you can directly control the number of columns through the Columns property.

Note that in this case, you never add a radio button to the form—the radio group creates the radio buttons itself based on the strings that you enter. That's important because it means you can't actually move the radio buttons around individually. The entire group must be taken as a whole. It also means you can't ask for the state of a specific radio button to find out which is checked.

Instead, the radio group has an ItemIndex property that contains the number of the element that's currently selected. This can actually be a perfect mirror of an enumerated type in a situation where you have a type like this:

```
type
    Suit = (Clubs, Diamonds, Hearts, Spades);
```

Now, the ItemIndex property will exactly match the ordinal values of the enumerated types. So you could do something like:

```
var ASuit: Suit;
. . .
case AGroupBox.ItemIndex of
    Ord(Clubs): ASuit := Clubs;
    Ord(Diamonds): ASuit := Diamonds;
    Ord(Hearts): ASuit := Hearts;
    Ord(Spades): ASuit := Spades;
    end;
```

And, you could even take advantage of an Object Pascal feature called *typecasting*. Typecasting allows you to circumvent Pascal's strong typing features by telling the compiler to "treat this as a (whatever) regardless of what you think it is." To typecast, you simply enclose the variable that you want to treat differently with parentheses, and precede it with the name of the type, as in:

```
AType(AVariableOfADifferentType);
```

Typecasting is generally a bad idea, since the whole point of type checking is to prevent the problems that arise from confusing types. However, used judiciously, it can streamline code. The preceding suit example could become

```
var ASuit: Suit;
. . .
case Suit(AGroupBox.ItemIndex) of
    Clubs: ASuit := Clubs;
    Diamonds: ASuit := Diamonds;
    Hearts: ASuit := Hearts;
    Spades: ASuit := Spades;
    end;
```

or even just:

```
var ASuit: Suit;
. . .
ASuit := Suit(AGroupBox.ItemIndex);
```

Example: Rock-Scissors-Paper

Bring back up the RSP project and its form (RSPForm). Then change the three radio buttons in each box to have the captions Rock, Scissors, and Paper. (Observe that you can select controls from only one group box at a time. Delphi does not let you select the two top radio buttons and rename them at the same time.) Change the Checked property of the two Rock radio buttons to be True.

> **Note:** In general, one radio button in a group of radio buttons should always be checked. When you add radio buttons to a form, Delphi has no way of knowing which one you want set. Select the one you do want checked and change the Checked property to True. Radio buttons will not act correctly if no items are checked or if more than one item is checked.

Change the Name property of the three radio buttons on the left to YourRock, YourScissors, and YourPaper. Then change the Name property of the buttons on the right to MyRock, MyScissors, and MyPaper. Next, change the caption of the box on the left to read Your Choice, and change the one on the right to read My Choice.

You're going to turn this program into the venerable Rock-Scissors-Paper game, which is sometimes used by children (and others) to settle disputes. In the real-world game, two contestants hold out their fists and shake them, once, twice, and on the third time hold out one of three hand formations: A bunched fist is a rock; the index and middle finger extended toward the opponent with the rest of the fingers tucked into the palm (like a peace sign aimed at the opponent) is scissors; the palm flat and facing down is paper. The winner is determined based on three simple rules: rock crushes scissors; scissors cuts paper; paper covers rock.

You're going to streamline this action a bit. When the user clicks on a radio button, that button is his choice of rock, scissors, or paper. The computer randomly selects its own choice, and the program then determines the winner.

To make this game more interesting, put a label at the top of the form telling who won, a label at the bottom explaining why that person won, and three labels on the side reporting the number of games played and wins and losses for both players. Call these labels Message, Why, Games, You, and Me. Set the Caption property of Message to a null string, since you don't want to display any message at the beginning of a game. Your form should look like the one shown in figure 14.3.

Figure 14.3

The Rock-Scissors-Paper form.

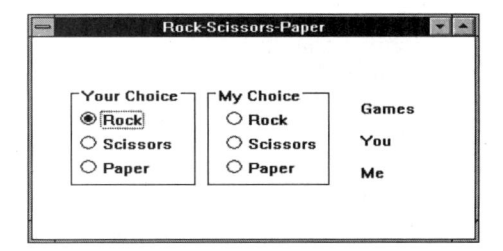

What are the variables for this program? You need one each to keep track of the games played, the user's wins, and the computer's wins. Place these variable declarations after the following Pascal-generated lines:

```
var
    Form1: TForm1;
```

Find the preceding lines and add the following:

```
GamesPlayed, YourWins, MyWins: Longint;
```

As with the calculator programs, you need to initialize these lines somewhere. Do that in the RSP project code window, right after the begin.

Next, find these lines:

```
program Rsp;

uses
  Forms,
  Rspform in 'RSPForm.PAS' {Form1};

begin
```

Then add the following:

```
Randomize;
GamesPlayed := 0;
YourWins := 0;
MyWins := 0;
```

Chapter 14 ◆ User-Defined Types and Enumeration

If you're going to use `Randomize`, calling it at the beginning of the program is best. Doing so sets up all the calls to `Random` used anywhere in the program.

These steps are easy enough. But you're not quite ready to code. To begin, you need two user-defined data types. In RSPForm, find this block:

```
var
    Form1: TForm1;
    GamesPlayed, YourWins, MyWins: Longint;
```

Then add the following code right *before* the preceding var block:

```
type
    RockScissorsPaper = (Rock, Scissors, Paper);
    ResultType       = (IWin, YouWin, Tie);
```

Just as with variable declaration, it doesn't really matter where you put this block of code, as long as the types are set up before any variables of that type are declared. So you can have the following:

```
var
    Form1: TForm1;
    GamesPlayed, YourWins, MyWins: Longint;

type
    RockScissorsPaper = (Rock, Scissors, Paper);
    ResultType       = (IWin, YouWin, Tie);
var
    WhoWon                : ResultType;
```

or this:

```
type
    RockScissorsPaper = (Rock, Scissors, Paper);
    ResultType       = (IWin, YouWin, Tie);

var
    Form1: TForm1;
    GamesPlayed, YourWins, MyWins: Longint;
    WhoWon                : ResultType;
```

But you cannot have the following:

```
var
    Form1: TForm1;
    GamesPlayed, YourWins, MyWins: Longint;
    WhoWon                : ResultType;   {No! Delphi doesn't know
                                            about ResultType yet!}
type
    RockScissorsPaper = (Rock, Scissors, Paper);
    ResultType       = (IWin, YouWin, Tie);
```

274

In the preceding example, `WhoWon` is declared before Delphi is told what `ResultType` is. As a result, the compiler will stop on that line.

Now you're ready to code. Start by double-clicking on the `YourRock` radio button. Delphi sets up the familiar code frame. Before you type anything, however, go back to the Object Inspector, select `YourScissors`, and set its clicked event to `YourRockClick`. Do the same thing with `YourPaper`. This way, they all call the same routine.

Think about the steps you have to take to implement this routine:

1. Declare the variables.

2. Figure out which radio button the user clicked.

3. Click on a radio button for the computer.

4. Figure out who won.

5. Change `Message` to tell who won. Increment the winner's win counts.

6. Explain why the winner won.

7. Update `Games`, `Me`, and `You` to accurately reflect the new count.

You should be able to code this program by using what you have learned up to this point in the book. If you were to go off and write this procedure, however, you would probably do some things differently than I did. That's perfectly okay. Keep in mind when you read the following code that how you do something is a matter of style and experience, but two people can take an entirely different approach to a problem and both can be right.

First, declare the variables (this code all goes in the `YourRockClick` method):

```
var WinType,
    UserChoice, MyChoice: RockScissorsPaper;
    I                  : Integer;
    Result             : ResultType;
```

Next, figure out which radio button was clicked:

```
begin
   If YourRock.Checked then UserChoice := Rock
   else If YourScissors.Checked then UserChoice := Scissors
   else UserChoice := Paper;
```

Click on a radio button for the computer:

```
MyChoice := Rock;
for I := 1 to 100 do
begin
   If MyChoice = Paper then MyChoice := Rock
   else MyChoice := Succ(MyChoice);
   case MyChoice of
```

Chapter 14 ♦ User-Defined Types and Enumeration

```
      Rock    : MyRock.Checked := true;
      Scissors: MyScissors.Checked := true;
      Paper   : MyPaper.Checked := true;
   end;
   Update;
   If Random(10) = 0 then break;
end;
```

The approach I've taken here is not one that everyone would take. I start out the computer's choice as Rock. Then I have it cycle through the possibilities 100 times, checking the appropriate radio button every time: rock, scissors, paper, rock, scissors, paper. (This approach creates a flickering effect in the group as buttons are selected and deselected.) Then, so that the choice is random, I put in some code to randomly break out of the loop.

> **Note:** The computer's choice could have been made in myriad ways, many far more efficient than the code here—for example, selecting a random number from zero to two. I picked this way because I like the effect it creates.

The next step is to figure out who won (here is another place where my approach might differ from the average):

```
case UserChoice of
   Rock    : case MyChoice of
      Rock    : Result := Tie;
      Scissors: Result := YouWin;
      Paper   : Result := IWin;
      end;
   Scissors: case MyChoice of
      Rock    : Result := IWin;
      Scissors: Result := Tie;
      Paper   : Result := YouWin;
      end;
   Paper   : case MyChoice of
      Rock    : Result := YouWin;
      Scissors: Result := IWin;
      Paper   : Result := Tie;
      end;
end;
```

It's usually a bad idea to nest Case statements as shown here. Keeping track of which choices go with which Case statement can be hard. However, in a situation where both Case statements are very simple, such as in the preceding code, this structure is very clear. The following is an alternative approach:

```
If MyChoice = UserChoice then Result := Tie
else case UserChoice of
   Paper   : If MyChoice = Scissors then Result := IWin
             else Result := YouWin;
   Scissors: If MyChoice = Rock then Result := IWin
             else Result := YouWin;
   Rock    : If MyChoice = Paper then Result := IWin
             else Result := YouWin;
   end;
```

Or you can abandon the `Case` statement altogether, like this:

```
If MyChoice = UserChoice then Result := Tie
else If (MyChoice = Scissors) then
begin
   If UserChoice = Paper then Result := IWin
   else Result := YouWin;
end
else If (MyChoice = Paper) then
begin
   If UserChoice = Rock then Result := IWin
   else Result := YouWin
end
else If (MyChoice = Rock) then
begin
   If UserChoice = Scissors then Result := IWin
   else Result := YouWin;
end;
```

You can even code without using `Begin-End` blocks by having complex `If-Then` statements:

```
If (UserChoice = MyChoice) then Result := Tie
else if (((MyChoice = Rock) and (UserChoice = Scissors))
    or  ((MyChoice = Scissors) and (UserChoice = Paper))
    or  ((MyChoice = Paper) and (UserChoice = Rock)))
    then Result := IWin
else Result := YouWin;
```

This last approach is the shortest and (from what I've seen) the most common approach to such a problem. At first, it can make your head reel—especially if you're dealing with code that you don't exactly understand. But once you figure out the parentheses, you see that three pairs of possibilities are being compared: `Rock-Scissors`, `Scissors-Paper`, and `Paper-Rock`.

Now consider how difficult code like this would be to read, if instead of `Rock`, `Scissors`, and `Paper`, you were dealing with the numbers 1, 2, and 3:

```
If (UserChoice = MyChoice) then Result := Tie
else if (((MyChoice = 1) and (UserChoice = 2))
    or  ((MyChoice = 2) and (UserChoice = 3))
    or  ((MyChoice = 3) and (UserChoice = 1)))
    then Result := IWin
else Result := YouWin;
```

Chapter 14 ♦ User-Defined Types and Enumeration

It doesn't matter which approach you take; the code definitely becomes less readable.

The next step is to change Message to show who won and increment the winner's win counts:

```
case Result of
    IWin  : begin
                Message.Caption := 'I Win!';
                Inc(MyWins);
                WinType := MyChoice;
            end;
    YouWin : begin
                Message.Caption := 'You Win!';
                Inc(YourWins);
                WinType := UserChoice;
            end;
    Tie   : Message.Caption := 'Tie.';
end;
```

Then you must explain why the winner won. In the last step, besides setting Message.Caption and incrementing the appropriate variable, I also set WinType. WinType now holds Rock, Scissors, or Paper, based on which selection the winner made. Using this approach makes the following step easy:

```
If Result = Tie then Why.Caption := ''
else case WinType of
        Rock    : Why.Caption := 'Rock crushes scissors.';
        Scissors: Why.Caption := 'Scissors cuts paper.';
        Paper   : Why.Caption := 'Paper covers rock.';
    end;
```

Finally, update the Me, You, and Games labels to reflect the current scores:

```
Inc(GamesPlayed);
Games.Caption := 'Games: '+StrFn(GamesPlayed);
You.Caption   := 'You:   '+StrFn(YourWins);
Me.Caption    := 'Me:    '+StrFn(MyWins);
end;
```

And, of course, you need to put the StrFn function into your code. It should go immediately before the YourRockClick procedure statement:

```
function  StrFn(L: Longint): String;
var S   : String;
begin
   str(L, S);
   StrFn := S;
end;

{procedure header is added by Delphi, of course}
```

```
procedure TForm1.YourRockClick(Sender: TObject);
```

The preceding code has one limitation: you can't select the same item twice. To get the computer to make its choice, you have to select a different item than the last one. Otherwise, YourRockClick never gets called. Typically, actions in Windows are done when the user clicks on a button, so you could put a button called Go on the form and move all the code from YourRockClick to the GoClick method. You could also create a new global variable called Pass, initialize it with a value of 3, and place the following code at the beginning of the YourRockClick code:

```
begin
   Dec(Pass);
   If Pass <> 0 then exit;
   Pass := 3
   . . .
```

The user makes three choices in this version; the third choice forces the computer to make its choice. (This code mimics the way the game is played in real life.)

The Exit procedure tells the program to leave the current procedure, thus preventing you from having to code something like this:

```
If Pass = 0 then
begin
   Pass := 3;
   {The rest of the code in the procedure would go here}
end;
```

Just as Break and Continue enable you to disrupt loops, Exit provides you with an easy way to disrupt the normal flow of the subroutine.

Enumeration Limitations

Enumerated types have their place. They also have limitations, some of which you have seen already. The elements of an enumerated type have to follow the standard rules for identifiers, meaning you can't use numbers or Pascal keywords. You can't transfer the name of an element directly to a string, which occasionally forces you to build code like this:

```
case UserChoice of
   Rock    : S := 'Rock';
   Scissors: S := 'Scissors';
   Paper   : S := 'Paper';
end;
```

Chapter 14 ◆ User-Defined Types and Enumeration

Also, an identifier in one enumerated type cannot be used in a different enumerated type. In other words, the following code would be flagged as an error by the compiler:

```
type
    Suit = (Spades, Hearts, Diamonds, Clubs);
    Gems = (Rubies, Emeralds, Sapphires, Diamonds);
```

`Diamonds` can't be an element of both `Suit` and `Gems`, and although you would never confuse the two, Pascal doesn't allow duplicates like this.

As programs become bigger and bigger, the likelihood of a "duplicate identifier" increases. A common practice these days is to prefix identifiers with anywhere from one to four characters that describe their context. For example, you might code the preceding as follows:

```
type
    Suit = (sSpades, sHearts, sDiamonds, sClubs);
    Gems = (gRubies, gEmeralds, gSapphires, gDiamonds);
```

or perhaps

```
type
    CardSuits    = (csSpades, csHearts, csDiamonds, csClubs);
    PreciousGems = (pgRubies, pgEmeralds, pgSapphires, pgDiamonds);
```

or even

```
type
    Suit = (suitSpades, suitHearts, suitDiamonds, suitClubs);
    Gems = (gemsRubies, gemsEmeralds, gemsSapphires, gemsDiamonds);
```

Summary

In Pascal, you can create data types suited to a particular program. This capability increases readability and allows Delphi to apply type checking, thus preventing one possible type of bug.

One kind of data type you can create is an enumerated type. You declare an enumerated type in the type section of a Pascal program by giving the compiler a list of identifiers, each representing a possible value that a variable of that type may have. Without enumerated types, programmers must keep relationships between values and concepts in their heads. (Instead of being able to deal with, for example, the rank and suit of a particular card directly, they must remember that 13 equals a king, 12 equals a queen, and so on.) Enumerated types are ordinal, but frequently the point of creating an enumerated type is to get away from the idea that a certain concept has a specific number.

`Ord` returns the ordinal value of an element for an enumerated type. You can use `Pred`, `Succ`, `Inc`, and `Dec` with enumerated types. Any user-defined data type must be declared before a variable of that type is declared. Elements of enumerated types must be unique. A subrange type may be declared from an enumerated type. A subrange type may also be declared from any ordinal type. Data types can be cast as other types, though this should be done with great caution.

Exit allows you to leave a procedure immediately.

Radio buttons are collected in groups. The TRadioGroup object facilitates creating a group that only has radio buttons. Exactly one radio button in any group is checked at any time. You use the group box to group radio buttons and other controls. A group box is said to be a "parent" to the controls within it, which are called its "children." The controls may not be moved outside of a group box, and if a group box is deleted, all the controls inside it are also deleted. The Top and Left properties of a control reflect its distance from the Top and Left edges of its owner, respectively. The TabStop property dictates whether the user can use the Tab key to get to a particular control.

Review Questions

1. What is a user-defined data type?
2. What is an enumerated type?
3. Why use an enumerated type?
4. In the enumerated type

   ```
   VIBGYOR = (Violet, Indigo, Blue, Green, Yellow, Orange, Red);
   ```

   what is the ordinal value of Blue?

5. Using the VIBGYOR type described in question 4, what does the following return?

   ```
   Pred(Orange)
   ```

   What does this example return?

   ```
   Succ(Red)
   ```

6. What does the Ord function do?
7. What is a subrange type? Why do you use one?
8. Can you use the same identifier in different enumerated types?
9. How can you reduce the likelihood of an identifier in an enumerated type being duplicated elsewhere while still maintaining readability?

Chapter 14 ♦ User-Defined Types and Enumeration

Review Exercises

1. In a project with no forms, use the project code window to declare a number of enumerated types.

2. Make a project that uses an enumerated type with 10 or 12 elements and translates user input into one of those elements. (You can do this through the radio buttons or even using the WinCRT unit and ReadLn, if you want.) From this you should be able to see that it is less work to deal with enumerated types internally than to translate input into an enumerated type.

3. In Chapter 13, Review Exercise 4, you built a calculator program that used push buttons to indicate the operator that should be used to make a calculation. Change that program so that the operators are part of a group of radio buttons. Use an enumerated type and case statement to handle a clicked radio button.

4. I mentioned that Pascal's data types can be well represented by various controls: The scrollbar illustrates the integer concept well, the edit line illustrates the string, and so forth. In a practice project, pair up the data types with different controls than the ones you've used so far. An easy example would be using a radio button group to illustrate a Boolean. A tougher example might be using a scrollbar with an enumerated type.

CHAPTER 15

The Set Type

In Chapter 14, you saw how the user-defined type can make a program more readable and can help prevent certain types of bugs. Another kind of data type that comes to your aid when programming is the *set* type.

Suppose that you were collecting information on people for a political candidate. You could store the information in a string,

```
AVoter := 'Party: Democrat, Sex:Male, Opinion of Candidate: Low'
```

or you could store it in a series of integers,

```
Party   := 1;   {1 is Democrat; 2 is Republican; 0 is other}
Sex     := 1;   {0 is male}
Opinion:= 3;    {On a scale of 1 to 10, 10 being "highly favorable to
 candidate"}
```

or taking a clue from the last chapter, you could store it in a series of enumerated variables:

```
Party    := Democrat;
Sex      := Male;
Opinion  := Low;
```

But what if there were a number of Boolean attributes about the voter that were all you cared about? What if you only wanted to know whether the voter was male, a Democrat, and liked the candidate? This situation would be an appropriate circumstance to use a set. Then, in one line you could sum up an entire voter. (This is in English.)

```
The Voter is Male, Democrat and Dislikes Candidate
```

With any given set describing any particular voter, you could ask a question like,

```
Is the Voter Male?
```

Declaring the Set Type

Sets are declared in a type section of the program, and are declared almost identically to enumerated types:

```
type
    VoterDataSet = set of (Democrat, Republican, Male, Female, LowOpinion,
    ↪HighOpinion, Confused);
```

The only difference is the keywords *set* and *of*. Just as with enumerated types, defining a set consists of telling the compiler that you are defining a set, followed by the elements that may make up that set. A set can have a maximum of 256 elements.

Sets can also be of user-enumerated types or a subrange of user-enumerated types.

```
type
    {This is an enumerated type}
    VIBGYOR     = (Violet, Indigo, Blue, Green, Yellow, Orange, Red);
    {The following two are sets of this type}
    ColorSet    = set of VIBGYOR;
    BluishColors = set of Violet..Green;
```

You can't define an element as being part of an enumerated type and then redefine it as being part of a set, however.

```
type
    Suits = (Spades, Hearts, Diamonds, Clubs);
    BlackSuits = set of (Spades, Clubs);   {No!  This won't work!}
```

Sets contain ordinal values; therefore, it's impossible to skip a value to make up a set. And, as you can see from the preceding snippet, trying to declare a set of two non-consecutive elements (Spades and Clubs in this exmaple) would look to the compiler like trying to redefine elements of an enumerated type as part of the set.

If, on the other hand, *Suits* were declared like this

```
    Suits = (Spades, Clubs, Hearts, Diamonds);
```

you could define two sets that were subranges of the black and red suits:

```
    BlackSuits = set of Spades..Clubs;
    RedSuits   = set of Hearts..Diamonds;
```

In actual fact, this code

```
type
    Suits = (Spades, Clubs, Hearts, Diamonds);
    SuitSet = set of Suit;
```

is identical to *this* code

```
type
    SuitSet = set of (Spades, Clubs, Hearts, Diamonds);
```

except that you don't have an enumerated type for the suits in the second example. *Spades, Clubs, Hearts,* and *Diamonds* have the same ordinal values in the second example as they do in the first, and can be used in the same way.

You also are allowed to have a set of byte, char, or Boolean, or a subrange of byte, char, or Boolean.

```
type
    Chars   = set of Char;
    Bytes   = set of Bytes;
    Bool    = set of Boolean;
    Letters = set of 'A'..'Z';
    Numbers = set of '0'..'9';
```

After you've declared a set type, you can declare a variable of that type just as you would any other variable:

```
var
    Voter : VoterDataSet;
    Color : ColorSet;
    Lets  : Letters;
```

Set Operators

Once you have a set, what do you do with it? Say that you put together the simple *VoterDataSet* you saw earlier. If you had a variable *Voter* of that type, and you wanted to indicate that the voter represented by the variable liked your candidate, you could assign a value to it.

```
Voter := [HighOpinion];
```

Sets in Pascal are indicated by using the square brackets. If you subsequently found out that the voter in question was a Democrat and a male, you could add those elements to *Voter* by using the '+' operator.

```
Voter := Voter + [Democrat];
Voter := Voter + [Male];
```

The set that you're adding is not restricted to one element. You could reduce these two lines to the following:

```
Voter := Voter + [Democrat, Male];
```

by using a comma to separate the elements of a set.

If you later discover that the voter was not, in fact, male, you could remove that element from the set by using the '-' operator.

```
Voter := Voter - [Male];
```

'+' and '-' should be thought of as "add an element" or "remove an element" and not as arithmetic addition and subtraction. An element can only be removed or added once meaningfully.

```
Voter := Voter + [Male];    {Adds the Male element to the Voter set}
Voter := Voter + [Male];    {Has no effect.  Male is already in voter}
Voter := Voter - [Male];    {This removes Male element from Voter}
Voter := Voter - [Male];    {Has no effect.  Male has already been
➥removed}
```

If you wanted to find out whether the voter had a high opinion of your candidate, you could test *Voter* with the *in* keyword.

```
If HighOpinion in Voter then SendTheVoterFlowers;
```

Here, *HighOpinion* is an element, not a set, so it does not need to be enclosed in square brackets. You can't ask whether a set is in another set with in. The following is illegal:

```
If [HighOpinion, Male] in Voter then SendAFootballPhone;   {Won't work!}
```

You can figure out if one set has any elements in common with another set with another set operator called the *intersection* operator, indicated by an asterisk. Say you wanted to send a football phone (as a gift) to males with a high opinion of your candidate:

```
MailingCriteria := [HighOpinion, Male];
ResultSet := MailingCriteria * Voter;
```

ResultSet will have all of the elements that are in both *MailingCriteria* and *Voter*. If *Voter* contains both the *HighOpinion* and *Male* elements, *ResultSet* will be equal to *MailingCriteria*.

```
If ResultSet = MailingCriteria then SendAFootballPhone;
```

A set can have zero elements in it, and this is called the *empty* set, represented by two square brackets with nothing in between. If *ResultSet* is empty, you don't want to mail to that person. If it isn't empty, you know that *Voter* has met at least one of your mailing criteria (that is, is either male *or* has a high opinion of the candidate) and you might send that voter a simple campaign letter.

```
If ResultSet = MailingCriteria then SendAFootbalPhone
  else if ResultSet <> [] then SendCampaignLetter
  else DontMailAnything;
```

Table 15.1 sums up these operators.

Table 15.1. Operators to add, remove, or test for elements in a set.

Operator	Description	Example
+	Add elements in a set	ASet := ASet + AnotherSet;
-	Remove elements in a set	ASet := ASet - AnotherSet;
*	Remove not in both sets	Aset := ASet * AnotherSet;
in	Test for element	Bool := AnElement in ASet;

Set Tips

Programmers often do things because they don't like to type—or perhaps more accurately, they like to type as little as possible. As a result, you might be inclined to declare your sets like this:

```
type
   SuitSet = Set of (Spades, Heart, Diamonds, Clubs);
```

The problem with this approach is that you can't have a variable that represents a member of the set. (Think about it. How would you declare it? There is no enumerated type declaration.) Consider the advantages of typing an extra line.

```
type
   Suits = (Spades, Heart, Diamonds, Clubs);
   SuitSet = Set of Suits;
```

This approach allows you to do this later on:

```
var
   ASuit  : Suits;
   ASuitSet: SuitSet;
. . .
   ASuit := Spades;
   SuitSet := [ASuit];   {SuitSet is now equal to [Spades]}
. . .
   If ASuit in SuitSet then DoSomething;
```

This approach only costs one extra line of typing and makes your set considerably more useful.

Chapter 15 ♦ The Set Type

Check Boxes

Just as radio buttons served as a good tutorial on enumerated types, check boxes can illustrate how sets might be used. Whereas a group of radio buttons must have exactly one button checked at all times, a group of check boxes may have many items selected, one item selected, or no items selected. Check boxes don't need to be grouped together in a group box, but they usually are.

The property that indicates whether a check box is checked or not is called, appropriately enough, *Checked*. *Checked* is a Boolean field, and if true, you'll add the element to a set, otherwise you won't.

Example: Set Logic

In Chapter 10, "On One Condition," you put together a little program that used switches to show how the logical operators AND, OR, and XOR worked. Now you'll use check boxes to show how the set operators +, - and * work.

Start a new project called "SETLOGIC" and a form called "SETLOGF." You're going to set up *five* group boxes, three of which will appear identical to the user. (See fig. 15.1.) The first, third, and fifth form will contain seven check boxes each, each labelled "Violet," "Indigo," "Blue," "Green," "Yellow," "Orange," and "Red"—I'll refer to these groups as the *colors* groups.

Figure 15.1

The Set Logic form.

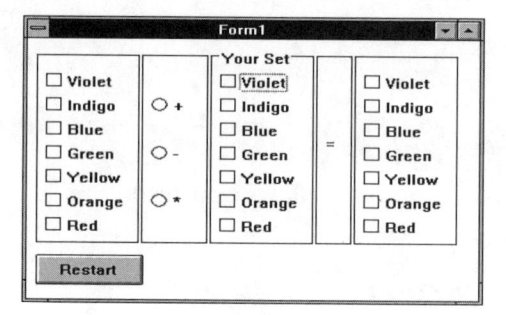

The check boxes in the first group should be called (when I say "called" technically I mean "change the *Name* property to") *Violet1, Indigo1, Blue1,* and so on. The second group should have the same names, except ending with a 2, as in *Violet2, Indigo2,* and so on. The check boxes in the third group should end with 3.

> **Note:** The speediest way to set up the color group boxes is to set up the first group exactly the way you want it: Add a group box and to that add seven check boxes. Change the check boxes' *Caption* and *Name* properties. (Change the *Name* property *first* and the *Caption* property will change to match the name, leaving you only to delete the "1" at the end of each caption.) Now arrange and size the controls until the seven check boxes look acceptable. Use the "Align..." and "Size..." dialog boxes to align the check boxes along the left, to make them all the same width, and to space them evenly vertically.
>
> Now, *copy* the group to the clipboard (using the Edit menu's Copy selection), then paste them back (using the Edit menu's Paste selection). If you select the group box, it and all of the controls it owns will be copied to the clipboard.
>
> You'll still have to change the *Name* properties of the check boxes, which will revert to CheckBox1, CheckBox2 and so forth in the copy. (Pascal isn't smart enough to alter your numbers.)
>
> The second group box should now look identical to the first. Repeat this process for the third group box.

Squeeze a group box in between the first and second colors box. This box should contain three radio buttons, marked with a '+', '-', and '*' sign. Call these radio buttons *Combine, Remove,* and *Intersect*. Set the *Checked* property of *Combined* to True.

Between the second and third colors box put another group box that has a label in it. Change the label's caption to '='. (This group box is purely decorative and included to make the form appear more symmetrical.) Underneath the group boxes put a button named *Restart*.

The idea behind this program will be that the *Restart* button creates a random set of colors in the first colors group. The user can check off colors in the second colors group and then click on a radio button representing one of the set operators. The result of the operation performed on the two sets will appear in the third color group.

The first and third colors groups should have their *Enabled* property set to false. This will *disable* them, making it impossible for the user to change them. (It's a good idea to disable controls or groups of controls if the program is using them for display and the user is not supposed to change them.)

This program will be considerably simpler than some of the others you've done. The restart button only needs to do two things. It must create a new set for the first color group, and then it must check and uncheck the appropriate check boxes in the

Chapter 15 ♦ The Set Type

first colors group. The radio buttons group box has only three things to do: Build a set based on which boxes in the second colors group are checked, perform the operation selected, and then check and uncheck the appropriate check boxes in the third colors group.

Based on what you've done so far, you should be able to implement this program on your own. The next paragraphs will walk you through the process.

First, describe the types and declare the three Set variables in the "SETLOGF" code window.

```
type                             {Add}
   Colors = (Violet, Indigo, Blue, Green, Yellow, Orange, Red);   {add}
   VIBGYOR = Set of Colors;                        {add}

var
   Form1: TForm1;
   Set1, Set2, Set3 : VIBGYOR;                     {add}
```

(The first two lines of the var section are generated by Pascal. Add only the lines indicated.)

Now, in your main program—the project code—"SETLOGIC" add in a *Randomize* statement, and initialize the three set variables.

```
begin
   Randomize;     {Add this}
   Set1 := [];    {And this}
   Set2 := [];    {And this}
   Set3 := [];    {And this}
   Application.Run(Form1);
end.
```

Again, add only the lines indicated.

Double-click on *Restart* to get Pascal to generate the *RestartClick* code frame. Start by going through each of the colors, from Violet to Red, giving each color a 50 percent chance to be added to the set.

```
procedure Tsetlogf.restartClick(Sender: TObject);
var Color: Colors;
begin
   Set1 := [];
   For Color := Violet to Red do
      If Random(2) = 0 then Set1 := Set1 + [Color];
```

Did you forget that enumerated types can be used in For loops? This feature is easy to forget because it isn't done very often. When you need to run through an enumerated type, however, this is the simplest approach to take.

After creating the set, check and uncheck the first color group's check boxes accordingly:

```
    Violet1.Checked := Violet in Set1;
    Indigo1.Checked := Indigo in Set1;
    Blue1.Checked   := Blue in Set1;
    Green1.Checked  := Green in Set1;
    Yellow1.Checked := Yellow in Set1;
    Orange1.Checked := Orange in Set1;
    Red1.Checked    := Red in Set1;
```

(Copy this block of code to the clipboard. You'll use it again in just a moment.)

Now, double-click on the *Combine* radio button. Build *Set2* based on the check boxes the user has checked.

```
procedure TForm1.CombineClick(Sender: TObject);
begin
    Set2 := [];
    If Violet2.Checked then Set2 := Set2 + [Violet];
    If Indigo2.Checked then Set2 := Set2 + [Indigo];
    If Blue2.Checked   then Set2 := Set2 + [Blue];
    If Green2.Checked  then Set2 := Set2 + [Green];
    If Yellow2.Checked then Set2 := Set2 + [Yellow];
    If Orange2.Checked then Set2 := Set2 + [Orange];
    If Red2.Checked    then Set2 := Set2 + [Red];
```

Perform the math:

```
    If Combine.Checked then Set3 := Set1 + Set2
    else If Remove.Checked then Set3 := Set1 - Set2
    else Set3 := Set1 * Set2;
```

Now, copy that code back out of the clipboard and change all the "1"s to "3"s.

```
    Violet3.Check := Violet in Set3;
    Indigo3.Check := Indigo in Set3;
    Blue3.Check   := Blue in Set3;
    Green3.Check  := Green in Set3;
    Yellow3.Check := Yellow in Set3;
    Orange3.Check := Orange in Set3;
    Red3.Check    := Red in Set3;
end;
```

Tip: The quickest way to change the "1"s to "3"s is to copy the code from the clipboard, select it, and then bring up the Replace dialog box. (From the Search menu select "Replace..." or type Ctrl+Q+A.) Type "1" in the first edit line and "3" in the second. In the Option group, make sure nothing is checked. In the Scope group, make sure the "Selected text" radio button is selected, and in the Origin group, select "Entire Scope." (It doesn't matter which item in the Direction group is selected.)

When you're sure you've got it right, click on the "All" button. This step tells Pascal to change all the "1"s in the selected block to "3"s.

Chapter 15 ◆ The Set Type

This program is much simpler than some of the others you've done. That's all it takes to make it work. Run the code and try it out. Press Restart to get a pattern. You make selections in the second colors box, press an operator radio button, and the third box reflects that operation done on the two boxes.

One thing you wanted to do with the "LOGIC" project that you did earlier was disable the last set of switches so that the answer was always accurate—that is, the user couldn't change the result set so that it displayed a wrong answer. With this program, when you press *Restart* and when you are marking boxes, the third colors group is inaccurate. It remains inaccurate until you select a new operator. Can you fix this?

Making the check boxes in the second group update the third group is really pretty easy. You've done similar things before. Select all the check boxes in the second colors group and change to the Events page of the Object Inspector. Select *OnClick* and press the down arrow that appears to the right. This step presents a list of the forms methods that you can call. Select *CombineClick*, and now all the check boxes will call *CombineClick* when checked or unchecked.

Having *Restart* call *CombineClick* is another matter. You definitely want it to call the *RestartClick* routine, and you just happen to want it to call the *CombineClick* routine as well. An event cannot be linked to two routines, however. But maybe if *RestartClick* triggered an event, you could hook that event up to the *CombineClick* event.

RestartClick does, in fact, trigger an event. If this code:

```
Red1.Checked := Red in Set1;
```

changes *Red1*, it creates an *OnClick* event for *Red1*. So, if you tie the *OnClick* events of all the controls in the first group box to the *CombineClick* event, that should have the desired effect. Link the check box's *OnClick* event in the first color group to *CombineClick* and try the modified program.

> **Note:** You might wonder why changing a property for an object would create an event. This feature reflects the idea that the program and the form should not have to know about what goes on with any given object. The check box object has a special code that checks it or unchecks it based on several possibilities: the user mouse-clicked on it; the user pressed the space bar when it was the focused control; some other part of the program changed the *Checked* property.
>
> So, the *OnClick* event is really a message sent to the rest of the program from the check box object saying, essentially, "I've been changed!" The program doesn't need to know any of the details—the message is just a way for the program to update itself accordingly.

Set Limitations

There are a few limitations on sets. As mentioned earlier, a set can have a maximum of 256 elements. Also, although it is easy enough to turn an element into a set through the use of square brackets:

```
AnElement := Violet;
ASet := [AnElement]
```

there is no easy or graceful way to get an element out of a set. If you set up an enumerated type, you can get the elements out of a set with a simple For loop:

```
For Color := Violet to Indigo do If Color in ASet then SetHas(Color)
```

Also missing is a keyword or procedure that tells you how many elements are in the set. An enumerated type can help you here, too:

```
For Color := Violet to Indigo do If Color in ASet then Inc(Count);
```

As with enumerated types, identifiers used as elements in one set cannot be used as elements in another.

```
type
   SuitSet = set of (Spades, Hearts, Diamonds, Clubs);
   GemSet  = set of (Emeralds, Rubies, Sapphires, Diamonds);  {This
   ➥causes an error!}
```

However, you could have different types of sets based on the same enumerated type:

```
type
   VIBGYOR = (Violet, Indigo, Blue, Green, Yellow, Orange, Red);
   BluishColors = set of Violet..Green;
   ReddishColors = set of Green..Red;
```

Knowing this, you could merge several enumerated types together, and base sets on portions of them:

```
type
   Stuff = (Spades, Hearts, Clubs, Diamonds, Emeralds, Rubies, Sap
   ➥phires);
   SuitSet = set of Spades..Diamonds;
   GemSet  = set of Diamonds..Sapphires;
```

I advise against this, because it can easily lead to confusion. The categories of card suits and precious gems don't really belong together.

What you can do with sets is create a variable designed to filter out unwanted types. Given the *SuitSet* above, you could set up two variables of that type designed to distinguish between red and black cards:

```
BlackCards := [Spades, Clubs];
RedCards := [Hearts, Diamonds];
```

Chapter 15 ♦ The Set Type

This tactic is often useful.

Knowing this, you *could* create an enumerated type like the following:

```
type
    KitchenSink = (Clubs, Crowbars, Daggers, Diamonds, Emeralds, Hearts,
    ↪Lungs, Spades, Swords);
```

and then set up variables to group the like items together:

```
Tools := [Crowbars, Spades];
Weapons := [Clubs, Daggers, Swords];
Suits := [Spades, Hearts, Diamonds, Clubs];
Gems := [Diamonds, Emeralds];
Organs := [Hearts, Lungs];
```

This idea is bad. The elements of *KitchenSink* don't really belong together, and by putting them together you make *Emeralds, Lungs, Swords,* and *Crowbars* all type compatible. Your best bet is to separate the enumerated types and prefix the identifiers with some kind of category code, as shown in the following:

```
type
    ToolType = (ttCrowbars, ttSpades);
    WeaponType = (wtClubs, wtDaggers, wtSwords);
```

and so on.

Another thing you can do with sets that is extremely useful but also can lead to errors is create a set "on the fly." Instead of setting up *BlackCards* and *RedCards,* as above, you could just create the set when you need it, as in the following:

```
If Card in [Hearts, Diamonds] then IsRed(Card);
```

The following is particularly handy when trying to determine the value of a char variable.

```
If AChar in ['A'..'Z'] then IsUpperCaseLetter[AChar];
```

The subrange punctuation ".." works here as before. If *AChar* is in the set of the characters from "A" to "Z," it is an uppercase letter. More than one subrange can be specified by using a comma:

```
If AChar in ['A'..'Z', 'a'..'z'] then IsALetter(AChar);
```

You can, of course, mix single elements and subranges.

```
If AChar in ['A'..'Z', 'a'..'z', '_'] then OKAsFirstLetterOfIdentifer :=
true;
```

You could have used something like this in the parsing routine from Chapter 12. You had a line that you used to detect whether a character was a valid part of a word, if you'll recall:

```
If ((T >= '0') and (T <= '9')) or
   ((T >= 'A') and (T <= 'Z')) or
   ((T >= 'a') and (T <= 'z')) or
   (T = '_') then
```

which, were *T* a char variable, you could have reduced to:

```
If T in ['0'..'9','A'..'Z','a'..'z','_'] then
```

(You'll actually make this change in an upcoming chapter.)

While this feature is useful, building sets on the fly has some liabilities. For example, you can build a set of bytes, and test for the value of any integer type:

```
If Element in [0..10, 240..255] then OnTheEdge(Element);
```

Element should be a byte, but it also could be a shortint, integer, word, or longint, and Pascal will not flag it as an error. Which means that, if *Element* is an integer, the code will compile, and this

```
Element := -1;
If Element in [0..10, 240..255] then OnTheEdge(Element);
```

will cause *OnTheEdge* to be called. Pascal wraps the *Element* variable value of -1 around to a valid byte value (255) just as you experienced first-hand in Chapter 7, "Using Numbers." This won't even cause a range error.

Summary

A set type consists of a number of elements, any of which may or may not be present in an actual set of that type. Sets can be declared as being of an enumerated type or of a subrange of an enumerated type, and while this is not mandatory, it is a good idea. Set operators allow you to combine two sets, remove all the elements from one set that are in another, or remove all the elements in two sets that are not in both. The `in` keyword allows you to determine whether or not a particular element is in a set.

A group of check boxes may have many items checked, one item checked, or no items checked.

Review Questions

1. What is a set good for?
2. How do you declare a set type?
3. Why should you declare a set using an existing enumerated type?

Chapter 15 ♦ The Set Type

4. What are the four set operators?

5. What value would *Set1* have after this line?
```
Set1 := ['B','L'] + ['A', 'E', 'K'];
```

6. What value would *Set1* have after this line?
```
Set1 := ['A'..'M'] * ['L'..'Z'];
```

7. Is *Bool* true or false after this line?
```
Bool := '@' in ['0'..'Z'];
```
(Use Appendix A to figure this out if necessary.)

8. Can you think of any reason why you would *not* want a set to be declared of an existing enumerated type? In other words, is there any reason to prefer the first code in the following example, or the second?
```
SuitSet = set of (Spades, Hearts, Diamonds, Clubs)
SuitSet = set of Suits;
```

Review Exercises

1. Define some sets that you think might be useful.

2. Write a WinCRT program that asks the user to enter "Y" or "N" and uses ReadLn to get a character from the user. Use a set to determine that the user typed in either or a "Y" or an "N" and nothing else. Allow lowercase "y" and "n" as well.

3. In Chapter 11, Review Exercise 2, you built a "multiple choice" program. Build or modify a multiple choice program that verifies that the user entered a valid response by using a set.

4. The edit object has an event called OnKeyPress, through which you can generate a code frame for using the object inspector. OnKeyPress passes as a parameter the *Key* char variable that contains the key-pressed. Go back to the calculator program you built in the exercises for chapter 13 and modified in exercise 2 of Chapter 14, and modify this program again so that the edit objects' OnKeyPress method checks to see whether Key is a legal numeric value.

CHAPTER 16

The Record

As much as you know about Delphi (and if you've read the preceding 15 chapters, you've learned the lion's share of the basics), there are still some programming questions that you might have trouble answering.

What if you wanted to write a program that catalogs books? You could probably set up a good form with entry fields, check boxes, radio buttons, and so on. But what would you do with the data once the user typed it in? How would you store it?

In more concrete terms, say you had a form like figure 16.1. The user had typed in all the data and pressed "OK." Then what? Well, you might declare several variables to store the information:

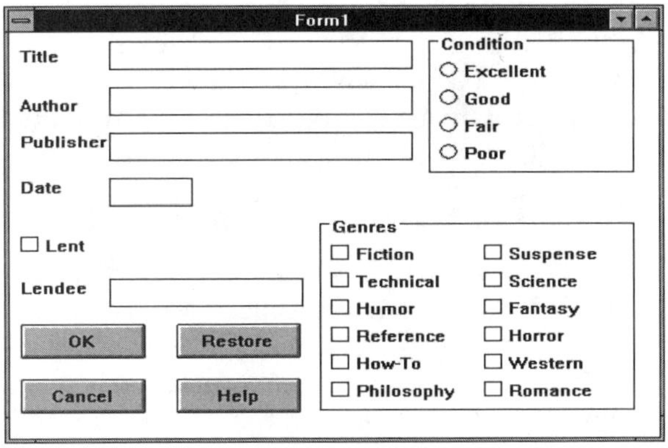

Figure 16.1

A data entry form for a book cataloging system.type.

Chapter 16 ◆ The Record

```
    Genres = (gFiction, gTechnical, gHumor, gReference, gHowTo,
    ➥gPhilosophy,
            gSuspense, gScience, gFantasy, gHorror, gWestern, gRomance);
    Conditions = (cExcellent, cGood, cFair, cPoor);

    GenreSet = Set of Genres;
var
    BookTitle, BookAuthor, BookPublisher : String;
    BookDate                             : Word;
    BookLentOut                          : Boolean;
    BookLendee                           : String;
    BookGenre                            : Genres;
    BookCondition                        : Conditions;
```

This approach is a little unwieldy, but you could probably make it work. But suppose that you wanted to let the user look at other book entries while making a new entry? In other words, what if you needed another set of these variables for your program? You would have to redeclare them all with slightly different names:

```
var
    ViewBookTitle, ViewBookAuthor,
    ViewBookPublisher, ViewBookDate : String;
```

and so on.

Or what if you had a procedure that performed a search on a database by using all the data from the catalog entry? The procedure would have to be called like this:

```
SearchFor(BookTitle, BookAuthor, BookPublisher, BookDate,
        BookLentOut, BookLendee, BookGenre, BookCondition);
```

A procedure header like this, as you might imagine, would be very hard to work with. It also would be frustrating because you consider all of these unstructured variables as parts of a whole, and you would wonder why the compiler wouldn't let you treat them all as one large data structure.

The Record Data Type

Delphi allows you to create a special kind of user type called a *record*. A record is a series of related variables, called *fields*, collected into one type.

Thus, for the previous example, you would create a record type that had fields for title, author, publisher, publication date, whether the book had been lent out, to whom the book had been lent, and the genre and condition of the book. You would put these elements into a data type called BookEntry or CatalogEntry or something similar.

> **Note:** Records are sometimes called *complex* types, because they are made up of other data types. Other data types, by comparison, are often referred to as *simple* data types.

The record is the programming predecessor of the object. In fact, if you think of fields as properties, you could consider a record like an object that has no methods. (You can explore this in detail in Chapter 21, "Objects.")

Declaring a Record

Declaring a record is like declaring many variables:

```
    Name, Address : String;
    PhoneNumber   : String[10];
    Relationship  : RelationshipTypes;
```

Before the list of fields for a record, you give the type name, followed by an equal sign, followed by the keyword *record*. After the list of fields, you use the keyword *end* to tell the compiler that the definition of the record type is complete.

```
type
    PhoneBookEntry = record
    . . .
end;
```

Going back to the book catalog example, you might do the following:

```
type
    LibraryEntry = record
        BookTitle, BookAuthor, BookPublisher : String;
        BookDate                             : Word;
        BookLentOut                          : Boolean;
        BookLendee                           : String;
        BookGenre                            : Genres;
        BookCondition                        : Conditions;
end;
```

and declare one or more variables of this type in the usual way:

```
var
    DataEntry, ViewEntry: LibraryEntry;
```

Note that the record definition can contain user types, like *Genres* and *Conditions*. It can even contain other records. Suppose that you created a record to hold dates:

```
type
    DateType = record
        Day, Month: Byte;
        Year      : Integer;
end;
```

you could then include that in any of your other records.

```
type
   PhoneBookEntry = record
      Name, Address : String;
      PhoneNumber   : String[10];
      Relationship  : RelationshipTypes;
      BirthDate, AnniversaryDate
                    : DateType;
end;
```

Using Records

To use a record, you need only to define the record type and declare variables of that type. You address the fields of a record by appending a period and the field name after the variable that you want to access. For example:

```
var
   Entry : LibraryEntry;

begin
   Entry.Title := 'Delphi by Example';
   Entry.Author := 'Blake Watson';
   Entry.Publisher := 'QUE';
   Entry.Date := 1994;
   Entry.LentOut := False;
   Entry.Lendee := '';
   Entry.Condition := cExcellent;
   Entry.Genre := [gTechnical];
   . . .
```

Unfortunately, there is no way to assign all the fields in one pass.

```
Entry := ('Moby Dick', 'Herman Melville', 'Penguin', 1832, False, '',
➥cFair, [gFiction]);   {No!  Not allowed}
```

In most cases, you have to deal with the fields individually. However, you can assign the values in one record to another of the same type:

```
Entry := ANewEntry;
```

You can't compare entire records or perform math on records. You can, however, return a record type from a function, a feature that distinguishes Delphi from standard Pascal.

```
var ARec, Brec : ARecordType;
begin
   . . .
   If ARec > BRec then ;  {No! Can't be done!}
   Arec := ARec + Brec;   {Also an error!}
   Arec := GetRecord;     {This is okay}
   . . .
```

You can do math or comparisons on any individual field of a record (as long as the field's type allows it, of course).

```
    If Arec.AField > BRec.AField then DoSomethingWith(Arec);
    Arec.NumberField := Arec.NumberField + BRec.NumberField;
    Arec.AField := GetRecordField;
```

In fact, you can treat the fields of a record as you would any variable of the same type.

```
    If ARec.AField > 12 then DoSomethingWith(ARec);
    Inc(ARec.NumberField, 42);
    If ARec.ElementField in SomeSet then DoSomethingElse;
```

And, you can use an entry record as a parameter to a procedure, and that may be a *var* parameter.

```
Bool := SearchFor(ARec);
GetNextRecord(ARec);      {could be a routine to fill ARec with data from
➥user}
```

Choosing Data Types

When you work with record types, choosing the right variables for fields becomes very important. When you go through the trouble to set up a record type, that usually means you're going to be using this data a lot. Often a record type is at the center of a large application. If you make bad choices when creating a record type, often those mistakes will be repeated thousands of times in an application.

Questions to ask yourself include: which data types will work?; which data will take up the least space?; which data types will be the fastest to work with?; and which data types will be the easiest to work with, considering such issues as possible changes that may need to be made, and access with outside programs like databases, spreadsheets, and word processors?

You know most of the data types used by Pascal at this point. You also know that you can create your own. Sometimes the best results can be achieved by creating a data type that gets used repeatedly within the same record, or across several records in the same program. Consider the two types of records used as examples so far:

```
type
   PhoneBookEntry = record
      Name, Address : String;
      PhoneNumber   : String[10];
      Relationship  : RelationshipTypes;
      BirthDate, AnniversaryDate
                    : DateType;
end;

type
   LibraryEntry = record
      BookTitle, BookAuthor, BookPublisher : String;
      BookDate                             : Word;
      BookLentOut                          : Boolean;
      BookLendee                           : String;
```

```
        BookGenre                           : Genres;
        BookCondition                       : Conditions;
    end;
```

Notice that the two records have several fields that seem to be related. This can be a good place to optimize. For example, there is a *DateType* record used by the *PhoneBookEntry* record to store dates. In the course of programming, you may write many subroutines that work by using the DateType record. Why not turn *BookDate* into a DateType?

Between the two records are three fields meant to hold people's names: *PhoneBookEntry.Name, LibraryEntry.BookAuthor,* and *LibraryEntry.Lendee.* You can set up a special data type to hold names, and then write subroutines that work with that data type which can then be used with both PhoneBookEntry and LibraryEntry.

```
function GetLastName(Name: NameType): String;
function GetDearMrOrMrs(Name: NameType): String;
```

Look for a moment at the LibraryEntry data type. This record type is meant to hold data about books in a library or catalog. There may be tens or hundreds of thousands of books in a library. Is this the best data structure you can use? For example, is it too big?

The *SizeOf* Function

Knowing what you know about the sizes of certain data types, you should be able to determine how much space the *LibraryEntry* record type takes. To help you, Pascal has a built-in function called *SizeOf* that tells you the size of any given data type.

Start a new project in Pascal and remove any forms. Go to the code window and take out the code. Replace it with the following:

```
program TestSize;

type
    Genres = (gFiction, gTechnical, gHumor, gReference, gHowTo,
    ↪gPhilosophy,
             gSuspense, gScience, gFantasy, gHorror, gWestern, gRomance);
    Conditions = (cExcellent, cGood, cFair, cPoor);

    GenreSet = Set of Genres;

    LibraryEntry = record

        BookTitle, BookAuthor, BookPublisher   : String;
        BookDate                               : Word;
        BookLentOut                            : Boolean;
        BookLendee                             : String;
        BookGenre                              : Genres;
```

```
        BookCondition                           : Conditions;
    end;

    begin
    end.
```

You shouldn't have to run this program, just compile it, open up the Evaluate/Modify dialog box (from the Debug menu select Evaluate/Modify...), and in the first edit line type the following:

SizeOf(LibraryEntry);

You should see something like figure 16.2. (If the Evaluate/Modify dialog box refuses to give an answer, start the program by stepping through it, and then try Evaluate/Modify again.)

Figure 16.2

The Evaluate/Modify dialog box showing the size of *LibraryEntry*.

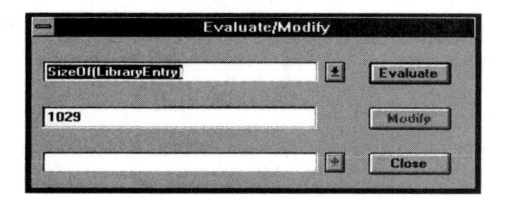

SizeOf returns the size of a data type in bytes, which means that *LibraryEntry* is over 1K long. Thus, a thousand books would take about a megabyte of memory. One megabyte seems like a lot, particularly when you consider that you aren't really storing that much information. How much space can a few names take?

Four of your fields representing the Author, Title, Publisher, and Lendee are all string type variables. Do you remember from Chapter 6, "Variables," how much space a string variable takes? 256 bytes! So, with four, you're already up to 1K. The remaining 5 bytes are taken by the rest of the fields. This gives you a good place to start when considering how to improve a record type. Few names are longer than 30 characters. You could shave the record down considerably by changing the record like so:

```
LibraryEntry = record
    BookTitle, BookAuthor, BookPublisher    : String[30];
    BookDate                                : Word;
    BookLentOut                             : Boolean;
    BookLendee                              : String[30];
    BookGenre                               : Genres;
    BookCondition                           : Conditions;
end;
```

Recompile the program and check out the size of *LibraryEntry* now. 129 bytes! You've reduced it to almost a tenth of its original size, just by making a sensible reduction in the string variables.

Example: Multiple Forms in Pascal

When you write a program, you'll often find that you need to use more than one form. With a book catalog, for example, you might have one form the user can use to browse books and another that the user can use to add or edit an entry. Pascal, naturally, allows for this multiple form possibility.

This would seem to be a pretty simple task on the surface. After all, Pascal allows you to add and remove forms from a project easily. Open a project now and set it up to have two forms. (You can use the form icon on the speedbar; also, you can add a form by accessing the File menu and choosing New Form.)

Now, run the project. You'll discover that *Form1* is the only form visible. How do you allow the user to call up *Form2*? All forms have a method called Show, which causes a form to do exactly that: make itself visible. (The application automatically shows the first form when it starts up.)

You can probably figure out from this explanation that you need to add the following line to make the second form show:

```
Form2.Show;
```

You can add a button to Form1 that makes Form2 appear when clicked; however, you need to do one more thing to make it all work. You need to give Unit1 access to Unit2. Otherwise, the compiler will stop on Form2 and tell you Unknown Identifier.

Units are covered in detail in Chapter 20, "Units." For now, just find the lines in Unit1 that read as follows:

```
uses
    SysUtils, WinTypes, WinProcs, Messages, Classes, Graphics, Controls,
    The code generated by Pascal now routinely looks like this:
```

and add a comma and Unit2 at the end, before the semi-colon.

```
uses
    SysUtils, WinTypes, WinProcs, Messages, Classes, Graphics, Controls,
    Forms, Dialogs, Unit2;
```

Now, your button code should work.

```
procedure TForm1.Button1Click(Sender: TObject);
begin
    Form2.Show;
end;
```

When using more than one form, it is important to understand that the primary form—the one first shown by the Application object—is special to the program. You can open and close additional windows as much as you want, but if you close the first one, the program ends.

The first form run is often called the *primary* form or window. Other forms run are sometimes called *secondary* forms or windows. Closing the primary form ends the application.

Considerations When Using Multiple Forms

Using what you've learned thus far, do you think you can build a program that has a form with a single button, where pushing that button calls up a different form (for data entry) like the one pictured in figure 16.1? As strange as it may seem, when writing your own programs, you probably won't start by designing the data entry forms. Instead, you'll start by designing the record type first and deciding on the data types for the fields. Then you'll match the data types to Pascal controls and arrange those controls on a form.

You will have to juggle many different concerns as a programmer. For example, the user doesn't particularly care if you store data as an enumerated type or a byte. The user won't notice—or *shouldn't* notice—anything at all about how the data is structured. If you made the Genre field an enumerated type instead of a set, for example, and the user goes to enter a book that fits into the categories of *Horror, Humor,* and *Fiction*—then the user will become aware of your data structure. He will not be able to class the book in several different genres (as he would have if you had made the Genre field a set), and he will not like it. It limits him and keeps him from doing what he wants.

Also, if you use full-length strings—256 characters each—everywhere, and the user discovers that his disk space is being consumed by your program's library, once again he will become aware of your data structure—and once again you will curry his disfavor. If you've limited *Title* and the other string fields to 30 characters, as discussed earlier, and he goes to enter the book *I HAVE NO MOUTH AND I MUST SCREAM,* getting stopped at the last "E," once again you will have drawn his attention to your data structure—with the same unpleasant results.

Get the idea? Generally, if the user accidentally becomes aware of the way you've structured the data, you've probably done something he doesn't like. A very big part of programming is balancing the user's needs with real-world programming issues. The user wants to be able to enter a title of any length, but you can't allow hundreds of bytes for each title, or you'll take up too much disk space—something else the user will not like. The shorter you make your string fields, however, the more likely the user is to run into some name or title that doesn't fit and be forced to abbreviate it in some way. (For now, assume that the last version of *LibraryEntry*—the one with the 30-character limitation on names—is adequate.)

The next question to resolve is how the form should be designed. This is another interesting question, because the form is your basic means of interacting with the user. The form shown in figure 16.1 is okay, but probably far from ideal. For example, you have two fields designed to store a person's name—Author and *Lendee*. The way the form is designed currently, some users will enter names like this:

```
Hunter J. Thompson
```

and some like this:

```
Thompson, Hunter J.
```

and still others will enter different variations. You can't solve all of these problems, no matter how smart you are, because some people are walking around with names like David Allen and Peter Paul. There is no way to tell which is a first name and which is a last. You can help the user get this right, however, by having a form with two or three separate fields: one for last name, and one or two for the last name and middle name or initial.

The liability of having more entry fields is that the larger a form is and the more controls it has, the harder it will be to work with. Larger forms are more likely to cover up other information that the user may need. Forms with more controls are more likely to result in confusion.

Another problem raised by many controls—especially those not arranged in a neat, logical manner—is the question of "Where will I go when I press the Tab key?". Figure 16.1 is particularly bad in that regard. The controls can be grouped in a number of ways. When doing a form that will be used for data entry, it is best to order the objects in a way that is natural for the eye to track. In this culture, that's usually left-to-right and top-to-bottom. Data enterers develop rhythms and pattern to speed data entry—if the flow of the form makes that difficult or uncomfortable, your program will be less successful.

> **Tip:** As a general rule, anything in a form that calls attention to itself, and thereby away from the user's intentions, is a bad idea.

Record Limitations

Records within records, as previously stated, are allowed by Pascal. In fact, you can have records within records within records, and so on. You can access these records normally, including accessing their fields by typing the sub-record name followed by a period followed by field name. Given the last declaration of the *PhoneBookEntry* type, you could access the year of someone's birth like this:

```
var
    AFriend : PhoneBookEntry;
begin
    AFriend.BirthDate.Year := 1966;
    . . .
```

This can be carried to extremes:

```
type
    Genders = (Male, Female, Both, Neither);
    PetSpecies = (Dog, Cat, Bird, Fish, Snake, Horse, Rodent, Mold);
```

```
   Date = record
      Day, Month : Byte;
      Year       : Word;
   end;

   Organism = record
      Gender : Genders;
      Birth  : Date;
   end;

   Pet = record
      BasicInfo : Organism;
      Kind      : PetSpecies;
   end;

   Child = record
      BasicInfo   : Organism;
      FavoritePet : Animal;
   end;

   Careers = record
      Position : String;
      Boss     : Organism;
   end;

   Adult = record
      BasicInfo  : Organism;
      Occupation : Careers;
   end;

   NuclearFamily = record
      Mother, Father : Adult;
      Son, Daughter  : Child;
   end;
var
   Family : NuclearFamily;
   Today  : Date;
   Message, Pronoun
          : String;
begin
   . . .
   If Family.Mother.Boss.BasicInfo.BirthDate = Today then
      SendTheBossALovelyCard(Family.Mother.Boss);
   . . .
   If Family.Son.Pet.BasicInfo.Birthdate = Today then
   begin
      If Family.Son.Pet.BasicInfo.Gender = Female then Pronoun := 'her'
      else if Family.Son.Pet.BasicInfo.Gender = Male then Pronoun :=
         'him'
      else Pronoun := "it';
      Message := 'Wish '+pronoun+' a happy birthday!';
   . . .
```

Chapter 16 ◆ The Record

This may seem cumbersome—or absurd—but every record has a specific purpose, and at least there's no chance of getting the boss's birthdate confused with the son's pet's birthday, or any other similar field. In many cases, you'll have subroutines set up to handle specific situations that arise with each specific record. That neatens things up considerably.

```
function GetPronoun(Who: Organism): String;
begin
   case who.gender of
      Female: GetPronoun := 'her';
      Male  : GetPronoun := 'him';
      else GetPronoun := 'it';
   end;
end;

function WishAHappyBirthdayTo(Who: Organism): String;
begin
   If Who.Birthday <> Today then WishAHappyBirthdayTo := ''
   else WishAHappyBirthdayTo := 'Wish '+GetPronoun(Who)+' a happy birthday!';
end;

. . .
begin
   . . .
   Message := WishAHappyBirthdayTo(Son.Pet.BasicInfo);
   . . .
```

You can see how the liberal use of subroutines can simplify code. The same code used to greet the son's pet can be used for the mother's boss:

```
Message := WishAHappyBirthdayTo(Mother.Occupation.Boss.BasicInfo);
```

An important limitation to realize from this example is that *Boss* could not be an *Adult* type record because it was used in defining the *Adult* record type. While you can have records within records, you cannot have a record that contains itself:

```
type
   Adult = record
      BasicInfo : Organism;
      Job       : String;
      Boss      : Adult;   {No! Will not compile!}
   end;
```

By extension, and also because a type must be declared before being used as a variable or in another type, you cannot have a record that contains a record type that contains itself:

```
type
   Tail = record
      Length: Byte;
      Owner : Dog;  {Will stop here!  Dog type is undefined.}
   end;

   Dog = record
      MyTail : TailRecord;
   end;
```

The reason this restriction exists is fairly obvious when you think about it. When you have a record containing a field of the same type (either directly or indirectly through another record) you've created an impossible situation—an endless data loop. A variable of type, *Tail* has a field *Owner*. *Owner* is a dog type which contains a field *MyTail* that is a variable of type Tail. A variable of type Tail has a field, *Owner*. You don't have to worry about doing this accidentally—Delphi won't let you. (There are ways to indicate the relationship between a dog and its tail that don't create this situation.)

You might wonder if there isn't some kind of speed penalty to your programs when you code a line like this:

```
Family.Mother.Boss.BasicInfo.Birthdate.Year := ThisYear;
```

After all, it certainly takes a long time to read!

There is no penalty. Variables are names for locations in RAM, as discussed many chapters ago. This is true of a record variable, too. This grouping of RAM into a complex, logical form that suits your purpose is ultimately changed by the compiler into a simple memory location, so the preceding expression is not much different than if you had two simpler records that assigned a field from one to the other.

```
ARecord.SomeField := AnotherRecord.SomeOtherField;
```

The *With* Keyword

Pascal has a feature that simplifies referring to records and their fields, and is particularly useful when doing a number of operations on the same record. The keyword *with* essentially says, put this record name in front of all the fields I'm about to list so that I don't have to repeat it each time. With is followed by a do.

```
With Family.Son.Pet.BasicInfo do
   if (Gender = Female) and (Birthdate = Today)
   then WishHerAHappyBirthday;
```

Delphi realizes that *Gender* and *Birthdate* are both fields of the *Organism* record *Family.Son.Pet*, and basically translates the above lines into the following:

```
If (Family.Son.Pet.Basic.Info.Gender = Female)
and (Family.Son.Pet.BasicInfo.Birthdate = Today) then . . .
```

Chapter 16 ◆ The Record

The Do may be followed by a begin, allowing you to perform a block of operations on a record:

```
With Family.Son.Pet.BasicInfo do
begin
   Gender = Female;
   BirthDate := Today;
end;
```

You can nest With statements. This nesting can be complementary, as in

```
with Family do
begin
   with Son do                         {With family.son}
   begin
      BasicInfo.BirthDate := Today;
      ↪{Family.Son.BasicInfo.Birthdate}
      with Pet Do                      {with family.son.pet do}
      begin
         Pet.Kind := Snake;            {Family.Son.Pet.Kind}
         Pet.BasicInfo.Gender := Female;
         ↪{Family.Son.Pet.Kind.BasicInfo}
      end;
   end;
   with Daughter do
   . . .
```

or can be unrelated to the outer With, though this can get confusing:

```
var
   Family, Friends: NuclearFamily;
   Joe, Steve    : Adult;

begin
   . . .
   with Family do
   begin
      Family.Father := Joe;
      ↪GetFamilyOfCoWorker(Joe, Friends);         {Routine that puts
Joe's CoWorker's family into var Friends}
      with Friends do
         Father := Steve;              {Friends.Father = Steve}
   . . .
```

In this example, *Friends.Father* is *Steve* and *Family.Father* is still *Joe*. Given the likelihood for confusion, this code is probably better expressed this way:

```
with Family do
begin
    Family.Father := Joe;
    GetFamilyOfCoWorker(Joe, Friends);
end;
with Friends do
    Father := Steve;
    . . .
```

Inside a With block, a record's field takes precedence over any variable of the same name:

```
procedure MyProc(var Family: NuclearFamily);
var Father : Adult;
begin
   Father := Steve;
   with Family do
   begin
      Father := Joe;    {Family.Father := Joe}
      Mother := Sue;
   end;
. . .
```

In this code, at the end of the With block, *MyProc's Father* variable is still *Steve*, but *Family.Father* has been changed to *Joe*. Here again is another confusion to be avoided. Often, because you're dealing with records and you don't really think of their fields as individual variables that you might get confused with local variables, you don't realize you have a conflict until you do something like this:

```
with Family do
begin
   Father := Father;   {Whoops!}
```

This can be remedied by changing the name of the non-record variable, or by ending the With block.

```
var Dad: Adult;
. . .
   Father := Dad;
. .
```

or

```
with Family do
begin
   . . .
end;
Family.Father := Father;
```

> **Note:** A lot of confusions and conflicts with records can be resolved by using objects, as shown in Chapter 20, "Units."

Although you're likely never to notice it, there *is* a slight speed penalty using a record over using a simple variable. Where a simple variable, like an integer, refers to an area in RAM that is treated as a whole, a record refers to an area where sections (the fields) may be accessed individually. So, in the following:

Chapter 16 ♦ The Record

```
var I: Integer;
    R: SomeRecordType
. . .
    I := 1;
    R.SomeField := 1;
. . .
```

whereas *I* can be translated and acted upon instantly, your program must first figure out where *R* is (as it would with *I*) and then also have to figure out where in the area of memory described by *R* the *SomeField* field begins. This doesn't take long, but could conceivably add up, particularly in a situation like this:

```
R.SomeField := 1;
R.NextField := 2;
R.ThirdField := 3;
```

where the calculations occur over and over again.

With reduces that time somewhat by telling the compiler that a number of fields that are going to be used in this block of code all come from the same area of memory. So,

```
with R do
begin
    SomeField := 1;
    SomeField := 2;
    SomeField := 3;
    end;
```

This should be faster than the previous snippet, although again you'd only notice it if you called this code many thousands of times.

Example: A Data Entry Form

The example for this chapter is to build the data entry form pictured in figure 16.3. And to build a simple project where the main form consists of a single button that calls up the data entry form. Then, store the data from that form in a record. Save the unit as PRIFORM and the project as TWOFORMS.

The difference between this and other examples in the book is that this example requires only that you build a data entry form *functionally* the same as the one pictured. You can build exactly the same form; you can build a form that doesn't separate out first and last name; you can build a form that uses a different control (maybe a spin button) for the publication date field; and you can build a form that's essentially the same but rearranged.

Figure 16.3

The redesigned Book Data Entry form.

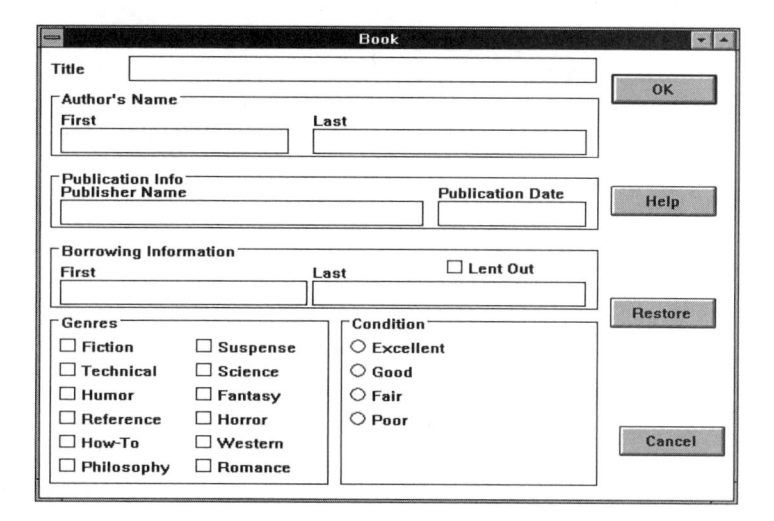

[Book form screenshot showing fields for Title, Author's Name (First, Last), Publication Info (Publisher Name, Publication Date), Borrowing Information (First, Last, Lent Out checkbox), Genres (Fiction, Technical, Humor, Reference, How-To, Philosophy, Suspense, Science, Fantasy, Horror, Western, Romance), Condition (Excellent, Good, Fair, Poor), and buttons OK, Help, Restore, Cancel.]

> **Note:** When building a complex form with many controls, keep in mind that you don't have to name *every* control. For example, if a label is going to have the same caption throughout the program, why does it need a name other than *Label5* or whatever Pascal makes up?
>
> A "trick" I use is to name the edit fields that the labels are describing after the caption in the label field. So if the label reads "Title," I name the edit line *Title*. I'll use the group box as a prefix, too, so that "First" in the Author group box becomes the name *AuthorFirst* for the edit line.
>
> However, it is *vitally important* that you name your components *before* referring to them in your code! **Pascal will *not* change your code to match a change in a component name.** If you forget to name your form, for example, and you have something like this in your code:
>
>   Form2.Show;
>
> and you subsequently change Form2 to *AddBook*, Pascal will not change that line (or any other) and will give you an `unknown identifier` error!

My choices reflect my personality. Edit objects are grouped together because I think that makes the form easier to look at. I also like figure 16.3 because the tab order is fairly natural: Title, Author First, Author Last, Publisher, Date, Lent To checkbox (this is the one bump in the flow of data entry), Borrower First, Borrower Last, Genre, Condition, and then the buttons.

Chapter 16 ◆ The Record

It is customary in a data entry form to have the "OK" button be the default, which means that it will be selected by the user pressing Enter. In terms of the program, clicking the OK button is the user saying "I'm done with this record. Enter it into the database."

> **Tip:** Which button should be default is a common sense issue: A good rule of thumb is make the default button the one that causes the least damage when the user selects it.

If the form is meant to be used for one record, you remove the form after the user presses Enter. If it is to be used for many records, you position the user back at the top of the form, in the Title field, ready to type in the next entry. You might also clear out the edit controls in the form and reset the radio buttons and check boxes.

There's very little code to show; most of the effort is in building the screen. Add the LibraryEntry, Genres, and Conditions types before the var section in Unit2 (which you should save as LIBDE):

```
type
   Genres = (gFiction, gTechnical, gHumor, gReference, gHowTo,
   ➥gPhilosophy,
            gSuspense, gScience, gFantasy, gHorror, gWestern, gRomance);
   Conditions = (cExcellent, cGood, cFair, cPoor);

   GenreSet = Set of Genres;

   LibraryEntry = record
      BookTitle, BookAuthor, BookPublisher: String[30];
      BookDate                            : Word;
      BookLentOut                         : Boolean;
      BookLendee                          : String[30];
      BookGenre                           : GenreSet;
      BookCondition                       : Conditions;
   end;

var              {These lines generated automatically by Pascal}
   Form2: TForm2;
```

(Notice that I changed BookGenre to be a GenreSet to accommodate the possibility of a book being in more than one genre.) After the place where Form2 is declared, add a record for holding the data.

```
Book : LibraryEntry;
```

Now, double-click on the OK button. Basically what has to be done at this point is to place the data the user has put into the data entry form into the record variable. This is pretty straightforward stuff. One place where I added a twist is in building the Genre set. Instead of doing this:

```
If Fiction.Checked then BookGenre := BookGenre + [Fiction];
```

I built a procedure that streamlined the process somewhat:

```
AddGenreToSet(BookGenre, Fiction, Fiction.Checked);
```

This adds the element specified in the second parameter to the set specified in the first parameter, but only if the third parameter is true.

Other than that, there isn't much to getting the data (except for the three lines noted, you have to type all this in):

```
implementation                   {Pascal generates this}

{$R *.FRM}                 {Pascal generates this}

procedure AddGenreToSet(var ASet: GenreSet; AGenre: Genres; DoIt: Boolean);
begin
   If DoIt then ASet := ASet + [AGenre];
end;


procedure TForm2.OKClick(Sender: TObject);          {Pascal generates this}
begin
   with Book do
   begin
      BookTitle    := Title.Text;       BookAuthor   := AuthorLast.Text +
       ', '+AuthorFirst.Text;
      BookPublisher:= PublisherName.Text;
      BookDate     := 0;
      BookLentOut  := LentOut.Checked;
      BookLendee   := LendeeLast.Text + ', '+LendeeFirst.Text;
      BookGenre    := [];

      AddGenreToSet(BookGenre, gFiction, Fiction.Checked);
      AddGenreToSet(BookGenre, gTechnical, Technical.Checked);
      AddGenreToSet(BookGenre, gHumor, Humor.Checked);
      AddGenreToSet(BookGenre, gReference, Reference.Checked);
      AddGenreToSet(BookGenre, gHowTo, HowTo.Checked);
      AddGenreToSet(BookGenre, gPhilosophy, Philosophy.Checked);
      AddGenreToSet(BookGenre, gSuspense, Suspense.Checked);
      AddGenreToSet(BookGenre, gScience, Science.Checked);
      AddGenreToSet(BookGenre, gFantasy, Fantasy.Checked);
      AddGenreToSet(BookGenre, gHorror, Horror.Checked);
      AddGenreToSet(BookGenre, gWestern, Western.Checked);
      AddGenreToSet(BookGenre, gRomance, Romance.Checked);

      If Excellent.Checked then BookCondition := cExcellent
      else if Good.Checked then BookCondition := cGood
      else if Fair.Checked then BookCondition := cFair
      else if Poor.Checked then BookCondition := cPoor;
   end;
end;
```

You'll have to adjust the names of the controls to whatever you called them, but there really should be little difference between the way I coded this and the way you coded it.

From here you can add code to make the Restore button. That basically consists of reversing the actions done here. Simply take the data out of Book and put it back in the appropriate on-screen components.

You'll use the LIBDE unit and form again in Chapter 19.

Summary

Record data types allow you to store a great deal of information in one neat package. Records may have many fields of any Pascal data type, including other records. The symbol '.' is used to access a record's field. A record variable may be assigned to another record variable of an identical type. A record type cannot be returned from a function, but can be used as a var parameter in a procedure. Choosing the right data type for a field in a record is very important. The same record type may be used as a component in many different records to great advantage. A record type cannot be used in its own definition. Referring to the fields of a record variable can be simplified through the judicious use of the With keyword. Mixing With blocks can be either helpful or confusing depending on how you use them.

Program design often begins with record data types, not with the visual forms that the user sees. Users don't want to know or care about the data structures used in your program. Forms must be designed for clarity and easy for the user to enter data. Breaks in the flow of data entry or anything that otherwise calls attention to the form (and away from the task) must be avoided. Designing a good form for the user to interact with is very important and also very subjective. People's opinions will differ as to what is better or worse.

The SizeOf built-in function returns the size of any data type in bytes.

Pascal allows a program to have many forms. These forms can be made to hide or show themselves through the Hide and Show methods.

Review Questions

1. What is the purpose of a record?
2. What is a field?
3. Can a record type contain another record?
4. How are fields of a record accessed?
5. If *S* and *T* are record types, which of the following will Pascal allow?

```
S := T;
S := T + 1;
If T<>S then . . .;
T := AFunction(S);
AProcedure(S, T);
```

6. What does the SizeOf function do?

7. Given this block of code, what does each reference to *Age* in the main block of the program actually refer to?

```
type
   Wine = record
      Area: String;
      Age : Longint;
   end;

   Person = record
      Name        : String;
      Age         : Byte;
      FavoriteWine: Wine;
   end;

var
   Age        : Word;
   Bordeaux : Wine;
   Fred       : Person;

begin
   . . .
   Age := Random(1000);
   with Bordeaux do Inc(Age);
   with Fred do
   begin
      Age := 1992 - SomeDate;
      with FavoriteWine do
      begin
         Age := Fred.Age div 2;
      end;
      Age := -1;
   . . .
```

8. Will this line in the preceding program compile?

```
      Age := -1;
```

Chapter 16 ◆ The Record

9. Will the following compile?

```
type
   Fish = record
      ScaleType    : Integer;
      AvgWeight    : Integer;
      FavoriteFood : Fish;
   end;
```

10. Should you hesitate to code something like this because it will be too slow? What could you do to make it easier to read?

```
APerson.Mom.FavoriteFlower.Color.Hue = Blue;
```

11. Can you have a record inside a record inside record and so forth until there was a record that was eight layers down? How many layers down could it go?

12. Why is it important to select the data types for fields carefully?

13. Why would you want to create a common data type that worked for all similar fields of all the records in a program—or even in every program you write?

14. What are some considerations you might have when building a data entry form?

15. Is it a good thing to make the users aware of your data structures?

16. When requiring the user to enter a name, what are the pros and cons of having two entry objects (one for first name, one for last) versus having just one?

17. What are some problems with having many controls on a form?

Review Exercises

1. Embellish the example library program by adding a library ID number to the Borrower Information group box. (And, of course, to the LibraryEntry record.)

2. Cause all the controls in the Borrower Information group box except LentTo to be disabled if `LentTo.Checked` is `False`.

3. Set up some simple records to handle the data that would go into a phone book, an address book, an appointment calendar, and a customer list. Decide what each type of record should hold and define those types. Locate the commonality between the types and set those into their own records that are used by the other record types. For example, you might be able to reuse a Person record in a number of those or a Date record.

4. Set up a program with various buttons that show forms based on the record types you set up in exercise 3.

5. Fix the Data Entry program built in this chapter so that the restore button works. (It should put the data in Book back into the various controls.) This exercise is not especially tricky, except that you'll have to parse the two names to put them back in their separate fields. From this you may decide that the data entry form should always mirror the data type.

6. Rewrite the Data Entry program so that values get assigned to the Book variable from each of the controls. For example, in a new TForm2.TitleChange, you would put this:

```
Book.BookTitle := Title.Text;
```

This way, every time you type a key, Book is already up to date. This step can make code more manageable. Here again, however, the code to update the names will be more difficult, and this may encourage you further to make sure that the entry form matches the data record as exactly as possible. (In a situation like this, the OK button could be used to commit the new entry to disk.)

7. After you complete exercise 6, the Restore button won't work because Book is being changed constantly. Fix this function.

CHAPTER 17

The Array

The record is an extremely valuable tool, as you saw in the last chapter. By allowing you to group variables together into a single data type, the record removes a lot of the drudgery of programming. But what if you wanted to keep handy a group of records—an array of 10 or 20 records perhaps—to display to the user? Currently you'd be forced to do something like this:

```
var
    Rec1, Rec2, Rec3, Rec4, Rec5, Rec6, Rec7, Rec8, Rec9, Rec10:
    ➥ARecordtType;
```

For all your sophistication in creating data types, this stuff is pretty ugly. Also, if you want to work with each of these records based on the contents of one of their fields, you'd have to do it like this:

```
If Rec1.Bool then DoThis(Rec1);
If Rec2.Bool then DoThis(Rec2);
If Rec3.Bool then DoThis(Rec3)
```

This is no better than repeating the same block of code over and over again instead of using a subroutine, or declaring a bunch of individual variables instead of organizing them into a record.

The Array Data Type

Enter the *array*. An array is a data type that represents a certain number of variables of the same type. The Pascal array may be used with any of the standard data types (integers, strings, reals, booleans) or with any of the user data types, including enumerated types, sets, and records. An array can be used to declare a simple (that is, a non-record) variable or as part of the definition of a record type.

To declare a variable that is an array requires you to provide an identifier, use the *array* keyword, specify the bounds of the array in square brackets, and tell the compiler what type the array is to hold:

```
var
    Data : Array[1..100] of string;
```

The range punctuation '..' is used to indicate that *Data* is an array of 100 strings numbered "from 1 to 100." This range implies that an array does not have to be numbered from one. It does not. An array can be numbered from zero:

```
var
    Kelvin: Array[0..1000] of Temperatures
```

It can be nowhere near zero or one, positive, or negative:

```
var
    TwentiethCentury: Array[1901..2000] of Events;
    LessThanZero: Array[-999..-400] of shortint;
```

An array can be expressed in terms of characters:

```
var
    DigitValues: Array['0'..'9'] of byte;
    SecretCode : Array['A'..'Z'] of char;
```

Or, in fact, almost any ordinal type, including your own enumerated types:

```
type
        Rank = (Ace, Two, Three, Four, Five, Six, Seven, Eight, Nine, Ten,
        ↪Jack, Queen, King);
var
    Deck: Array[Ace..King] of Cards;
```

Using an array that you have declared is as simple as requesting the specific element in brackets after the identifier name:

```
var
    Book     : LibraryEntry;
    Catalogue: Array[1..100] of LibraryEntry;
begin
...
    Book := Catalogue[50];
...
```

Of course, the *index*—the value in between the brackets—must be a value compatible with the type that you declared the array's range to be. In the preceding example, this

```
    LibraryEntry = Catalogue[-1];
```

would cause an error. And the *Deck* type earlier could not be accessed like this:

```
    Card := Deck[1];
```

but would instead have to be accessed by using an element from Rank:

```
Card := Deck[Ace];
```

The most important part about accessing arrays, however, is that the index can be a variable rather than a literal amount:

```
type
     Rank = (Ace, Two, Three, Four, Five, Six, Seven, Eight, Nine, Ten,
     ↪Jack, Queen, King);
var
   Deck: Array[Ace..King] of byte;
   Index: Rank;
begin
   Index := Jack;
   Deck[Index] := 12;
   . . .
```

If it can be indexed by a variable, that means the same operation can be performed on all of the elements of the array without duplicating code, as in:

```
For Index := Ace to King do Deck[Index] :=  Random(52)+1;
```

Or, going back to the first example in the chapter:

```
For I := 1 to 10 do If Rec[I].Bool then DoThis(Rec[I]);
```

Example: Sort

No book on beginning programming is complete without showing an example of how to sort. (Sorting data is the process of putting data in some kind of order.) Although sorting can be done many ways, almost all beginning books on programming demonstrate the *bubble* sort. Why they do this is a mystery, because it is one of the least efficient sorting algorithms around. It works by comparing one data item to its immediate neighbor, and swapping the two if they are out of order. This process looks something like this:

```
Q L B C      <--- Q is compared with L and swapped
L Q B C      <--- Q is compared with B and swapped
L B Q C      <--- Q is compared with C and swapped
L B C Q
```

From here, L is compared with B, then with C, and then with Q. This procedure is continued until you pass through all the data without swapping any of the items.

This sorting is called "selection sort" and is a little more straightforward (and considerably faster) than sorting by the bubble method. You'll scan through the data to find the lowest item and put that first. Then you'll scan through the remaining items to find the next lowest item. You'll do this until you get to the last two items.

Chapter 17 ♦ The Array

```
Q L B C <—Q is comapred with L, B and C, and swapped with B
B L Q C <—L is compared with Q and C and swapped with C
B C Q L <—Q is compared with L and swapped
B C L Q
```

This method of sorting is good because the further along you get, the less time you spend scanning. By the time you get to the next to last item, you only have to compare (and possibly swap) it with the last item and you're done.

You can use a very basic form to show how this sort works. Set up a form like the one shown in figure 17.1. Inside the group box with the caption "List" is a label with the *Name* of List that will show your sorted and unsorted data. (I called the project "SORT," the unit "SORTFORM," and the form "TestSort.")

Figure 17.1

Setting up the TestSort form.

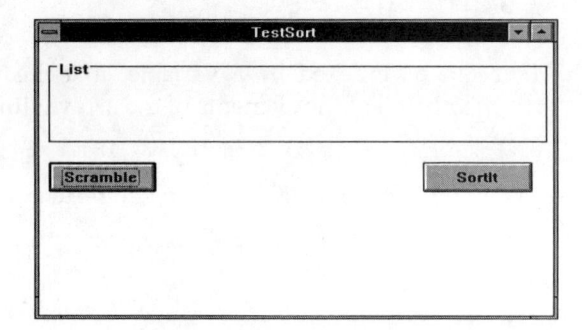

The data will be an array of 30 characters, which you will randomly fill with data when the user presses the *Scramble* button, and then sort when the user presses the *SortIt* button.

To get the random characters, you'll use a Pascal function called *Chr*. Given a byte value, *Chr* returns the ASCII character with that ordinal value. If you look at Appendix A, you'll observe that the letters A through Z are ASCII 65 through 90. You can generate a random character with this code:

```
Chr(Random(26)+65);
```

All that remains is to assign the result to an array so that you can then display it and sort it. You should be able to create the procedure for *Scramble* easily. These next sections will walk you through the process.

Declare the array that will hold the data after Pascal generated var section:

```
var
  TestSort : TTestSort;
  Data : Array[1..30] of char;                {Add this line only}
```

Double-click on the *Scramble* button. In the *ScrambleClick* procedure, create a loop that cycles 30 times, generates a random character, and puts it into the *Data* array:

```
procedure TTestSort.ScrambleClick(Sender: TObject);
var I: Integer;
begin
   List.Caption := '';

   For I := 1 to 30 do
   begin
      Data[I] := Chr(Random(26)+65);
      List.Caption := List.Caption + Data[I] + ' ';
      Update;
   end;
end;
```

Here *List.Caption* is being updated 30 times. A more efficient approach would have been to substitute a string variable for *List.Caption* and then assign *List.Caption* its final value outside the loop.

```
For I := 1 to 30 do
begin
   Data[I] := Chr(Random(26)+65);
   S := S + Data[I];
end;
List.Caption := S;
```

I prefer the first version only because this is a demonstration program and gives you a feel for what is happening while it happens.

The sort code is somewhat more complex. It should have an outer loop traversing the array, and then an inner loop looking for the lowest character remaining. Based on what the inner loop discovers, the remaining code should swap the characters that aren't in the right order.

Here's the outer loop:

```
For I := 1 to 29 do
begin
   Low := I;
```

You start by assuming that the current character is in the right place. By the end of the inner loop, *Low* will contain the lowest character not yet sorted. Here's the inner loop:

```
   For J := I+1 to 30 do
      If Data[J] < Data[Low] then Low  := J;
```

Straightforward enough. You're now going to swap the characters—but only if the current character isn't in the right place.

```
      If I<>Low then
      begin
         Hold := Data[I];
         Data[I] := Data[Low];
         Data[Low] := Hold;
      end;
```

Every now and again, a programmer will write the preceding code something like this:

```
Data[I] := Data[Low];
Data[Low] := Data[I];
```

This code won't work to swap the values, because the value in *Data[I]* is destroyed by the first line. You end up with both positions having the same value and the original value being lost. (Pascal, mysteriously, does not have a built-in *Swap* procedure for swapping two variables' values.)

Finally, you should set up *List.Caption* to have the new values.

```
{Redraw list caption code}
List.Caption := '';
For Index := 1 to 30 do
begin
    List.Caption := List.Caption + Data[Index] + ' ';
    Update;
end
```

Again, for illustration purposes, I took the liberty of putting the code to refresh *List.Caption* within the inner loop. Here's how I put the whole procedure together:

```
procedure TTestSort.SortItClick(Sender: TObject);
var I, J, Low, Index: Integer;
    Hold     : Char;
begin
   For I := 1 to 29 do
   begin
      Low := I;
      For J := I+1 to 30 do
         If Data[J] < Data[Low] then Low  := J;
      If I<>Low then
      begin
         Hold := Data[I];
         Data[I] := Data[Low];
         Data[Low] := Hold;

         {Redraw list caption code}
         List.Caption := '';
         For Index := 1 to 30 do
         begin
             List.Caption := List.Caption + Data[Index] + ' ';
             Update;
         end;
      end;
   {Redraw code really belongs here}
end;
```

If you put the redraw code where the comment is, you'll notice that the code runs a lot faster. Where I put it, every time two characters are swapped, *List.Caption* redraws itself. Depending on the speed of your computer, you can actually track the progress of the sort as *List* flickers with its new values. *List.Caption* flickers faster and faster as the sort approaches the end.

> **Caution:** This procedure will tie up Windows until it is completed. The procedure shouldn't take long, however, even on a slow computer—so don't be alarmed.

If your machine is *really* fast, so that you can't see what's going on at all, try a larger array. The sort is also much easier to follow with the eye if you alter the *List.Caption* update code as in the following:

```
If I<>Low then
begin
   Hold := Data[I];
   Data[I] := Data[Low];
   Data[Low] := Hold;

   {Redraw list caption code}
   S := '';
   For Index := 1 to 100 do
      S := S + Data[Index] + ' ';
   List.Caption := S;
   Update;
end;
```

using a temporary string variable *S* to hold the values for *Data*. Otherwise, *List* gets redrawn 100 times and the flickering is difficult to look through.

A Deck of Cards

You've toyed with the concept of card types a number of times already but the idea of trying to emulate a deck of cards without using an array is distasteful at best. (Most kinds of games, as a matter of fact, require some array usage, whether it be to hold data that represents a hand in poker; the playing board in chess, checkers, or Monopoly; or the map for the terrain of a strange world.)

Chapter 17 ◆ The Array

> **Note:** If you're using the Visual Solutions Pack, you have a control that allows you to present cards on the VBX page of your tool bar. You can use that object in place of the three label objects you're going to use.
>
> You might be wondering if you'll need 52 card controls to get a deck. You don't. The control is not a single *card* but a *stack* of cards. The control can show only one card at a time, but it can change its rank and suit, as though cards were constantly being pulled out of a deck.
>
> To get a feel for how this might work, find the *Value* property for the control. Right now it says, "0 - Back." Indeed the card appears to be face down. Select that property and click on the down-arrow that appears. A list of ranks from "0 - Back" to "13-King" appears. Select "1 - Ace" and the card becomes an Ace of Clubs.
>
> The card also has a *Suit* property, which can be changed from "0 - Clubs" to "3 - Spades." Change that and the card's appearance changes.

Start a new project. The key to building a card game in Delphi is to decide how many cards are going to be shown at once. For each card, you'll need one label (or card deck, if you have the Visual Solutions Pack).

In Blackjack, you might need four. The player is dealt two cards, the dealer is dealt two cards. You might have an additional two as well: there is a deck from which the cards are dealt and a discard pile. These two would always be face down.

The other thing to remember is that even the deck of control cards (in the Visual Solutions Pack) doesn't give you any help in actually keeping track of what cards have been dealt. Two controls might show Ace of Spades. (If you think about it, this makes sense—the deck of cards control can't know how many decks you're playing with.) That leaves it up to you to keep track of the cards.

Example: Hi-Lo

To exercise your array muscles a bit, write a simple card game. One of the simplest card games I know is called "Acey Deucy" or "Hi-Lo." The dealer deals two cards, and the player makes a bet as to whether the next card dealt will fall between the first two.

Start a new project ("HILO") and unit ("HILOFORM").

To create this program you'll use five of the deck of cards controls (if you have the VSP) or five labels representing cards (if not). Three will show the cards that the user is betting on, one will be the deck, and one will be the discard pile. When the user clicks on the deck, that will cause a card to be dealt to one of the first three piles. When the user clicks on the discard pile, that will cause the deck to be reshuffled.

You're going to start by declaring enumerated types for the suits and ranks. Before doing this, if you're using the deck of cards control it would be wise to heed the deck control itself. The ranks are listed as "0 - Back," "1 - Ace" and so on down to "13 - King." The suits are listed from "0 - Clubs" to "3 - Spades." It would seem to make sense to have your enumerated types match the ordinal types of the control:

```
type
    Suits = (Clubs, Diamonds, Hearts, Spades);
    Ranks = (Back, Ace, Two, Three, Four, Five, Six,
            Seven, Eight, Nine, Ten, Jack, Queen, King);
```

(Use this order even if you aren't using the deck of cards control. If nothing else, it will make using that control or a similar one easier.)

The next step is to declare a record type to represent an individual card, and a deck type to represent the whole deck.

```
Cards = record
    Suit: Suits;
    Rank: Ranks;
    end;

CardDeck = array[1..52] of cards;
```

Before getting to the procedures, you should declare the variables to hold the deck, to keep track of how many cards have been dealt from the deck, and to keep track of the user's funds. You'll also declare a special enumerated type and variable to keep track of how many cards have been dealt in this game—none, one, two, or three. (When three have been dealt, the program should notify users whether they have won or lost.)

Here are the complete type and var sections in "HILOFORM."

```
type
    Suits = (Clubs, Diamonds, Hearts, Spades);
    Ranks = (Back, Ace, Two, Three, Four, Five, Six,
            Seven, Eight, Nine, Ten, Jack, Queen, King);

    Cards = record
        Suit: Suits;
        Rank: Ranks;
    end;

    CardDeck = array[1..52] of cards;

    GameState = (NoCards, OneCard, TwoCards, ThreeCards, Reset);

var                     Form1: TForm1;
    Deck : CardDeck;
    State: GameState;
    Dealt: Byte;
    Funds: Integer;
{You need this line if you aren't using the deck of cards control.}
    CardNames: Array[Ace..King, Clubs..Spades] of string[20];
```

Chapter 17 ◆ The Array

Remember that these two lines

```
var
    Form1: TForm1;
```

are generated by Pascal.

Now you should set up the the subroutines to initialize the values in a deck and to shuffle the cards. (The first two lines of code shown here are generated by Delphi.) If you haven't got the Visual Solutions Pack and the deck of cards control, you'll need an extra bit of code to create the text names of the cards. (If you have the deck of cards control, it will *show* the appropriate card.)

```
implementation

{$R *.FRM}

procedure InitializeDeck(var Deck: CardDeck);
var I    : Integer;
    Rank : Ranks;
    Suit : Suits;
    R,S  : String;
begin
   I := 1;
   For Suit := Clubs to Spades do
      For Rank := Ace to King do
   begin
      Deck[I].Suit := Suit;
      Deck[I].Rank := Rank;

{Special code for non-card-deck users}
      case Suit of
         Clubs   : S := 'Clubs';
         Diamonds: S := 'Diamonds';
         Hearts  : S := 'Hearts';
         Spades  : S := 'Spades';
      end;
      case Rank of
         Back : R := 'Back';
         Ace  : R := 'Ace';
         Two  : R := 'Two';
         Three: R := 'Three';
         Four : R := 'Four';
         Five : R := 'Five';
         Six  : R := 'Six';
         Seven: R := 'Seven';
         Eight: R := 'Eight';
         Nine : R := 'Nine';
         Ten  : R := 'Ten';
         Jack : R := 'Jack';
         Queen: R := 'Queen';
         King : R := 'King';
```

```
end;
      CardNames[Rank, Suit] := R + ' of ' + S;
{End special code for non-card-deck users}

      Inc(I);
   end;
end;
procedure ShuffleDeck(var Deck: CardDeck);
var Hold: Cards;
    I, J: Integer;
begin
   for I := 1 to 52 do
   begin
      Hold := Deck[I];
      J := Random(52)+1;
      Deck[I] := Deck[J];
      Deck[J] := Hold;
   end;
end;
```

And, you'll definitely need the old *StrFn* routine to convert the *Funds* variable into a string that you can display on your form.

```
function StrFn(L: Longint): String;
var S: String;
begin
   Str(L, S);
   StrFn := S;
end;
```

The interesting thing to notice at this point is that you haven't done anything that restricts this program to the *Hi-Lo* game. You're more or less set up for *any* card game, except for the *GameState* enumerated type, which would be different for different games.

Now set up the form (see fig. 17.2). The three decks that form an upside-down triangle are *Card1*, *Card2*, and *HiLo*. The cards dealt will appear there. These three controls start out hidden, because no cards have been dealt yet.

Note: If you aren't using the deck of cards control, replace the five card controls shown with simple label controls.

The descriptions of how to program this include notes on using both tools.

Chapter 17 ◆ The Array

Figure 17.2
The Hi-Lo form.

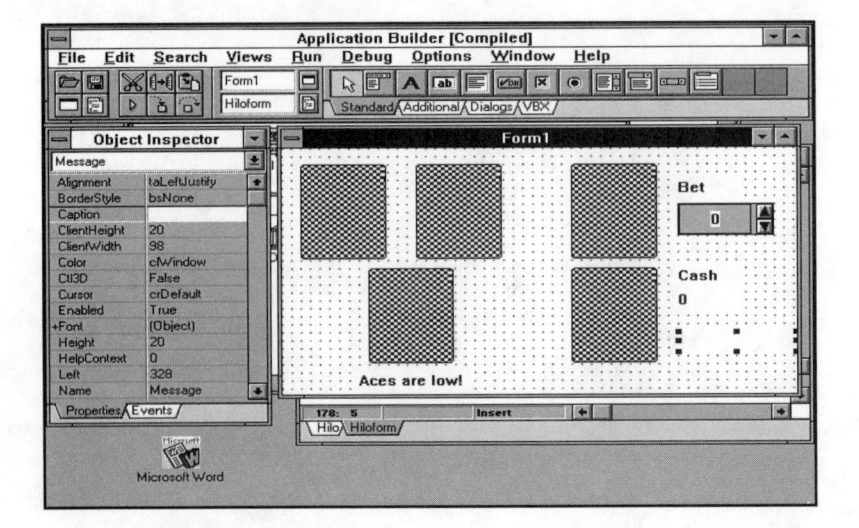

On the right side of the form are *Stack*, where the cards will "be dealt," and *Discard*, where the cards will "be discarded" after the game is over. At first, *Discard* should be hidden, because no cards have been discarded yet. (The real value of *Stack* and *Discard* will be to give the user access to events that will cause cards to be dealt and the deck to be shuffled.)

There is also a spin button, *Bet*, representing the bet that the user wants to place. This should have a *Min* property of 0, because a large part of the game is not betting when you think you can't win. It should have a *Max* property of however much cash the user has at the moment. Set it to 0. (You'll set it to the correct amount when the game begins.)

There are five labels on the form, three of which are not specially named. The label with the *Caption* "Bet" is there to decribe the *Bet* spin button. The label with the *Caption* "Cash" is there to describe the *Cash* label. The "Aces are low!" label is just a friendly reminder to the player.

Underneath the *Cash* label is a label named *Message*, which along with the *Cash* label will change as the program runs. *Cash*, of course, will display the *Funds* variable. *Message* will display a message such as "You won" or "You lost."

The "HILO" program has at least two events to handle: *StackClick* and *DiscardClick*. Before going into those, look at another event that can be useful for initializing data—the *Create* event.

The *Create* event happens when a program starts and the form is first displayed to the user. Up to this point, you've done all your initialization in the main block of the program:

332

```
begin
   {Initialization code here}
   Application.Run(Form1);
end.
```

You could just as well do it by creating a special procedure that gets called when the *Create* event occurs. Click on a blank spot of the form for the game and switch to the event page in the Object Inspector. Double-click on the entry field for the *Create* event. In this code frame, you'll put the code to set up the deck of cards:

```
procedure TForm1.FormCreate(Sender: TObject);
begin
   State := NoCards;
   Dealt := 0;
   Funds := 100;
   Bet.Max := Funds;
   InitializeDeck(Deck);
   ShuffleDeck(Deck);
   Cash.Caption := StrFn(Funds);
end;
```

This procedure is self-explanatory. (You built the *InitializeDeck* and *ShuffleDeck* procedures a few pages ago, remember?) The next event procedure you'll look at is *DiscardClick.* (If you're using the card controls, double-click on *Discard.* If not, switch the event page for *Discard* and double-click to the right of the *OnClick* event.) This procedure is also pretty simple:

```
procedure TForm1.DiscardClick(Sender: TObject);
begin
   Discard.Visible := False;
   Stack.Visible := True;
   HiLo.Visible := False;
   Card1.Visible := False;
   Card2.Visible := False;

   State := NoCards;

   ShuffleDeck(Deck);
   Dealt := 0;
end;
```

The most interesting procedure in the program is the *StackClick* method. (Double-click on *Stack* if you're using the card control, otherwise switch to the event page for *Stack* and double-click to the right of *OnClick* again.) This program is the first one you've written that reacts differently according to context—in other words, clicking on Stack can produce one of four possibilities:

- Deal a card to the first stack.
- Deal a card to the second stack.

Chapter 17 ◆ The Array

- Deal the Hi-Lo card and figure out if the player wins or loses.
- Clear the cards for the next game.

In computer programming, these contexts are called *states*. A code block that acts differently according to the current context of the program is called a *state machine*. You'll look at how to code a state machine in a moment. First, however, look at your states again:

```
GameState = (NoCards, OneCard, TwoCards, ThreeCards, Reset);
```

No cards, one card, two or three cards have been dealt. The *Reset* state tells you that the cards have been cleared from the table, and the program will be set back in a *NoCards* state. In code, the state machine will look something like this:

```
case State of
   NoCards: DealACardToStack1;
   OneCard: DealACardToStack2;
   TwoCards: DealTheHiLoCardAndCalculateWinsAndLosses;
   ThreeCards: ClearTheTable;
end;
Inc(State);
If State = Reset then State := NoCards;
```

This block is the basic framework for the *StackClick* method. Here's how the code should react according to each state:

```
case State of
   NoCards: begin
             Inc(Dealt);
      {Use this code for the deck of cards control}
             Card1.Value := Ord(Deck[Dealt].Rank);
             Card1.Suit  := Ord(Deck[Dealt].Suit);
      {Use this code for the label control
             Card1.Text := CardNames(Deck[Dealt].Rank,
             ↪Deck[Dealt].Suit);
      }
             Card1.Visible := True;
         end;
```

> **Note:** The code commented out is the code that sets a label control to the name of the card. I'll be using this code throughout the rest of the example to distinguish between that and the code to work with the VSP card deck control.

If no cards have been dealt, change the *Value* and *Suit* properties of *Card1* (or the *Text* of *Card1*) to the next card in the deck. The only lines of interest, really, are these:

```
Card1.Value := Ord(Deck[Dealt].Rank);
Card1.Suit  := Ord(Deck[Dealt].Suit);
```

Ord, recall, returns the ordinal value of an enumerated type. So the *Ord* of any rank in *Deck* should return from 1 to 13, where your 1, an Ace, matches the deck control's 1, also an Ace. If you didn't use *Ord* here, you'd have to do something like this:

```
case Deck[Dealt].Rank of
   Ace: Card1.Value := 1;
   Two: Card2.Value := 2;
    . . .
```

and so on, all the way down to King. (In some ways, you can see how the label control is actually easier to work with, if not as glamorous as the deck of cards component.) You'd have to do a smaller version of the same thing for the suits. The next state, *OneCard*, is handled almost identically as was *NoCards*.

```
      OneCard: begin
         Inc(Dealt);
{Code for the deck of cards control}
         Card2.Value := Ord(Deck[Dealt].Rank);
         Card2.Suit  := Ord(Deck[Dealt].Suit);
{Code for the label control
         Card2.Text := CardNames(Deck[Dealt].Rank, Deck[Dealt].Suit);
}
         Card2.Visible := True;
      end;
```

The only difference here is that *Card2* is the control being affected, not *Card1*. The *TwoCards* state starts out the same as *NoCards* and *OneCard*,

```
     TwoCards: begin
         Inc(Dealt);
{Code for the deck of cards control}
         HiLo.Value := Ord(Deck[Dealt].Rank);
         HiLo.Suit  := Ord(Deck[Dealt].Suit);
{Code for the label control
         HiLo.Text := CardNames(Deck[Dealt].Rank, Deck[Dealt].Suit);
}
         HiLo.Visible := True;
```

but then includes the code to handle wins and losses. This first section figures out which of the first two cards dealt is the highest in rank:

```
            If Deck[Dealt-1].Rank > Deck[Dealt-2].Rank then
            begin
               HiRank := Deck[Dealt-1].Rank;
               LoRank := Deck[Dealt-2].Rank;
            end
            else begin
                  HiRank := Deck[Dealt-2].Rank;
                  LoRank := Deck[Dealt-1].Rank;
               end;
```

Chapter 17 ♦ The Array

If *Hi-Lo* falls between them, then the user has won if he has bet money.

```
        If Deck[Dealt].Rank in [LoRank..HiRank] then
        begin
           If Bet.Value = 0 then Message.Caption := 'Too bad!'
           else begin
                   Inc(Funds, Bet.Value);
                   Message.Caption := 'You won!';
              end;
        end
```

If it doesn't, the user wins by not having bet anything:

```
        else begin
           If Bet.Value = 0 then Message.Caption := 'Smart move.'
           else begin
                   Dec(Funds, Bet.Value);
                   Message.Caption := 'You lost.';
              end;
        end;
   end;
```

To give the user a chance to read the messages and check on his funds, you leave the table with the cards all facing up until the user clicks on the stack again. Now the game should be in the *ThreeCards* state:

```
     ThreeCards: begin
{Code for deck of cards and label controls are the same here}
                   Card1.Visible := False;
                   Card2.Visible := False;
                   HiLo.Visible := False;
                   Discard.Visible := True;
              end;
end;
```

This code "clears the table" by turning the various controls invisible. Now look at the entire routine. You use a case statement to determine which block of code to execute:

```
procedure TForm1.StackClick(Sender: TObject);
var HiRank, LoRank : Ranks;
begin
   case State of
      NoCards: begin
         Inc(Dealt);
         Card1.Value := Ord(Deck[Dealt].Rank);
         Card1.Suit  := Ord(Deck[Dealt].Suit);
{        Card1.Text := CardNames(Deck[Dealt].Rank, Deck[Dealt].Suit);}
         Card1.Visible := True;
      end;
      OneCard: begin
         Inc(Dealt);
         Card2.Value := Ord(Deck[Dealt].Rank);
```

```
Card2.Suit   := Ord(Deck[Dealt].Suit);
{       Card2.Text := CardNames(Deck[Dealt].Rank, Deck[Dealt].Suit);}
        Card2.Visible := True;
    end;
    TwoCards: begin
       Inc(Dealt);
       HiLo.Value := Ord(Deck[Dealt].Rank);
       HiLo.Suit  := Ord(Deck[Dealt].Suit);
{      HiLo.Text := CardNames(Deck[Dealt].Rank, Deck[Dealt].Suit);}
       HiLo.Visible := True;

       If Deck[Dealt-1].Rank > Deck[Dealt-2].Rank then
       begin
          HiRank := Deck[Dealt-1].Rank;
          LoRank := Deck[Dealt-2].Rank;
       end
          else begin
                 HiRank := Deck[Dealt-2].Rank;
                 LoRank := Deck[Dealt-1].Rank;
          end;

       If Deck[Dealt].Rank in [LoRank..HiRank] then
       begin
          If Bet.Value = 0 then Message.Caption := 'Too bad!'
          else begin
                   Inc(Funds, Bet.Value);
                   Message.Caption := 'You won!';
             end;
       end
          else begin
             If Bet.Value = 0 then Message.Caption := 'Smart move.'
             else begin
                      Dec(Funds, Bet.Value);
                      Message.Caption := 'You lost.';
                end;
             end;

       Bet.Max := Funds;
       Cash.Caption := StrFn(Funds);
    end;

    ThreeCards: begin
                   Card1.Visible := False;
                   Card2.Visible := False;
                   HiLo.Visible := False;
                   Discard.Visible := True;
                end;
end;

Inc(State);
If State<>ThreeCards then Message.Caption := '';
If State = Reset then State := NoCards;
If Dealt = 51 then Stack.Visible := False;

end;
```

Chapter 17 ◆ The Array

(Again, the three lines that are commented out work with the label controls.)

After passing through the case statement, you increment *State*'s value, so that it accurately reflects what has happened. You clear out the *Message* so that it doesn't say "You won" or "You lost" when the player has moved on to the next game. You also make the *Stack* control invisible when all the cards have been dealt.

> **Note:** The reason you stop at 51 instead of 52 is that you're playing a three-card game. With a single deck the user can play 17 games and have one card left over. Since you can't play a game with one card, you force him to shuffle the deck at that point by making *Stack* invisible.

The last two lines ensure that *Bet*'s Value can never exceed the amount of money the player has, and that *Cash*'s Caption accurately reflects the value in *Funds*.

Complex Arrays

An array can hold any Pascal data type. In the past few pages you've used arrays of characters and arrays of your own record type. What if you wanted to write an array to hold values in a spreadsheet, or a chessboard, or perhaps even the locations of stars in space? The arrays you've seen have all been *one-dimensional*—they have had only one index.

You can, however, have an array of arrays:

```
Deck := Array[Ace..King] of Array[Clubs..Spades] of Cards;
```

This declaration can be shortened to simply:

```
Deck := Array[Ace..King, Clubs..Spades] of Cards;
```

To access an element of a variable of type *Deck* requires *two* indices, separated by commas.

```
ADeck[Ace, Spades];
```

This same thing can also be phrased by separating the indices out into separate square brackets:

```
ADeck[Ace][Spades];
```

Arrays can have three or more dimensions.

```
ThreeDChess : Array[1..8,1..8,1..8] of byte;
ComplexArray: Array[1..2,1..2,1..2,1..2,1..2,1..2,1..2] of byte;
```

The thing to keep in mind when using multi-dimensional arrays is that the amount of RAM taken up by the arrays increases exponentially for each dimension.

In other words,

```
ALine: Array[1..10] of byte;
```

takes 10 bytes, while

```
AnArea: Array[1..10,1..10] of byte;
```

takes 100 bytes (10 x 10), and

```
AVolume: Array[1..10,1..10,1..10] of byte;
```

takes 1,000 bytes (10 x 10 x 10) of memory.

Array Limitations

Arrays are so useful in some circumstances and so easy to use that programmers often wish they were unlimited. Unfortunately, there are some severe restrictions on the use of arrays, however, and in some circumstances they simply aren't appropriate.

The biggest limitation on arrays, which is not imposed by the Pascal language so much as it is by the DOS/Windows environment, is that one array cannot occupy more than 64K of space. This condition is a throwback to an earlier era, to pre-80386 computers that could only operate in blocks of 64K.

> **Note:** This 64K limit applies to *all* Pascal data structures, not just arrays. You can't have a record that's larger than 64K, either. This limit is usually not a problem with data types other than arrays, however.
>
> This limit would not apply to the version of Delphi that Borland has promised for Windows 95. Although neither of these products is available at the time of this writing, both are supposed to ship sometime in 1995.

If you were planning to program a great space epic, and had hoped to declare an array like this:

```
Space: Array[1..100,1..100,1..100] of byte;
```

you can forget it. This structure would take up 1M of memory.

Even for a library catalog program, if you use the 129-byte *LibraryEntry* structure that you developed in the previous chapter, you have room for only around 500 entries.

The other liability to using arrays this large is that, if you declare an array like this:

```
Catalog :  Array[1..500] of LibraryEntry;
```

the *Catalog* variable is going to take up 64K of memory, regardless of whether 1 entry, or 500 entries, are in it. This limit is also true of a variable like this:

```
Space: Array[1..100,1..100] of byte;
```

If you're going to use *Space* as a map of some kind, you may find that it is 90% empty, which means 9,000 of the 10,000 bytes of space it occupies will contain nothing but zeroes.

There are more-advanced methods of data storage that don't have these liabilities; unfortunately, however, they don't even come close to arrays in ease of use.

Arrays share many of the record's limitations. You cannot do math with an entire array, or compare two arrays, but you can get an array back from a function.

```
AnArray := AnArray + AnotherArray;    {No!};
If AnArray >= AnotherArray then DoSomething;    {No!}
AnArray := SomeFunction; {This works!}
```

You can, however, assign one array to another array:

```
AnArray := AnotherArray;
```

Delphi has no way for you to assign a value to every item in an array, except through a For loop:

```
AnArray := 0;   {Not Allowed!}
For I := 1 to 100 do AnArray[I] := 0;   {OK}
```

Just as with records, an array may be used as a var parameter in procedures, as you saw with the *DeckShuffle* and *DeckInitialize* procedures.

The Character Array

You've been dealing with arrays from your first step as a Pascal programmer. The string data type is very much like an array of characters. In fact, a string type is essentially identical to this:

```
type
    StringType : Array[0..255] of char;
```

except that Pascal makes special allowances for the string data type so that you can treat it as a whole.

But, although you can treat a string as a unit, the string also retains its array properties. For example, you can get the first character of a string this way:

```
AChar := AString[1];
```

The 0th entry in the string type's array is the length byte. You can get the length of a string by using the *Length* function, or by doing this:

```
I := Ord(String[0]);
```

(Remember, String[0] is a char, just like the rest of the array. To turn it into a byte, use the *Ord* function.)

The hazard of accessing the string's characters like this is that you can easily do this:

```
AChar := AString[10];
```

even when *AString* is only nine characters long. AChar will be set to some undefined character—in other words, to garbage.

I can't tell you not to use it, because there is no other way in Pascal to convert a character in a string to a char type variable. As long as you keep track of how long the string is, you shouldn't have difficulty.

Summary

An array is a group of many variables of the same type, indexed by one or more ordinal ranges. An array can be of any type, including records and other arrays. An array may have many dimensions, but the amount of RAM taken up by an array increases accordingly. An array must not exceed 64K in the DOS/Windows environment. An array takes up the same amount of space regardless of what it contains. Arrays may not be used (as a whole) in math or comparison operations but they can be returned from a function. An array can be assigned the value of another array, but an entire array cannot be assigned one value through a simple assignment statement. A string is essentially a character array that is treated specially by Delphi.

The *Chr* function returns the ASCII character with a specific ordinal value.

There are many approaches to sorting data. The *Bubble* sort is one, but it's not a very good approach. A better approach is the *Selection* sort. A block of code can be made to act differently according to the different states of the program. This is called a *state machine*.

The deck of cards control allows you to easily represent cards in a Pascal program. When using the deck of cards it is best to match your enumerated types for rank and suit with the control's. When a form is first displayed, it results in a *Create* event. The *Create* event is a good time to initialize program data.

Review Questions

1. What is an array good for?
2. What is the *index* of an array?
3. Can you declare an array like this?

   ```
   type ArrayType = array['A'..'Z'] of Longint;
   ```

Chapter 17 ♦ The Array

4. How would you set a variable *A* of this *ArrayType* type declared above to all zeros?

5. What is a bubble sort? What is a better way to sort things?

6. How is a string like a character array? How is it not?

7. What is a state machine? Why build one?

8. Does Pascal pose a limit on the number of dimensions an array can have? What would the limit be for Pascal?

9. How large can a Pascal data structure be? Is this a feature of the Delphi language?

10. Why is the bubble sort so bad and why is the selection sort better? (This question is answered best by demonstration or by a mathematical equation.)

11. In the "HILO" program, the deck of cards was declared as an array of 52 *Cards* type records. Would it have been better to make it a two-dimensional array of 4 by 13?

12. Examine the Data Entry form example of the last chapter, the Set Logic example of Chapter 15, and the Parser example of Chapter 12. One of these previous examples in this book has a state machine in it, but I didn't really call it that. Which one was it? (Hint: It only had *two* states.)

Review Exercises

1. Set up some arrays. Discover how large you can make arrays of various data types before the compiler stops you.

2. Modify the Hi-Lo game so that unless the range expressed by the high and low cards is exclusive—meaning that the Hi-Lo card itself has to fall in between the two ranks but *cannot* be either of those ranks. Right now, in other words, if the low card is an Ace and the high card is a King, the player can't lose. Make it so that an Ace or King would lose in that situation.

3. Add "Jokers" to the Hi-Lo game developed in this chapter. A Joker in the low spot would be an Ace; a Joker in the high spot would be a King; and a Joker as the middle card would always be a win.

4. Adapt the sorting program from the beginning of the chapter to sort whole words rather than just characters.

5. Using the CALCINT program as a template, write a program that displays a random number. Then, when the user pushes a button, the random number clears and he must replay that number. With each round, have the computer display more numbers. So, at first it might display "1" and the user would have to clear that and enter "1." Then, it might display "1 7," and the user would have to clear that and enter "1 7." Then it might display "1 7 5," and so on.

6. Write a program that lets the user enter two strings, and analyzes the second string based on the first so that if the first string is AEIOUaeiou and the user types "CATO" as the second string, the program responds with something like "'CATO' contains two elements of the set of "AEIOUaeiou." (Hint: You will need to use the concept of sets here as well as the concept of arrays.)

7. Write a program that uses a two-dimensional array (of, for example, bytes) and displays it in a meaningful fashion (like a grid). Write this program by using WinCRT and then using a Pascal form.

8. Go back to the last chapter and modify the data entry program built there so that it can store multiple records. Make it so that the user can flip back and forth between the store records.

9. Build a card program to play Blackjack. Keep it as simple as possible while retaining the essential elements of the game.

10. Build a card program to play five card stud poker. You needn't get elaborate. Just make the program deal out five cards for itself and a player, pausing in between to accept bets. You can use several arrays here: one for the deck of cards and one each for the players' hands.

Part VI

File Handling

CHAPTER 18

File Basics

Serious applications—and even most games—demand that the user be able to save the work done in a program from session to session. In modern terms, saving work means storing it on a disk drive. Standard Delphi procedures provide you with a simple and straightforward way to work with disk files.

These procedures bend no rules: A disk file in Delphi must comply with the naming conventions of the DOS/Windows environment as described in Chapter 2.

In Delphi, files are represented by variables, and these variables must be declared as any other variable using one of two file types. Delphi allows you to declare a file as consisting of a particular data type, including records—a very handy tool.

However, there is a common file format that you are doubtless quite familiar with (whether you know it or not) and that you should learn to work with first before learning about typed files.

The Text File

The text file is the most common type of file around. Every general purpose application knows how to read this type of file, and most of them can also write out their data in this format. All the code you write in Pascal gets saved with the PAS or PRJ extension, but are in fact text files and you could read them into any word processor or text editor, or even a spreadsheet program.

Text files are used (naturally) to store text. But there is more than just text in there. For example, if you had some text like this:

```
"The time has come," the Walrus said,
"To talk of many things."
```

which you stored to a file, if a text format held *just* the characters, how would a program know where to break up the lines? It would come back like this:

```
"The time has come," the Walrus said,"To talk of many things."
```

The secret code used in text files to separate lines is called a *carriage return, line feed* sequence (CR-LF). Why? Well, instead of this text being called up on-screen, imagine it going to an old-style daisy wheel or dot-matrix printer, or some similar typewriter device. The device would output character after character, and then at the end of the line what would have to happen? The *carriage,* which holds the paper, would have to *return* to the beginning of the line. And, to keep the next stream of characters from printing over the same text, it would have to move down a *line.* Telling the printer to move down a line is called a *line feed.*

If this sounds archaic to you, you're not alone. The CR-LF sequence is one of the oldest things in computing. It is in such broad use, however, that the notion of it ever completely going away seems unlikely. Printers all still understand this sequence. In fact, writing information to a text file is very similar to writing information to a printer, as you'll see.

File Handling

There are four steps that must be taken when using a file, and those steps have to be followed in the exact order prescribed, every time a file is used. A file variable (sometimes called a file *handle*) must first be associated with an external file name, and then it must be opened (to read an existing file) or rewritten (to write over an existing file) or created (to write to a new file). It can then be read from or written to. When you have completed all your file work, the file must be closed.

Assign, Open, Read/Write, and Close. Leave out any of these steps and the program will fail, sometimes immediately, sometimes in a subtle way that you may not notice for a while.

You may wonder what a file variable really is inside. Is it a longint, a string, or a special record type? The answer is, that's none of your business. Delphi takes great care to insulate you from the complex and arcane details of Windows file management so that you don't have to care what is inside a text variable.

Declaring a File Variable

Declaring a file variable is just like declaring any other kind of variable. The type of a text file variable is called *Text.*

```
var MyFile: Text;
```

The identifier, *MyFile* in this case, is a standard Delphi identifier and has no connection with the name of the file that it will access. In other words, *MyFile* can refer to a file on the disk called "MYFILE" but it could just as well refer to a file called "AUTOEXEC.BAT."

After declaring a file variable, you must take the four steps just outlined, starting with associating the variable with a file name. This is done through the *Assign* procedure. The *Assign* procedure takes two parameters. The first is a file variable, the second, a valid DOS/Windows file name.

```
Assign(MyFile, 'TestFile.TXT');
```

TESTFILE.TXT need not exist at this point. If it doesn't exist the program will, of course, have to create it. In most cases, you'll probably want to be more specific than just a file name. That is, you'll probably want the data for a program to go into a specific directory. A directory and sub-directories can be specified as part of the file name, with the backslash character used to separate the directories from each other and the file name:

```
Assign(MyFile, '\BOOKPAS\TestFile.TXT');
```

You can even specify a particular disk drive, with that disk drive's letter and a colon, as in

```
Assign(MyFile, 'C:TestFile.TXT')
```

When writing to a different disk drive than the default, it is probably even *more* important to specify a specific directory:

```
Assign(MyFile, 'Q:\BOOKPAS\TestFile.Txt');
```

This would refer to a TESTFILE.TXT file in the BOOKPAS directory on the Q drive.

Notice that here I've been using an extension of ".TXT" for the files. This is the common extension for text files. However, it is not mandatory and certainly not enforced by Delphi. The above declaration could just as well have been:

```
Assign(MyFile, 'Q:\TestFile.PDQ');
```

or even with no extension:

```
Assign(MyFile, 'Q:\TestFile');
```

Opening the File

The next step in handling a file is to open the file. Delphi gives you three ways to open a text file, the easiest of which is through the *Rewrite* procedure. Its only parameter is the file variable:

```
Rewrite(MyFile);
```

This will create a new file called whatever was specified in the *Assign* procedure for this variable. In your case that would be "TESTFILE.TXT." If a "TESTFILE.TXT" already exists in the directory specified by the *Assign* (or the current directory if none was specified) that file will be *erased.* Wiped out. Gone forever. Even if you

Chapter 18 ◆ File Basics

have an undelete or unerase utility, it won't help. The file hasn't been deleted, you've just told DOS/Windows that there's no information in it.

Obviously, you aren't going to want to use *Rewrite* every time. Delphi has another procedure, *Reset*, that opens an existing file. Its only parameter is the file variable:

```
Reset(MyFile);
```

Using *Reset* prompts this question: What if the file isn't there? To find out what happens, start a new project, with a single button form, double-click on it and set up the procedure this way:

```
procedure TForm1.Button1Click(Sender: TObject);

var F: System.Text;
begin
   System.Assign(F, 'C:\Testfile.Txt');
   Reset(F);
```

> **Note:** For reasons that will become apparent in Chapter 20, you must prefix references to the Text data type and the *Assign* procedure with the word "System" followed by a period, as shown above.
>
> Make sure there is no "TESTFILE.TXT" file in your root directory.

Run this program. What happens when you push the button? (See figure 18.1.) Delphi puts up the error message `File not found` and stops the program. If you have the Break On Exception option set (**O**ptions menu, **E**nvironment notebook, in the Debugging section), your program will stop first on the `File not found` line, and you will have to continue the program (press F4) to see the error message your program would show a user if a file was not found.

Figure 18.1

The `File not found` error message.

The compiler feature that is causing your difficulty is called *I/O checking*. (I/O is a computer abbreviation for input/output, meaning anything that reads from or writes to the disk.) If you pull down the Options menu and select Project from the sub-menu you'll see a dialog showing all the options for a project. You looked at this earlier when investigating range checking. One of the options is called "I/O checking" and you'll notice that it is checked.

To eliminate the message that pops up when you try to open a nonexistent file, you could un-check that box. But that would mean that all of the file accesses in

350

every part of your program would not get the benefit of I/O checking, which may not be what you want.

The solution to this dilemma comes in the form of a special kind of program "comment" called a compiler *directive*. Using a compiler directive, you can tell Delphi to not present a message that occurs as a result of a file error.

A compiler directive is surrounded by curly braces, begins with a '$' sign, and has a one-letter code indicating its purpose. The letter is usually followed by a '+' sign or a '-' sign depending on whether the directive is to turn on or turn off some compiler feature.

The code for turning I/O checking on and off is the letter *I*. Add in "{$I-}" and "{$I+}" around the *Reset* statement.

```
begin
    Assign(F, 'Testfile.Txt');
    {$I-}
    Reset(F);
    {$I+}
end;
```

The error message will not appear. I/O checking is turned off for the call, then turned back on immediately after.

Now all you need to do is figure out whether or not the *Reset* statement worked. When I/O checking is off, the result of every I/O operation is stored and can be found from the built-in function *IOResult*. *IOResult* can return many different error codes. The only one you need to be interested in right now is 2. 2 means "file not found."

> **Note:** You may wonder why there isn't some enumerated type somewhere that would allow you to use *FileNotFound* instead of the number 2. There isn't, and curiously there never has been.
>
> As a result, DOS and Windows Delphi programmers throughout the ages have learned that the number 2 means *FileNotFound*.

Here is how the code would look using the I/O compiler directive and the *IOResult* function.

```
var F: Text;
    I: Integer;
begin
    Assign(F, 'Testfile.Txt');
    {$I-}
    Reset(F);
    {$I+}
    I = IOResult;
    If I = 0 then {everything went ok}
    else if I = 2 then Rewrite(F)
    else {there is some other problem.}
end;
```

Chapter 18 ◆ File Basics

Calling the *IOResult* function clears out the error number, so that if you call it twice in a row,

```
If IOResult = 0 then {Everything went ok}
  else If IOResult = 2 then Rewrite(F);  {No! IOResult will always be 0!}
```

the second call always results in zero. That's why it is necessary to copy *IOResult* to a variable before testing it.

> **Note:** There are two other compiler directives of interest to you. The first is the {$R+}/{$R-} directive which affects range checking. {$R-} will turn it off and {$R+} will turn it back on. This is one way you can selectively decide where you want Delphi to generate range checking errors for you.
>
> The other compiler directive takes the format of {$R filename} and it tells Delphi to include a particular resource file in the compiled program. Resource files can contain many things, including bitmaps and dialogs, but most commonly (in Delphi) they contain the descriptions of the forms that you have been designing throughout the book.
>
> You're not going to go into depth about Resource Files in this book, but you should recognize that compiler directive because Delphi puts it in every unit you write that has an associated form! That compiler directive usually appears as {$R *.DFM} or {$R *.RES} meaning "include the Delphi form file that matches the name of the unit or the resource file that matches the name of the application."

Delphi also allows you to check to see whether a file exists through the `FileExists` function, which requires the name of the file to be checked and returns true if the file does exist.

```
If not FileExists('C:\CONFIG.SYS') Then ThatWouldBeBad;
```

Closing a File

After reading and writing to a file (the details of which you'll cover momentarily) it is very important to *close* the file you've been working with. This is done through the *Close* procedure.

```
Close(F);
```

As you can see the *Close* procedure takes just one parameter, the file variable that you are done with.

Closing the file is important when reading from a file, because Windows keeps track of open files, and this takes up a certain amount of RAM. Windows also has a finite number of files that it will allow open at any time, and if you keep a file open after you need it, that resource will be unavailable for your own or other programs later on.

Closing a file is *crucial* when writing to files, however. When you write information to a file, it does not necessarily all get written to the disk immediately. Writing to the disk takes time and both Windows and Delphi reserve the right to hold off writing until it is most efficient.

> **Note:** Writing many small bits of data takes longer than writing one large block. Windows and Delphi both recognize this, and try to make writing to files more efficient by grouping many requests to write to the disk together.

If you forget to close a file after writing to it, some of the data may be lost.

Write and *WriteLn* Revisited

This brings you back to the *WriteLn* statement. I mentioned much earlier in this book that the *WriteLn* statement was the cornerstone of all Pascal tutorials before the Age of the Graphical User Interface, which essentially made Writeln an obsolete mode of communicating to the user.

The advantage to Writeln was that it was used to communicate with the user and to write things to the disk and printer. *WriteLn* was the most ubiquitous Pascal procedure— you would have been hard pressed to find a program without at least one call to *WriteLn*.

Even though you no longer use it to communicate with the user, it still is one of the main procedures for storing data on disk and is still used for creating printer output. Technically, what *WriteLn* does is output a string of characters to the disk or the printer (or the screen) followed by a carriage return-line feed sequence to force the next line. The *Write* procedure, which you have not looked at up to this point, does exactly the same thing, but does *not* add the carriage return-line feed sequence at the end.

You haven't used the two procedures much, but they can actually output *any* of the basic data types: integers, reals, Booleans, characters, and strings, and they can output any number of them in one call. These are all legal calls to *WriteLn*:

```
Writeln(AString, AnotherString, AThirdString, AByte, AReal);
Writeln(AByteArray[10], ARecord.AField);
Writeln('Hello, ',YourNameHere,'. Today is ',day,month,year,'.');
```

These same calls are valid with *Write*. Notice that you can mix literal strings with variables.

WriteLn will not let you output entire arrays or records.

```
Writeln(AnArray);    {No!}
Writeln(ARecord);    {No!}
```

WriteLn has some meager formatting options as well. You can specify the length of an item that is output by following the item with a colon and a number.

Chapter 18 ♦ File Basics

```
Writeln(S:20);
```

S, whether string, byte, or real, will take up a *minimum* of 20 spaces—on-screen, on disk, or on paper. If S happens to be longer than 20 characters, it will take more, however.

Write and *WriteLn* will even let you specify the decimal places that a real number should have. This parameter should follow the length parameter. For example,

```
var R: Real;
begin
   R := 1;
   Writeln(R:1:0)
   Writeln(R:1:1);
end;
```

will print out the real number *R* as "1" and "1.0". Remember, the length parameter specifies the *minimum* amount of space. Printing out *R* with one decimal place requires three spaces, and that's how much space it will take.

Does this sound familiar to you? It should. The *Str* procedure uses the same formatting conventions as *Write* and *WriteLn,* and produces exactly the same output. For further details on how this formatting works, refer to the *Calculator, Version 1.0* program in Chapter 13.

Example: Writing to a Text File

So, how do *Write* and *WriteLn* work with files? Both will take, as their *first* parameter, a file variable. As simple as that.

```
program EZWrite;
var F: Text
begin
   assign(F, 'SomeFile.TXT');
   rewrite(F);
   writeln(F, 'Hello, Text file');
   close(F);
end.
```

Enter this into the project code window of a project with no forms, compile, and run. You can see what was done by loading up the file by using WRITE, your word processor, or, if you know DOS, the EDIT program or the TYPE command. Actually, as an experiment, you might want to see how many programs you have that will read the output from this program.

This code also illustrates the four steps you need to take whenever using a file. This tiny bit of code will create a file called 'SomeFile.TXT', and this file will have one line in it with the characters 'Hello, Text file' followed by the CR-LF sequence.

Write is different from *WriteLn* in that it doesn't include that sequence, which makes it possible for you write out a line in pieces. Declare some integers I, J, and K and give them some value so that you can try out this code in the program.

```
Write(F, I);
Write(F, J);
Write(F, K);
Writeln(F);
```

Ultimately, however, you must write out the CR-LF sequence, which can be done by calling *WriteLn* with just a file parameter and nothing else. The same results could be achieved by doing this, of course,

```
WriteLn(F, I, J, K);
```

but sometimes it is handy to write out a line item by item. You can also build a line to write out using a string variable:

```
S := StrFn(I);
S := S + ' ' + StrFn(J);
S := S + Format(K);
Writeln(F, S);
```

Different approaches are useful for different situations.

To write to a text file, you will generally open it using the *Rewrite* procedure. If you try to write to a text file you have opened with *Reset*, your program will fail when you run it.

Appending to Text Files

This doesn't mean that you can only read or entirely rewrite a text file. If you know that a text file exists, you can open it with the *Append* procedure.

```
Append(F);
```

This will allow you to add text to the end of a file. The *Append* procedure has the same liabilities as the *Reset* procedure. If the file is not there, *Delphi* will display an error message. (Unless you have overridden that through the {$I-} directive.)

You cannot, under any circumstances, rewrite a particular line of a text file. You can add to the end of it, or rewrite it completely, but never write to the middle of it.

Read and *ReadLn*

The complements of *Write* and *WriteLn* are *Read* and *ReadLn*. These two procedures allow you to read data back from a text file. *Read* and *ReadLn* were once as ubiquitous as their counterparts. If you wanted data from a user, you got it by using the *ReadLn* procedure. These procedures are still used for getting data off the disk.

By far the most commonly used procedure is *ReadLn*, with a string parameter to hold all the data for the line or from the user. Then, if the data is in several parts, you parse out the elements you want. (You built a simple parser in Chapter 12.)

So, if you read in this line,

```
Give Letter To Mom
```

you would have a parse routine that fished out each word and interpreted what the user wanted done.

ReadLn can take more than one parameter. If you know you have data in a text file in this format:

```
1 50 Bird
2 25 Snake
3 60 Dwarf
```

You can read in the data this way:

```
Readln(F, AByteValue, AnIntegerValue, AString);
```

If you're certain of what you are doing, you can even use *Read*.

```
Read(F, AByteValue);
Read(F, AnIntegerValue)
Read(F, AString);
```

Ultimately, to get to the next line of the file, you must use *ReadLn*.

```
Readln(F);
```

Using multiple variables with *Read* or *ReadLn* requires a great deal of caution and awareness of a few things. First of all, if you have a text file with data organized like this:

```
1 2 Buckle my shoe 3 4 Shut the door
```

You cannot read it back like this:

```
Readln(I, J, Str1, K, L, Str2);
```

I will have a value of 1 and *J* a value of 2. But *Str1* will have a value of "Buckle my shoe 3 4 Shut the door" and at that point the program will put up an error message because the program is trying to read a null string value into integer variable *K*. Delphi cannot tell where the string *Str1* is supposed to end, so it puts everything from the current point to the end of the line into that variable.

Anything you try to read into a number variable must be a string completely type-compatible with the variable. If you have a file containing the value "1.0" and you try to read that into an integer variable, you'll get an error.

My blanket advice is not to use either of these approaches because you don't really know what is in any given text file. Even if your program was the one that wrote the file, just about any program around will read it and allow the user to change it. *Notepad*, for example, which comes with Windows, will read in and allow the alteration text files.

The best approach for reading data from text files is just to read in the entire line, and parse it according to how your program thinks it should be laid out. That way, you can handle any errors accordingly.

EOF

A cruicial built-in function that you need for any file code is *EOF*. EOF is short for "End of File." Without the *EOF* function you have no way of knowing when to stop reading a file. *EOF* is a Boolean function that returns true when you have read the last line in a file. Otherwise, it returns false.

Example: Reading in a Text File

One of the most common blocks of code you'll see is this:

```
repeat
   readln(F, S);
   {Do something with S}
until eof(F);
```

This reads in an entire text file. Replace the code from the last example with this:

```
program EZRead;
uses WinCRT;   {So you can see what you're reading.}
var F: Text
    S: String;
begin
   assign(F, 'SomeFile.TXT');
   reset(F);
   readln(F, S);
   writeln(S);
   close(F);
end.
```

(Notice that you use WinCRT here to display on-screen what you're reading.)

You might find it worthwhile to see if you can make Write and other programs output a text file so that you can read the file using this program, basically to the reverse of what you did in the previous example.

A Note on Text Files

Text files are useful at least in part because they are so common. If you store program data in a file and the user wishes to look at that data *outside* of your program, he can do so with any number of tools. This is good news and bad news since it also makes it easy for the user to change things without necessarily knowing what he's doing.

Chapter 18 ◆ File Basics

Liabilities of text files are that they are slower than other kinds of files to read and write, that they can't be changed in the middle (you either have to append or rewrite), and that they can't store many data types in Delphi's native format. You can't store a byte field as a byte in a text file—you have to store it as the string representation of the value. In other words you can't store a 13 as a 13 or a 10 as a 10— you have to store them as '13' and '10'.

This is because certain values have special meaning within a text file, namely the values 13 and 10, which are the carriage return and line-feed characters. (See the ASCII table in Appendix A.) These very limitations are also why text files are so common and easy to modify— they can be edited "as is;" no translation has to occur to turn a byte value 13 into an editable string "13."

One very important feature of text files is that a printer can be treated as a "write-only" text file. (You can't read any data from the printer.)

The printer has a specific name—"LPT1." You can write data to the printer like this:

```
var F: Text;
begin
   assign(F, 'LPT1');
   rewrite(F);
   writeln(F, 'Hello, Printer!');
   close(F);
end;
```

(If you have a printer hooked up to a second parallel port, that can be accessed through the name "LPT2.")

You can use all the formatting capabilities of *WriteLn* when outputting to the printer, and basically treat it as you would any text file— except that you can't read from it.

> **Note:** You've probably seen your printer create some pretty spectacular text and graphics output. There are volumes of technical manuals on how this is done, but most don't relate directly to Delphi.
>
> When complex graphics are used in printing, the printer is no longer acting as a simple text file.

Example: Cryptographer

A cryptograph is a message written in secret code. Most programs can read a text file, but you could use a cipher, or secret code, to encrypt data so that although any program could load the text file, no one but you would be able to make sense out of it. You'll do this now, and use the opportunity to test text files, as well as review some concepts and controls.

Set up a form like the one shown in figure 18.2. You've had a similar form before for the "PARSE" program, but this program will actually be simpler. Users will type their names into the *Name* entry field. They can then use the edit line beneath that and the add button to put text into the list box *Storage*.

Figure 18.2

The Cryptographer Form.

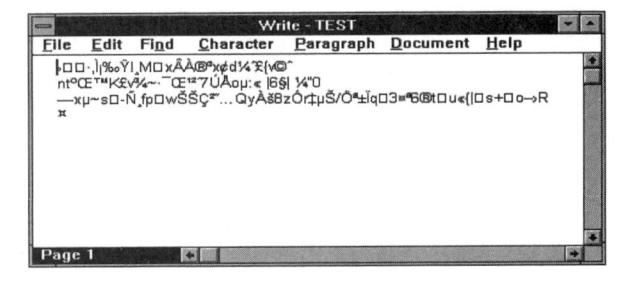

When they've entered all the data they want, they can type a file name into the Entry field just above the *Store* and *Load* buttons. They press *Store* and the data gets saved to the file. The catch is, the data was encrypted by using their name as a key. (I'll show you how to do this in a moment.)

Later, to retrieve the data, the users can enter their name in the Name field and the file name above the *Store* buttons, and the program will read it back, and unencrypt it. Somebody else putting in a different name will not be able to read the data.

Let's start by adding the code for the *Add* button.

```
procedure TForm1.AddClick(Sender: TObject);
begin
   Storage.Items.Add(Entry.Text);
end;
```

Remember that a list box has as a property the Items object. The Items object has a method *Add* that allows you to add a text string to it.

What you didn't discuss before was that Items is very much like an array of strings numbered from zero to the total strings it contains less one. The first string in a list can be accessed like so:

```
S := Storage.Items[0];
```

The Items property *Count* tells you how many strings are currently in the list. That means you could write a For loop like so:

```
For I := 0 to Storage.Items.Count - 1 do
   writeln(F, Storage.Items[I]);
```

If *F* is an appropriately assigned and opened text file, this will copy the data from the list box into the text file.

The only other thing you need to come up with is a good encryption scheme for the data that works off of the user's name. Delphi has a built-in secret-code maker in the *Random* function. You can change all the characters in the entered strings to random values and no one will ever be able to read it.

But, of course, neither would you, and while the data would be secure, it would also be worthless. The thing to keep in mind here is that *Random* really isn't. It's a series of numbers that are duplicative. In an earlier program, this was a problem— the program kept coming up with the same "random" numbers. You had to call *Randomize* to get the numbers to be different.

There is a pre-declared variable called *RandSeed,* upon which all the random numbers are based. When you call *Randomize* that puts a value into *RandSeed* based on the system clock— the number of seconds past midnight or something. Well, if you create a number based on the user's name and use that for the *RandSeed,* what will happen? You'll get the same "random" numbers every time for any given name.

Double-click *Store* and enter the following code:

```
procedure TForm1.StoreClick(Sender: TObject);
var S : String;
    L : Longint;
    I,J: Integer;
    F : System.Text;
begin
   If (Name.Text <> '') and (FileName.Text<>'') then
   begin
      {Create Code}
      S := Name.Text;
      L := 0;
      for I := 1 to Length(S) do Inc(L, Ord(S[I]));
      RandSeed := L;
      system.assign(F, FileName.Text);
      rewrite(F);
      for I := 0 to Storage.Items.Count-1 do
      begin
         S := Storage.Items[I];
         For J := 1 to Length(S) do
            S[J] := Chr(Random(100) + Ord(S[J]));
         writeln(F, S);
      end;
      system.close(F);
   end;
end;
```

You should be able to read this pretty easily, but a few lines could stand some explanation:

```
If (Name.Text <> '') and (FileName.Text<>'') then
```

If the user hasn't entered in a file name and his own name, then don't do anything.

```
for I := 1 to Length(S) do Inc(L, Ord(S[I]));
```

This builds the code that you'll put into *RandSeed*. It goes through each character and builds a number by adding all the ordinal values of those characters together. This is far from a sophisticated system. Names like "ANNA" and "NANA" will have the same code.

The tricky thing about this is that because it uses the ASCII values and doesn't shift the string to upper case, typing "George" is not the same as typing "GEORGE" or "GeORge" or anything except exactly those characters. (So, "Anna" and "Nana" will generate different secret codes.)

```
For J := 1 to Length(S) do
    S[J] := Chr(Random(100) + Ord(S[J]));
```

This code actually translates the characters to some encoded value, and does so simply by adding a "random" value to the ordinal value of the character, and putting that new character where the old one was.

The code to load the data back is complementary to the storage code. In practical terms, that means you can start by double-clicking on the *Load* button, and then copying the entire store routine over to the *LoadClick* procedure.

```
procedure TForm1.LoadClick(Sender: TObject);
var S  : String;
    L  : Longint;
    I,J: Integer;
    F  : System.Text;
begin
   If (Name.Text <> '') and (FileName.Text<>'') then
   begin
      {Create Code}
      S := Name.Text;
      L := 0;
      for I := 1 to Length(S) do Inc(L, Ord(S[I]));
      RandSeed := L;
      system.assign(F, FileName.Text);
      reset(F);
      repeat
         readln(f, S);
         For J := 1 to Length(S) do
            S[J] := Chr(Ord(S[J]) - Random(100));
         Storage.Items.Add(S);
      Until eof(F);
      system.close(F);
   end;
end;
```

Very little difference exists between the two routines except that this routine resets the file rather than rewriting it, decodes the data instead of encoding it, and so on.

```
For J := 1 to Length(S) do
   S[J] := Chr(Ord(S[J]) - Random(100));
```

You decode the data by subtracting the "random" number from it.

If the user has typed in the wrong name or is simply trying to read someone else's file, it will look for all the world like the computer is swearing at him in cartoon-ese.

Summary

The users of most programs expect to be able to save data to disk. The most common format in which to save data is the text file. A text file is a series of characters broken into lines that are delineated with carriage return-line feed sequences. Files are broken into four steps: assign, open, read/write, close. The *Text* keyword identifies a variable as a text file handle. The procedure to associate a variable with an actual file is *Assign*. A text file can be opened with *Rewrite* (which allows the file to be written to but destroys any data already in the file), or with *Reset* (which allows the file to be read), or with *Append* (which allows data to be added onto the end of an existing file). Opening a non-existent file with *Reset* and *Append* will cause an error message to appear unless I/O checking is disabled through the {$I-} directive or the Project Options dialog. A file is closed by using the *Close* procedure. A file that is not closed will waste resources. A file that has been written to and that is not closed may result in lost data. Text files are slower and sometimes less efficient than other ways of storing data. A printer can be accessed like a write-only text file through the name "LPT1."

Write and *WriteLn* are the procedures used to write data to text files. They can format variables passed as parameters somewhat before outputting them to files. *Read* and *ReadLn* will read data from text files. The best way to read data from text files is to read in entire lines and then parse them as necessary. The *EOF* function returns true when you have read the last information out of a file.

The IOResult function contains the last error code of the last I/O operation performed, or zero if the operation was successful. The *RandSeed* variable determines what "random" numbers the *Random* function will generate.

Compiler directives tell Delphi to turn off and on certain features. The {$I-} and {$I+} compiler directives turn I/O checking off and on, for example.

The *List* object property of a *Listbox* can be accessed as an array. It has a property, *Count*, which indicates how many strings it has.

Review Questions

1. What are the four steps to file handling?
2. What does *Assign* do?
3. What are the differences between *Reset*, *Rewrite*, and *Append*?
4. What is a compiler directive?
5. What are the two hazards of not closing a file?
6. What is the printer's "name"?
7. What are the two formatting parameters of *WriteLn*?
8. What is a text file, technically speaking?
9. What is a file handle?
10. Which compiler directive turns off I/O checking? Why would you want to do that? What hazards would that involve?
11. Would the following code work? Why or why not?

    ```
    {$I-}
    Reset(F);
    {$I+}
    If IOResult = 2 then FileNotFound
    else if IOResult = 0 then
    begin
         . . .
    ```

12. What byte values represent the carriage return and line feed?
13. What is the value that represents "File not found"?
14. If a text file contains the following line:

    ```
    1 2 3 4 5 6 7
    ```

    what will the following code set I, J, K, and S to? Will the code run?

    ```
    var I, J, K: Integer;
        S      : String;
    begin
       . . .
        Read(F, I, J, S, K);
    ```

15. The *RandSeed* variable has a special purpose. What is it?

Chapter 18 ◆ File Basics

Review Exercises

1. Write a program that allows the user to enter "commands" through a readln and then responds to those commands in some way. Have the program store everything entered by the user and all the computer responses. The program might look like this:

   Command?

   > **Slay the Jabberwock.**

   Ok. Status Green. Command?

   > **Stow the mizzenmast.**

   Error***Program malfunction.

   You can have the computer randomly generate responses to whatever is entered. The key thing is to end up with a complete log of everything that transpired.

2. Write a program like the crypto program built in this chapter, only don't encrypt the user's data. (In other words, just store the data directly in a text file.)

3. The memo object (on the Standard page of the toolbar) is, in itself, like a mini-text editor. Use the memo object to create a form that allows the user to enter whatever and then saves that data to a file— call it MEMO.TXT. The memo object saves its data with its Lines property. Lines is an object *just like* the Items property of the listbox.

4. Modify the programs from Review Exercises 1 and 3 so that they don't ever erase their text files. (Use Append instead of Rewrite.)

5. Write a program that reads in one of your programs (DPR or PAS file) and writes it to the printer.

6. Use the parsing skills learned in Chapter 12 and the text file skills learned here to write a program that reads any text file and prints out statistics about that file. How many lines? Longest line? Shortest line? How many characters? How many words? If you want to get really fancy, create a program that shows how often each letter of the alphabet is used in the file.

7. Write a program that reads in a text file and writes each line out backwards. (Remember that you can treat a string as an array.) A file like this

    ```
    One
    Two
    Three
    Four
    ```

    would become

    ```
    enO
    owT
    eerhT
    ruoF
    ```

    The more advanced version of this is to write the *entire* file out backwards, so that the first line of the converted file is the last line of the unconverted file, only backwards. The same file above would come out:

    ```
    ruoF
    eerhT
    owT
    enO
    ```

CHAPTER 19

Typed Files and Random Access

Alhough you can make text files work for many (perhaps all) kinds of data storage, they clearly have limitations. For example, if you're storing a series of bytes, why should you be forced to store them as their character representation? That could take anywhere from one to three bytes of space, plus two bytes for the CR-LF, as noted in the preceding chapter. Thus, you would be consuming anywhere from three to five bytes of space to store a single byte value. Not only that, but also if you want to find the 10th byte in the file, you have to read the previous nine records.

These shortcomings would be multiplied, for example, in the book cataloging program that you worked with in Chapter 16. You not only would have to write the byte data as strings, but also would have to figure out how to store the enumerated type that contains the condition and the set type that contains the genre for each book.

What you need is something that acts like an array on disk. Something that allows you to store records in such a fashion that you can retrieve or replace specific records. A text file will not serve you well here.

Typed Files

Delphi allows you to write Pascal data types directly to files, rather than forcing you to convert them to strings for text files. A byte takes a byte, and set types and enumerated types may be stored as-is. This feature is provided through *typed* files.

A typed file is a file containing only one data type, like a byte or a string—or more usefully, your own custom data type, such as a record.

In a typed file, the data is exactly the same as it is in RAM. In other words, if you had an array of bytes that contained the values 65, 66, 67, and 68, they would be stored as those byte values. If you looked at the file through a text file viewer or editor, those bytes would look like an "A," "B," "C," and "D." This finding may seem surprising until you realize that the data is stored as byte values, but a text file viewer can only see them as characters—the character that corresponds to their ASCII values.

This situation is one reason why you can't actually load a Pascal typed file into a program expecting a text file. If you store 10- and 13-byte values, those values will be interpreted as a line feed or carriage return, respectively. Many text file editors and browsers will tell you that the file is not a text file.

Another reason is that the records are not delineated with a CR-LF. In fact, they aren't delineated at all. Because they are values of all the same type, they all take exactly the same number of bytes. (You can figure out how many by using the *SizeOf* function with the file's data type as a parameter.) This type of file is sometimes called a *flat* file or a *fixed* file.

Because each record is a fixed length, a specific record may be retrieved without retrieving all the previous records. To understand why this is possible, consider the concept of a library card file where each book can take one or more cards, or perhaps just a fraction of a card. To find the tenth book in this system, you'd have to look at all of the cards until you found the 10th book, which can be anywhere in the file. This is analogous to a text file.

If, on the other hand, one card contains all the information of exactly one book, you can go straight to the 10th book by going to the 10th card. This is analogous to a typed file.

Typed files are faster than text files, and don't require any conversions to be made. They can also require less space than text files, but that depends on the data. If you have a record that contains 10 string fields, for example, where each string can be 100 characters long, then each record in the fixed file will be 1010 characters, no matter what. (The extra 10 bytes come from the 10-length bytes.) In a text file, the records would take only the actual length of the strings, plus the carriage return and line feed for each field. The other advantages of a typed file, such as speedier access, will still apply, so sometimes you'll see fixed files being used even though they take up more space than text files would.

Declaring

Typed files are declared by using the *file* keyword. File is then followed up with an *of* and the data type identifier.

```
var
    F: file of char;
    G: file of string;
    H: file of longint;
    I: file of real;
```

Of course, the typed file can be used with user types as well.

```
var
   F: file of MyRecordType;
   G: file of MyEnumeratedType;
   H: file of MySetType;
```

The most common kind of typed file is probably the one based on a user record type.

Opening, Creating, Appending

The four steps of working with files (assign, open, read/write, close) apply to typed files just as they do to text files. In fact, there are only a few differences between the way the two are used.

Assignment is the same:

```
Assign(F, 'AFile');
```

And, you can start a new file from scratch, as with a text file.

```
Rewrite(F);
```

However, with typed files the *Append* procedure is not used. Instead, for reading an existing file *or* reading, writing, and appending, the *Reset* procedure is used.

```
Reset(F);
```

(As with text files, you must turn I/O checking off and use the *IOResult* function to determine whether a file exists or not, or use the *FileExists* function.)

Records in a typed file can be considered numbered, like elements of an array. The first record is considered record zero. Pascal keeps track of the file *position*, which identifies the location of the current record. When *Reset* is called with a typed file, the file position is set to zero.

The *Write* procedure is used with typed files, just as it was with text files.

```
Write(F, AVar);
```

As with text files, you could use `write` to write many variables at once:

```
Write(F, AVar, BVar, CVar);
```

Every call to `Write` increments the file position by one record for each record written. (That way, successive writes are done one after the next instead of one over the other.)

Read also works the same as it did with text files.

```
Read(F, AVar);
Read(F, AVar, BVar, CVar);
```

Read increments the file position by one record for each record read. (That way the entire file can be read in with successive reads.)

Chapter 19 ♦ Typed Files and Random Access

> **Note:** *Read* and *Write* work *almost* the same in a text file as in a typed file. However, in a text file, *Read* and *Write* can be used to write out various data types (which are all represented as strings in the file) while a typed file will only allow *one* type to be written to it. If it is a record, of course, the record may contain many different data types, but only one kind of record may be output.

In no case would you use *ReadLn* or *WriteLn* with a typed file. After all, those procedures are used to write the CR-LF characters at the end of a record in a text file. The compiler won't allow you to make this mistake.

When done with the file, you close it, just as before.

```
Close(F);
```

The Typed File Subroutines

I mentioned that Pascal keeps track of the current record in a typed file, and that when a file is reset the current record is considered to be zero. You can find out where you are in a file at any time by using the *FilePos* function.

```
CurrentPosition := FilePos(F);
```

You can find out how big a file is, in number of records, by using the *FileSize* function.

```
FSize := FileSize(F);
```

And, you can change the current file position by using the *Seek* procedure. This would seek the first record in a file.

```
Seek(F, 0);
```

You can use these last two calls together to get an effect like the text file *Append*:

```
Seek(F, FileSize(F));
```

Remember, the records are numbered from zero, so the last record is

```
LastRecord := FileSize(F) - 1;
```

To append, you want to be positioned *after* the last record.

With typed files, you don't absolutely need to use the *EOF* function. You can use the *FileSize* function in a For loop to read all the data in a file.

```
For I := 0 to FileSize(F)-1 do
begin
    Seek(F, I);
    Read(F, ARecord);
    DoSomethingWith(ARecord);
    Seek(F, I);
    Write(F, ARecord);
end;
```

Notice that you can write a record back in the same place it was written, but that you have to use *Seek* to get it to that place because *Read* and *Write* both change the file position (by moving it forward one record).

A file where any record can be accessed at random, that is, without all subsequent records being accessed, is called a *random-access file.* Text files are not random-access.

Random Updates

Typed files really *can* be used like arrays. Using *Seek,* you can access, read, and write a particular file component just as you might read and write a particular element of an array.

You can even sort a typed file without loading the whole thing into memory and, of course, loading an entire data file into memory as an array may not even be possible if there is a lot of data. (Arrays are restricted to 64K—see Chapter 17, "The Array.") In fact, look at some of the code from that chapter:

```
For I := 1 to 99 do
begin
    Low := I;
    For J := I+1 to 100 do
        If Data[J] < Data[Low] then Low  := J;
    If I<>Low then
    begin
        Hold := Data[I];
        Data[I] := Data[Low];
        Data[Low] := Hold;
    end;
end;
```

There doesn't seem to be any reason that the code can't be used almost as is, substituting the array accesses with seeks and reads.

```
For I := 0 to FileSize(F)-2 do
begin
    Low := I;
    Seek(F, I);
    Read(F, LowRec);
    ReplaceRec := LowRec;

    For J := I+1 to FileSize(F)-1 do
    begin
        Seek(F, J);
        Read(F, CurrentRec);
        If LowRec < CurrentRec then
        begin
            Low := J;
            LowRec := CurrentRec;
        end;
    end;
    If I<>Low then
```

```
        begin
            Seek(F, I);
            Write(F, LowRec);
            Seek(F, J);
            Write(F, ReplaceRec);
        end;
end;
```

This is not commonly done, however, because it would be extremely *slow*. It works by reading through the file many times—the more records there are the more it reads through the file. Read and Write take a lot more time than shuffling records around in an array in memory. Much more complicated algorithms are typically used to sort a file. But it *can* be done this way and for a small file the simplicity may make this basic approach worthwhile.

Deletes

If the typed file can be used like an array, how do you think you would *delete* something from it? Deleting from a typed file is a cumbersome process, but it can be done. If you have a file of byte with 10 entries, like this:

```
12 4 5 99 0 128 67 1 200 144
```

and you want to delete the fifth entry (the "0"), you have to copy over the sixth entry into the fifth spot, the seventh entry into the sixth spot, and so on to the 10th entry. The code to do this looks like the following:

```
reset(f);
for I := 5 to 9 do {remember Seek(5) will return the sixth entry}
begin                {because typed files are zero based}
   seek(I);
   read(F, B);
   seek(I-1);
   write(F, B);
end;
```

When you're done, you end up with a file that looks like this:

```
12 4 5 99 128 67 1 200 144 144
```

The last 144 is left over—there was nothing to copy over it. However, while with an array you are stuck with a fixed number of entries, with a typed file, you can cut the file off at the current file position through the Truncate procedure. This is simple enough:

```
seek(F,8);   {The beginning of the 9th entry}
truncate(f); {However big F used to be, it is now 8 entries long}
```

> **Caution:** Don't confuse the `truncate` procedure, which reduces the size of a file, with the `trunc` function, which returns the integer portion of a real.

Accessing Delphi's Database Power

If you work with large amounts of data, the smart decision is to use a database *engine*—a program written to handle nonvisual aspects of programming.

A database engine (like Paradox or dBASE) comes with subroutines that you can call to access an existing database, or to write your own program's data into a new database.

These engines give you a tremendous amount of power to manipulate data in various ways. The downside of this approach is that the database engine will not recognize special Pascal data types, like your record types, which means that you have to feed those records into the database field by field.

The Desktop edition of Delphi comes with the Borland Database Engine, which allows you to access dBase and Paradox files. The client/server edition of Delphi provides easy interfacing with a number of popular high-end databases such as Oracle and Informix.

Example: Catalog, Version 1.0

For this example, open the project you created in Chapter 16 (TWOFORMS) and save it as "LIB," save the main form unit as "LIBMAIN," and change the form's name to "LibraryBrowser." As you'll recall, pushing the button on the main form calls up the data entry dialog box ("LIBDE" from Chapter 16). This is a good starting point for a program that catalogues books.

Now change the main form so that it matches figure 19.1. You'll need four buttons—AddButton, EditButton, DeleteButton, and ExitButton, continuing the tradition of naming buttons after their captions.

The big blank control in the center is a listbox. A standard listbox has no horizontal scrollbar, which means that if the items in it are too wide to fit within the box, the user can't see the rest of the data. Because of that feature, I've made the listbox very wide.

> **Note:** It would be possible, of course, to modify the listbox to have a horizontal scrollbar, but that would distract you from the purpose of this chapter—to learn about typed files.

Chapter 19 ♦ Typed Files and Random Access

Figure 19.1

The main Catalog form.

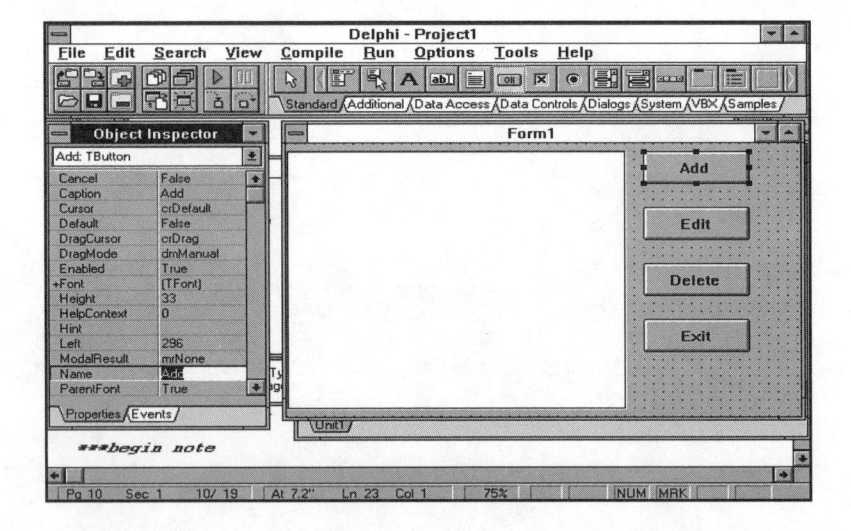

The Items field of the listbox will display the book descriptions. The Add button will call up the dialog box and allow the user to enter a new book entry. The Edit button will call up the same dialog box but fill the dialog box's fields with the current selection. If users click OK in this dialog box (regardless of whether they are adding or editing), the program will instantly add a record or change the current record. The Delete button should ask users if they really want to delete that record, and upon receiving an okay perform the delete. Exit will just close the form. (There's no reason to ask users whether they want to save any changes before exiting, because all changes take place immediately!)

> **Note:** Although this approach highlights using typed files for data storage, it is just one of several approaches to this kind of program. Another approach loads all the records into memory and performs all the actions in memory, but does not affect the external data file unless the user saved his changes. For example, Delphi (or, for that matter, any word processor) doesn't make any changes to a file you're editing until you save it.

The program works this way:

♦ When the program first begins, text describing all the books is loaded into the listbox.

♦ Pressing Add calls up the data entry form. Pressing OK writes the new entry to the end of the file.

♦ Pressing Edit calls up the data entry form. Pressing OK rewrites the new data over the old record.

- Pressing Delete confirms, and then deletes, if OK.
- Ending the application closes the file.

To do this the program will also have to translate the LibraryEntry data type to a string. This process is sort of like a reversal of the code used in Chapter 16 to convert all the control data into the LibraryEntry record format. Here's the way I coded it:

```
function  DateToString(Date: Word): String;
begin
   Str(Date, Result);
end;

function  GenreToString(G: GenreSet): String;
var S: String;

   procedure Add(T: String);
   begin
      If S<>'{' then S := S + ', ';
      S := S + T;
   end;

begin
   S := '{';
   If gFiction    in G then Add('Fiction');
   If gTechnical  in G then Add('Technical');
   If gHumor      in G then Add('Humor');
   If gReference  in G then Add('Reference');
   If gHowTo      in G then Add('How-to');
   If gPhilosophy in G then Add('Philosophy');
   If gSuspense   in G then Add('Suspense');
   If gScience    in G then Add('Science');
   If gFantasy    in G then Add('Fantasy');
   If gHorror     in G then Add('Horror');
   If gWestern    in G then Add('Western');
   If gRomance    in G then Add('Romance');

   GenreToString := S+'}';
end;

function  ConditionToString(C: Conditions): String;
begin
   Case C of
      cExcellent: Result := 'Excellent';
      cGood     : Result := 'Good';
      cFair     : Result := 'Fair';
      cPoor     : Result := 'Poor';
   end;
end;
```

```
function  FieldToString(LE: LibraryEntry; Field: BookFields): String;
begin
   Result := '';
   case Field of
      BookTitle    : Result := LE.BookTitle;
      B???Blake    : Result := LE.BookAuthor;
      BookPublisher: Result := LE.BookPublisher;
      BookDate     : If LE.BookDate<>0 then Result :=
        DateToString(LE.BookDate);
      BookLendee   : If LE.BookLendee<>'' then Result := LE.BookLendee;
      BookGenre    : Result := GenreToString(LE.BookGenre);
      BookCondition: Result := ConditionToString(LE.BookCondition);
   end;
end;

function  BookToString(Book: LibraryEntry): String;
var I: BookFields;
    S: String;
begin
   Result := '';
   For I := BookTitle to BookCondition do
   begin
      S := FieldToString(Book, I);
      If (I <> BookCondition) and (S<>'') then S := S + '\';
      Result := Result + S;
   end;
end;
```

There's hardly anything new in this code, so I won't spend much time on it here. It does reflect certain stylistic choices. Here, as elsewhere in the book, I avoid creating long routines. Smaller routines are easier to understand and debug. (On the other hand, they can make tracing through a program harder.)

Notice the procedure Add *inside* the function GenreToString. Unlike many other languages, Delphi allows you to *nest* routines. Mostly this is done for organizational reasons—nothing outside a routine can see that routine's nested procedures and functions. In other words, no routine but GenreToString can use Add. That's exactly why I put it in there: No other routine *should* use Add.

I put all the preceding code into LibMain before any other routines that the unit might have.

With this code, you can easily code the five steps needed to make this program functional. Start by double-clicking on the FormCreate event for the LibraryBrowser form.

```
procedure TLibraryBrowser.FormCreate(Sender: TObject);
var J: Longint;
begin
   Assign(Lib, 'LIBRARY.FIL');
   {$I-}
   Reset(Lib);
   {$I+}
```

```
   If IOResult<>0 then
   begin
      {$I-}
      Rewrite(Lib);
      If IOResult<>0 then {end program};
      {$I+}
   end;

   For J := 1 to FileSize(Lib) do
   begin
      Read(Lib, Book);
      BookList.Items.Add(BookToString(Book));
   end;
end;
```

Notice that I use the $I compiler directive *twice*—the first time to see whether the file exists, the second time to create the file if it doesn't. If the attempt to *create* the file fails, then the program can obviously not proceed.

> **Tip:** File creation could fail if, for example, the disk were flawed, or in a network situation where a user didn't have the authority to create a file.

After all this, the code to actually read in the file is laughably simple:

```
For J := 1 to FileSize(Lib) do
begin
   Read(Lib, Book);
   BookList.Items.Add(BookToString(Book));
end;
```

Perhaps the code for adding a new record is more complex. Here is AddButton.Click:

```
procedure TLibraryBrowser.AddButtonClick(Sender: TObject);
var Result: Integer;
begin
   Result := BookEntry.ShowModal;
   If Result = mrOK then
   begin
      Seek(Lib, FileSize(Lib));
      Write(Lib, Book);
      BookList.Items.Add(BookToString(Book));
   end;
end;
```

If anything, that's even easier. If the user presses OK, then the Result variable gets set to OK, the code seeks the end of the file, writes the new entry, and adds a description for the new entry to the BookList listbox.

For the Delete and Edit buttons, you need to do a little more work. First, use the Object Inspector to set their Enabled properties to False. To Edit or Delete an entry, you must first *select* an entry, right? You'll have to add code to the listbox to enable

Edit and Delete when an item is selected. Double-click on the Booklist listbox and fill it in with the following code:

```
procedure TLibraryBrowser.BooklistClick(Sender: TObject);
begin
   If BookList.SelCount = 0 then
   begin
      DeleteButton.Enabled := false;
      EditButton.Enabled := false;
   end
   else begin
         DeleteButton.Enabled := true;
         EditButton.Enabled := true;
      end
end;
```

SelCount is the Booklist attribute that tells you how many items have been selected. (Although you'll only be using a single-select listbox here, it is possible to enable the user to make multiple selections.) If it's zero, that means no items have been selected.

Now, for the edit button's clicked routine, the code is very straightforward:

```
procedure TLibraryBrowser.EditButtonClick(Sender: TObject);
var Result: Integer;
    J     : Longint;
begin
   J := BookList.ItemIndex;
   Seek(Lib, J);
   Read(Lib, Book);
   {Put Book into BookEntry's controls}
   Result := BookEntry.ShowModal;
   If Result = mrOK then
   begin
      Seek(Lib, J);
      Write(Lib, Book);
      BookList.Items.Delete(J);
      BookList.Items.Insert(J, BookToString(Book));
   end;
end;
```

ItemIndex gives the currently selected item. You seek that position, Read that record into Book, put Book's data into the BookEntry form's fields, and then show BookEntry. If the user made changes and wants to commit those to the file, he pressed OK, so you seek out that position in the file and write out the new data. Then you delete the updated item from the listbox and create a new item from the new data.

What you might notice here (and you'd definitely notice if you ran the program) is that BookEntry's fields *don't* contain the data from Book. You're not going to implement that part of the code here, because it just would be a matter of taking all of Book's fields and putting them into BookEntry's controls—the complement of what you did in Chapter 16, when you converted all the fields *from* the control data *into* Book's fields. (Also, you'll be better able to do this by using techniques from the next two chapters.)

The DeleteButton code is a little trickier, and not as obvious as some of the other code you've looked at, so I've included it here, heavily commented:

```
procedure TLibraryBrowser.DeleteButtonClick(Sender: TObject);
var I, Offset: Longint;
begin
   Seek(Lib, 0);
   Offset := 0;
   I := 0;
   while (I<>BookList.Items.Count) do
   if BookList.Selected[I] then
   begin
      BookList.Items.Delete(I); {remove selected items from list}
      Inc(Offset) {Don't write them out, but instead adjust }
   end             {where subsequent records will go}
   else if Offset > 0 then
   begin
      Inc(I);
      Seek(Lib, I);       {Get Record I}
      Read(Lib, Book);
      Seek(Lib, I-Offset);{Adjust Position}
      Write(Lib, Book);   {Write over old data}
   end
   else Inc(I);
   If Offset>0 then
   begin
      Seek(Lib, FileSize(Lib)-Offset);
      truncate(Lib);      {New size is old size less deleted.}
   end;
   DeleteButton.Enabled := False;
   EditButton.Enabled := False;
end;
```

You can just use `ItemIndex` here, as in `EditButtonClick`, but this code was specifically written with the idea that multiple items might have been selected. The main loop goes through all the items in `Booklist` and does one of three things. If the item is selected, the loop deletes it from `Booklist` and increments the `Offset` variable. (Notice that the record is *not* read in or written out. By *not* writing it to the file, you will essentially be deleting it.)

If `Offset` is greater than zero, this means that a record has been deleted. If a record is deleted from a fixed file, this means that all subsequent records move up a position in the file. The record is read in and written back at the new, "earlier" position.

If the Item is *not* selected and `Offset` is *not* greater than zero, then the main loop does nothing but increment `I`.

One of the most important things to note about this code is that `I` is used as the control variable for the loop. The loop terminates when `I` is equal to the number of items in `Booklist`. `I` also indicates which item is currently being looked at. So when a record is deleted, I is *not* changed, because all the records are going to move up a notch in Booklist, too.

Otherwise, I *must* be incremented or you'll get an endless loop. You might be surprised how easy it would be to forget the last else statement.

```
else Inc(I);
```

> **Efficiency**
>
> You should know that this is *not* wildly efficient code. What happens, for example, if you have 1,000 book entries and you delete the very first entry? You have to rewrite the remaining 999 records to their new positions. In dBASE—the original flat-file PC database—records had a Boolean field that indicated whether they had been "deleted." They were still there but dBASE ignored them.
>
> An advantage of this approach was that dBASE utilities could "undelete" records. A disadvantage was that "deleted" records still took space on the disk. But dBASE could also *pack* records, which meant rewriting the file just as you have here. You couldn't undelete records after packing, of course, because they weren't there, but the records no longer took any space.

As mentioned previously, Pascal's file handling is perfectly adequate for some tasks, but if you were going to implement a large-scale book catalog for a library, you would probably want to make your life easier by using a database engine. (On the other hand, you might be interested in building your own database engine with Pascal, if you had the time and inclination.)

Summary

Typed files allow you to store data in its native Pascal format. Typed files are set up for both reading and writing when opened. *Read* and *Write* are used to read and write records to a typed file. Records in a typed file can be considered numbered. The first record is zero. The last record is the total number of records in the file less one. *Seek* can be used to position the file to a specific record. The *FilePos* routine tells what the current file position is. *FileSize* tells how many records are in the file. A typed file is called a random-access file because any record in the file can be read or written without interfering with any other record.

Review Questions

1. List some of the pros and cons of using typed files over text files.
2. Does a typed file record end with a CR-LF?

3. What is it about a typed file that makes it possible to randomly access records?

4. What do Seek, FilePos, and FileSize do?

5. Records in a typed file can be accessed as though numbered. What is the first record numbered? The last?

6. Why buy a database engine product to use in your own programs?

7. Explain how a typed file can be treated like an array.

8. Is a typed file more efficient than a text file?

Review Exercises

1. Design a very simple data management program, such as one that allows entering a person's name and phone number. Make the program store the data to a file and allow the user, through "Forward" and "Backward" buttons, to look at all the data in the file. (You can use material from Chapter 16, exercises 3 and 4, for this and variations on this.)

2. Improve on the results of Exercise 1 by allowing the user to edit the current record and replace it on disk through an Update button.

3. Improve on the results of Exercise 2 by adding a sort button that puts the file in alphabetical order by name.

4. Improve on the results of Exercise 3 by adding a delete button, so that the user can remove records from the file. Take the necessary steps to *pack* and *truncate* the file so that there is no wasted space in it.

Part VII

Advanced Programming Concepts

CHAPTER 20

Units

You've looked a bit at units already—and you've done most of your work in units—but until now you weren't ready to examine the unit in detail. Without knowing how Delphi works and how real programs are written, you couldn't meaningfully explore units.

Before you get too deeply into this chapter, recap what you know about units:

- ♦ They can contain objects that your main program needs to access, as you saw early on.

- ♦ They contain the methods for those objects, as demonstrated throughout this book through the examples of writing various event handlers (like ButtonClick, and so on).

- ♦ They can contain subroutines that your main program needs to access (remember the WinCRT unit?).

- ♦ They can contain variables that the main program can access, as in the calculator programs where the applications set up the unit's variables.

That's actually quite a bit. You know *what* units can do, you just don't know *how* or *why*. The rest of this chapter is dedicated to *how*. Explaining *why* requires a little bit of history:

In Chapter 8, "Subroutines," I explained that subroutines were developed as a way to keep from constantly repeating the same code. Repeating code is like reinventing the wheel—it invites you to make errors doing things that you (or others) have done and perfected dozens or hundreds of times already.

Subroutines are a good thing. The question arises, however: Where should they go? The original answer was to develop a compiler directive that allowed integrating an external file into any given program. This file was called an *include* file, and you can still do this in Pascal.

```
program MyProg;
{$I MySubs}
var
   S : String;
   I : Integer;
begin
   GetString(S);   {From the MySubs.Pas file}
   I := StrFn(S);  {From the MySubs.Pas file}
   . . .
end.
```

Here you can see the {$I} directive in its second duty. Earlier you saw how {$I} and {$I+} turn I/O checking on and off. And how {$R} could be used to turn range checking on and off or to include a resource file. {$I filename} includes the file specified into your program file. Pascal adds a PAS extension to the file name by default.

The text from the *include* is inserted into the program where specified. So the preceding program will actually look like this to the compiler:

```
program MyProg;
{Code from MySubs}

procedure GetString(var S: String);
begin
   {GetString code here}
   . . .
end;

function StrFn(S: String): Longint;
begin
   {StrFn code here}
   . . .
end;

{Code from MySubs ends here}
var
   S : String;
   I : Integer;
begin
   GetString(S);   {From the MySubs.Pas file}
   I := StrFn(S);  {From the MySubs.Pas file}
   . . .
end.
```

This *include* file technique is still common in many languages, but it has drawbacks. The code for the *include* file has to be completely available to the person using it (commonly called *the client*), which makes it difficult for people trying to sell the code they've developed to protect their secrets. The second drawback is that the code has to be compiled and recompiled every time the main program is compiled and recompiled. But, the code really is not supposed to change, or change much. The idea is that it has already been tested and checked out—so why should it constantly be recompiled?

The next solution, probably the most common today, takes advantage of the fact that compiling code is done in two steps. The first is to turn the code into machine language or *object* code, as discussed in Chapter 2, "Traditional Programming,"—this step is properly referred to as *compiling*. The second step is to turn this object code into an executable program—this step is called *linking*. (Delphi artfully hides the whole linking process from you.) The linking step actually attaches any code that the OS (Windows in Delphi's case) requires of every program in order for that program to be executable.

If you wrote a number of routines that you wanted to sell to other people, or that you didn't want to continually recompile, you could compile the routines just once, and have your progam *link* in the object code for those routines. Now the source code doesn't have to be available to the person using the code, and the source code doesn't have to be continually recompiled by every programmer who uses it. (You may, in fact, have some files on your disk that have an OBJ extension—these are probably object files.) An object file meant to be called by other programs is sometimes called a *library*.

> **Caution:** Although there is similarity between the terminology of *objects* and *object code*, the two are not related in any way. A compiler produces *object code* (machine language) from *source code* (Delphi text).
>
> This is the only place in this book you'll see a reference to *object code*.

The drawback with using object libraries is that they give the calling program no way of knowing what subroutines are actually in them or how those routines are to be called. In other words, if you had purchased an object library that handled decks of cards, you might expect to have a routine called *ShuffleDeck*, so you would code:

```
ShuffleDeck(Deck);
```

Then, when you went to compile and link your program, your linker might say

```
ShuffleDeck procedure unknown
```

or something like that. The object library came with documentation, but that documentation says the procedure name is *ShuffleDeck*. In actual fact, the procedure name might be *DeckShuffle*, or *ShuffleTheDeck* or anything. If the documentation is wrong, you're out of luck.

The next problem that could arise is this:

```
DeckShuffle(Deck);
```

What if *DeckShuffle* is the name of the procedure but *Deck* is not the right data type to pass? Say the library can handle a number of data types, like:

```
FullDeck: array[1..52] of cards;
ShortDeck: array[1..24] of cards;
```

and some of the routines handle the *FullDeck* type and some handle the *ShortDeck* type.

Not only is type checking unavailable in object libraries, but also *only* subroutines can be transferred. So if the object library defines a type like this:

```
FullDeck: array[1..52] of cards;
```

you have to do the same thing in *your* program, and you'd better know what kind of data type *Cards* is, too, or you're courting disaster. (To circumvent the lack of type declarations, programmers generally have made the source code describing the data types that work with their libraries available to users of their code.)

> **Note:** DLLs have most of the shortcomings of OBJs and were really developed to address different issues from the ones we're talking about here.

Realizing the shortcomings of both of these approaches, Borland implemented a system for Delphi that is widely regarded as a good, efficient approach to handling subroutines, data types, and so on. This system is the *unit*. The unit allows the *compiler* to be aware of the subroutines in it, so that this:

```
ShuffleDeck(Deck);
```

will generate an error immediately if *ShuffleDeck* is not a correct name. The code will also generate a type-mismatch error if the *Deck* data type is not the correct data type to pass to the routine. The code also will allow you to declare *Deck* as a data type defined in the unit, so that you don't have to worry about the internal details.

Unit Structure

Now that you know *why* units exist and the problems they resolve, look at *how* they work. A unit begins with the keyword *unit* (mandatory) followed by the name of the unit.

```
unit MyUnit;
```

The name for a unit must follow all the usual rules for identifiers. (It cannot start with a number and so on.) The following would be valid:

```
unit ASuperLongUnitName;
```

Interface

The unit approaches the problems of reusable code by beginning with an *interface* section. The interface section declares all the types, variables, and routines to which a program using the unit (a *client* program) has access. The interface section immediately follows the unit name and is noted by the keyword *interface*.

```
unit MyUnit;
interface
```

The interface section can have only declarations in it. You can declare types,

```
type
   MyRecord = record
      A, B, C: String;
end;
```

you can declare variables,

```
var
   S, T: String;
```

and you can even declare procedures and functions.

```
procedure MyProcedure;
function  MyFunction: Integer;
```

In previous chapters, you have always declared and coded subroutines in the same place. The subroutine header declares the subroutine, and is followed by the type and var sections, and then the Begin-End code block. In the interface section of a unit, you include only the header.

If *MyUnit* has an interface section like this:

```
unit MyUnit;
interface
type
   MyRecord = record
      A, B, C: String;
end;
var
   S, T: String;
procedure MyProcedure;
function  MyFunction: Integer;
```

A client could use the *MyRecord* type, the *S* and *T* string variables, and *MyFunction* and *MyProcedure*.

Chapter 20 ◆ Units

The interface section of a unit also serves as a starting point for documentation for the unit. Although the interface section doesn't tell what the subroutines do or how the variables are used, it does tell you the names of the routines, variables, and types, and how the routines are called—that is, which data types are used in the parameters to those routines.

> **Tip:** With the liberal use of comments, a unit's interface *can* be used to completely document a unit.

Implementation

The code for subroutines declared in the interface section goes into the second section of the unit, called the *implementation* section. This section is noted with the keyword *implementation* and always follows the interface section.

```
implementation

procedure MyProcedure;
begin
   S := 'Something';
end;

function  MyFunction: Integer;
begin
   MyFunction := Random(10);
end;

end. {ends the unit}
```

The unit must end with the keyword *End* followed by a period.

On closer examination, the *implementation* section is virtually identical to a regular program. It can declare data types, declare variables, have its own subroutines, and even have a main block of code:

```
implementation

type
   MyHiddenRecord = record
       A, B, C: String;
end;

var
   MR1, MR2: MyRecord;

procedure MyHiddenProcedure;
begin
   . . .
```

390

```
end;

begin  {This is the main block of code}
   S := 'Hello, World!';
end.
```

The Hidden Elements of a Unit

The key thing to realize about types and variables declared in the implementation section of a unit is that they are *invisible* to the client programs. In other words, a client program could not use *MR1*, *MR2*, the *MyRecord* type, or the *MyHiddenProcedure* routine.

Subroutines, variables, and types are hidden from clients for a number of reasons. One reason is that they might really be none of the client's business. This might seem like an odd thing to say, but if a unit is meant to provide certain services, adding in extras that the client doesn't need to know about can complicate things for the client. Keeping elements of the unit hidden also allows you to *change* those elements, if you decide that the unit could be improved by doing so.

If you change something in the interface part of a unit, a good chance exists that clients will have to change as well. This is called *breaking* code, because code that used to work with your unit no longer will. If you change something in the implementation section *only*, client code will be unaffected in how it calls your code. (You might change the code to make it faster, more efficient, or to correct a bug, but in the process you shouldn't change the interface to the code.)

The Unit's Main Block

The main block of the unit code is executed before the first line of the program. Thus, if you had a program that used the preceding unit,

```
begin
   DoSomething;
end.
```

before *DoSomething* ever got called, *S* in the unit would have been set to 'Hello.' This feature allows you to initialize variables in a unit before a program starts. You could have used this feature in the calculator programs. You put this code in the main program, remember:

```
   Total := 0;
   Operator := '+';
   Complete := True;
```

But it really belongs in the main block of the unit code. With this code in the main block, *all* programs using that unit get the *Total*, *Operator*, and *Complete* fields initialized, and don't have to worry about forgetting to initialize them themselves.

The unit "knows" that if it is used by another program, certain variables must be initialized in order for it to work properly. Thus, the main block of unit code exists in part to minimize the chance that the calling program will make an error by forgetting to initialize crucial variables.

The End in the main block of unit code serves to end the unit as well—but the End (followed by a period) has to be there regardless of whether there is a main block—a Begin—or not.

The *Uses* Clause

A unit is accessed through the *Uses* clause, which you saw early on in the book. In fact, your first real program had the Uses clause in it so that you could make your program emulate a teletype.

```
uses WinCRT;
```

The WinCRT contained the special routines you needed to make this emulation happen. You also looked at Uses in a genuine Windows program, which illustrated the one variation on Uses

```
uses
  Forms,
  Unit1 in 'UNIT1.PAS' {Form1};
```

and mentioned how the Forms unit made it possible for your program to be a Windows program (containing the Application object), and how the *Unit1* unit gave you access to *Form1*.

```
uses ALongUnitName in 'AFILE.PAS';
```

Ironically, the place you've seen this the most has been in Delphi-generated cases such as this:

```
uses
  Apps,
  Unit1 in 'UNIT1.PAS' {Form1};
```

Here, it's not even necessary.

Example: Units and Uses

Units may have Uses clauses, too. In fact, just as with programs, if units want to use subroutines, data types, and variables defined in other units, they must have a Uses clause. Delphi begins every form unit with a substantial Uses clause:

```
uses
  SysUtils, WinTypes, WinProcs, Messages, Classes, Graphics, Controls,
  Forms, Dialogs;
```

You might wonder if all these units are necessary to your form unit. To find out, try reducing the Uses clause to just:

```
uses Forms;
```

and compiling the form. Sure enough the form will compile and the program will run. So what is all that other stuff?

Well, the WinTypes and WinProcs units contain functions and variables that you need to program the Windows Application Programming Interface (API), a complex set of functions that allow you to do things like draw windows and buttons in your application. With Delphi, you'll rarely need to use the Windows API, but there are some, more advanced tasks where it might come in handy.

In fact, everything other than the Forms unit was put there by Delphi as a convenience. The folks at Borland thought you *might* need an object from Dialogs or a function from WinProcs, so they added it into the Uses clause so it would be available to you.

The obvious concern that you might have is whether all the code from the unused units ends up in your compiled program. The answer is, fortunately, no. Delphi won't put any code in your application that your application doesn't call.

So there's really no harm in having all those units listed in your Uses clause. Theoretically, more units should cause the program to compile more slowly, but I've never experienced a significant change in speed from changing the Uses clause.

Try this out. Start a new project and set it up so that you can see the form and the Code Editor for the form and the entire length of the Uses clause. Now, drop a control on the form and compile the program. Did the Uses clause change? That depends. If you added a control from the Standard page, probably not. If you added, say, the gauge from the VBX page, you'll see the GAUGE and VBXCtrl units added. If you reduce the Uses clause to just "Uses Forms;" you'll find that any control you add ends up adding one or more units to the Uses clause.

> **Tip:** The change doesn't occur until you try to compile the code.

> **Note:** Customarily, a unit contains many subroutines and data types that are related. For space reasons, most of your examples have just one or two routines in them.

Notice that the Uses clause comes *after* the interface keyword. Consider the following code:

Chapter 20 ♦ Units

```
unit AUnit;
interface
type
   SpecialDataType = array[1..100] of char;
implementation
end.
```

Suppose you had another unit, one that used *SpecialDataType*. The code might look like this:

```
unit Another;
interface
uses AUnit;
procedure DoSomething(AParm: SpecialDataType);
implementation
procedure DoSomething(AParm: SpecialDataType);
begin
   {Code to do something}
end;
end.
```

The Uses clause must be in the interface section because *DoSomething*, a procedure that uses *ASpecialDataType,* is declared in that section. The following also will work, however:

```
unit Another;
interface
uses AUnit;
implementation
procedure DoSomething(AParm: SpecialDataType);
begin
   {Code to do something}
end;
end.
```

DoSomething is now a hidden routine—unavailable to client programs. The Uses clause for the interface section, as you can see, also applies to the implementation section. However, the implementation section can *also* have a Uses clause. This same unit could be as follows:

```
unit Another;
interface
implementation
uses AUnit;
procedure DoSomething(AParm: SpecialDataType);
begin
   {Code to do something}
end;
begin
   {Do something important here.}
end.
```

(As you can see from this example, you *can* have an empty interface section. A unit like this would exist only to do something in its main block, like calling hidden subroutines coded in the implementation section.)

The previous variations are all legal. The following variation will not work.

```
unit Another;
interface
procedure DoSomething(AParm: SpecialDataType);    {No!  Will not compile}
implementation
uses AUnit;
procedure DoSomething(AParm: SpecialDataType);
begin
   {Code to do something}
end.
end;
```

The Uses clause has to appear before any of its subroutines, data types, or variables are used.

You might come to the conclusion that it is best to just put all the units in the interface's Uses clause. However, there is one drawback with that approach, as covered in the following section.

Circular References

Sometimes you may find yourself with two units, where one unit is using a data type declared in the other, and the other is using a data type declared in the first. In other words, in a situation like

```
unit AUnit;
interface
uses Another;
type
   NameType = record
      First, Last, Middle: String[30];
   end;
procedure PrintAddress(Address: AddressType);
implementation
end.
```

where *Another* is a unit that uses *AUnit*

```
unit Another;
interface
uses AUnit;
type
   AddressType = record
      Name: NameType;
      Address: String[30];
   end;
implementation
end.
```

these two units will cause a "Circular Unit Reference" error. You've told Delphi that you want to use *AUnit*, so it goes to compile *AUnit*. *AUnit* requires *Another* to be compiled, so Delphi goes to compile that. But *Another* requires *AUnit*, so Delphi cannot proceed.

The interface section of a unit tells Delphi everything it needs to know about compiling the unit, so it would be acceptable for *AUnit* to access *Another* even though *Another* accesses *AUnit* as long as they don't both do these accesses in the interface section. In other words, if *AUnit* were

```
unit AUnit;
interface
type
    NameType = record
        First, Last, Middle: String[30];
    end;
implementation
uses Another;
procedure PrintAddress(Address: AddressType);
end.
```

then Delphi would not be stumped.

This is a trumped-up example, obviously. *AUnit* and *Another* would probably be just one unit. There's certainly no logical reason to have the *AddressType* subroutine in the unit that defines *NameType*. It would either be in *Another* or in a unit all of its own.

However, some circular references are not that obvious. Thus, as a general rule it is best to put as many units as possible in the implementation's Uses clause instead of the interface's.

Relationship of the Unit to the Project

The nature of Delphi really makes it impossible for you to not deal with units from the start. Each form—the main visual design element of Delphi—is set up in its own unit. You've put most of the associated code for the forms in those units—and you could move the code you *did* put in the main program into the main block of the appropriate units.

This has a greater significance than is immediately obvious. Any project you work on from now on can use any of the forms you've already built. If you need a calculator, you've got that. If you want to include a dialog box that allows the user to enter a message to be "secret coded," you can use the *CrypForm* unit. And so on.

What is probably obvious to you is that a unit cannot use a type, procedure, or variable declared in the project.

```
program AProject;
uses Windows,
     Unit1 {Form1}
type
   MyType = record
      Field1: String;
      Field2: Integer;
   end;

procedure MyProc;
begin
   {DoSomething}
end;

var M: MyType
begin
   {DoStuff}
end.
```

AProject can use any type, variable, or function declared in the interface section of *Unit1*. *Unit1*, on the other hand, has no right or access to *AProject*—it cannot use *MyProc*, *MyType*, or the variable *M*.

You can deduce from this discussion that, if you're going to write code that has any possibility of use in another program, you shouldn't put it in the project file. Traditionally, most Delphi programs do have substantial project code. In *Delphi*, however, the project code is usually limited to a couple of lines:

```
Application.CreateForm(TForm1, Form1);
Application.Run;
```

Constants

A Pascal program or unit has several sections, as you have seen. There is a type section, a var section, and a procedure section (where procedures are coded or, in the case of a unit's interface section, merely declared.) A Pascal program can have yet another section called the *constant* section. The constant section begins with the keyword *const*, and in this section, identifiers are used to represent specific values:

```
const
   HelloWorldString = 'Hello, World!';
   Programname = 'Super-Program';
   Version = 1.5
   ElementsInArray = 100;
```

A constant can be any of the simple types—Delphi figures out which type based on the value of the constant. Unlike a variable, a constant cannot be changed—hence, the name. A constant can be used any place you have used literals. For example:

```
WriteLn(HelloWorldString);
For I := 1 to ElementsInArray do Something;
```

All Delphi does when it comes across a constant in a program is substitute the literal for that identifier. Thus, like the enumerated type, a constant is for you, the programmer. By the time the program is actually run, the constant identifier is gone—replaced with the appropriate value.

Enumerated types are very similar to constants. If you have the following definition:

```
type
    Color = (Violet, Indigo, Blue, Green, Yellow, Orange, Red);
```

Violet has a value of zero, *Indigo* a value of 1, and so on. But these are ordinal values, and cannot be used with the same freedom that a series of constants could be:

```
const
    Violet = 0;
    Indigo = 1;
    Blue = 2;
    Green = 3;
    Yellow = 4;
    Orange = 5;
    . . .
```

In the enumerated type, you can't substract 2 from *Orange* by coding

```
Int := Orange - 2;
```

although this would be perfectly acceptable if *Orange* were a constant with a value of 5. Very often, Delphi programmers use constants as a way to circumvent type checking but to retain the readability benefits of enumerated types.

A more valid use of constants is to improve readability, when an enumerated type is inappropriate. For example:

```
const
    DaysInWeek = 7;
    HoursInDay = 24;
    DaysInYear = 365;
    DaysInLeapYear = 366;
```

An even better use for constants, however, is as names for numbers that might change as the program develops. Earlier, you had an example of a 30-element array being sorted. You may have changed that array to 100 elements. To make the program work properly, you had to find every instance of the literal 30 and change that to 100. If you'd had a constant,

```
const ElementsInArray = 30;
```

and then used the constant instead of the literal 30,

```
    Data : Array[1..ElementsInArray] of char;
...
    For I := 1 to ElementsInArray do
...
    For I := 1 to ElementsInArray-1 do
...
    For J := I+1 to ElementsInArray do
...
    For Index := 1 to ElementsInArray do
```

instead of having to make *five* changes to the program, you would have had to make only *one*.

```
const ElementsInArray = 100;
```

This is a remarkably valuable tool. Imagine dozens of other units having used the *SortForm* unit and coding 30, 30, 30, every time they wanted to do something with the *Data* array. Now imagine trying to track down all these units after having changed *Data* to have 100 elements.

The Typed Constant

It is possible to specify the type of a constant. In the constant section, follow the identifier with a colon and a data type, then follow that with an equal sign and a value.

```
const
    MyName : String[18] = 'D. S. Blake Watson';
```

You can also use this to declare a more complex constant.

```
type
    Data = array[1..10] of byte;
const
    D : Data = (1, 2, 3, 4, 5, 6, 7, 8, 9, 10);
```

The elements of an array are given values in order, where each value is separated by a comma, and the series of values are surrounded by parentheses. You must specify each element in the array.

Records may be similarly declared, except the declaration is accordingly more complex:

```
type
   MyRecord = record
      Name: String;
      Age : Integer;
      Male: Boolean;
   end;

const
   Me : MyRecord = (Name: 'Blake Watson',; Age:0; Male: True);
```

The data is surrounded by parentheses, as with arrays, but the field name must be given, followed by a colon, followed by a value. This action is admittedly a little strange, because Delphi will not allow you to present the fields in any order other than the order in which they were declared. In the preceding example you couldn't put *Age* before *Name* or *Male* before *Age*. Also, you're not allowed to leave fields out in the middle. You couldn't specify the preceding as:

```
Me : MyRecord = (Name: 'Blake Watson',; Male: True);
```

or just:

```
Me : MyRecord = (Male: True);
```

Even stranger still—you *may* leave fields off the end. Either of these would be valid:

```
Me : MyRecord = (Name: 'Blake Watson',; Age:0);
Me : MyRecord = (Name: 'Blake Watson',);
```

Even this is acceptable:

```
Me : MyRecord = ();
```

You also can declare an array of records, which involves combining the punctuation for the two types. The array elements are separated by commas and surrounded by quotes, as before. However, because the array elements are records, between the commas are another set of parentheses for each element, wherein zero or more of the fields are declared:

```
Everybody: array[1..5] of MyRecord = (
   (Name: 'Jean';  Age: 0; Male: False),
   (Name: 'Cleo';  Age: 0),
   (Name: 'Loki'),
   (Name: 'Sarah'; Age: 4; Male: False),
   ()
   );
```

I keep the record parentheses separate from the array parentheses by specifying the array parentheses on separate lines. Note that if a field is not specified, its value is undefined, just as if you declared a variable and didn't assign a value to it.

A file type can never be a typed constant (or a regular constant for that matter). To achieve the effect of having a "constant" file the best approach is to declare the file's *name* as a constant.

Now the strangest part of all: You can *change* a typed constant. And to understand why, I should first informally define the word *kludge* (pronounced like "clue" with a "j" at the end). A kludge is a modification *to* something that was not planned and *for which* that something was *not designed*. It is also the process of making such a modification (the verb, "to kludge"). Many roads in Europe designed for pedestrians and horses, for example, were kludged to allow for cars.

Delphi was never designed to allow for variable initialization in the same step as declaration. Something like this

```
var S: String = 'Hello!';
```

is not allowed, and probably was deliberately excluded. In traditional Pascal, which didn't have units or objects, the main program file might get to be very long. As a result, you might define a variable hundreds or thousands of lines before it was actually used. Therefore, allowing variables to be initialized when they were declared could result in some confusion. Imagine having a variable declared and initialized:

```
var AnInteger = 12345; {Hypothetical, won't work}
```

Then imagine paging through all your code to see the line:

```
    AnInteger := AnInteger * 2;
```

What was `AnInteger` initialized to again? You could easily forget and end up paging back and forth through your code.

However, many programmers do like to preinitialize their variables. Some programmers forget to initialize when they first use them, and end up with mysterious bugs. As someone who has coded hundreds of thousands of lines in Pascal, I'm used to the Pascal way, but Borland felt the need to allow for preinitialized variables, and came up with typed constants.

The concept isn't as dumb as it sounds. They really *are* constant, in a special way that serves a particular purpose. Typed constants occupy a specific place in memory. When the program starts, their place in RAM is decided and does not change throughout the program.

This may seem like no big deal, particularly if you're thinking about global variables. Global variables never change their location in RAM either. But what about subroutine variables?

```
procedure SomeProc;
var A: String;
begin
end;
```

The first time you call *SomeProc*, *A* will be at one place in RAM; the next time, it probably will be in a different place. Remember: subroutine variables come and go with the subroutine.

Typed constants, on the other hand, stay put. They always occupy the same place in RAM. This makes it possible to do things like this:

```
procedure SomeProc;
const  BeenCalledBefore: Boolean = false;
begin
   If BeenCalledBefore then
   begin
      {some code}
   end
   else begin
         BeenCalledBefore := true;
        {some different code}
      end;
end;
```

SomeProc will now act differently the first time it is called than it will on subsequent calls.

The variable need not be Boolean either. You could have a longint variable that kept track of how many times a routine was called, a variable or set of variables that kept track of the last parameters used when calling the subroutine, and so on. You'll use this in a practical example later on.

Scope Revisited

All constants, types, variables, procedures, and functions have a scope. You've talked about scope with regard to variables in subroutines and record fields. You can now expand your understanding of scope to include units. Consider the following, simple example:

```
unit A;
interface
var S: String;
implementation
end.

unit B;
interface
var S: String;
implementation
end.

program C;
uses A,B;
begin
   S := 'Hello!';
end.
```

Which *S* do you suppose is being set by program *C*? Logically, it could be either, but in Delphi the *last* unit in the Uses clause has precedence, so it is the *S* variable of the *B* unit that is being altered. You can change that by reordering the Uses clause.

```
Uses B, A;
```

I don't recommend this approach. You should (first) try to avoid having identical identifiers from unit to unit. That's not always possible, because you might be using somebody else's units.

Fortunately, Delphi allows you to specify the unit name before any identifier, thereby removing any ambiguity. Program *C* could look like this:

```
program C;
uses A,B;
begin
   A.S := 'Hello!';
   B.S := 'World!';
end.
```

The identifier before the period specifies the unit; the identifier after the period specifies what feature (variable, subroutine, or object class) is to be used.

> **Note:** The name of the unit containing the built-in procedures and functions is *System*. *System* is part of a group of units that get used automatically whenever you program in Delphi. (You never need to include it in your Uses clause.)
>
> In Chapter 18, "File Basics," when you wanted to close a file, you entered this line:
>
> ```
> System.Close(F);
> ```
>
> instead of just *Close*. The reason for that is because the Form object has a method called *Close* (which would close the form—that is, remove it from the screen), which has precedence over the system command to close a file. By specifying *System* first, you indicated that you wanted the standard built-in *Close* procedure, not the Form's method.

Unit Design

Unit design is an important part in making reusable code. If you developed a series of routines that would draw geometric images on the form, you could group these all together in a single unit, perhaps called *DrawGeo*.

Later, should you need a function to draw a sphere, you could look through your existing units and spot the *DrawGeo* unit as a good place to look for it.

If you had also included in that unit a routine that sorts strings, or that does math, or something unrelated, you will have reduced the chance of your reusing that code, simply because you might not be able to find it, and you might not think of looking in a unit called *DrawGeo* for a routine to sort strings. This is no different from keeping a well-ordered file cabinet, or your books, records, and tapes in alphabetical order. As long as you're trying to keep track of only a few things, you can be as messy as you want. Once you start getting into the hundreds (or even dozens) of items, organization becomes more and more important.

Right now, you should create a sub-directory in the DELPHI directory called GPUNITS, for General Purpose Units. These are units that you might use over and over again in many different projects.

Before Delphi can find units in your GPUNITS directory, you have to tell it to look there. To do so, follow these steps:

1. Open a project if one is not open already. It doesn't matter what the project is.

2. Pull down the Options menu and select Project. A notebook will appear with several tabs along the bottom.

3. Select the tab labelled "Directories/Conditionals." (You can turn the page of a notebook in Delphi by pressing Ctrl+Tab.)

4. Underneath the Help button on this page of the notebook is a checkbox marked "Default." Check that box. This makes any changes made on this page the default for *all* projects.

5. In the ComboBox labeled "Search Path," enter the full name of the path you want Delphi to search for your files. (For this example, enter "D:\DELPHI\GPUNITS" where "D:" is the drive on which you have installed Delphi.

It's a peculiarity that you must have a project open to make changes to the defaults, but as you can see, Delphi allows you to customize the options in each project as well as make changes to all projects.

Example: A General Purpose Unit

You're going to violate the rule expressed in the preceding section about giving units descriptive names and grouping them like procedures and functions together. You're going to create a unit called GENERAL, which will contain a number of routines that you're likely to use in almost every program you write.

I've had a general unit for years. At this point, it contains almost 60 subroutines, mostly functions. Ironically, when writing the previous section I discovered that the routines in the unit were all closely related after all—they all have to do with converting strings to numbers or numbers to strings, or some other kind of string manipulation.

Your starting GENERAL unit should contain the *StrFn, ValFn* functions (you've certainly used those a lot), the code to convert real numbers to strings, and perhaps the code to parse a string that you developed. These seem like things you might want to do quite a bit.

```
unit General;

interface

type CharSet = set of Char;

function StrFn(A: longint): string;
function ValFn(S: String): longint;
function WordCount(Line: String): byte;

var Delims : CharSet;

implementation

function StrFn(A: Longint): string;
var s: string;
begin
   Str(A,S);
   StrFn := s;
end;


function ValFn(S: String): longint;
var L: LongInt;
    code: integer;
begin
   val(S,L,code);
   ValFn := L;
end;

function WordCount(Line: String): byte;
var I, WC: byte;
    InWordNow, InWordBefore
         : Boolean;
begin
   WC := 0; InWordBefore := false;
   For I := 1 to Length(Line) do
   begin
      If Line[I] in Delims then InWordNow := false
      else InWordNow := true;
      If InWordNow and not InWordBefore then Inc(WC);
      InWordBefore := InWordNow;
   end;
   WordCount := WC;
end;

begin
   Delims := [' '];
end.
```

Decide for yourself how you want to integrate the code to convert real numbers into the GENERAL unit. You can have a function to use just the standard *Str* procedure, which allows the user to specify the width and number of decimals. Or you can take the code from the CALCREAL project, letting the user specify the width and letting the function decide how many decimal places should be shown, translating into scientific notation if necessary. Or you might want both.

I think of the GENERAL unit as very personal—it should reflect the functions and procedures that you need most. I've included three handy ones here as a starting point. What you add will depend entirely on you.

Instead of including the parsing code from the PARSE project, I give you the *WordCount* function. This function essentially is a stripped-down version of the parsing code. It has also been modified to reflect what you have learned since you wrote that procedure—the use of sets and treating strings as arrays. The *WordCount* function could be the first in a series of string manipulation subroutines.

Standard Units

A big part of being productive with Delphi is knowing what subroutines are a part of the product. Delphi comes with a complete reference of these subroutines in the form of the help files, to which you should refer frequently. Often, instead of wondering "How can I do this?" you should be wondering "Has someone else done this for me?"

> **Tip:** Browse the Delphi on-line help to search for any routines that might assist you in your task.

The Timer

So far, whenever you have written any kind of complex code, you have allowed it to tie up the computer completely. You have, in essence, frozen Windows. This is counterproductive, and a program that does this is likely to end up scratched from the hard disk.

Also, up to this point, the only objects from the Component Bar that you've included on your forms have been *controls*. Controls are visible objects with which the user interacts. *Delphi* also allows you to add components that are used strictly for program control. One such object is the *timer*.

The timer, located on the additional page of the object bar, can help resolve your problem. Start a new project, and put a timer on the blank form. The Timer object only has a few properties, and *Left* and *Top* are properties that have no impact on the program because the timer is not visible.

The two properties of greatest interest are the *Enabled* property and the *Interval* property. When enabled, a timer creates an event every *Interval* milliseconds. This interval is by no means precise: it depends on the speed of your computer, for one thing. It can also depend on what else is happening on your computer.

Switch the Object Inspector over to the event page and you'll observe that the timer has only one event it responds to: *OnTimer*. Every time *Interval* passes (approximately), an *OnTimer* event is generated.

One way to keep a complex program from freezing Windows, then, is to break the task into small pieces—pieces that would take relatively little time to complete. You can do those pieces at spread-out intervals—as *OnTimer* events occur—leaving the user free to continue working in other programs.

If, for example, you were writing a program to count the number of words in a file, you can write a routine that counts the words in one line of the file at a time.

The Open Dialog

First you need some way to get a file name from the user. Before, in the CRYPTO project, you let the user type in a file name. A better move might be to offer the user the standard Windows file dialog box, with which he is doubtlessly familiar, and which allows him to see what is currently on the disk before guessing at a name.

On the Dialogs page of the Component Bar, you'll find a number of standard dialog boxes used in Windows. The icon resembling an open file folder is an Open dialog. Put one of those on the form.

Notice that it looks a bit like the timer object. It doesn't expand out into the full dialog, and it takes little space on the form. Like the timer, the icon that represents the dialog will not actually appear in the running program. It is simply a resource you can easily call up.

To use the file dialog, you typically have a button or some other control that was meant to begin a process that required a file name. In the event handler you would use the *Execute* method.

```
procedure TSelectForm.SelectClick(Sender: TObject);
begin
   If OpenDialog.Execute then
   begin
```

If *Execute* returns False, that means the user quit the operation without selecting a file name. If *Execute* returns True, that means the dialog's *FileName* property contains the name of the file selected.

The Open dialog has one other property of interest to you right now, and that is the *Filter* property (see fig. 20.1). The box in the lower left corner labeled "List Files of Type" shows the filters available for this file dialog.

Chapter 20 ◆ Units

Figure 20.1
The Open Dialog.

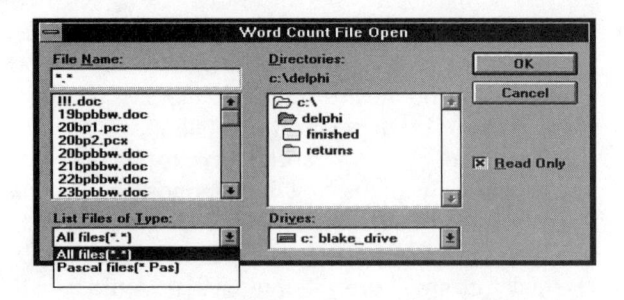

In the Object Inspector, you can set this property by selecting the filter property and clicking on the triple-dash that appears to the right of the entry line. This brings up a simple filter editor dialog that has two columns. On the left, enter the name of the filter, such as "Pascal Programs." On the right, enter one or more file masks, such as "*.DPR" and "*.PAS." If you have more than one file mask for a given filter, separate them with semicolons. So, a file filter for Pascal programs would look like this:

Pascal Programs   *.PAS; *.DPR

File Masks

File masks are a common part of DOS. But while they are less important in Windows, you should understand what they are. A file mask is a *template* that represents a set of file names. Variables in the template are indicated with either a question mark (?) or an asterisk (*).

The question mark means, "Any character is okay here as long as there is a character here." The asterisk means, "Zero or more characters are okay here to the end of the name."

For example, the mask "A*" would represent all files beginning with the letter "A." The mask "DEL?HI" would accept files like "DELAHI" or "DELPHI."

In a file mask, the extension is treated separately, so "A*" actually represents all files beginning with the letter "A" that don't have extensions. To make it *all* files that begin with the letter "A" regardless of extensions, you would have to use "A*.*."

Commonly, as noted in the early chapters of this book, extensions are used to denote a certain kind of file, not file names. So, a Pascal file mask would be "*.PAS" or (for a project file) "*.DPR." A text file is often "*.TXT." Delphi form files are "*.DFM."

The `Filter` property can also be set by typing the file type description, followed by a pipe (|), followed by a file mask. So, for example, this would list all the files:

```
All Files |*.*
```

To do more than one file type, you would add another pipe, and repeat the process. The following would set up filters for all files and for Pascal files:

```
All files |*.*|Delphi files |*.PAS;*.DPR
```

Example: Word Counter

To illustrate everything you've done in this chapter, you'll put together a simple program to count the words in a text file. Put together a form like the one in figure 20.2.

Figure 20.2
The WordCount form.

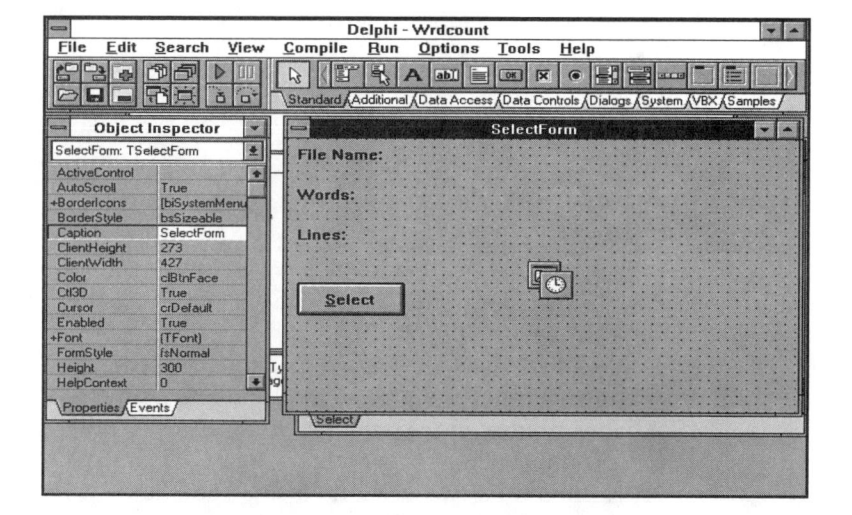

The labels that read "Filename," "Words," and "Lines" are followed by labels (without captions and therefore not visible in the figure) that are actually named *Filename*, *Words*, and *Lines*. *Filename* stretches across the top of the form, and will hold the file name. *Words* will hold the number of words in the file. *Lines* will hold the number of lines in the file. Below *Lines* is another label (also not shown) called *CountMessage* that the program will use to communicate error messages and such to the user. The *Select* button will call up the file dialog and activate the counting process. The form itself is called *SelectForm*, the project WRDCOUNT, and the form unit, SELECT. The file dialog is *OpenFileDialog*, and the timer is *CountTimer*. Remember that it does not really matter where these appear on the form, as they will not show up in the running program. Give *OpenFileDialog* a filter to accept text (*.TXT) files.

Chapter 20 ◆ Units

> **Tip:** Remember that, in general, if a form has only one button, consider setting that button's `Default` property to True.

Ironically, although this is one of the most sophisticated programs you've written, it's also simple and small. You can use the *WordCount* function from the GENERAL unit, and the file dialog really gives the application a bit of class without your having to do any work at all. You need two event handlers to make the program work.

Double-click on *Select*. *SelectClick* calls up the file dialog; if it is not cancelled, it stores the file name where the timer routine can get to it; and activates the timer. Oh yes, and it should disable itself so that the user doesn't try to count a second file while the first file is still counting.

```
procedure TSelectForm.SelectClick(Sender: TObject);
begin
   If OpenFileDialog.Execute then
   begin
      FileName.Caption := OpenFileDialog.FileName;
      CountTimer.Enabled := true;
      Select.Enabled := false;
   end;
end;
```

There it is. Instead of using a global variable, I've chosen to use the *FileName* label to store the file name. This makes the current file visible to the user and available to the word-counting procedure.

Set the *CountTimer Interval* property to 1 (the smaller the interval, the more frequently the routine will be called) and make sure to set its *Enabled* property to false. Now, double-click on the timer icon. This is where the code should go that actually counts the words in a file.

There should be two sections to the code, and each section should itself be divided into two sections. The first section should open the file. If the open fails, the user should be notified, and the appropriate controls in the form should be set up so that the user can select another file. If it doesn't fail, the routine should be set up to count words on the next call and any previous messages should be cleared.

The second section should first read in a line of the file, count the number of words in that line, and update all the appropriate variables and controls. Then, if the line read was the last line in the file, the user should be notified, the file should be closed, and the controls should be set up so that the user can select another file. You should be able to code this routine.

> **Note:** When I say you "should be able to" code something, I don't mean that you should be able to code it perfectly the first time. Programming often involves a lot of trial and error, seeing how things work, and correcting typos.

Here is how I coded the routine:

```
var CountFile: Text;

procedure TSelectForm.CountTimerTimer(Sender: TObject);
const
   TotalWords : Longint = 0;
   TotalLines : Longint = 0;
   NewFile    : Boolean = true;
var
   S          : String;
begin
   If NewFile then
   begin
      system.assign(CountFile, FileName.Caption);
      {$I-}
      reset(CountFile);
      {$I+}
      If IOResult<>0 then
      begin
         CountMessage.Caption := 'Error opening file.';
         CountTimer.Enabled := false;
         Select.Enabled := true;
         end
      else begin
         NewFile := false;
         CountMessage.Caption := '';
         end;
   end
   else begin
      readln(CountFile, S);
      Inc(TotalWords, WordCount(S));
      Words.Caption := StrFn(TotalWords);
      Inc(TotalLines);
      Lines.Caption := StrFn(TotalLines);
      If EOF(CountFile) then
      begin
         CountMessage.Caption := 'Count completed';
         TotalWords := 0;
         TotalLines := 0;
         NewFile := True;
         System.Close(CountFile);
         CountTimer.Enabled := False;
         Select.Enabled := True;
         end;
   end;
```

It's fairly long, but simple and quite legible. I used local typed constants to keep track of things—global variables would have served just as well. (And, in fact, a global constant was necessary for the typed file.) Notice that I also availed myself of the *StrFn* function and the *WordCount* function of the GENERAL unit. To make this code work, you need to add GENERAL to the Uses clause of the SELECT unit. You can add it to the interface Uses clause, or you can start a new one, right after the implementation keyword.

```
implementation

{$R *.FRM}

uses General;   {Add this line}
```

Summary

Units were created so that the full range of Delphi features could be communicated between a prewritten library and a client program. Unlike *include* files, a unit does not give the client program complete access to the code and does not force code to be continually recompiled. Unlike precompiled object libraries, a unit alerts the compiler to the available routines, data types, and other features of the unit.

Units are specified with the keyword unit, followed by a legal DOS file name. Units are divided into two sections: the interface, which determines what the client program can be aware of; and, the implementation, which contains the code for subroutines declared in the interface section, and any "secret" code of which the client cannot be aware. The interface section of a unit can be the basis for documenting the unit. The implementation section of a unit can have a main block of code, which is executed before the program's main block. This is good for initializing variables.

The Uses clause allows a program (or unit) to use units. A unit must be mentioned in the Uses clause before any of its components are used in the client code. Two units that refer to each other in their interface sections will cause a "circular unit reference error." If two units declare the same identifier, the unit that appears *last* in the Uses clause will have precedence. Rather than relying on precedence, however, the identifier may be preceded with the unit name and a period, just as though the identifier were a field and the unit were a record.

Constants are identifiers that are replaced at compile time with specific values. Constants are used to clarify code and to make code changes throughout a program easy. The typed constant is a way to allow Delphi to have preinitialized variables. It also allows a subroutine to have a variable that retains its value every time the subroutine is called.

In Windows, it is best not to have a subroutine that takes a long time to execute. When possible, the task should be broken into small pieces that allow Windows to keep the user in control.

The timer object can be set to create events at specific intervals. The file dialog object can be used to get a filename from the user through the standard Windows file dialog.

Review Questions

1. What is a *client* of a unit?
2. True or False: Data types, constant values, variables, and subroutines can be communicated through units.
3. Why use a constant instead of a literal?
4. What is the interface section of a unit for?
5. What is the implementation section of a unit for?
6. How do you declare a procedure or function in the interface section of a unit?
7. If the implementation section contains a procedure not declared in the interface section of the unit, can this procedure be used by a client program?
8. How does one unit or program become a client of a unit?
9. Can a unit use variables declared in a client project?
10. When is the main block of a unit executed?
11. What happens to constants when a program is compiled?
12. What is a kludge?
13. Can you change a typed constant?
14. Can you preinitialize variables in Delphi?
15. What is an *include* file?
16. How is a typed constant constant? How is this handy?
17. Which unit in the Uses clause has precedence?
18. What does the compiler do, as distinguished from what the linker does?
19. What is an object library?
20. True or False: Data types, constant values, and variables, as well as subroutines, can be communicated through object libraries.

Chapter 20 ◆ Units

Review Exercises

1. Think of some of the simple routines that you've coded in this book. Try transplanting some of the code from the object methods into standalone routines that might be generally useful. Do not try to transplant any code that deals with objects until the next chapter.

2. Write a simple program that allows you to enter two times and that gives the amount of time passed between the two times. For example, if you entered "9:50" and "11:30" it would return "1:40." Put the time math code into a unit. I'll leave to you how you would like to handle AM vs. PM, but a word of advice: accepting only military times—so that 1:00pm is 1300, 2:00pm is 1400, and so on—can make the math easier.

3. Expand the program in exercise 2 to include a date, so that a person can enter "January 1st 1994 11:30 AM" and "January 3rd 1994 1:00 AM" and get back "37 hours and 30 minutes." Which user input controls you use can make a big difference on the ease or difficulty of this program. Put the math routine on date and time in the same unit as the one you used for exercise 2.

4. Write a unit that handles the *CardDeck* data type created in Chapter 17, "The Array." Make the unit capable of initializing the deck, dealing the cards, *and* handling what happens when a request for a card is made, but there are no cards left in the deck. (Do you deal from the discards, re-shuffle, or what?)

CHAPTER 21

Objects

You've dealt with objects throughout this book, but with little attention to technical details. Without knowing how they work, you've plugged them into your code and used what you did know to build programs. In actual fact, to understand objects in Delphi fully is no trivial task; however, there's no reason you can't get a good start on the road to understanding them now.

Having *some* understanding of how objects work is absolutely vital. There are still a few lines in every Pascal-generated form unit that you don't yet understand, and it is important to understand these. While this code is unlikely to cause any bugs in your programs, it will leave you with a question mark floating around in your head every time you use Delphi.

Fortunately, Delphi simplifies things somewhat. You don't have to know all the details about how and why objects do what they do. You can write programs, even build your own objects, using the features that we'll cover here. Then, when you feel ready to tackle more complex concepts than those detailed in this book, you'll have a strong base on which to stand.

What Is an Object?

An object is very much like a record with associated subroutines. In fact, you could use an object in many of the same circumstances you would a record. It is a user type and can have fields. An object is declared by using the keyword *class*. Consider the following:

```
type
    Point = class
          X, Y: Longint;
    end;

    ScreenThing = class
          Location: Point;
          Color: Word;
    end;
```

Point is an object type that holds screen coordinates. ScreenThing is an object type that holds screen coordinates and a value for color.

In traditional object-oriented programming (OOP)—that is, programming with objects—Point and ScreenThing would be called *classes*. A class is analogous to a data type.

Variables of a class are declared in the same fashion as any other type, in a var section of the program.

```
var
    APoint: Point;
    AThing: ScreenThing;
```

If we think of APoint and AThing in traditional Pascal terms, they are simply variables of a data type. In OOP they would be called *instances* of their respective classes.

Fields of an object are accessed in exactly the same way that record fields are.

```
APoint.X := 100;
APoint.Y := 101;
AThing.Location.X := 100;
AThing.Color = 20;
```

You can also use with..do to simplify the accessing of an object.

```
with APoint do
begin
    X := 100;
    Y := 101;
end;
```

There is a lot more to objects than this, of course. As you already know, an object can have methods. Object methods are declared just as they would be in the interface section of a header, and within the block started by the class keyword. So, if ScreenThing was supposed to draw itself, it might have a Draw method.

```
ScreenThing = class
      Location: Point;
      Color: Word;
   procedure Draw;
end;
```

The actual code for Draw would go any place you might put a procedure or function—in other words, before the main block of the program or (more likely) in the implementation section of a unit. The header for the method is coded exactly the same as for any other procedure or function *except* that the method name is preceded by the object type name and period. This should look familiar:

```
procedure ScreenThing.Draw;
```

You've seen this same thing dozens of times already—almost every time you added code to a Pascal application.

```
procedure TForm1.Button1Click(Sender: TObject);
```

Every time you double-click on a component (or on an event in the Object Inspector) so that Pascal generates a code frame, what is actually created is a new method for the TForm1 (or whatever you call the form) object type.

The method itself is no different from any other subroutine, except that it has access to the object's fields. Draw could access the Location and Color fields to draw ScreenThing, almost as if there were a with..do before the procedure begins:

```
procedure ScreenThing.Draw;
var X: Integer;
    C: Word;
with ScreenThing do   {This line not really here.}
begin
   X := Location.X;
   C := Color;
   {Code to do something based on location and color}
end;
```

An object's class determines the fields and methods it has, as shown above. The ScreenThing class is different from the Point class. They have different fields. ScreenThing has the Draw method.

Different instances of the ScreenThing class will call Draw and get different results, insofar as their Location and Color fields are different, not unlike passing different parameters to a subroutine would get different results.

Inheritance

The preceding examples don't really illustrate why objects were necessary. After all, you could easily define a series of procedures to work from a specific record type, and code those procedures with an actual with..do block.

But what if you wanted to design a new record type, like the old one, but with some additional fields? You could no longer use the same subroutines—they're designed to work with a specific type. Objects are different from records in that a class can *inherit* fields and methods from another class. Consider this class:

```
type
   ThreeDPoint = class(Point)
        Z: Longint;
   end;
```

If `Point` is the class described above, `ThreeDPoint` has a total of three fields. X and Y from `Point`, and the new Z field. `Point` is said to be an *ancestor* of `ThreeDPoint`. `ThreeDPoint` *inherited* two fields from `Point`, and is said to be a *descendant* of `Point`. A new class's ancestor is put in parentheses after the class keyword, as shown.

```
var Pt3D: ThreeDPoint;
begin
   . . .
   Pt3D.X := 1;          {inherited}
   Pt3D.Y := 2;          {inherited}
   Pt3D.Z := -12;        {new}
   . . .
```

As you can see, accessing an ancestor's fields is no different from accessing fields that are original to the class.

Inheritance goes all the way back to the original object. In other words, you could define a new class based on `ThreeDPoint`,

```
type
   FourDPoint = class(ThreeDPoint)
        Z2: Longint;
   end;
```

and it would have all of the fields of both `Point` and `ThreeDPoint`.

As previously stated, an object inherits not just an ancestor's fields, but also its methods.

```
type
   NamedScreenThing = class(ScreenThing)
        Name: String[30];
   end;
```

`NamedScreenThing` has the `Location` and `Color` fields, and a new field `Name`. It also has the `Draw` method.

```
var NST: NamedScreenThing;
begin
   . . .
   NST.Location.X := 1;        {Ancestor's}
   NST.Name := 'Hello.';       {Original}
   NST.Draw;                   {Ancestor's}
```

It is important to understand that classes inherit the methods of their ancestors, because every class in Delphi has a *default* ancestor, even your `Point` and `ScreenThing` classes above. The default ancestor is a class called `TObject`.

```
type
   Point = class(TObject)
   . . .
   ScreenThing = class(TObject)
   . . .
```

Note: By tradition, classes in Pascal are given a descriptive identifier preceded by the letter *T*. So, if you had a class for a deck of cards, you might call it `TDeck` or `TCardDeck`.

Similarly, if you had a form class, you might call it `TForm`.

`TObject` is a class with no fields but several useful methods that, for example, can provide information about a class's ancestors. If you specify a class without specifying an ancestor, `TObject` becomes your new class's ancestor. In other words, this class definition

```
type NewClass = class
```

is the same as this one:

```
type NewClass = class(TObject);
```

Note: Every object is ultimately descended from `TObject`. `TObject` is called the *root* class.

Constructors and Destructors

Object instances are different from other variables in that you can't simply declare them and use them. They must be prepared through a special kind of method called a *constructor*. When you are done with a particular object instance, you destroy it with a *destructor*.

A constructor might look like this:

```
type
   TPoint = class
      X, Y, Z : Longint;
      constructor Init;
   end;

constructor TPoint.Init;
begin
   X := 0; Y := 0; Z := 0;
end;
```

whereas a destructor might be something like this:

```
type
   TFile = class
         SourceFile: Text;
      destructor Done;
   end;

destructor TFile.Done;
begin
   Close(SourceFile);
end;
```

In other words, they're just special procedures where you can initialize variables (constructor) or wrap up any unfinished business that the object might have (destructor). A lot more than this happens behind the scenes, but we don't have to care about that.

A constructor is special in one other way. An object instance never calls a constructor. In essence, the constructor is you asking the class to set aside some memory and create an instance of itself. So, in order to actually use an object you must first declare a variable of that class and then ask that class to create an instance of itself. If you had the TPoint class above, you could use it in this way:

```
var APoint: TPoint
begin
   APoint := TPoint.Create;
   APoint.X := 1;
   . . .
```

You absolutely *must* call a constructor (like TObject Create constructor) before trying to use the instance.

You *should* call a destructor (like TObject Destroy) after you have finished with an object instance, because this will free up the memory that your object instance has been allocated.

Replacing Object Methods

Inheriting methods is well and good, but sometimes the inherited method is of little use with the new class. Consider these two classes:

```
type
   TScreenThing = class
         X, Y : Longint;
      procedure Draw;
      function    SomeFunc: Longint;
      procedure SomeProc;
   end;

   T3DScreenThing = class(TScreenThing)
      Z: Longint;
   end;
```

Imagine that `TScreenThing.Draw` draws an image on-screen based on the coordinates in the *X* and *Y* fields. `T3DScreenThing`, on the other hand, is supposed to draw a different kind of image— a three-dimensional image that needs to take into account the *Z* field. An object can replace an ancestral method, simply by declaring a method with the same name in its definition.

```
T3DScreenThing = class(TScreenThing)
   Z: Longint;
      procedure Draw;
   end;
```

Nothing special has to be done in the code for `T3DScreenThing.Draw`. Instances of this class will automatically call their own class's `Draw` method. The new `Draw` method is said to have *replaced* the old one.

Sometimes you need to add something to an ancestral method, but you don't want to have to re-code the whole thing, just because you changed one small aspect of it. To allow you to call the ancestral method from the new method, Pascal provides the keyword `inherited`. `Inherited` is usually followed by a method name and means simply, "Call my ancestor's method."

```
procedure T3DScreenThing.Draw;
begin
   inherited Draw;   {Calls TScreenThing.Draw};
   {Add new drawing code here.}
end;
```

This capability is particularly important in one case, as you'll see later on.

Object Type Compatibility

Objects, like records, are not things that you can compare or do math with. If *Q* and *R* are `TScreenThing` objects, you can't do any of these things:

```
If Q = R then . . .
Q := Q + R;
If Q>R then   . . .
Q := R;   {Works but not as expected.}
```

The last assignment will compile, by the way, but it probably doesn't do what you might expect. It doesn't copy all of R's fields onto Q, but instead actually makes Q and R refer to the *same* object, so just don't do it for now.

A curious thing about object types is that a class is compatible with all of its descendants. The following code illustrates:

```
type
   TScreenThing = class
       X, Y : Longint;
      procedure Draw;
   end;
```

Chapter 21 ♦ Objects

```
    T3DScreenThing = class(TScreenThing)
       Z: Longint;
    end;
procedure ResetScreenThing(T: TScreenThing);
begin
   T.X := 0; T.Y :=0;
   T.Draw;
end;

procedure Reset3DScreenThing(T: T3DScreenThing);
begin
   T.X := 0; T.Y :=0; T.Z := 0;
   T.Draw;
end;

var
   Q : TScreenThing;
   R : T3DSceenThing;

begin
   . . .
   ResetScreenThing(Q);
   ResetScreenThing(R);      {This works!}
   Reset3DScreenThing(Q);    {This does not!}
   . . .
```

When you think about it, this makes sense. After all, the descendant has all the fields of the ancestor, so all the fields in the ancestor can be accounted for. In the case of Reset3DScreenThing, however, this line of the procedure makes no sense with a TScreenThing object:

```
T.Z := 0;
```

because a TScreenThing object has no z field.

Note: The interesting upshot of this is that *every* object created in Delphi is compatible with *TObject*. This will prove to be quite useful.

Example: Understanding Delphi

Finally, now you can understand the code that Delphi generates when you build a form. Start a new project and follow along as I get into the mechanics of how Delphi works.

Set up the form and code windows so that you can see both (see fig. 21.1). You don't really care what the form looks like — you're only going to use it to see what happens behind the scenes. Make sure the Code Editor is open to UNIT1, not to the project.

Figure 21.1

Code and form windows side-by-side.

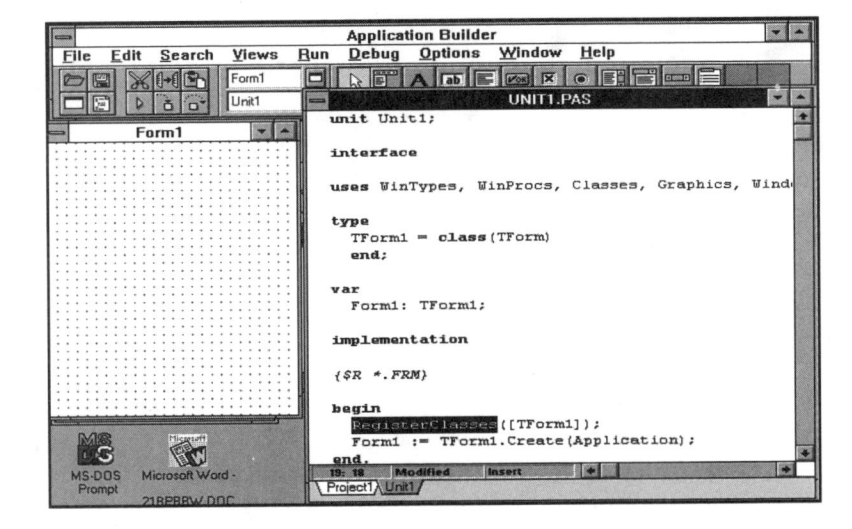

By now, you've covered almost everything that Delphi puts in the form unit and main code. Unit, uses, interface, implementation, the compiler directives, and the main block of code are all known to you. From the previous sections on objects, you can deduce that any form you build in Delphi has the TForm object as an ancestor; TForm1 is always a descendant of TForm. That leaves just one line in the main program.

Application.CreateForm(TForm1, Form1); Form1 is declared in the var section of the unit as being of the type TForm1. In the main block of the program, before Application.Run is called, Form1 is created. You can imagine that the CreateForm method of Application has a line that looks something like:

```
Form1 := TForm1.Create;
```

which actually sets the Form1 variable.

Look at what happens to your unit code when you change things in Delphi. Position the form and code windows so that both are visible. Change the Name property of the form to TestForm. Every case of TForm1 is replaced with TTestForm.

Now, add a button to the form. The TTestForm gets a field called Button1. If you change the name of Button1 in the Object Inspector the field name will change as well. Add a label to the form. A field called *Label1* gets added to TTestForm. Now delete the label from the form and the field goes away. (The fields are all, of course, declared as being of the appropriate class for the control. Buttons are TButton objects, labels are TLabel objects, and so on.) This does not work in reverse! You cannot delete a field from an object in the code window to make a change in the form.

Chapter 21 ◆ Objects

> **Note:** The *TForm* class is said to *own* all components placed on it.
>
> The *TForm* class automatically creates and destroys all the components it owns, so you never have to call the constructors or destructors of components added to a form.

Now, double-click the button object. Delphi generates a code frame and positions you to edit it. Page up to find out what happens to the class; it gets a new procedure method called `Button1Click`. All of the controls in Delphi notify the application when an event occurs, which allows the form to handle the event rather than the control.

So, when you have a blank form in Delphi you are creating a new class. When you add controls to that form, you are adding fields to the class. When you generate event handlers, you are adding methods to the class.

If controls didn't work this way that would mean that every time you wanted to add a button to a form that did something, you would have to create a new button class that acted the way you wanted. (This approach has its uses, but having the form handle all of the events is much easier to manage.)

And this, at long last, gives you a clue to the parameter of the event handler.

```
procedure TForm1.Button1Click(Sender: TObject);
```

`Sender` is the object that received the event! In this case it would be the button, but it could be a button, label, listbox, or any component you've used in this book. Because `TObject` is the root of all objects, any object in Delphi can be passed as a parameter declared `TObject`.

Typecasting

You might wonder why even bother to pass `TObject` as a parameter. Sure, any object can be passed, but so what? `TObject` has no fields and only two methods, neither of which is likely to be of any use to you. Pascal provides a way to "change" `TObject` into an object that you can actually use. This is done through *typecasting*.

> **Note:** You looked at a form of typecasting earlier on in the book (Chapter 14) that used parentheses to cast one variable as a variable of a different type.

Typecasting is done with the keyword `as`, often in conjunction with a `with..do`.

```
with Sender as TButton do
```

If `Sender` isn't compatible with `TButton`, this line will cause a run-time error. If you have some reason to think that different objects may call the same event handler, you can ask the object's type first with the `is` key word:

```
If Sender is TButton then
with Sender as TButton do
begin
   . . .
end
else if Sender is TLabel then
with Sender as TLabel do
. . .
```

This can be incredibly useful, as shown in the next few examples.

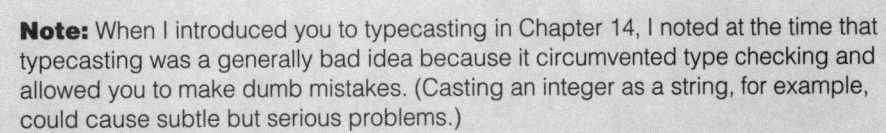

> **Note:** When I introduced you to typecasting in Chapter 14, I noted at the time that typecasting was a generally bad idea because it circumvented type checking and allowed you to make dumb mistakes. (Casting an integer as a string, for example, could cause subtle but serious problems.)
>
> The keywords `as` and `is` take the danger out of using typecasts, as they will generate an obvious error message if you make a bad cast. And typecasting is vital to productive OO programming.

Example: Calculators Revisited

Remember the CALCINT and CALCREAL programs? They had a great deal of code in them that all did basically the same thing:

```
procedure TForm1.OneClick(Sender: TObject);
begin
   If Complete then Entry.Text := '';
   Entry.Text := Entry.Text + '1';
end;
```

This was repeated nine times. Suppose we took all these methods out of the program (including their declarations in the `TForm1` class type), and added a new one:

```
procedure NumberClick(Sender: TObject);
```

Now, select all the number keys and flip the Object Inspector over to the Event page. If you get the list of available methods for `OnClick`, you'll see that `NumberClick` is one of them. This is handy to know: you can add a method in the form's definition and then hook it as an event handler.

Select `NumberClick` so that each number button will now call that method when clicked. How would you write this procedure so that the correct number is added?

Chapter 21 ♦ Objects

To do so, you should know that the button component's class name is `TButton`. (Hint: Each button has its number as its *Caption* property.) The code follows:

```
procedure TForm1.NumberClick(Sender: TObject);
begin
   If Complete then Entry.Text := '';
   with Sender as TButton do
      Entry.Text := Entry.Text + Caption;
end;
```

Pretty simple, actually. And it sure beats having 10 copies of the same code, doesn't it? Now, can you do the same thing for the operator keys? Remember, only +, -, * and ÷ (and mod for the integer version) are the operators. The equal sign has a fair amount of other code in it.

Give it a try, then come back and check out the code below.

```
procedure TForm1.OperatorClick(Sender: TObject);
begin
   with Sender as TButton do
      Calculate(ValFn(Entry.Text),Caption[1]);
   Entry.Text := StrFn(Total);
end;
```

You might have handled the fact that `Caption` is a string one of two ways. You could have picked the first character of the caption, as above, or you might just have changed the `Calculate` procedure to accept a string instead of a char.

While you're at it, you can clean up the code in some other ways, too. Pushing the `AllClear` button is like pushing the `Clear` button, and then zeroing the total. Well, you can now push the `Clear` button:

```
procedure TForm1.AllClearClick(Sender: TObject);
begin
   ClearClick(Clear);
   Total := 0;
   Operator := '+';
end;
```

A trickier situation is this: every time you call `Calculate` you update `Entry.Text`. Why not just do that in the `Calculate` procedure? For one thing, this won't work:

```
Entry.Text := StrFn(Total);
```

You should be able to figure out why. What is `Entry` and what is its scope?

`Entry` is a field in the `TForm1` class. `Calculate` is a standalone procedure — it doesn't know the `TForm1` class even exists. Therefore, `Entry` is outside of `Calculate`'s scope.

There are several approaches we could take here to remedy the situation. First of all, you could just add the variable name `Form1` before the `Entry`.

```
Form1.Entry.Text := StrFn(Total);
```

This works because `Form1` is declared *before* the `Calculate` procedure, so `Calculate` knows about it. But, if you're going to tie the procedure to the form, why not make it another method? Change the header to:

```
procedure TForm1.Calculate(Number: Longint; NextOp: Char);
```

(You'll have to add the following to the TForm1 class, too.)

```
procedure Calculate(Number: Longint; NextOp: Char);
```

And as long as you're neatening things up, shouldn't these variables

```
        Total    : Longint;
        Complete : Boolean;
        Operator : Char;
```

actually be object fields? That way, if there are two calculators in one program, they each have their own set, not the same global variables — which would cause no end of trouble.

This is more a matter of principle in this case, as it is somewhat unlikely that you would actually *have* two calculators in one program. Someday, however, you'll probably need two of *some* form, and when possible, you want them to rely entirely on their own methods and fields — not external variables.

Now, if you compile, you'll find that these lines in the project are no longer valid:

```
    Total := 0;
    Operator := '+';
    Complete := True;
```

Just as well — they don't really belong in the main program. The initialization of the form's fields should happen when the form gets created, right? Not only that, this setup is kind of saying, "When I am activated, push the AC button." So, why not just do that?

```
procedure TForm1.FormCreate(Sender: TObject);begin
    AllClearClick(AllClear);
end;
```

The examples given here apply to both calculator programs equally well. Not only that, you can extrapolate them to apply to almost every example you've coded in this book. It would be an excellent idea right now to go back through the examples and the text and see where an example could have been improved by incorporating fields and methods into an object rather than using global variables and isolated procedures and functions. (And, when you have procedures and functions that *aren't* part of methods, shouldn't they be in units so that they can be re-used?) We'll do one more example of this below, with the HILO program.

Example: A Deck Of Cards Engine

Not all objects are visual objects. Non-visual objects, or *engines*, can be as complex as a database management system (discussed in Chapter 19) or very, very simple. One good engine candidate is an object to manage a deck of cards. The Visual

Chapter 21 ♦ Objects

Solutions Pack comes with a control that you can use to represent a deck of cards, covered in Chapter 17, but if you'll recall, *you* had to write the code that shuffled the cards and dealt them out.

If you wanted to build a new card game, you'd have to transfer the code out of the HILO program into the new one. You could put the code more or less directly into a unit of standalone procedures and functions, but take the approach of turning it into an object.

You'll start by figuring out what fields the object should have: it should have an array to hold the cards and a byte value to keep track of how many cards have been dealt.

Then, you'll decide on the methods: it should have a method to set up the values of the cards appropriately, like the InitializeDeck procedure in the HILO program. It should have a method to shuffle the cards. It should also have a method to deal the cards. And, we know that the HILO program is going to need to know what the rank of previously dealt cards is, so we should have a method for that. For the sake of symmetry, we might as well add a method to return what the suit of a previously dealt card is, too.

The object should look like this:

```
TCardDeck = class
      Dealt       : byte;
      Deck        : Array[1..52] of cards;
   constructor Create;
   function    CardName(R: Rank; S: Suit): String;
   function    Deal: Cards;
   function    RankOfLastDealt(Depth: Byte): Ranks;
   procedure   Shuffle;
   function    SuitOfLastDealt(Depth: Byte): Suits;
end;
```

This code fragment displays my aesthetic preference when designing objects: I set the fields six spaces from the left and the methods three spaces. I also keep the fields and methods in alphabetical order, except for constructors, which I always put first. And, I prefer to space the method names so that they line up under each other, rather than staggered the way Pascal does them.

Notice that I gave the method a constructor, Create. TCardDeck's Create constructor will set up the cards exactly the way InitializeDeck did. Since the deck is useless without the cards set up, and since the client program has to call Create before using an instance of the class, it seems a logical marriage.

Before writing new code, you'll first find out how much of the code from HILO we can use: the Suits and Ranks enumerated types; the Cards record; and the Shuffle and InitializeDeck routines should be object methods. Now, because you used the same field names, you can practically transfer the procedures directly.

At this point, you should be able to code the object yourself. Below is the listing showing my approach:

```
unit DeckCard;

interface

type
   Suits = (Clubs, Diamonds, Hearts, Spades);
   Ranks = (Back, Ace, Two, Three, Four, Five, Six,
            Seven, Eight, Nine, Ten, Jack, Queen, King);

   Cards = record
      Suit: Suits;
      Rank: Ranks;
   end;

   TCardDeck = class
         Dealt      : byte;
         Deck       : Array[1..52] of cards;
      constructor Create;
      function    CardName(R: Ranks; S: Suits): String;
      function    Deal: Cards;
      function    RankOfLastDealt(Depth: Byte): Ranks;
      procedure   Shuffle;
      function    SuitOfLastDealt(Depth: Byte): Suits;
   end;

implementation

constructor TCardDeck.Create;
var I    : Integer;
    Rank : Ranks;
    Suit : Suits;
begin
   inherited Create;
   I := 1;
   For Suit := Clubs to Spades do
      For Rank := Ace to King do
      begin
         Deck[I].Suit := Suit;
         Deck[I].Rank := Rank;
         Inc(I);
      end;
end;

function    TCardDeck.CardName(R: Ranks; S: Suits): String;
var Q, K: String;
begin
   case R of
      Ace   : Q := 'Ace';
      Two   : Q := 'Two';
      Three : Q := 'Three';
      Four  : Q := 'Four';
      Five  : Q := 'Five';
```

```
      Six   : Q := 'Six';
      Seven : Q := 'Seven';
      Eight: Q := 'Eight';
      Nine : Q := 'Nine';
      Ten  : Q := 'Ten';
      Jack : Q := 'Jack';
      Queen: Q := 'Queen';
      King : Q := 'King';
   end;
   case S of
      Spades  : K := 'Spades';
      Hearts  : K := 'Hearts';
      Diamonds: K := 'Diamonds';
      Clubs   : K := 'Clubs';
   end;

   CardName := Q + ' of ' + K;
end;

function TCardDeck.Deal: Cards;
begin
   Inc(Dealt);
   Deal := Deck[Dealt];
end;

function  TCardDeck.RankOfLastDealt(Depth: Byte): Ranks;
begin
   RankOfLastDealt := Deck[Dealt-Depth].Rank;
end;

procedure TCardDeck.Shuffle;
var Hold: Cards;
    I, J: Integer;
begin
   for I := 1 to 52 do
   begin
      Hold := Deck[I];
      J := Random(52)+1;
      Deck[I] := Deck[J];
      Deck[J] := Hold;
   end;
end;

function  TCardDeck.SuitOfLastDealt(Depth: Byte): Suits;
begin
   SuitOfLastDealt := Deck[Dealt-Depth].Suit;
end;

begin
   Randomize;
end.
```

This object will deal cards, and is ready to use with any form that uses the Visual Solutions Pack deck of cards control— or any other card control that comes along.

Restricting Access to Object Features

By default, any object field is accessible by any client of that object. Fields and methods (which are sometimes collectively referred to as *features* or *attributes*) that are generally accessible are said to be "public." Delphi allows you to specifically control which clients through for keywords: Public, private, protected, and published.

Public, as mentioned, is the default: any client can access a public feature. Published features, too, can be accessed by any client. (You'll see the difference between a public feature and a published one below.) A private feature can be accessed by any client of an object *within the same unit!* So, given the following unit

```
Unit Protect;

interface

type
   TAnObject = class
   private
        AField: Integer;
   end;

   TAnotherObject = class
      procedure DoSomething(AO: TAnObject);
      end;

implementation

function Zero(AO: TAnObject): boolean;
begin
   Zero := AO.AField = 0;
   end;

procedure TAnotherObject.DoSomething(AO: TAnObject);
begin
   AO.AField := 42;
   end;

end.
```

both the Zero function and the TAnotherObject class can access AO's AField feature. Anywhere outside the Secretive unit, however, AField is *not* accessible. For example, the main program file can't read it or change it:

```
program Test;

uses Secretive;

var AO: TAnObject;
begin
   AO := TAnObject.Create;
   AO.Field := 6;   {No!  Won't compile}
   end;
```

A feature may also be protected, which means that a descendant of the class may use it, but no one else.

```
Unit Protect;

interface

type
   TAnObject = class
   protected
         AField: Integer;
   end;

   TAnotherObject = class(TAnObject)
      procedure DoSomething;
      end;

implementation

function Zero(AO: TAnObject): boolean;
begin
   Zero := AO.AField = 0;   {Won't compile}
   end;

procedure TAnotherObject.DoSomething;
begin
   AField := 42;
   end;

end.
```

So the function `Zero` cannot use `AField`, but the descendant can.

You might wonder how important any of this is, but recall back to Chapter 8, where you lamented the fact that if you passed a variable to a subroutine, that subroutine could change that variable whether you wanted it to or not. An object has complete control over which fields can and cannot be changed.

A published feature includes about itself certain information that can be used by the Delphi object inspector. It is through the published keyword that you could write your own components.

Example: HILO Revisited

As another example of using objects to improve a program's readability, go back to the HILO program and clean it up while incorporating the TCardDeck object into it. In the process, look for features of the various classes you might want to restrict access to. The following text describes the process of cleaning the code up from top to bottom.

Add a Deck field to the form, of type TCardDeck.

Remove from the form unit the CardDeck type and the Ranks and Suits enumerated types, as well as the Cards record— these are all in the DECKCARD engine. GameState is specifically a HILO type, so keep that. Take the variables Deck and Dealt out. State and Funds should be fields of the form, so remove them from the var section and add them to the form. Change State and Funds to be *protected*.(Why should any code other than the HiLo form itself have access to these fields?) Move the GameState type so that it is defined before the form, since State is now a field in the form.

From the implementation section remove StrFn, InitializeDeck, and Shuffle. Now, about this StackClick method. It looks pretty bad. You have the same code duplicated three times: once to set the value for Card1, once for Card2, and once for HiLo. Set up a form method to set the card value. Use this

```
        procedure SetCardValue(var CardObject: TVBXMhCardDeck; Card:
    ➥Cards);
```

if you have the VSP, or if you're using a label object,

```
        procedure SetCardValue(var CardObject: TLabel; Card: Cards);
```

This would give a VBX card deck control (or label control) the value specified in Card. That way, the code for StackClick can look like this:

```
    case State of
       NoCards : SetCardValue(Card1, Deck.Deal);
       OneCard : SetCardValue(Card2, Deck.Deal);
       TwoCards: begin
          SetCardValue(HiLo, Deck.Deal);
```

The next section of code in StackClick won't work with the Deck object, so we'll have to change it.

```
            If Deck[Dealt-1].Rank > Deck[Dealt-2].Rank then
            begin
               HiRank := Deck[Dealt-1].Rank;
               LoRank := Deck[Dealt-2].Rank;
            end
            else begin
                    HiRank := Deck[Dealt-2].Rank;
                    LoRank := Deck[Dealt-1].Rank;
                 end;

            If Deck[Dealt].Rank in [LoRank..HiRank] then
            begin
```

Chapter 21 ◆ Objects

You could access the array of cards directly, but instead, use the object's `RankOfLastDealt` method. My preference here is to remove the next bit of code (this code figures out which card is high and which is low and what the rank of the last card dealt was) from `StackClick` altogether and make it its own method. You might rightfully disagree, since the method would only likely be called by `StackClick`. My rationale for separating it is simply that smaller subroutines are easier to debug and to follow than large ones. I would set up the method like this

```
procedure GetHiLo(var HiRank, LoRank, HiLoRank: Ranks);
```

that could be called from `StackClick`.

```
GetHiLo(HiRank, LoRank, HiLoRank);
```

You'd have to add a `HiLoRank` variable to make this work and change the test line, which used to deal directly with the deck array.

```
If HiLoRank in [LoRank..HiRank] then
```

The reference to `Dealt` in `StackClick` has to be replaced with `Deck.Dealt`. From `FormActivate` we have to remove all references to `Dealt`, `InitializeDeck` and `Shuffle`, and replace them with code to construct the `Deck` object and shuffle the deck. The code to call `Shuffle` in `DiscardClick` has to be replaced with a call to the `Deck` object's `Shuffle` method. Then finally, we have to set up the `SetCardValue` and the `GetHiLo` methods.

Here is the new, improved code:

```
unit Hilo2;

interface

uses WinTypes, WinProcs, Classes, Graphics, Windows, Controls, Mhcd200,
   VBXCtrl, Mhsn200, DeckCard;
{Your uses clause may vary.}

type
   GameState = (NoCards, OneCard, TwoCards, ThreeCards, Reset);

   TForm1 = class(TForm)
        . . . {Delphi added components here}
      procedure DiscardClick(Sender: TObject);
      procedure FormActivate(Sender: TObject; Value: Boolean);
      procedure GetHiLo(var HiRank, LoRank, HiLoRank: Ranks);
      procedure SetCardValue(var CardObject: TVBXMhCardDeck{or TLabel};
      ➥Card: Cards);
      procedure StackClick(Sender: TObject);
   protected          Funds  : Integer;
        State   : GameState;
   end;

var
   Form1: TForm1;
implementation
```

```delphi
{$R *.FRM}

uses General;

procedure TForm1.StackClick(Sender: TObject);
var HiRank, LoRank, HiLoRank : Ranks;
begin
   case State of
      NoCards : SetCardValue(Card1, Deck.Deal);
      OneCard : SetCardValue(Card2, Deck.Deal);
      TwoCards: begin
         SetCardValue(HiLo, Deck.Deal);
         GetHiLo(HiRank, LoRank, HiLoRank);

         If HiLoRank in [LoRank..HiRank] then
         begin
            If Bet.Value = 0 then Message.Caption := 'Too bad!'
            else begin
                   Inc(Funds, Bet.Value);
                   Message.Caption := 'You won!';
                 end;
         end
         else begin
            If Bet.Value = 0 then Message.Caption := 'Smart move.'
               else begin
                      Dec(Funds, Bet.Value);
                      Message.Caption := 'You lost.';
                    end;
            end;
         end;

      ThreeCards: begin
                     Card1.Visible := False;
                     Card2.Visible := False;
                     HiLo.Visible := False;
                     Discard.Visible := True;
                  end;
   end;
   Inc(State);
   If State<>ThreeCards then Message.Caption := '';
   If State = Reset then State := NoCards;
   If Deck.Dealt = 51 then Stack.Visible := False;

   Bet.Max := Funds;
   If Bet.Value > Funds then Bet.Value := Funds;
   Cash.Caption := StrFn(Funds);
end;

procedure TForm1.FormActivate(Sender: TObject; Value: Boolean);
begin
   State := NoCards;
   Funds := 100;
   Bet.Max := Funds;
```

Chapter 21 ♦ Objects

```
      Deck := TCardDeck.Create;
      Deck.Shuffle;
         Cash.Caption := StrFn(Funds);
      end;

      procedure TForm1.DiscardClick(Sender: TObject);
      begin
         Discard.Visible := False;
         Stack.Visible := True;
         HiLo.Visible := False;
         Card1.Visible := False;
         Card2.Visible := False;

         State := NoCards;

         Deck.Shuffle;
      end;

      {USE ONLY ONE OF THE FOLLOWING SETCARDVALUE METHODS!!!!}

      {This procedure handles the deck of cards control}
      procedure TForm1.SetCardValue(var CardObject: TVBXMhCardDeck; Card:
      ↩Cards);
      begin
         CardObject.Value := Ord(Card.Rank);
         CardObject.Suit  := Ord(Card.Suit);
         CardObject.Visible := True;
      end;

      {This procedure handles the label control}
      procedure TForm1.SetCardValue(var CardObject: TLabel; Card: Cards);
      begin
         CardObject.Text := CardName(Rank, Suit);
         CardObject.Visible := True;
      end;

      procedure TForm1.GetHiLo(var HiRank, LoRank, HiLoRank: Ranks);
      var A, B: Ranks;
      begin
         A := Deck.RankOfLastDealt(1);
         B := Deck.RankOfLastDealt(2);
         If A > B then
         begin
            HiRank := A;
            LoRank := B;
         end
         else begin
               HiRank := B;
               LoRank := A;
            end;
```

```
    HiLoRank := Deck.RankOfLastDealt(0);
  end;

end.
```

Summary

The last chapter of this book discusses planning and walks you through a sample project in a fashion that is more appropriate than the seat-of-the-pants method used so far. An object is like a record with associated subroutines. An object data type is called a class, and variables of that type are called *instances.* Object fields and methods are accessed just as record fields are, through the '.' symbol. An object method is declared as part of the class, and then usually implemented in the implementation section of a unit, where the method name is preceded by the class name and a '.'. As part of the class, a class method has access to the instance's fields, as though there were a with...do statement around the code block. Classes can be descended from other classes: they inherit the fields and methods of their ancestors. TObject is the root class of all objects in Delphi. It supplies the Create constructor and the Destroy destructor. A constructor is a class method, which means that it is called by referring directly to the class, not an instance of the class. Every instance of an object must first be assigned the result of the Create constructor. When done with an object, it should be destroyed with Destroy, which frees up the resources that the object instance used. Classes can replace inherited methods, and still call the inherited methods from the new methods. Object instances are backwardly compatible: they can be assigned to ancestral object instances. Objects may not be assigned to their descendants, however. Typecasting causes an object to be seen as another object by the compiler. This can be done safely through the as keyword. An object can be tested to see if it is an object type through the is keyword.

A TForm object keeps a list of all the objects in it. A descendant class may have specific fields to refer to those objects.

Review Questions

1. What is the root of all Delphi classes?
2. Why typecast? What do is and as do?
3. What does OOP stand for?
4. What feature of non-OOP Pascal is an object class comparable to?
5. What feature of non-OOP Pascal is an object instance comparable to?

Chapter 21 ◆ Objects

6. What does inheritance mean? How would you allow a new class to inherit fields and methods of an existing class?

7. Which comes first, the ancestor or the descendant?

8. Does an object instance have to do anything special to use inherited fields or methods?

9. True or False: once you've inherited a method, you're stuck with it.

10. True or False: an object instance is compatible with its ancestors.

11. What is a constructor? What is a destructor?

12. Would you ever call a constructor from an instance of the class?

Review Exercises

1. Right now, the Hi-Lo game is coded as part of the form object. As an exercise, take *all* of the logic for the Hi-Lo game and put it in its own object. (The object can be part of the Hi-Lo form unit.) The form must *ask* the object for the values of the cards, and the outcome of the game.

2. In the last chapter, you wrote a little program (Word Counter) to count the number of words in a file and you used a lot of typed constants and a global file variable. Rewrite that program by converting the typed constants and global variable to object fields.

3. Write a program that calls up *two* copies of the main form from Word Counter. It should be possible to count two separate files at once, and neither process should stop Windows.

4. Create an object that mimics a slot machine. Then create a form that communicates with the object to present the state of the slot machine to the user. You can do this by using labels to describe the slot machine (as in "Bar," "Bell," "Lemon"), or if you feel adventurous, through the Image component found on the Additional page (it appears on the component palette as the sun over the sea). You'll have to draw the bitmaps representing slot possibilities yourself.

CHAPTER 22

Better By Design

The examples given in this book, although functioning programs, were created to illustrate certain points. It's generally a bad sign if you go back in your programs and find all sorts of duplicated code or illogically organized projects. Poor planning can cause all kinds of problems. Up to this point, you've done no planning at all.

This book was designed to teach you the basics of Delphi. The examples you have worked with thus far have been designed to show facets of the language rather than to serve as models of how to program. The term for the kind of programming you've done here is *hacking*.

Hacking

Sources have it that the word *hack* (as used in computers) originated at the Massachusetts Institute of Technology, where the term meant "a good joke." A "computer hacker" was at first a computer prankster, then any computer enthusiast. In recent years, *hacker* has come to mean a programmer who analyzes a problem too quickly, then immediately begins coding.

Chapter 22 ◆ Better By Design

> **Hacker**
>
> Up until the 1980s, a hacker was a computer enthusiast who enjoyed learning everything about a computer system and, through clever programming, pushing the system to its highest possible level of performance.
>
> During the 1980s, the press redefined the term to include hobbyists who break into secured computer systems. Sensationalist news accounts of the dangerous activities of "hackers" created a "hacker hysteria." In 1989, for example, the New York Times published an article headlined "Invasion of the Data Snatchers," culminating in a ridiculous series of Secret Service raids in which the computer systems of these "dangerous" persons were confiscated.
>
> Although some hackers are indeed *crackers* who enjoy the challenge of breaking into corporate and organizational computing systems, the media's redefinition of the term has cast a shadow over the activities of many of the most creative computer users.

I like to think of a *hacker* as someone similar to a person with a machete. A person who tackles a programming problem without giving it considerable thought beforehand is like the jungle adventurer hacking through the underbrush with a machete. He may get through all right, but he never knows what he is going to run into, and woe to him if something should take him off course.

However, I would recommend that right now, you take what you've learned in this book, and start hacking. Think of some simple programs you can write and just sit down and code them. Do two or three or a dozen, until you feel good about what you've learned.

Hacking out code will show you what you know and don't know. You may find yourself twisting a programming problem around because you don't like arrays or you aren't comfortable with objects. Hacking can show you your prejudices. A popular saying among programmers is, "When the only tool you have is a hammer, everything begins to look like a nail." In more concrete terms, if you're really comfortable with declaring simple variables, and not with defining record types, your programs will be full of disjointed variables, instead of record types that would serve better.

> **Note:** Although it's a popular saying among programmers, the "hammer and nail" quote was originated by American psychologist Abraham Maslow.

Most importantly, as you are hacking out your programs, you'll discover the importance of design. One of your small programs will get a little bigger, or you'll want to vary it in some way, and you'll discover that you have to do a lot more work to progress than you would have if you'd thought the problem through in the first place. In some cases, it is easier to start from scratch—to completely rewrite the program—than it is to change a badly hacked program.

Design

The key to smooth programming is design. To *design* a computer program is to lay it out in as much detail as possible, to predict and avoid the pitfalls that would otherwise emerge as code was being written. Code is written in interlocking pieces, and if one piece has to change, the change has the unfortunate tendency to "break" other pieces. Proper use of units and objects can reduce the amount of breakage, but nothing beats a good design as a preventative to disaster.

Many programmers hate design. If they're not a few clicks away from the compiler, they feel their time is wasted. Many (maybe most) programmers would rather spend hours or days tracking down a bug than a few minutes or hours on a design that could have prevented the bug. Most programmers might never admit to this, but the fact that so many programmers spend little time designing, and much time debugging, indicates otherwise.

Unfortunately, while design is crucial, it is also extremely controversial. Programmers are often steeped in controversy: Which language is the best? Which compiler? What design philosophy?

I'm not going to engage in any arguments—you'll get plenty of those from other programmers you meet. What I'm going to do in this chapter is suggest ways of approaching and solving programming problems that have worked successfully for me. I'll also warn you away from a few dangerous practices. Ultimately, however, I make no claims of being right or better, and you should use what works for you.

To take you through the design process, as I envision it, you will imagine a problem, and design an application to solve that problem.

The Problem

Computers are like any tool—they exist to create solutions. Given this, the genesis of any computer program is from a problem. To solve the problem, you first have to understand what the problem really is. You do that by surveying people who have the problem. Find out from them what it is. Remember that many people might have a different view of the same problem, and that all these views might be valid. At the same time, the views might be incomplete. Then, examine the situation for yourself. You might see things that no one else does. Problems often have many layers to them, and the people with the problem often are stuck looking at the outermost layer. Fortunately, the problem you'll be working with here is rather simple.

The problem you'll use is this: I can't seem to remember people's birthdays, anniversaries, or other important dates.

This is a pretty easy problem, of course. If you were going to build a commercial application (one that you packaged and sold to others), your best approach would be to survey people about their needs in this regard. Some problems mentioned will be outside the scope of your program, and others will only seem that way. Consider that you need to be reminded of dates, but you don't turn on your computer every day. Can a program do anything about that?

A Modest Proposal

The approach I take at this point is not a common one for programmers. In fact, I don't know of any other programmer who does this. After analyzing the problem, I write the documentation for the program. The end user documentation—not a technical reference, but a book that anyone can pick up and figure out how the program (were it written) works.

My method isn't as far out as it sounds—most design methods suggest that the problem be expressed in English and the objects, records and other types, variables, subroutines, and so on should be culled from this English language description. Then, a lot of methods encourage *prototyping*. This is the development of a user interface—easily done in Delphi—that shows how the final project will work. You give the prototype to the users and let them try it out to see how they like it. Subsequently, you incorporate their feedback into the project, making changes where necessary and hammering out differences that might occur.

I use the documentation a bit differently than this, however. I create the documentation almost as though it were a perfect world, and I could create the perfect program, with the perfect user interface. The program in the documentation becomes my *goal*. Invariably, there are changes from the near-perfect program envisioned to one that actually works—usually as a result of hardware limitations (computers that aren't fast enough or can't store enough data are two of the most common problems)—but the ideal is always there as I program.

Usually, after writing the end-user documentation, I write the technical reference, which explains what everything is and how it works. The idea behind writing both sets of documents is that any programmer or programming team can take these documents and build the program from them.

The Description

Because including the full documentation for even a simple reminder program would be too long, I'll leave it up to you to explore the documentation approach as a possible tool. It has worked quite well for me.

However, a clear description of the problem to be solved and how the program is going to solve it is vital to the program's success. The dangers you face by not having this description and not knowing how the program is going to solve the problem are twofold: you'll miss something, or you'll get sidetracked and start adding feature after feature to your program.

> **Feature Bloat**
>
> Feature bloat is a common situation in today's competitive application market. Companies with competing applications feel forced to add features to their products, and often do so without ever asking their customers if they need the feature.
>
> This situation comes about partially because computer trade magazines often compare products feature-by-feature. Thus, if your word processor doesn't chart astrological forecasts, but a competing word processor does, this shortcoming might show up in the magazine's rating system, which doesn't necessarily bother to find out what percentage of the population actually needs that feature.
>
> Even without trade magazines, computer programmers are always looking to make programs better, and sometimes this comes out as an irresistable urge to add *more* to the program.

Start with a clear description of what the program is to do. When ideas start to spring up—and they definitely will spring up while you're coding—write them down and look at them *after* the program is complete. That's why programs are *updated*.

Descriptions of programs typically begin in general terms, then become more and more detailed. From the descriptions of the program, you can subsequently pick out objects and subroutines that need to be written.

Example: REMINDME

The program, called REMINDME, will allow the user to set "reminders." These can be set to go off on and around specific dates, and should show a message, the current date and time, and the reminder date. The program should be able to provide the list of current reminders for editing. The program also should keep a record of the last date it was run, so that it can present all the important dates from the first run to the most current.

> **Note:** This solves the problem of the user who doesn't turn on the computer every day. You can't make the user turn on his computer daily, but you can compensate for his being off-line for a period of days.

Reminders will be a message associated with a certain date that the user enters into the program. The message should appear on the date, or every day within a certain number before the date (as specified by the user). The user should be able to "clear" the reminder so that if he doesn't want the message to come up anymore, it won't—even if the date has not arrived. He should also be able to set any reminder to have a "nag" mode, so that if he doesn't clear the reminder, it keeps nagging him—even after the date has passed.

To allow the same reminders to be used year after year, reminders should be given an active or inactive status. An active reminder is one that, *on the current day*, presents a message to the user, or would present a message if not cleared. An inactive reminder is one that wouldn't present a message. When an inactive reminder becomes active, it is automatically given a status of "not cleared." This way, the user gets a message, clears it, and can forget about it until next year when it becomes active again.

After the program starts, it should check the reminder file for any reminders that should be activated on the current date. It should present these reminders (if not already cleared) one at a time. Once completed with the active reminders, it should allow the user to view, modify, remove, or add reminders. It should also let the user review the active reminders.

Reminders should be a date (special data type), a message (string), a window (byte), a cleared field (Boolean), an active field (Boolean) and a nag field (Boolean). This is the user interface: a form that displays the active reminders, a form that displays all the reminders in the file, and a form that allows editing of the files.

The Prototype

After deciding how the product should work, the next step is prototyping. The prototype should demonstrate how everything in the description that the user is going to control will be done. Of course, you've been doing a lot of that in this book, but the choices made reflected what you needed to learn rather than what would be best for the user.

> **Note:** You've covered only a fraction of the total components in Delphi. There are controls you can use that aren't even included in Delphi, but are available through bulletin boards and commercial packages. Remember, you aren't restricted to controls created in Delphi. You can also use some Visual Basic controls in Delphi.

The key to prototyping is to set up something, and then use it. Make the conditions under which it is tested as close as possible to the conditions under which the product would actually be used. Try the prototype on a number of people. Ideally, the people testing the prototype should represent as broad a range of users as possible. If you're expecting the program to be used by people who don't know much about computers, get a few of them to test it out. If you're expecting the program to be used by fellow hackers, try it out on them. If you're expecting it to be used by carpenters…well, you get the idea. Realism counts heavily when testing prototypes.

Example: REMINDME, the Forms

Figure 22.1 shows how I set up the three forms described in the description section. The form in the lower-right corner shows the reminder list, where reminders can be displayed. That form has buttons to edit, remove, or create new reminders, and also a button named "Remind" to review the active reminders. This is the main form—the one that will call the other forms.

Figure 22.1
The REMINDME Forms.

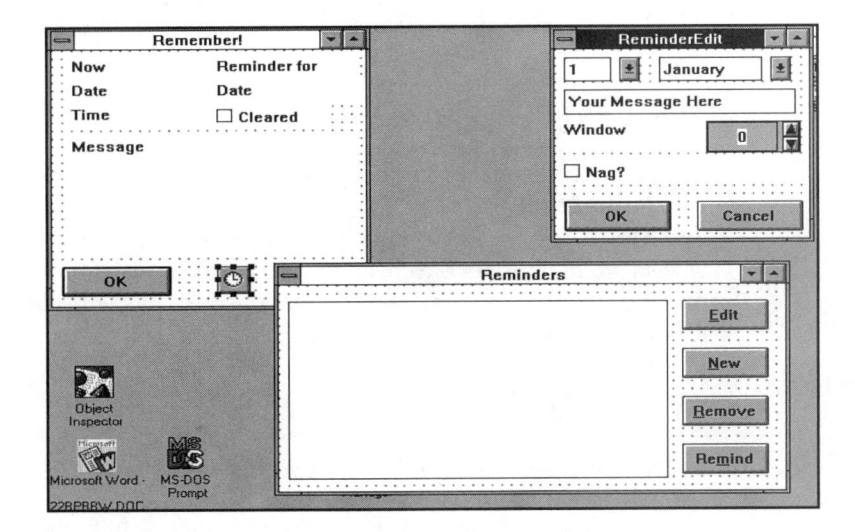

The form in the upper left is the actual reminder form. It shows the current date and time, the message, and the date of the reminder. It has a timer control so that the time label can be updated.

The last form is the editing form. It has controls for the user to create and edit reminders.

Chapter 22 ◆ Better By Design

> **Note:** The month control at the top of the ReminderEdit form is called a *combo box*. Combo boxes allow you to make one of several choices. You specify the choices through the *Items* property, which is the same object used by the *ListBox* control. I've set up the month combo box to have the months from January to December. I've also set the *Style* property to csDropDownList, which prevents the user from entering any data into the combo box—the user can only select from the list.
>
> In this case, I'm using the combo box as a list box that doesn't take up as much space.
>
> You may find, especially as a beginner, that you are constantly discovering new tools and objects to use in your programs, and this may make it seem like you'll never really master Delphi. But keep in mind that building a user interface is an art form, and therefore subject to a million interpretations.
>
> One of the first things you should do when programming on your own is to explore all the controls you can find. See which are the most useful—and which suit your taste.

The Objects

The next step in designing is to find the objects in the program and decide what general functions they should have. You can find the objects by looking at the description. *What* is being talked about? In a checkbook balancing program those objects might be a check, a checkbook, and an account. In a card game, those objects might be a deck of cards, the piles that the various cards can be dealt to, and cash to bet with. And, of course, there are the form objects that are a part of every Delphi program.

Spotting the objects is sometimes simple, but as it often happens there sometimes is an object lurking under the surface that you don't notice on first glance. Remember the HILO program? You originally did not have an object that dealt cards. Looking at the card deck control, you might have thought it was unnecessary.

One key to keeping things straight is to realize that you aren't yet writing any code. If you're building a card game, you include the deck of cards as part of the design, even though you've written that object already. It is still part of the program, and the functions that it has to serve should be generally noted.

Example: REMINDME, the Objects

REMINDME has the three form objects, a reminder object, and a reminder reader object that handles the reminder file. The `TReminderList` form serves to display the reminders in the file. The `TRemember` form serves to display an active reminder. The

TReminderEdit form allows the user to edit or add reminders. The TReminder object contains the message, the date, and the other information pertinent to the reminder. The TReminderReader loads and retrieves reminders on request, but also has a Reminders method that will go through the entire file reminder by reminder and return the active reminders.

You'll also descend a "special" TReminder object which you'll call TCatchUp. The TCatchUp reminder object will be the first object in any reminder file and will contain the *last* day the program was used. When the program begins, this reminder will set a field (LastDay) in the TReminderReader object.

Defining the Objects

Now that you've "discovered" the objects, you need to define them in technical terms. What methods will they have? What fields? It is here that you'll notice a certain "fallout" from earlier phases of the design. You're now talking—not actually coding, but talking—in technical terms. What object is going to do what, and through what methods, and what data types should fields be?

You decide here, for example, which object in the checkbook program is going to be responsible for printing checks, printing reports, saving data to the file, and so on. In a card game, you decide which pile of cards is designated for what purpose. This step extends to deciding what methods the form's controls will call, if any.

This is also the place where you decide, in general terms, how to manage the data for your program. Will you use text files or typed files? Purchase a database engine?

The definition of the objects is not so complete that you've actually coded the methods, but complete enough so that no major part of the program has gone unseen. After this point, objects may have methods not discussed here, but they should be methods like the *GetHiLo* method from Chapter 21—things done to keep code logically neat, rather than to fill a design gap.

This is also where you decide *responsibility*. When you created the *TCardDeck* object, you gave it two methods (*RankOfLastDealt* and *SuitOfLastDealt*) that could have resulted in an error. If the client requested the fourth card from the top, and only one card had been dealt, *TCardDeck* would be accessing its *Deck* array at -3. This would have resulted in a run-time error at best, and incorrect answers at worst.

At this point in the design, you specify what is okay and not okay to pass a method. If designing the *TCardDeck* object, you might say of those two methods: "These methods must be passed a valid value or they will result in the program giving incorrect results or ending in an error."

Alternatively, you could have added code that detected an invalid value being passed and returned some kind of error code. This step would also be noted at this point: "These methods will detect invalid values passed and will return the values *InvalidRank* or *InvalidSuit* if called with an invalid value. This should be detected by the client program."

Chapter 22 ♦ Better By Design

The alternative isn't particularly useful here because if the client program has to check for an error, it might as well just check to see that it is not passing an invalid value to begin with. But these are the decisions you'll have to make.

Example: REMINDME, Object Definition, Etc.

Reminder object (engine):

Message : String[100]

Date : date data type

Window for Reminder (in days): byte

Active : Boolean (Should the message be active today?)

Cleared : Boolean (If true, an active message will not be displayed.)

Nag : Boolean (If true, a reminder is active past its actual date.)

method Create(Message, date, window, Nag) (Create object and set all fields.)

method Destroy; (not needed)

method IsActive(Today): Boolean; (Should the method be active today? This method juggles the active, cleared, and nag fields to determine whether message should be displayed for a given reminder.)

method Describe: String (Put the object's fields together in one string, for display.)

method Replace(Reminder Record): (Replace the object's current data with a new Reminder.)

As a rule, I like to start with the constructor and destructor methods. Here, Create would set all the fields of the object. You really don't need a special destroy, because there are no files to close or anything—but it should be noted that the method is unnecessary and not just forgotten.

> **Note:** For purposes of this example, you are going to put all the fields of the reminder object into a stand-alone record. This step will allow you to have a typed file containing all the reminder data.
>
> It is possible, and perhaps even preferable, to store objects in external files. The mechanics of this step are, unfortunately, beyond the scope of this book.

Reminder Reader object (engine):

filename: String

handle: typed file of Reminder

Last: Date (last access)

method Create(filename): (create file, inserts first record)
method Destroy (close file)

method GetReminder(Number): Reminder; (Create TReminder object from file data.)

method NumberOfReminders: Longint; (How many reminders in file?)

method PutReminder(Number, Reminder); (Replace existing reminder in file with reminder passed as parameter. If Number is higher than the NumberOfReminders in the file, this works as an add.)

method RemoveReminder(Number); (Delete reminder from file.)

When you get to RemoveReminder, you have to question how this is going to be done. How are you actually going to delete reminders from a file? There are a number of ways to do something like this: You could copy all the reminders over the one to be deleted and then truncate the file, or you could incorporate one of the ideas introduced in Chapter 19, "Typed Files and Random Access" (see the sidebar on efficiency).

For this application, you might as well use the same approach you used for the book cataloguing example in Chapter 19. A few hundred reminders would be a *lot* so, in this case, you have the luxury of using the method you used before.

You'll also need several date manipulation routines. Now, ideally, you would have a TReminder object that had a TDate object, and both would be stored directly to the disk, but as noted, storing objects isn't covered in this book. Normally you'd have to start a new general purpose unit that declares a TDate type and routines to manipulate it, but Delphi comes with a date type and functions built-in.

> **Tip:** One advantage of the SysUtils TDate type is that it is implemented as a double-type real, where the non-fractional part represents the days. Therefore, you can figure out the number of days between two dates merely by subtracting them!

After establishing what the engines need to do, then figure out what the forms are going to do.

ReminderList object (form) in unit REMMAIN:

ReminderListBox: ListBox;

Edit (disabled), New, Remove (disabled), Remind: Button;

ReminderFile: Reminder reader object

Chapter 22 ♦ Better By Design

OnActivate: If the form has been activated for the first time, create the reminder reader object, call RemindClick, and then for each reminder in the file get the string representation of the reminder and store that in the ReminderListBox.

OnClose: destroy the reminder reader object.

ReminderListBoxClick: Enable Edit and Remove.

EditClick: Set the control values in ReminderEdit to the current selection in ListBox and call up the ReminderEdit form. Set the caption of the ReminderEdit form to "Edit a Reminder." If ReminderEdit returns OK then update the ListBox.

NewClick: Same as OnEditClick, but set some value in ReminderEdit so that it knows to add the reminder as new, rather than replacing an old one. Set the caption of the ReminderEdit to "Add a Reminder." If ReminderEdit returns OK, then update the ListBox.

RemoveClick: Call the Reminder file object's RemoveReminder method. Disable Edit and Remove. Update the ListBox.

RemindClick: For each active reminder present a message to the user by setting all the fields in the Remember form and showing it.

> **Note:** The Remember and ReminderEdit forms (described below) both should pop-up when called, require that the user handle them, and then go away. The user should not be able to go back to the main form while either Remember or ReminderEdit is present.
>
> When a form shuts off access to other parts of the program, it is called modal. In previous chapters we've used the `Show` procedure to show forms, but here we'll use `ShowModal` to show both Remember and RemEdit.

Remember object (form) in unit REMINDER:

"Now": label

"Reminder for": label

CurrentDate: label

CurrentTime: label

ReminderDate: label

Cleared: checkbox

Message: label

OK: Button;

Timer: Timer; (Disabled)

Reminder Reader Object: (set by the client form reminder list)

reminder number: (set by calling form reminder list)

OnActivate: Enable the timer. OnTimer: Every second, change CurrentTime.

OKClick: Close the form. (This will be done automatically when ModalResult is set to mrOK.)

OnClose: If Cleared has been checked, clear the reminder.

> **Note:** If all you want a button press to do is close a modal form and return some value to the client code, set the button's ModalResult property to one of the listed values in the object inspector. The Remember form's OK button ModalResult property is set to mrOK.

Hmmm. Clearing the reminder would involve getting the reminder from the reminder file object, setting the cleared field, then calling PutReminder. Maybe what you need here is another method for the reminder file object:

(for Reminder file object)

Clear(ReminderNumber)

This is a situation where you have to establish which method is going to be responsible for the *ReminderNumber* parameter being valid. If it is the client code, then that code must ensure that *ReminderNumber* refers to a valid record, somewhere between zero and *TReminderFile.TotalReminders*- 1.

Conveniently, Pascal objects and files tend to be zero based, but this is another point to consider: What is a reminder number? Is it from 1 to *TotalReminders* or from 0 to *TotalReminders-1*. We've already planned to use reminder zero to store the date of last access, so the numbering will have to be based on one instead of zero.

With *Clear* the best approach is probably this: The only way *ReminderNumber* could be invalid is if there were some serious error in the program. If the program crashes because of it, that's actually good—it will alert you to a problem you can weed out before letting users run the program.

The last object to detail is the form to edit reminders.

Reminder Edit object (form):

Day: spin edit

Month: combo box

[Year: combo box?]

Message: edit line

Chapter 22 ◆ Better By Design

"Window": label

Window: spin button

Nag: checkbox

Cleared: checkbox

OK: Button (disabled)

Cancel: Button

ReminderNumber: Longint; (Set by calling reminder list form)

Reminder file object: (set by calling reminder list form)

MonthClick: Set the Day spin edit to have a maximum value according to the number of days in the current month. Also enable the OK button. This way, in order for the user to press OK, there must be a valid date showing.

OKClick: Put the current reminder using the reminder file object. The calling form must specify the ReminderNumber, which should be set to zero to add a record or otherwise must contain the number of the reminder to be updated. Close the form. (Done automatically by setting ModalResult to mrOK.)

CancelClick: Close the form. (Done automatically by setting ModalResult to mrCancel.)

Notice that I added a combo box for *year* in square brackets. This step was a spontaneous thought like: "What if I want to mark my 10th year anniversary or something?" At this point, you would go back a step to ask yourself whether you really wanted to add this level of functionality to the program now or in a later version (or not at all), how difficult it would be to implement, and so on.

This ends the object definition section for REMINDME.

> **Note:** You may have observed a "bug" with the program, already, although this is a program limitation that I didn't forsee with the design phase rather than something that will cause your program to behave badly.
>
> Because you made no provision for the Year in your program, the user cannot set a reminder for February 29th. You could do any number of things at this point to accommodate leap years, but instead you'll presume that a future version of the program will resolve this issue, if necessary.

Miscellaneous Subroutines and Data Types

If any activities in the program have not been assigned a particular object, or if any data storage needs don't seem to be met by an object, they should be handled by setting up nonobject subroutines and data types.

Subroutines can involve string operations, like *ValFn* or *StrFn*, or parsing operations like *WordCount*. Data types can involve dates, times, enumerated types (like the ranks and suits of cards), set types, and so on.

As a rule, these data types and subroutines should not be big parts of the program. They may perform handy (even crucial) services, but preferably not services that are very tied up in the engines and forms of the program. If they are, that's a good sign that one of the object definitions is incomplete.

This phase of design includes searching the Pascal manuals and on-line help for existing subroutines and data types that fulfill the program's needs. It is usually better to use a standardized data type or subroutine than to write your own. The standardized data types and subroutines are usually bug-free and cause fewer problems down the line if you need to interact with other people's code.

Example: REMINDME, Subroutines and Data Types

REMINDME requires access to the current date and current time. It also will require some procedures to do math on the current date, so that it can figure out whether today's date falls within a message's window.

Scanning the manuals reveals that Delphi has a `TDateTime` record and a host of routines that work on that data type. You might be inclined to build your own simple routines for your own `TDateTime`. Arguably, you can say that REMINDME is meant to be a yearly reminder program, and therefore requires only a month and day, not a year and certainly not an hour.

But, on the other hand, why *not* include the year? Doing so doesn't add much to the data, and doesn't make anything more difficult. Also, you could add the year combo box speculated on earlier at no extra charge, as it were.

In addition, consider how this program might be used: users put it into their startup folder, and it pops up every time they turn on their machine. A logical outgrowth of this program could be an alarm clock—something that reminds the user to eat or to get his children off the schoolbus.

Is this feature bloat? That's a judgement call. For this example, it hardly matters. This program is a small one; you can benefit from building the routines on your own, or you can just as well argue: since Pascal has its own routines, why should you? In the listings that follow, I'll use the standard TDateTime data type.

Implementation

You can see that design is a very involved process, of which actually coding something is a small part. Even the steps outlined earlier are a rather basic approach. Design is a subject that fills volumes. If you actually took some time to hack a few programs (as suggested in the begining of the chapter) you probably have a good feel for why design is so detailed. At every keystroke you type as a programmer, you have to make a decision. Later on, you may not remember the *problem*, much less the actual decision you made. This situation can make changing the program, adding on to the program, or finding and correcting bugs in the program very difficult.

Finally, a program is ready to be implemented. But even while coding, there still are design considerations. You might find that the design process left out some crucial point. You might discover issues that have not been resolved by the design process, issues that emerge in the details of coding—especially regarding how subroutines should interact with each other. Ideally, this means going back to the drawing board to examine where the design failed. Often, however, programmers just silently make decisions so that no one (even themselves) will ever know the decision was made—until something goes wrong.

This brings you the final issue: Comments. There are a lot of different schools of thought on how you should use comments in your code. Some say that each block of code should begin with a detailed description of the code; others say that each line of code should have a comment to its right.

My opinion on this matter, based on my experience reading my own and other people's code, is one I've never heard expressed by anyone else, so you may take it accordingly:

Comments are no substitute for clear code.

The English language is not well-suited for describing what happens in code. Let me show you what I mean:

```
function WordCount(Line: String): byte;
var I, WC: byte;
    InWordNow, InWordBefore
         : Boolean;
begin
   WC := 0; InWordBefore := false;
   For I := 1 to Length(Line) do
   begin
      If Line[I] in Delims then InWordNow := false
      else InWordNow := true;
      If InWordNow and not InWordBefore then Inc(WC);
      InWordBefore := InWordNow;
   end;
   WordCount := WC;
end;
```

This is the *WordCount* procedure from the GENERAL unit. Here is an English description of this procedure:

> *The WordCount procedure goes through each character of the line passed to it as a parameter. If the current character is a delimiter, this character is not part of a word. If the previous character was* **not** *a delimiter, then the WC variable—representing the total number of words in the string—is incremented.*

So, which is clearer, the code or the English description? The English description is not nearly as precise, and might even be misleading in some cases, particularly cases where the code is complex.

Perhaps more than any other computer language, Pascal is easy to read. Keep your code simple. Some programmers do things with their code that is clever or fast. Unfortunately, this approach often amounts to entertaining themselves at the cost of program clarity.

Sometimes the code has to be made to go faster, or the problem has to be solved by doing something not obvious. When this happens, don't waste time detailing what every line does. Explain the overall method used and the reason *why* the approach was taken, and detail only lines or blocks of code that require it.

My rules of thumb are these: If I have to think very hard about the code that I'm writing, then what I'm doing or why probably isn't obvious, so I'll comment that code. If I have to constantly debug a piece of code, then I'm missing some subtlety. When I discover it, I comment *that* in the code so that someone else (or I a few months later) can understand why something was done.

Finally, don't be afraid to comment code with more code. In other words, if you have a block of code that works, but you need to make it faster, comment out the slower code and leave that behind. Later on, you'll be able to figure out exactly what the purpose of the faster code is by looking at the simpler code left behind.

Example: REMINDME, the Source

```
program Remindme;

uses
  Forms,
  Remmain in 'REMMAIN.PAS' {ReminderList},
  Reminder in 'REMINDER.PAS' {Remember},
  Remedit in 'REMEDIT.PAS' {ReminderEdit};

{$R *.RES}

begin
  Application.CreateForm(TReminderList, ReminderList);
  Application.CreateForm(TRemember, Remember);
  Application.CreateForm(TReminderEdit, ReminderEdit);
```

```
  Application.Run;
end.
unit Remeng;

interface

uses SysUtils;

type
   TReminderRecord = record
      Message : String[100];
      Date    : TDateTime;
      Window  : byte;
      Active  : Boolean; {Should the message be active today?}
  Cleared : Boolean; {If true, active msg not displayed.}
      Nag     : Boolean; {If true, is active past its due date.}
      end;

   TReminder = class
        Data    : TReminderRecord;
      constructor Create(Msg: String; D: TDateTime; Win: Byte; N, C:
      ↪Boolean);
{     destructor  Destroy;   (not needed)}
      function    Describe: String;
      function    IsActive(Today: TDateTime): Boolean;
      procedure   Replace(NewData: TReminderRecord);
      end;

   TReminderFile = file of TReminderRecord;

   TReminderReader = class
        filename : String;
        handle   : TReminderFile;
        Last     : TDateTime;
      constructor Create(filename: String);
      destructor  Destroy;
   {Valid record numbers used in GetReminder and RemoveReminder
    are from 1 to NumberOfReminders.}
      function    GetReminder(Number: Integer): TReminder;
      function    NumberOfReminders  : Longint;
      procedure   PutReminder(Number: Integer; Reminder: TReminder);
      procedure   RemoveReminder(Number: Integer);
      procedure   SetClear(Number: Integer; Clear: Boolean);
      function    SinceLastChecked(Number: Integer): boolean;
      end;

implementation

{The DATE function is from the SYSUTILS unit and returns the
 current date.}
```

```
constructor TReminder.Create(Msg: String; D: TDateTime; Win: Byte; N,C:
↪Boolean);
begin
   with Data do
   begin
      Message := Msg;
      Date := D;
      Window := Win;
      Cleared := C;
      Nag := N;
      Active := IsActive(Date);
      end;
   end;

{In this version of the program, Today might just as
 well be returned by the SysUtil function Date— that
is, the current date.  But we might want to add
 functionality later to allow the program to ask:
 Would this reminder be valid on a certain date,
 where that date wasn't today.  This could be useful,
 for example, if we were going to add a monthly
 calendar that showed the active dates for a
 reminder.}
function    TReminder.IsActive(Today: TDateTime): boolean;
var Distance, ReminderDate: TDateTime;
    Y, M, D : Word;
begin
   {Whatever year the reminder was written in,
    it should be compared as though the date
    were the same year as today. This might
    change in a later version.}
   ReminderDate := Data.Date;
   DecodeDate(ReminderDate, Y, M, D);
   ReminderDate := ReminderDate - Y;
   DecodeDate(Today, Y, M, D);
   ReminderDate := ReminderDate + Y;

   with Data do begin
      Distance := Abs(Int(Today) - Int(Date));
        {If we've passed the Reminder's date then Nag must be true
         in order for the Reminder to still be active.}
      Data.Active := ((Today <= Date) and (Distance <= Window)) or Nag;
      end;

   IsActive := Data.Active;
   end;

function    TReminder.Describe;
begin
   with Data do
   begin
      If Active then Result := '!' else Result := '';
      If Nag then Result := Result + '(nag)';
```

```
         if Cleared then Result := Result + 'x';
         Result := Result + ' ' + DateToStr(Date)+ ' ';
         Result := Result + message;
      end;
   end;

procedure    TReminder.Replace;
begin
   with Data do
   begin
      Message := NewData.Message;
      Date := NewData.Date;
      Window := NewData.Window;
      Cleared := NewData.Cleared;
      Nag := NewData.Nag;
      Active := IsActive(Date);
 end;
   end;

constructor TReminderReader.Create(filename: String);
var Error: Integer;
    First: TReminder;
begin
   assign(handle, filename);
   {$i-}
   reset(handle);
   {$i+}
   Error := IOResult;
   If Error<>0 then
   begin
      If Error<>2 then fail;
      {$I-}
      rewrite(Handle);
      {$I+}
      end;

   If NumberOfReminders<1 then
   begin
      {Create a "last access" date so that a new file may
       be treated like an existing file after being created.}
      First := TReminder.Create('Created', Date, 0, False, False);
      PutReminder(0, First);
      First.Destroy;
      end;

   First := GetReminder(0);
   Last := Trunc(First.Data.Date);
   First.Destroy;
   {Now that we know what the last access date was,
    set the last access date for the file to today.}
   First := TReminder.Create('Last access', Date, 0, False, False);
   PutReminder(0, First);
```

```delphi
   First.Destroy;

   end;

destructor TReminderReader.Destroy;
begin
   Close(Handle);
   end;

function    TReminderReader.GetReminder(Number: Integer): TReminder;
var R   : TReminderRecord;
    B,E : TDateTime;
begin
   Seek(Handle, Number);
   Read(Handle, R);
   Result := TReminder.Create(R.Message, R.Date, R.Window, R.Nag,
   ➥R.Cleared);

end;

function    TReminderReader.NumberOfReminders  : Longint;
begin
   {Subtract 1 because first "reminder" is, in fact, last access.}
   NumberOfReminders := FileSize(handle)-1;
   end;

{Up to client to pass a valid record number.}
procedure   TReminderReader.PutReminder(Number: Integer; Reminder:
➥TReminder);
begin
   Seek(Handle, Number);
   Write(Handle, Reminder.Data);
   end;

{Up to client to pass a valid record number}
procedure   TReminderReader.RemoveReminder(Number: Integer);
var R: TReminderRecord;
    I: Longint;
begin
   Seek(Handle, Number);
   for I := Number to NumberOfReminders-1 do
   begin
      Seek(Handle, I+1);
      Read(Handle, R);
      Seek(Handle, I);
      Write(Handle, R);
      end;
   Truncate(Handle);
   end;

{Up to client to pass valid reminder number.}
procedure   TReminderReader.SetClear(Number:Integer; Clear: Boolean);
var R: TReminder;
```

```
begin
   R := GetReminder(number);
   R.Data.Cleared := Clear;
   PutReminder(number, R);
   R.Destroy;
   end;

function    TReminderReader.SinceLastChecked(Number: Integer): boolean;
var T: TDateTime;
    R: TReminder;
begin
   SinceLastChecked := false;

   T := Trunc(Date); {today! (days only)}
   R := GetReminder(Number);

   while (T<=Last) do
   begin
{If reminder was active then became inactive it s/b uncleared;
      if reminder was inactive then became active it s/b uncleared.}
      If R.Data.Active<>R.IsActive(T) then SetClear(Number, False);
      If R.Data.Active and not R.Data.Cleared then
      begin
         SinceLastChecked := true;
         break;
         end;
      T := T + 1;
      end;

   R.Destroy;
   end;

end.
unit RemMain;

interface

uses
  SysUtils, WinTypes, WinProcs, Messages, Classes, Graphics, Controls,
  Forms, Dialogs, StdCtrls,
  RemEng;

type
  TReminderList = class(TForm)
    ReminderListBox: TListBox;
    Edit: TButton;
    New: TButton;
    Remove: TButton;
    Remind: TButton;
    procedure FormClose(Sender: TObject; var Action: TCloseAction);
    procedure EditClick(Sender: TObject);
```

```
    procedure ReminderListBoxClick(Sender: TObject);
    procedure RemindClick(Sender: TObject);
    procedure NewClick(Sender: TObject);
    procedure RemoveClick(Sender: TObject);
    procedure FormActivate(Sender: TObject);
  private
    { Private declarations }
  public
    { Public declarations }
  protected
        ReminderFile: TReminderReader;
  end;

var
  ReminderList: TReminderList;

implementation

{$R *.DFM}
uses RemEdit, Reminder;

procedure TReminderList.FormClose(Sender: TObject;
  var Action: TCloseAction);
begin
   ReminderFile.Destroy;
end;

{This code counts on the fact that Edit is only
 enabled and therefore "clickable" when the user
 has made a valid selection in the list box.}
procedure TReminderList.EditClick(Sender: TObject);
var R: TReminder;
    M, D,
    Year: Word;   {Year Not used in this version}
begin
   {The listbox is zero based but the reminders
    are from one to n.}
   R := ReminderFile.GetReminder(ReminderListBox.ItemIndex+1);
   {DecodeDate from SysUtils}
   DecodeDate(R.Data.Date, Year, M, D);
   with ReminderEdit do
   begin
   {The month combo-box is zero based, but Decode date
    returns 1-31 and 1-12 for day and month.}
      Month.ItemIndex := M-1;
      Day.Value := D;
      Window.Value := R.Data.Window;
      Message.Text := R.Data.Message;
      Nag.Checked := R.Data.Nag;
      Cleared.Checked := R.Data.Cleared;
      ReminderNumber := ReminderListBox.ItemIndex+1;
      end;
```

```
      ReminderEdit.ReminderFile := ReminderFile;
      R.Destroy;
   If ReminderEdit.ShowModal = mrOK then
        begin
        R := ReminderFile.GetReminder(ReminderListBox.ItemIndex+1);
        ReminderListBox.Items[ReminderListBox.ItemIndex] := R.Describe;
        R.Destroy;
        end;

     Edit.Enabled := false;
     Remove.Enabled := false;
     end;

procedure TReminderList.ReminderListBoxClick(Sender: TObject);
begin
   Edit.Enabled := true;
   Remove.Enabled := true;
end;

procedure TReminderList.NewClick(Sender: TObject);
var R: TReminder;
begin
   with ReminderEdit do
   begin
      Message.Text := 'New Reminder';
      {A ReminderNumber of Zero tells ReminderEdit
       to add a new reminder.}
      ReminderNumber := 0;
      end;
   ReminderEdit.ReminderFile := ReminderFile;
   If ReminderEdit.ShowModal = mrOK then
   begin
      R := ReminderFile.GetReminder(ReminderFile.NumberOfReminders);
      ReminderListBox.Items.Add(R.Describe);
      R.Destroy;
      end;
   end;

{RemoveClick counts on ReminderListBox having a valid
 selection in it.}
procedure TReminderList.RemoveClick(Sender: TObject);
begin
   {ReminderListBox is zero based,
   ReminderFile is one based.}
   ReminderFile.RemoveReminder(ReminderListBox.ItemIndex+1);
   ReminderListBox.Items.Delete(ReminderListBox.ItemIndex);
   Edit.Enabled := False;
   Remove.Enabled := False;
end;

procedure TReminderList.RemindClick(Sender: TObject);
var I: Integer;
    R: TReminder;
```

```
begin
   For I := 1 to ReminderFile.NumberOfReminders do
   begin
      If ReminderFile.SinceLastChecked(I) then
      begin
         R := ReminderFile.GetReminder(I);
         with Remember do
         begin
            Message.Caption := R.Data.Message;
{DateToStr from SysUtils}
            ReminderDate.Caption := DateToStr(R.Data.Date);
{Cleared.Check should always be false.}
            Cleared.Checked := R.Data.Cleared;
            ReminderNumber := I;
            R.Destroy;
            end;
         Remember.ReminderFile := ReminderFile;
         Remember.ShowModal;
         end;
      end;
end;

procedure TReminderList.FormActivate(Sender: TObject);
const FirstTime : boolean = true;
var   I: Longint;
      R: TReminder;
begin

   {This code can't be put in FormCreate because it
    requires that the reminder form already be
    created.}
   If FirstTime then
   begin
     {Note for next version of program:
         Allow user to specify the name of reminder file.
         Maybe allow user to open more than one file.}
     ReminderFile := TReminderReader.Create('Reminder.Lst');

     {"Click" the reminder button for the user.}
     RemindClick(Remind);
     FirstTime := False;

     For I := 1 to ReminderFile.NumberOfReminders do
     begin
        R := ReminderFile.GetReminder(I);
        ReminderListBox.Items.Add(R.Describe);
        R.Destroy;
        end;
     end;
   end;

end.
```

```
unit Reminder;

interface

uses
  SysUtils, WinTypes, WinProcs, Messages, Classes, Graphics, Controls,
  Forms, Dialogs, StdCtrls, ExtCtrls,
  RemEng;

type
  TRemember = class(TForm)
    Label1: TLabel;
    Label2: TLabel;
    Message: TLabel;
    Ok: TButton;
    CurrentDate: TLabel;
    CurrentTime: TLabel;
    ReminderDate: TLabel;
    Cleared: TCheckBox;
    Timer: TTimer;
    procedure FormActivate(Sender: TObject);
    procedure TimerTimer(Sender: TObject);
    procedure FormClose(Sender: TObject; var Action: TCloseAction);
  private
    { Private declarations }
  public
    { Public declarations }
    ReminderFile: TReminderReader;
    ReminderNumber: Longint;
  end;

var
  Remember: TRemember;

implementation

{$R *.DFM}

procedure TRemember.FormActivate(Sender: TObject);
begin
   Timer.Enabled := True;
end;

procedure TRemember.TimerTimer(Sender: TObject);
begin
   CurrentTime.Caption := TimeToStr(Now);
   CurrentDate.Caption := DateToStr(Date);
end;

procedure TRemember.FormClose(Sender: TObject; var Action: TCloseAction);
begin
   If Cleared.Checked then ReminderFile.SetClear(ReminderNumber, True);
   Timer.Enabled := False;
```

```pascal
  end;

end.
unit Remedit;

interface

uses
  SysUtils, WinTypes, WinProcs, Messages, Classes, Graphics, Controls,
  Forms, Dialogs, StdCtrls, Spin,
  RemEng;

type
  TReminderEdit = class(TForm)
    Label1: TLabel;
    Label2: TLabel;
    Month: TComboBox;
    Label3: TLabel;
    Message: TEdit;
    Label4: TLabel;
    Window: TSpinEdit;
    Nag: TCheckBox;
    Cleared: TCheckBox;
    OK: TButton;
    Cancel: TButton;
    Day: TSpinEdit;
    procedure OKClick(Sender: TObject);
    procedure MonthChange(Sender: TObject);
    procedure FormActivate(Sender: TObject);
  private
    { Private declarations }
  public
    { Public declarations }
    ReminderFile: TReminderReader;
    ReminderNumber: Longint;
  end;

var
  ReminderEdit: TReminderEdit;

implementation

{$R *.DFM}

procedure TReminderEdit.OKClick(Sender: TObject);
var
   RemDate      : TDateTime;
   Y,M,D        : Word;
   R            : TReminder;
begin
  {Get the current year.}
   DecodeDate(Date, Y, M, D);
```

```
      RemDate := EncodeDate(Y, Month.ItemIndex+1, Day.Value);
      R := TReminder.Create(Message.Text, RemDate,
                    Window.Value, Nag.Checked, Cleared.Checked);
      If ReminderNumber = 0
         then ReminderFile.PutReminder(ReminderFile.NumberOfReminders+1, R)
         else ReminderFile.PutReminder(ReminderNumber, R);
   end;

procedure TReminderEdit.MonthChange(Sender: TObject);
type
   Months = (Jan, Feb, Mar, Apr, May, Jun,
             Jul, Aug, Sep, Oct, Nov, Dec);
begin
   case Months(Month) of
      Jan, Mar, May, Jul,
      Aug, Oct, Dec       : Day.MaxValue := 31;
      Feb                 : Day.MaxValue := 28;
      Apr, Jun, Sep, Nov  : Day.MaxValue := 30;
      end;
   OK.Enabled := True;
   end;
procedure TReminderEdit.FormActivate(Sender: TObject);
begin
   If Month.ItemIndex<>-1 then Ok.Enabled := true;
end;

end.
```

Summary

One definition of hacking is programming without planning. Hacking can be a useful and productive exercise, but is not a good way to approach a complex programming problem.

Design is the process of laying out a program in as much detail as possible before actually coding, and anticipating problems and solving them before a great deal of code is written.

Programming starts with a problem to be solved, and you must understand the problem as well as possible before trying to solve it. Design starts with understanding the problem, moves to a description of the program, and then to prototyping, which gives a feel for how the program will finally work.

Objects are established from the program description. The objects are then defined in terms of fields and methods, and methods are given certain responsibilities to handle possibly bad parameters. At this point, technical details surface. Afterward, unhandled actions and data types are handled, either by assigning them to appropriate objects, or creating nonobject units that handle specific needs.

The design phase actually continues while coding is occurring. If the programmer finds himself constantly making decisions about how things should interact, it means the design plan was flawed, and should be reexamined. Comments are fine, but should be used sparingly, and not as a substitute for clear code.

Review Questions

These questions have no answers in the back, nor do they have any particular level. They are only things for you to consider before embarking on your own programs.

1. Why is design important?
2. What aspects of design are the most important and useful?
3. Is it okay to spend more time designing than actually coding?
4. Is it okay not to comment code at all?

Review Exercises

All levels. Make sure that when you do these exercises you *don't* write any code that ties up Windows for a long time. (See Chapter 20, "Units," about breaking up tasks.)

1. In Chapter 10, "On One Condition," you created "Guess It." Even a simple program like this can benefit from good design. Go back to that program now and design a better algorithm for guessing than just a random number. Then, figure out how to catch the user *lying* and design what should be done in such an instance. For example, the program guesses "50" and the user says "Too High," but later the program guesses "49" and the user says "Too Low."

2. In Chapter 12, "Repeating Yourself," you built a simple parser. As an exercise, design a more complex parser that parses an entire text file. Incorporate the following rules to make the parser more complex: A word is delimited by any non-letter or number, except the period; anything that appears within braces is a comment and should be ignored; any word that starts with a character is a regular word; any word that starts with a number is either a numeric value or an error (if it can't be converted to a numeric value, as in '9A'); anything else is a symbol. Display to the user the number of regular words, symbols and errors, as well as the number of numeric values and their sum.

3. Design and implement an application that stores peoples' names and phone numbers. Allow the user to search for a specific name. Allow the names to be stored to disk. As part of this exercise, try storing this data both as a text file and as a typed file. Find out which is faster and which

Chapter 22 ◆ Better By Design

takes more space. Find out how many records the application will work with before being too slow. (Hint: Design an additional program that writes out fake records to test.)

4. Design and implement a program that reads in a Pascal source file and *formats* it according to your preferences. (Allow the formatted file to be saved under a new name or printed to a printer.) To do this, you have to decide what your preferences are, first of all. (Do you like `begin` and `end` lined up together? How do you like to indent code? What about capitalization?) Then you need to analyze the source code as you read it in: look for begins and ends, of course. Also look for some of the keywords you know. Should `if` appear as "if," "IF," or "If"? And so on.

Appendixes

APPENDIX A

ASCII and Extended ASCII Codes

This appendix presents the ASCII, Extended ASCII, and Extended Function ASCII codes.

Dec X10	Hex X16	Binary X2	ASCII Character
000	00	0000 0000	null
001	01	0000 0001	☺
002	02	0000 0010	●
003	03	0000 0011	♥
004	04	0000 0100	♦
005	05	0000 0101	♣
006	06	0000 0110	♠
007	07	0000 0111	●
008	08	0000 1000	■
009	09	0000 1001	○
010	0A	0000 1010	■
011	0B	0000 1011	♂
012	0C	0000 1100	♀

Appendix A ♦ ASCII and Extended ASCII Codes

Dec X10	Hex X16	Binary X2	ASCII Character
013	0D	0000 1101	♪
014	0E	0000 1110	♪♪
015	0F	0000 1111	✱
016	10	0001 0000	►
017	11	0001 0001	◄
018	12	0001 0010	↕
019	13	0001 0011	‼
020	14	0001 0100	¶
021	15	0001 0101	§
022	16	0001 0110	▬
023	17	0001 0111	↕
024	18	0001 1000	↑
025	19	0001 1001	↓
026	1A	0001 1010	→
027	1B	0001 1011	←
028	1C	0001 1100	FS
029	1D	0001 1101	GS
030	1E	0001 1110	RS
031	1F	0001 1111	US
032	20	0010 0000	SP
033	21	0010 0001	!
034	22	0010 0010	"
035	23	0010 0011	#
036	24	0010 0100	$
037	25	0010 0101	%
038	26	0010 0110	&
039	27	0010 0111	'

Dec X10	Hex X16	Binary X2	ASCII Character
040	28	0010 1000	(
041	29	0010 1001	)
042	2A	0010 1010	*
043	2B	0010 1011	+
044	2C	0010 1100	,
045	2D	0010 1101	-
046	2E	0010 1110	.
047	2F	0010 1111	/
048	30	0011 0000	0
049	31	0011 0001	1
050	32	0011 0010	2
051	33	0011 0011	3
052	34	0011 0100	4
053	35	0011 0101	5
054	36	0011 0110	6
055	37	0011 0111	7
056	38	0011 1000	8
057	39	0011 1001	9
058	3A	0011 1010	:
059	3B	0011 1011	;
060	3C	0011 1100	<
061	3D	0011 1101	=
062	3E	0011 1110	>
063	3F	0011 1111	?
064	40	0100 0000	@
065	41	0100 0001	A
066	42	0100 0010	B

Appendix A ♦ ASCII and Extended ASCII Codes

Dec X10	Hex X16	Binary X2	ASCII Character
067	43	0100 0011	C
068	44	0100 0100	D
069	45	0100 0101	E
070	46	0100 0110	F
071	47	0100 0111	G
072	48	0100 1000	H
073	49	0100 1001	I
074	4A	0100 1010	J
075	4B	0100 1011	K
076	4C	0100 1100	L
077	4D	0100 1101	M
078	4E	0100 1110	N
079	4F	0100 1111	O
080	50	0101 0000	P
081	51	0101 0001	Q
082	52	0101 0010	R
083	53	0101 0011	S
084	54	0101 0100	T
085	55	0101 0101	U
086	56	0101 0110	V
087	57	0101 0111	W
088	58	0101 1000	X
089	59	0101 1001	Y
090	5A	0101 1010	Z
091	5B	0101 1011	[
092	5C	0101 1100	\
093	5D	0101 1101	]

Dec X10	Hex X16	Binary X2	ASCII Character
094	5E	0101 1110	^
095	5F	0101 1111	_
096	60	0110 0000	`
097	61	0110 0001	a
098	62	0110 0010	b
099	63	0110 0011	c
100	64	0110 0100	d
101	65	0110 0101	e
102	66	0110 0110	f
103	67	0110 0111	g
104	68	0110 1000	h
105	69	0110 1001	i
106	6A	0110 1010	j
107	6B	0110 1011	k
108	6C	0110 1100	l
109	6D	0110 1101	m
110	6E	0110 1110	n
111	6F	0110 1111	o
112	70	0111 0000	p
113	71	0111 0001	q
114	72	0111 0010	r
115	73	0111 0011	s
116	74	0111 0100	t
117	75	0111 0101	u
118	76	0111 0110	v
119	77	0111 0111	w
120	78	0111 1000	x

Appendix A ♦ ASCII and Extended ASCII Codes

Dec X10	Hex X16	Binary X2	ASCII Character
121	79	0111 1001	y
122	7A	0111 1010	z
123	7B	0111 1011	{
124	7C	0111 1100	¦
125	7D	0111 1101	}
126	7E	0111 1110	~
127	7F	0111 1111	DEL
128	80	1000 0000	Ç
129	81	1000 0001	ü
130	82	1000 0010	é
131	83	1000 0011	â
132	84	1000 0100	ä
133	85	1000 0101	à
134	86	1000 0110	å
135	87	1000 0111	ç
136	88	1000 1000	ê
137	89	1000 1001	ë
138	8A	1000 1010	è
139	8B	1000 1011	ï
140	8C	1000 1100	î
141	8D	1000 1101	ì
142	8E	1000 1110	Ä
143	8F	1000 1111	Å
144	90	1001 0000	É
145	91	1001 0001	æ
146	92	1001 0010	Æ
147	93	1001 0011	ô

Dec X10	Hex X16	Binary X2	ASCII Character
148	94	1001 0100	ö
149	95	1001 0101	ò
150	96	1001 0110	û
151	97	1001 0111	ù
152	98	1001 1000	ÿ
153	99	1001 1001	Ö
154	9A	1001 1010	Ü
155	9B	1001 1011	¢
156	9C	1001 1100	£
157	9D	1001 1101	¥
158	9E	1001 1110	P_t
159	9F	1001 1111	ƒ
160	A0	1010 0000	á
161	A1	1010 0001	í
162	A2	1010 0010	ó
163	A3	1010 0011	ú
164	A4	1010 0100	ñ
165	A5	1010 0101	Ñ
166	A6	1010 0110	a̲
167	A7	1010 0111	o̲
168	A8	1010 1000	¿
169	A9	1010 1001	⌐
170	AA	1010 1010	¬
171	AB	1010 1011	½
172	AC	1010 1100	¼
173	AD	1010 1101	¡
174	AE	1010 1110	«

Appendix A ♦ ASCII and Extended ASCII Codes

Dec X10	Hex X16	Binary X2	ASCII Character
175	AF	1010 1111	»
176	B0	1011 0000	░
177	B1	1011 0001	▒
178	B2	1011 0010	▓
179	B3	1011 0011	│
180	B4	1011 0100	┤
181	B5	1011 0101	╡
182	B6	1011 0110	╢
183	B7	1011 0111	╖
184	B8	1011 1000	╕
185	B9	1011 1001	╣
186	BA	1011 1010	║
187	BB	1011 1011	╗
188	BC	1011 1100	╝
189	BD	1011 1101	╜
190	BE	1011 1110	╛
191	BF	1011 1111	┐
192	C0	1100 0000	└
193	C1	1100 0001	┴
194	C2	1100 0010	┬
195	C3	1100 0011	├
196	C4	1100 0100	─
197	C5	1100 0101	┼
198	C6	1100 0110	╞
199	C7	1100 0111	╟
200	C8	1100 1000	╚
201	C9	1100 1001	╔

Dec X10	Hex X16	Binary X2	ASCII Character
202	CA	1100 1010	╩
203	CB	1100 1011	╦
204	CC	1100 1100	╠
205	CD	1100 1101	=
206	CE	1100 1110	╬
207	CF	1100 1111	╧
208	D0	1101 0000	╨
209	D1	1101 0001	╤
210	D2	1101 0010	╥
211	D3	1101 0011	╙
212	D4	1101 0100	╘
213	D5	1101 0101	╒
214	D6	1101 0110	╓
215	D7	1101 0111	╫
216	D8	1101 1000	╪
217	D9	1101 1001	┘
218	DA	1101 1010	┌
219	DB	1101 1011	█
220	DC	1101 1100	▄
221	DD	1101 1101	▌
222	DE	1101 1110	▐
223	DF	1101 1111	▀
224	E0	1110 0000	∝
225	E1	1110 0001	β
226	E2	1110 0010	Γ
227	E3	1110 0011	π
228	E4	1110 0100	Σ

Appendix A ♦ ASCII and Extended ASCII Codes

Dec X10	Hex X16	Binary X2	ASCII Character
229	E5	1110 0101	σ
230	E6	1110 0110	μ
231	E7	1110 0111	τ
232	E8	1110 1000	Φ
233	E9	1110 1001	θ
234	EA	1110 1010	Ω
235	EB	1110 1011	δ
236	EC	1110 1100	∞
237	ED	1110 1101	ø
238	EE	1110 1110	∈
239	EF	1110 1111	∩
240	F0	1110 0000	≡
241	F1	1111 0001	±
242	F2	1111 0010	≥
243	F3	1111 0011	≤
244	F4	1111 0100	⌠
245	F5	1111 0101	⌡
246	F6	1111 0110	÷
247	F7	1111 0111	≈
248	F8	1111 1000	°
249	F9	1111 1001	•
250	FA	1111 1010	•
251	FB	1111 1011	√
252	FC	1111 1100	η
253	FD	1111 1101	²
254	FE	1111 1110	■
255	FF	1111 1111	

APPENDIX B

Answers to the Review Questions

Chapter 1

1. The Central Processing Unit, or CPU.

2. Through disk drives and Random Access Memory.

3. A byte is 2 to the eighth power (eight bits) capable of holding 256 values.

4. Programs. (Software.)

5. Any eight letters or numbers, optionally followed by a dot and any three other letters or numbers will do. Other special characters are allowed (like the underscore "_"). To verify that your answer is correct, start a new document in Write and save it under the file name you chose. If your file name is not valid, Write will tell you.

6. Directories group related files together, instead of lumping all files into one mish-mash. The root directory is the top-most directory; that is, the *only* one that is not a sub-directory of any other directory.

7. DOS, OS/2, System 7 (for the MacIntosh), are the most common microcomputer OSs. Strictly speaking, Windows isn't an operating system but an operating environment that enhances DOS.

8. Instructions to the computer are called software. A group of instructions that perform a specific task is called a program.

Appendix B ◆ Answers to the Review Questions

9. No.
10. File extensions are the three characters of a file name after the dot that are usually used to indicate the type of the file. PAS is a file extension that indicates a Pascal file.
11. It's 1,000 times 1,000 bytes (1,000,000 bytes) or 1,000 times 1,024 bytes (1,024,000) or 1,024 times 1,024 bytes (1,048,576).

Chapter 2

1. A program is a series of instructions to the computer designed to accomplish a specific task. Programmers write them. Windows is a program.
2. No.
3. Anything that happens to an object is an event. Mouse clicks and double-clicks, key presses, computer clock "ticks" are all events.
4. An object is a computer simulation of a real-world "thing." Windows, buttons, scroll bars, and so on are all things.
5. Object properties are any of the characteristics that describe the object, like a window's color or a button's size.
6. Object behaviors are any of the actions that an object can take, like a button clicking or a window closing.
7. The world's almost-shortest Pascal program is:

```
program Hello;
begin
    end;
```

In Object Pascal the line containing the word `program` is optional.

8. It gives the name of the program, but actually has no effect on the behavior or file name of the program, and so is optional.
9. A compiler.
10. Machine Language. Like a series of numbers.
11. Typewriter style, without graphics.
12. An assembler takes short codes that represent machine language and turns them into machine language.

13. A class is a categorization of objects. You can have a class of windows or class of birds, of which any window or bird is an instance, respectively.
14. Focus is the computer's idea of which object the user's attention is currently centered around.

Chapter 3

1. A code unit is a file of Pasal code that is *not* associated with any form.
2. A project is a file of Pascal code that contains all the information necessary to compile the complete program.
3. Yes.
4. Yes.
5. All projects that use the form are affected, unless the changed form or unit is saved under a new name.
6. Delphi has no way of knowing how many different projects might use a specific form or unit, therefore it forces you to very deliberately delete a project and its associated files.
7. Yes.

Chapter 4

1. The 10 functions covered up to this point are "Save project," "Open project," "Open file," "Save file," "Add to project," "Remove from project," "Select form," "Select unit," "Toggle form/unit," and "New form."
2. It's to the right of the SpeedBar. It provides components to add to forms.
3. On forms. They're called "components," or if they're visible on-screen, "controls."
4. Into the Code Editor.
5. All the components in the current project.
6. Yes.
7. It is lost forever.

Appendix B ♦ Answers to the Review Questions

8. A search that requires the characters searched for be surrounded by non-word characters. So a search for "cat" would skip things like "catalogue" or "catastrophe."
9. Press the Shift key before selecting the component.

Chapter 5

1. Select an item from the Help menu. Press F1.
2. Press F9 or press the "Play" button on the SpeedBar.
3. Comments are notes to a person reading the program that explain elements of the program. You use them when some part of the code is not clear. They are delimited with curly braces, "{" "}".
4. Objects are referred to by their name. Object methods and properties are referred to by the object name followed by a dot followed by the method or property name.
5. Debugging is the action taken to remove errors from a program.
6. Syntax highlighting shows which words have special meanings in Pascal. It's useful because, if you make a typo, the word will *not* be highlighted.
7. With an error message, "String constant exceeds line." This would appear because the `Writeln` has an opening quote (') but instead of a closing quote there is a double quote (") which Pascal does not recognize.
8. Not really. It tells the compiler to treat the subsequent statements as a block.
9. With two consecutive single quotes ('').
10. Press F7 or F8 or press the "Step over" or "Trace Into" buttons on the SpeedBar.
11. WinCrt turns a Window into a typewriter-like device. You don't normally use it in a Windows program.
12. Select Add Breakpoint from the Debug menu or press F8.

Chapter 6

1. No.
2. `var`

3. The colon (:).

4. A variable can be up to 63 meaningful characters long. Yes. No. Yes.

5. A variable type determines the kind of information it may hold. The character type (char) or a string of characters (string) are the two types covered in this chapter.

6. With a plus sign. (+)

7. With the colon-equal. (:=)

8. No.

9. A specific area in RAM given a name for the programmer's convenience.

10. A generic example:

```
var AVar, AnotherVar, AThirdVar: AType;
```

11. The program will attempt to assign the literal string 'Hello, World' to s but s is not big enough to hold it; therefore, it will assign only the first six characters and s will have a value of 'Hello,'.

Chapter 7

1. A numeral is the character representation of a number. It does not represent a quantity.

2. No.

3. Except for the minus sign, no other punctuation is allowed. A minus sign may precede an integer.

4. The five integer types are shortint, byte, word, integer and longint, and their ranges are -128 to 127, 0 to 255, 0 to 65535, -32768 to 32768 and about -2 billion to about positive 2 billion, respectively.

5. No. Somewhat. (A character may be assigned to a string but a string may not be assigned to a character.) Yes.

6. W := -1; and B := -1; will not compile.

7. When range checking is on, the program will generate an error message. When range checking is off, B will have a value of 246.

8. The value of either variable is undefined.

Appendix B ◆ Answers to the Review Questions

9. Its value might be anything.
10. No.
11. Some other languages allow this.
12. An Integer.

Chapter 8

1. Subroutines are like mini-programs. They're used to organize programs and to keep programmers from having to repeat code.
2. Procedures and functions.
3. Yes. Yes.
4. The duration of the procedure.
5. To pass information to a procedure so that it may act differently according to the parameter.
6. Undefined. (You get the idea that this is an important concept or I wouldn't keep asking you, right?)
7. Undefined.
8. Yes.
9. By specifying var before the parameter name.
10. Writeln, Readln, ClrScr.
11. Yes. No.
12. By concatenating two smaller strings:

    ```
    Writeln('Hello, '+
            'World!');
    ```

13. It probably means that the variable isn't defined at all in the program, or that the variable isn't part of the current scope.
14. Scope is the life of a variable.
15. A global variable is a variable that many routines can see. A local variable can only be seen by the routine that declares it. Local variables take precedence.
16. Passes the actual parameter to the routine instead of just a copy.

Chapter 9

1. To prevent common programmer errors. Because the rules of automatic conversion are usually so complex as to make specific conversion by the programmer an easier choice that is less prone to errors.

2. `Str` turns a number into a string. It cannot fail.

3. `Val` turns a string into a number. It can fail if the string is *not* an acceptable number. The third parameter to `Val` will contain the first illegal character found if `Val` fails.

4. Copies part of a string to another string.

5. No. If a specific type of integer is defined as a `var` parameter to a routine, that exact type must be used.

6. Yes. The value returned by `DoSomething` could be outside of the range of `B`.

7. Yes. Yes.

8. The character '1'.

Chapter 10

1. A statement that presents code to be executed only if a certain condition is true.

2. A Boolean variable is a variable capable of handling only two values (true or false).

3. `True` and `False`.

4. Equal To, Not Equal To, Greater Than, Greater Than Or Equal To, Less Than, Less Than Or Equal To. (=, <>, >, >=, <, <=)

5. `Writeln('A is greater or equal to B')`

6. Generates a random number within a certain range.

7. They group code together into blocks. As a single statement.

8. Makes the "random" numbers returned by `Random` actually unpredictable. By default the "random" numbers generated are from a specific, repeatable series.

9. Yes.

10. `False. True. True. True. False.`

Appendix B ◆ Answers to the Review Questions

11. Like this:

```
If A>B then
   begin
      {block}
   end
else {single line of code}
```

12. No.

13. Zero and one.

Chapter 11

1. A `Case` statement neatens up what could otherwise be a very long series of `If-then-else` statements.

2. Yes. Yes. No.

3. No. (Literal characters are okay.)

4. No. (Literal values only may be used as part of a case statement.)

5. With a double dot. (..)

6. Yes.

7. Yes.

8. An ordinal type is any type that expresses an order. Boolean, character, any of the integer types.

9. No.

Chapter 12

1. It forces the program to jump to a different area, possibly unrelated to the current area.

2. If terminates a loop.

3. It forces a loop to skip to the next iteration.

4. The `While` loop is executed only if (and as long as) a condition is true. The `Repeat` loop is executed at least once (and as long as) a condition is true. They are different in that the `Repeat` loop is always executed at least once.

5. A way of solving a problem.
6. The variable that changes on each iteration.
7. The starting value for the control variable and the ending value for the control variable.
8. A label.
9. Causes a control loop to be decremented rather than incremented on its way from source to destination.
10. To break it up into pieces that the program can understand and use.
11. The loop will not stop. (Endless loop.)
12. A thing that indicates a boundary. For example, a space indicates the end of a word.
13. This is a matter of opinion. Current popular opinion says, "No, you shouldn't." In Pascal, you'll probably never be inclined to.
14. Yes.

Chapter 13

1. `+`, `-`, `*`, `div` and `mod`.
2. `mod`. (Real types have their own division, though it's not called `div`.)
3. Checking what values a certain variable has.
4. Determines the order that a control will be selected by the user pressing Tab.
5. Here's table 13.2 again:

Standard integer procedures and functions. (Integer refers to any of the five integer types.)

Routine	Type	Example	Equivalent	Returns
Dec(O)	Ordinal	Dec(O);	O := O - 1;	
Dec(O,n)	Ordinal	Dec(O,3);	O := O - 3;	
Inc(O)	Ordinal	Inc(O);	O := O + 1;	

Appendix B ◆ Answers to the Review Questions

Routine	Type	Example	Equivalent	Returns
Inc(O,n)	Ordinal	Inc(O,3);	O := O + 3;	
Pred(O)	Ordinal	O := Pred(O);	O := O - 1;	same
Succ(O)	Ordinal	O := Succ(O);	I := I + 1;	same
Hi(W)	Word	B := Hi(W);	B := W div 256;	byte
Lo(W)	Word	B := Lo(W);	B := W mod 256;	byte
Odd(I)	Integer	Bool := Odd(I)	Bool := (I mod 2)=1;	Boolean

6. Real, single, double, comp, extended. Comp.

7. Here's table 13.5 again:

The built-in Pascal Real routines. (Real refers to any of the five real types.)

Name	Example	Returns
Round(R)	L := Round(R);	Longint
Trunc(R)	L := Trunc(R);	Longint
Frac(R)	R1 := Frac(R2);	Real
Int(R)	R1 := Int(R2);	Real
ArcTan(R)	R1 := ArcTan(R2)	Real
Cos(R)	R1 := Cos(R2)	Real
Exp(R)	R1 := Exp(R2);	Real
Ln(R)	R1 := Ln(R2);	Real
Pi	R1 := Pi;	Real
Sin(R)	R1 := Sin(R2);	Real
SqrRt(R)	R1 := SqrRt(R2);	Real

8. It's a means of expressing very large numbers without using up a lot of space. An 'E'.

9. 0.000000001245

10. 5.7210624E+12

11. Locates a string inside of another string.

12. Inserts a string inside of another string.

13. Operator precedence is the order in which operations are done, and can affect programmers who are unaware of it, as the programmer may be evaluating expressions differently (like from left to right). Parentheses can force an expression to come out a certain way.

14. '890'

15. `Str`. It converts numbers to strings and takes the number, followed by an optional colon and number indicating length, followed by another optional colon and number indicating positions after the decimal point.

16. Code that must be evaluated and reduced to a single value. An expression consists of operators and operands.

17. Yes. Yes. No.

18. -511. 20,000. By default, the compiler will use the data type of the operands to evaluate an expression *or* an integer, whichever is largest.

19. Yes. Yes. No.

20. The significand and the exponent. Because the CPU cannot natively deal with the comp type.

21. Press and hold Alt, then tap out '2', '2' and '3' on the number pad.

Chapter 14

1. A type defined by the programmer to handle a specific need not covered by the basic Pascal data types.

2. A list of related programmer-defined items.

3. To make code clearer.

4. Blue's ordinal value is 2. It is third in the sequence.

5. Yellow. This would be a range error.

6. Gives the ordinal value of an enumerated or other ordinal type.

7. A type consisting of only some portion of another (ordinal) type. To limit the values a variable can have.

Appendix B ♦ Answers to the Review Questions

8. No.

9. Adding a prefix to the name that indicates the identifier's grouping.

Chapter 15

1. Describing a set of items, any combination of which may apply.

2. Use set of followed by square brackets containing the items.

3. Because you can then use the enumerated type as a basis for variables to manipulate individual elements of the set.

4. in, *, +, -

5. ['A','B','E','K','L']

6. ['L','M']

7. True.

8. When you *don't* want variables indicating elements to be possible, but instead force all manipulations to be done with sets only.

Chapter 16

1. To organize related variables in a structure way.

2. An element of a record.

3. Yes.

4. With a dot between the record and field name.

5. Yes. No. No. Yes. Yes.

6. Returns the size of the record type.

7. The global age variable will be set to a random number, the Bordeaux age field will be incremented, Fred's age will be set to "1992 - SomeDate", the age of Fred's favorite wine will be set to Fred's age divided by two, Fred's age will be set to "-1".

8. No, because *Fred.Age* is a byte variable.

9. No. A record cannot refer to itself in its definition.

10. No, the speed should be unaffected. Liberal use of with..do could make it easier to read.

492

11. Yes. There is no practical limit.

12. Because a record type is bound to be duplicated many times and bad choice of field data types could result in a lot of wasted space or time.

13. Because you could then have routines that handled that data type and you wouldn't have to constantly rewrite those routines for slight variations on those data types.

14. Flow of data entry is probably the biggest concern.

15. No!

16. Two entry fields requires more work for the user but allows the program to guarantee the format of the name.

17. The more controls there are the harder the form will be to read.

Chapter 17

1. Storing many variables of the same type together.

2. The *index* gives the particular array entry being referred to.

3. Yes.

4. A For loop.

5. A bubble sort repeatedly goes through each element in an array, swapping them if they are out of order, until they are in order. A selection sort is superior.

6. It can be seen as an array [1..255] of characters, except that its zero index is a byte that indicates the string length.

7. A state machine is a code loop that changes state according to certain factors in the program, and upon changing state executes different code. It can be good for parsing, or in any situation where any number of different blocks of code might be executed depending on what came before.

8. Not really. The limit for Delphi programs is simply that no array may exceed about 64K in size.

9. 16-bit Delphi is limited to exactly 65,520 bytes in size. This is a limitation of Windows. Windows 95 and a promised 32-bit Delphi could have structures 2 billion bytes in size.

Appendix B ♦ Answers to the Review Questions

10. The number of iterations required to sort something using a bubble sort is far greater than the number need by the selection sort.
11. Not really. A deck consists of fifty-two cards, and while their values may be seen to have two dimensions, the whole point of a deck of cards is to supply randomness— in other words to *not* distinguish one card from the next in any structural way.
12. The parser from Chapter 12 had two states: *InWord* and *not InWord*.

Chapter 18

1. Assign, Reset or Rewrite (or Append), Read or Write, Close.
2. Associates a file variable with an external file name.
3. Reset opens an existing file, Rewrite creates a new file or "empties" an existing file, Append adds to an existing text file.
4. A special code placed in a program that's designed to force the compiler to do something or to force it to *not* do something.
5. You use up resources and you may lose data.
6. "LPT1" or "LPT2" depending on which parallel port it's hooked up to.
7. As with str, a colon followed by a value for length, and a colon followed by a value for the number of places after the decimal.
8. A series of characters divided into lines by the carriage-return/line-feed sequence.
9. What it is in Pascal terms is hidden from programmers, but basically it's a way for Pascal to communicate with Windows about a specific file.
10. {$I-} To prevent an error from occurring if a file doesn't exist. Hazards include ignoring some other serious error as well as possibly forgetting to turn it back on.
11. No. Access to IOResult clears IOResult.
12. 13 and 10 respectively.
13. 2.
14. I would be set to 1. J would be set to 2. S would be set to '3 4 5 6 7'. The program would generate an error upon trying to read a value into K.
15. Duplicating "random" number sequences.

Chapter 19

1. Typed files can be faster, harder for other programs to read, and use space more efficiently. Text files are easier for other programs to read (which could be a pro or a con) and might use space more efficiently in some circumstances. A typed file may be treated as an array.

2. No.

3. A fixed size for each record.

4. Locates a spot within a file. Returns the current file position. Returns the total number of records in a file.

5. Yes. 0. Total number of records minus 1.

6. To add more data manipulation capabilities to your program.

7. A typed file can be treated as an array[0..FileSize(File)-1] of the record type involved via the `FileSize`, `Seek`, and, of course, the `Read` and `Write` routines.

8. Maybe. In cases where a large number of strings with wildly varying sizes might occur in the data, a text file could be more efficient in terms of space used. In terms of speed, a typed file is generally faster than a text file.

Chapter 20

1. A client is any code that uses a unit's features.

2. True.

3. To avoid repeating the same literal (and consequently having to change that literal many times over) over and over again.

4. Communicating with client code about which of the unit's features it can have access to.

5. Actually implementing all of a unit's features, including those hidden from clients.

6. With a header only.

7. No.

8. Through the `Uses` statement.

9. No.

Appendix B ◆ Answers to the Review Questions

10. Before the project's main block is.

11. They are replaced with literal values.

12. Something not originally planned for, the implementation of which is not consistent with the original design.

13. Yes.

14. No. (But you can pre-initialize typed constants.)

15. A file that gets included into your source file before compilation as if it were actually part of that file.

16. It always refers to the same location in RAM. It makes it possible for a procedure or function to have permanent local variables.

17. The last.

18. The compiler turns the Pascal code into machine language but the linker adds code that "prepares" the code for execution, as well as adding any object files that the program may use.

19. A sort of primitive kind of unit provided by most operating systems. You can access code in object libraries by linking the libraries into your programs.

20. False. Routines can be communicated only through object libraries.

Chapter 21

1. TObject.

2. Typecast an object to make it act like a more specialized descendent. Use Is to ensure that it actually can act like that type and as to do the actual casting.

3. Object-oriented programming.

4. A user defined data type (specifically, a record).

5. A variable.

6. Inheritance is the idea that a class can be "just like another class" only with a few modifications. Define the new class as

```
type
   NewClass = object(ExistingClass)
   ...
```

7. The ancestor comes first and has descendents.
8. No. (It *can* use the keyword `inherited` as needed, however.)
9. False. You can override inherited methods.
10. True.
11. They are methods designed to create and destroy objects.
12. No. A constructor is, in essence, you asking the class to create an instance of itself.

Index

Symbols

* (asterisk) character, 408
+ (plus) concatenation operator, 106
; (semicolon) following statements, 80
? (question mark) character, 408
_ (underscore) in variable names, 96
80X86 chips, 11

A

Abs procedure, 249
absolute values, 249
accessing records, 306-308
addition, 231, 240-241
algorithms, 217-219
aligning components, 56-58
Alignment Palette command (View menu), 58
AMD chips, 11
analog computing vs. digital, 13-14
AND operator, 172
Append procedure, 355
appending
   text files, 355
   forms to project files, 44-45
   listbox items, 217
   units to project files, 45

applications
   components, 53
   controls, 53
   see also software
arrays, 321-327
   character arrays, 340
   complex, 338-339
   constants, 398
   declaring, 322
   dimensions, 338
   Hi-Lo card game, 327-338
   multi-dimensional, 338
   one-dimensional, 338
   reading, 322
   records, 400
   returning with functions, 340
   size limits, 339
   sorting, 323-327
   typed constants, 399
as keyword, 424
ASCII character set, 113
assemblers, 22
Assign procedure, 349
assigning values to strings, 103-104

Index

assignment statements, 103
attributes (objects), 431-437
automatically generated code, 88
autosizing string variables, 107

B

background color, 195
Backspace key, 4
behavior (objects), 32-33
bits, 13
blocks, 80
   conditional code, 183-191
      Else statements, 184-185
      style, 185-186
bookmarks, 66
Boolean data type, 169-176
   comparison operators, 170-172
   declaration, 170
   logical operators, 172-176
   switches, 173-176
boundaries (integers), 119-120
Break statement, 225-228
breaking code, 391
breakpoints, 86-87
bubble sorts, 323
bugs, 83
   logic errors, 84-85
   syntax errors, 84
   see also debugging
building vs. compiling, 118
built-in subroutines, 239
button labels, 108
button objects, 104-106
bytes, 13-14

C

C (language), 156
CALC program, 425-427
CALCINT project, 234-239
CALCREAL project, 246-247
Calculate procedure, 426
calling
   constructors, 420
   destructors, 420
   subroutines, 128, 138
Caption property, 234
card game (Hi-Lo), 327-338
   bets, 332
   "clearing table," 336
   dealing, 333
   discarding cards, 333
   individual card declarations, 329
   shuffling cards, 330-331
   suit declarations, 328
Case statements, 196-204
   applicability, 197-198
   limitations, 200-204
   matching selections, 199
   nesting, 276
   ordinal types, 199-200
case-sensitivity, 170
Catalog, version 1.0, 373-380
CD-ROM installation steps, 38
centering components, 57
central processing unit, *see* CPU
character arrays, 340-341
character set (ASCII), 113
character variables, 98, 104-106
check boxes, 288-292
Checked property, 268
chips, 10
circular references (units), 395-396
class keyword, 416
classes, 29-30, 416
   compatibility, 421-422
   inheritance, 418
   root classes, 419
   TForm class, 424
   variables, 416
clearing screens, 130-133
click on events, 106
clicking (mouse), 4
clients, 386
Close procedure, 352

closing
  project files, 45
  text files, 352-353
  typed files, 370
code
  algorithms, 217-219
  automatically generated, 88
  blocks, *see* blocks
  bookmarks, 66
  breaking, 391
  breakpoints, 86-87
  comments, 78, 454
  counters, 209
  debugging, 83-87
  delimiters, 222
  double-dots, 197
  hacking, 439-440
  line length (code), 139-140
  literals, 104
  null statements, 82
  placeholders, 199
  prototyping, 442
  punctuation, 80-81
    checking, 81
    errors, 81-82
    semicolons (;), 80
  recompiling, 86
  REMINDME program, 454-466
  spaghetti code, 208
  states, 334
  stepping, 134
  tracing, 135
  see also conditional code; object code; units
Code Editor, 40, 63-71
  editing keys, 66-68
  finding text, 68-70
  replacing text, 70
  undo operations, 71
code frames, 88-90
color grid (objects), 195
combo boxes, 446

commands
  Compile menu, Syntax Check, 81
  Debug menu, Goto, 86
  Edit menu
    Find, 69
    Size, 55
  File menu
    Exit, 46
    New Project, 59
    New Unit, 45
    Open Project, 43
    Save Project, 44
  Help menu, Topic Search, 82
  machine language, 22
  Options menu, Environment, 85
  View menu
    Alignment Palette, 58
    Forms, 52
    Project Source, 42, 64
    Units, 52
    Watch, 133
commas in numeric expressions, 112
comments (code), 78, 454
comparison operators, 170-172
compatibility
  data conversion, 160-163
  integer types, 116
  objects, 421-422
Compile menu commands, Syntax Check, 81
compiler directives, 351
compiling, 23-24, 76-77, 387
  building comparison, 118
  I/O checking, 350
complex arrays, 338-339
complex logic, 177-180
complex types, 299
Component Palette, 53-59
components, 53
  aligning, 56-58
  Alignment Palette, 58

Index

centering, 57
deleting, 58
grid, 55
moving, 55
selecting, 55
sizing, 54-56
see also controls
compound statements, 83
computer-based tutors, 82
concatenation (strings), 106-107
conditional code, 169, 195-196
    blocks, 183-191
        Else statements, 184-185
        style, 185-186
    Boolean data type, 169-176
        comparison operators, 170-172
        declaration, 170
        logical operators, 172-176
        switches, 173-176
    Break statement, 225-228
    Case statements, 196-204
        applicability, 197-198
        limitations, 200-204
        matching selections, 199
        ordinal types, 199-200
    Continue statement, 225-228
    endless loops, 207
    GoTo statements, 208-209
    If-Then statements, 176-183
        complex logic, 177-180
        Else keyword, 182-185
        Random function, 180-181
        Randomize procedure, 181
    loops, 209-211
        For statements, 211-215
        GoTo statements, 209-211
        Repeat statements, 219-225
        While statements, 219-225
    parsing, 216-219
        code, 217-219
        While/Repeat statements, 221-224

const parameter, 143-144
constants (units), 397-402
constructors (objects), 419-420
context-sensitive help, 82-83
Continue statement, 225-228
control variables, 211
controls, 53
    Enabled property, 175
    form position, 62
    gauges, 119
    group box control, 268-270
    group boxes, 269
    naming, 313
    object classes, 424
    radio buttons, 267-270
    slider control, 157
    switches, 173-176
    tab stops, 270
    Visual Solutions Pack, 59
    see also components
converting data, 156-160
    edit line object, 157
    integers, 160-163
        Copy function, 163
        Label object, 162
    numeric to string, 158
    scrollbar object, 157-158
    strings to numeric, 159-160
Copy function (data conversion), 163
copying text, 65
counters, 209
    incrementing, 228
counting words (text files), 409-412
CPU (central processing unit), 10-11, 37
CR-LF sequences, 348
crackers, 440
Craps simulation, 201
cryptographs, 359-362
cursor keys, 4, 65
Cursor property, 62
customizing component grids, 55

cutting text, 65
Cyrix chips, 11

D

data, 16
data conversion, 156-160
  edit line object, 157
  integers, 160-163
    Copy function, 163
    Label object, 162
  numeric to string, 158
  scrollbar object, 157-158
  strings to numeric, 159-160
data entry forms, 312-316
data types, 261
  arrays, 321-327
    card game, 327-338
    character arrays, 340
    complex, 338-339
    declaring, 322
    reading, 322
    returning with functions, 340
    size limits, 339
    sorting, 323-327
  complex types, 299
  declaring, 263
  records, 298, 339
    accessing, 306-308
    addressing fields, 300
    comparisons, 300
    data entry forms, 312-316
    declaring, 299-300
    limitations, 306-309
    multiple form use, 304-306
    performance issues, 311
    returning from functions, 300
    selecting variables, 301
    SizeOf function, 302-303
    variable conflicts, 311
    with keyword, 309-312
  REMINDME program, 453
  returning ordinal value, 265

sets, 283
  check boxes, 288-292
  declaring, 284-285
  elements, 293
  identifiers, 293
  limitations, 293-295
  operators, 285-287
  situational uses, 294-295
  variable conflicts, 311
simple data types, 299
SizeOf function, 303
user-defined data types, 262
  declaring, 262-265
  Ord function, 265-267
  subrange types, 267
see also typed files
database engines, 373
deactivating range checking, 121-122
Debug menu commands, Goto, 86
debugging, 83-87
  breakpoints, 86-87
  integrated debuggers, 85
  procedures, 133-144
  stepping (code), 134
  subroutines, 141
  tracing, 85-86
see also bugs
Dec procedure, 240-241
decimal calculator project, 249-253
declaring
  arrays, 322
  Boolean variables, 170
  file variables, 348-349
  functions, 146-149
  global variables, 144-146
  integers, 114
  local variables, 146
  objects, 416
  record types, 299-300
  sets, 284-285
  string variables, 101-103

Index

typed files, 368-369
user-defined data types, 262-265
variables, 95, 100
   location, 99-100
   names, 95-98
   types, 98
decrementing loops, 212
defaults, 60
Delete procedure, 227
deleting
   components, 58
   forms, 46
   forms from project files, 45
   group boxes, 269
   project files, 46
   typed file data, 372-373
   units, 46
   units from project files, 45
delimiters, 222
Delphi
   hard disk requirements, 37
   installation, 37-38
   quitting, 46
design issues, 441
   documentation, 442-444
   problem analysis, 441-442
   REMINDME program
      code, 454-466
      data types, 453
      forms, 445-446
      objects, 446-452
      subroutines, 453
   units, 403-406
destination values, 212
destructors (objects), 419-420
dialog boxes
   Evaluate/Modify, 233, 303
   Fonts, 31
   Open, 407-412
   Project - Compiler Options, 117
   Search, 69
   Search and Replace, 70
   Size, 56
   Watch Properties, 133
   see also check boxes; radio buttons
Dialogs tab, 58
DICE project, 201-204, 224-225
digital computing vs. analog, 13-14
dimensions (arrays), 338
directories, 18-20
   File Manager (Windows), 19-20
   GPUNITS directory, 404
   naming, 19
   root directory, 19
   sub-directories, 19
division, 231
documentation (programs), 442-444
DOS, 16-17
double-clicking (mouse), 4
double-dots, 197
dragging/dropping (mouse), 4
dropping fractions, 244
duplicate identifiers (enumerated types), 280

E

edit line object, 157
Edit menu commands
   Find, 69
   Size, 55
editing
   Code Editor operations, 63-71
   events, 90-91
   properties, 61-63
   typed files, 371-372
   variables with subroutines, 140
elements (sets), 293
elements (variables), 262
ellipsis, 81
Else keyword, 182-185
Enabled property, 175
ending programs, 24
endless loops, 207, 215

engines, *see* database engines
enumerated types
   advantages, 264
   declaring user-defined types,
      262-265
   disadvantages, 279-280
   identifiers, 280
   Ord function, 265-267
   radio buttons, 267-270
   radio groups, 271-279
   RSP project, 272-279
   subrange types, 267
enumeration, 262
Environment command
      (Options menu), 85
EOF function, 357
errors
   punctuation, 81-82
   see also bugs; debugging
Evaluate/Modify dialog box, 233,
      303
event handlers, 424
event model, 26-27
events
   editing, 90-91
   naming, 106
exceeding boundaries (integers),
      119-120
executable files, 18
Exit command (File menu), 46
exponents, 248
expressions, 232
extended ASCII character set, 113
extensions (files), 18

F

failed Else statements, 183
feature bloat (programs), 443
features, *see* attributes
fields, 300, 416
file handles, 348
File Manager (Windows), 19-20, 46
file masks, 408

File menu commands
   Exit, 46
   New Project, 59
   New Unit, 45
   Open Project, 43
   Save Project, 44
files, 347
   adding to projects, 51
   executable, 18
   extensions, 18
   fixed files, 368
   flat files, 368
   I/O checking, 350
   include files, 386
   naming, 17-18
   PAS file extension, 386
   project files, 41
      appending forms, 44-45
      closing, 45
      creating, 43
      deleting, 46
      deleting forms, 45
      extensions, 44
      loading, 43
      saving, 44
      units, 45
   random-access files, 371
   removing from projects, 51
   SizeOf function, 368
   text files
      appending, 355
      closing, 352-353
      counting words, 409-412
      cryptographs, 359-362
      declaring, 348-349
      disadvantages, 358
      opening, 349-352
      printing, 358
      reading, 355-362
      writing, 353-355
   typed files, 367-380
      Catalog, version 1.0, 373-380
      declaring, 368-369
      deleting data, 372-373

Index

editing, 371-372
size, 368
subroutines, 370-371
see also units
FileSize function, 370
Filter property, 407-409
Find command (Edit menu), 69
finding text, 68-70
fixed files, 368
flat files, 368
focus (objects), 31-32
Font property, 62
Fonts dialog box, 31
For statements, 211-215
   applicability, 212-214
   limitations, 214-215
For-Downto statements, 212
foreground color, 195
form units, 89
forms, 39-41
   bringing to foreground, 52
   combo boxes, 446
   Component Palette, 53-59
   data entry, 312-316
   deleting, 46
   multiple form use, 304-306
   naming controls, 313
   placing objects on, 54
   primary, 304
   project files
      appending, 44
      deleting, 45
   REMINDME program, 445-446
   secondary, 304
   selecting, 51
   toggling, 53
   see also components
Forms command (View menu), 52
Frac procedure, 245
functions
   Copy function, 163
   declaring, 146-149
   EOF, 357

FileSize, 370
integer math, 240
IOResult, 351-352
Length, 218
Ord, 265-267
Random, 180-181, 360
SizeOf, 302-303, 368
WordCount, 406

G

gauges, 119
GENERAL unit, 404-406
gigabytes (G), 15
global variables
   declaring, 144-146
   precedence, 148
Goto command (Debug menu), 86
GoTo statements, 208-211
GPUNITS directory, 404
grids (components), 55
group box control, 268-270
group boxes
   deleting, 269
   TabIndex property, 269
group properties, 63
GUESSIT project
   loops, 213-214
   version 1.0, 178-180
   version 2.0, 187-191

H

hacking, 439-440
hard disk requirements, 37
Height property, 62
help
   computer-based tutors, 82
   context-sensitive, 82-83
   syntax, 83
Help menu commands,
      Topic Search, 82
Hi procedure, 242

Hi-Lo project, 328-338, 427-431
  bets, 332
  "clearing table," 336
  dealing, 333
  discarding cards, 333
  individual card declarations, 329
  object attributes, 433-437
  shuffling cards, 330-331
  suit declarations, 328
hiding SpeedBar, 51
Hopper, Grace, 84

I

I/O checking, 350
IBM extended ASCII character set, 113
identifiers, 97
  enumerated types, 280
  sets, 293
  units, 403
If-Then statements
  complex logic, 177-180
  Else keyword, 182-185
  Random function, 180-181
  Randomize procedure, 181
implementation section (units), 390-391, 394
Inc procedure, 240-241
include files, 386
incrementing counters, 228
inheritance (objects), 417-419
inherited keyword, 421
Insert mode (Code Editor), 65
installation, 37-38
Int procedure, 245
Integer variable type, 113
integers, 112-123
  boundaries, 119-120
  compatibility, 116
  data conversion, 160-163
    Copy function, 163
    Label object, 162
  declaring, 114

incompatibility, 160-163
math operations, 231-242
modulus, 122
range checking, 120-122
range errors, 117-119
real number variable comparison, 246-253
  scientific notation, 247-253
  subroutines, 248-258
subtraction, 117
wraparound, 122-123
integrated debuggers, 85
interface section (units), 389-390, 394
interfaces
  historical, 24-26
  user-controlled, 26-27
interpreters, 76-77
intersection operators, 286
Interval property, 407
IOResult function, 351-352
ItemIndex property, 271

K

keyboard input, 132
keywords, 98
  as, 424
  class, 416
  Else keyword, 182-185
  inherited, 421
  var, 100
  with, 309-312
  see also reserved words
kilobytes (K), 14

L

label keyword, 208
label objects, 104-106, 162
labels
  buttons, 108
  updating, 278
  word wrap, 107-108
leading zeros, 112

Index

Left property, 62
length bytes, 101
Length function, 218
LIBDE form, 314-316
libraries, 149-150, 387
line feeds, 348
line length (code), 139-140
linking, 387
listbox objects, 216-217
listing properties, 60
literal strings, 101
literals, 104
Lo procedure, 242
LoadClick procedure, 361
loading
   project files, 43
   units, 51
local variables, 146-148
logic errors, 84-85
logic, *see* Boolean data type
logical operators
   AND operator, 172
   Boolean variables, 172-176
   NOT operator, 173
   OR, 172
   XOR, 172
Longint variable type, 113
loops, 209-211
   control variables, 211
   destination values, 212
   endless loops, 207, 215
   enumerated types, 265
   For statements, 211
      applicability, 212-214
      limitations, 214-215
   For-Downto statements, 212
   GoTo statements, 209-211
   GUESSIT project, 213-214
   Repeat statements, 219-221
      DICE project, 224-225
      PARSE project, 221-224
   sorting arrays, 325-327
   terminating, 224
   While statements, 219-221
      DICE project, 224-225
      PARSE project, 221-224

M

machine language, 22, 387
main program files, 41
matching selections (Case statements), 199
math operations, 231
   absolute values, 249
   dropping fractions, 244
   exponents, 248
   expressions, 232
   integers, 231-242
   modulus, 232
   operators
      integers, 231
      precedence, 254-255
      real numbers, 243
   overflows, 232
   real number-integer variable
      comparison, 246-253
      scientific notation, 247-253
      subroutines, 248-258
   real numbers, 242-245
   rounding numbers, 244
   scientific notation, 247-253
   significand, 248
   significant digits, 243
   square roots, 245
   squaring numbers, 249
   subroutines
      integers, 239-242
      real numbers, 244-247
   see also numeric operations
maximum string length, 108
measuring RAM, 14-15
megabytes (M), 14
memory
   bits, 13
   bytes, 13-14
   gigabytes, 15

hard disk requirements, 37
kilobytes, 14
megabytes, 14
RAM, 11-15
    measuring, 14-15
    requirements, 37
    string declarations, 103
terabytes, 15
typed constants, 401
methods, 87
    parameters, 88
    prototyping, 442
    see also objects
microprocessors, 10-11
modulus, 122, 232
mouse
    click on events, 106
    clicking, 4
    drag/drop operations, 4
moving components, 55
multi-dimensional arrays, 338
multiple form use, 304-306
multiplication, 231

N

naming
    controls, 313
    directories, 19
    events, 106
    files, 17-18
    objects, 97
    procedures, 131
    programs, 24
    units, 389
    variables, 95-98
        numeric characters, 97
        reserved words, 98
        restrictions, 96-97
navigating Code Editor window, 65
negative values (numeric), 112
nesting
    Case statements, 276
    routines, 376

New Project command (File menu), 59
New Unit command (File menu), 45
NOT operator, 173
null statements, 82
null strings, 101, 107
numeric characters, 97
numeric operations, 112
    commas in numeric expressions, 112
    comparison operators, 171
    converting numbers/strings, 158-160
    integers, 112-123
        boundaries, 119-120
        compatibility, 116
        declaring, 114
        modulus, 122
        range checking, 120-122
        range errors, 117-119
        subtraction, 117
        wraparound, 122-123
    leading zeros, 112
    negative values, 112
    numeric types, 112-114
    see also math operations
NUMEXAM, 115

O

object code, 387
Object Inspector, 59-63
    object behavior, 63
    properties, 60-63
object methods, 135, 417
    see also procedures
objects, 387
    attributes, 431-437
    behavior, 32-33, 63
    buttons, 104-106
    CALC programs, 425-427
    classes, 29-30, 416
    color grid, 195

Index

compatibility, 421-422
constructors, 419-420
declaring, 416
destructors, 419-420
edit line object, 157
fields, 416
form, 39-40
group properties, 63
HILO program, 427-437
inheritance, 417-419
labels, 104-106, 162
listbox objects, 216-217
naming, 97
placing on forms, 54
properties, 87
   Checked, 268
   Cursor, 62
   defaults, 60
   editing, 61-63
   focus, 31-32
   Font, 62
   Height, 62
   Left, 62
   Top, 62
   Visible, 61
   Width, 62
REMINDME program, 446-452
replacing methods, 420-421
root classes, 419
scrollbar object, 157-158
sizing, 62
TForm class, 424
TObject class, 419
TRadioGroup, 271
typecasting, 424-425
see also components; events; methods; tabs
Odd procedure, 242
one-dimensional arrays, 338
OOP (object-oriented programming), 416
Open dialog box, 407-412
Open Project command (File menu), 43
opening
   files, 349-352
   projects, 51
operating systems, 16
   directories, 18-20
   file names, 17-18
operators
   comparison operators, 170-172
   concatenation (+), 106
   logical operators, 172-176
   math operations
      integers, 231
      real numbers, 243
   precedence, 254-255
   sets, 285-287
   subtraction, 117
Options menu commands, Environment, 85
OR operator, 172
Ord function, 265-267
ordinal types, 199-200
OS, *see* operating systems
overflows, 232
overriding file extensions, 18
Overwrite mode (code editor), 65

P

parameters, 81, 88
  procedures, 137-139
  splitting, 140
  subroutines, 132-133
     changing, 142
     const parameter, 143-144
     var parameter, 141
PARSE project, 217-219
  Continue/Break statements, 226-228
  While/Repeat statements, 221-224

parsing, 216-219
    code, 217-219
    Repeat/While statements, 221-224
PAS file extension, 386
pasting text, 65
PL/I variable assignments, 155
placeholders (code), 199
Pos procedure, 251
positioning controls, 62
precedence
    math operators, 254-255
    variables, 148
Pred procedure, 241
preinitializing variables, 401
primary forms, 304
printing text files, 358
problem analysis (program design), 441-442
procedures, 135
    Abs, 249
    Append, 355
    Assign, 349
    Calculate, 426
    Close, 352
    Dec, 240-241
    Delete, 227
    Frac, 245
    Hi, 242
    Inc, 240-241
    Int, 245
    integer math, 240
    Lo, 242
    LoadClick, 361
    local variables, 146
    naming, 131
    Odd, 242
    parameters, 137-139
    Pos, 251
    Pred, 241
    Random, 249
    Randomize procedure, 181
    Read, 355-356

ReadLn, 355-356
Reset, 350
Rewrite, 349
Round, 244
Seek, 371
Sqr, 249
SqrRt, 245
Str, 158, 249-250, 406
subroutines, 131
Succ, 241
Trunc, 244
Truncate, 372
unknown identifiers, 141
Val, 159-160
watch window, 133-144
Write, 353-355
WriteLn, 353-355
see also object methods
program design, 441
    documentation, 442-444
    problem analysis, 441-442
    REMINDME program
        code, 454-466
        data types, 453
        forms, 445-446
        objects, 446-452
        subroutines, 453
programs, 15-16
    assemblers, 22
    code frames, 88-90
    comments, 78
    compiler directives, 351
    compiling, 24, 76-77
    Craps simulation, 201
    debugging, 83-87
        breakpoints, 86-87
        integrated debuggers, 85
        tracing, 85-86
    ending, 24
    feature bloat, 443
    interpreters, 76-77
    naming, 24

Index

REMINDME, 443-444
  code, 454-466
  data types, 453
  forms, 445-446
  objects, 446-452
  subroutines, 453
resetting, 119
running, 76
starting, 24
suspended, 119
see also code
Project - Compiler Options dialog box, 117
project files, 41
  closing, 45
  creating, 43
  deleting, 46
  extensions, 44
  forms, 44-45
  loading, 43
  saving, 44
  units, 45
Project Manager, 42-46
Project Source command (View menu), 42, 64
projects
  adding files, 51
  CALCINT, 234-239
  CALCREAL, 246-247
  decimal calculator, 249-253
  DICE, 201-204, 224-225
  GUESSIT
    version 1.0, 178-180
    version 2.0, 187-191
  GUESSIT project, 213-214
  NUMEXAM, 115
  opening, 51
  PARSE project, 217-219
    Continue/Break statements, 226-228
    While/Repeat statements, 221-224
  removing files from, 51
  RSP project, 272-279
  saving, 51
  SETLOGIC, 288-292
  SUB project, 129
  unit role, 396-397
properties
  Caption property, 234
  defaults, 60
  editing, 61-63
  Enabled property, 175
  Filter, 407-409
  Interval, 407
  listing, 60
  Object Inspector, 60-63
  objects, 30-32, 87
    Checked, 268
    Cursor, 62
    focus, 31-32
    Font, 62
    Height, 62
    Left, 62
    Top, 62
    Visible, 61
    Width, 62
prototyping, 442
pseudocode, 16
punctuation (code)
  checking, 81
  errors, 81-82
  semicolons (;), 80

Q-R

quitting Delphi, 46

radio buttons, 267-270
radio groups, 271-279
RAM, 11-15
  measuring, 14-15
  requirements, 37
  string declarations, 103
  variables, 95
Random function, 180-181, 249, 360
random-access files, 371

random-access memory, *see* RAM
Randomize procedure, 181
Rand*See*d variable, 360
range checking, 120-122
range errors, 117-119
Read procedure, 355-356
reading
    arrays, 322
    keyboard input, 132
    text files, 355-362
    typed files, 369
ReadLn procedure, 132, 355-356
real numbers, 112
    integer variable comparison, 246-253
        scientific notation, 247-253
        subroutines, 248-258
    math operations, 242-247
recompiling code, 86
records, 298-306
    accessing, 306-308
    addressing fields, 300
    arrays, 400
    comparisons, 300
    data entry forms, 312-316
    data types, 301
    declaring, 299-300
    limitations, 306
    multiple form use, 304-306
    performance issues, 311
    records containing, 308-309
    returning from functions, 300
    size limits, 339
    SizeOf function, 302-303
    variable conflicts, 311
    with keyword, 309
recursion, 148
Redo capability (Code Editor), 71
refreshing displays, 130-133
REMINDME program, 443-444
    code, 454-466
    data types, 453
    forms, 445-446

    objects, 446-452
    subroutines, 453
Repeat statements, 219-221
    DICE project, 224-225
    PARSE project, 221-224
replacing
    object methods, 420-421
    text, 70
reserved words, 83, 98
    see also keywords
Reset procedure, 350
resetting programs, 119
restricting object attribute access, 431-437
Result variables, 149
returning
    arrays with functions, 340
    records from functions, 300
    string length, 218
    strings, 163
Rewrite procedure, 349
REXX, 155
root classes, 419
root directory, 19
Round procedure, 244
rounding numbers, 244
routines, *see* subroutines
RSP project, 272-279
running programs, 76

S

Save Project command (File menu), 44
saving projects, 44, 51
scientific notation, 247-253
scope
    units, 402-403
    variables, 134-136
scrollbar object, 157-158
Search and Replace dialog box, 70
Search dialog box, 69
secondary forms, 304
Seek procedure, 371

Index

selecting components, 55
selection sorts, 323-324
semicolons (;) following statements, 80
SETLOGIC project, 288-292
sets (set type), 283
sets
- check boxes, 288-292
- declaring, 284-285
- elements, 293
- identifiers, 293
- intersection operators, 286
- limitations, 293-295
- operators, 285-287
- situational uses, 294-295

shortening strings, 102
Shortint variable type, 113
significand, 248
significant digits, 243
simple data types, 299
Size command (Edit menu), 55
Size dialog box, 56
size limits
- arrays, 339
- records, 339

SizeOf function, 302-303, 368
sizing
- components, 54-56
- objects, 62

slider controls, 157
snap to grid feature (components), 55
software, 15-20
- data, 16
- operating systems, 16
  - directories, 18-20
  - file names, 17-18
- programs, 15-16
- *see also* applications

sorting
- arrays, 323-327
- bubble sorts, 323
- selection sorts, 323-324

source code, 387
spaghetti code, 208
SpeedBar, 50-52
splitting parameters, 140
square roots, 245
squaring numbers, 249
Standard tab, 58
starting programs, 24
statements, 103
- assignment statements, 103
- Break, 225-228
- Case statements, 196-204
  - applicability, 197-198
  - limitations, 200-204
  - matching selections, 199
  - ordinal types, 199-200
- compound statements, 83
- Continue, 225-228
- failed Else statements, 183
- For, 211-215
- For statements
  - applicability, 212-214
  - limitations, 214-215
- For-Downto, 212
- GoTo, 208-211
- If-Then statements, 176-183
  - complex logic, 177-180
  - Else keyword, 182-185
  - Random function, 180-181
  - Randomize procedure, 181
- null statements, 82
- parameters, 81
- Repeat, 219-221
  - DICE project, 224-225
  - PARSE project, 221-224
- While, 219-221
  - DICE project, 224-225
  - PARSE project, 221-224

states, 334
stepping (code), 134
Str procedure, 158, 249-250, 406

string variables, 101-108
  assigning values, 103-104
  autosizing, 107
  character variable relationship, 104-106
  concatenation, 106-107
  declaring, 101-103
  labels, 107-108
  maximum length, 108
  null strings, 107
  RAM issues, 103
  shortening, 102
strings
  comparison operators, 171
  converting numbers to, 158
  converting to numeric data, 159-160
  returning, 163
  returning length, 218
  WordCount function, 406
  writing, 132
strongly typed languages, 155
style guidelines (code), 185-186
SUB project, 129
sub-directories, 19
subrange types, 267
subroutines
  advantages over GoTo statements, 209
  built-in, 239
  calling, 128, 138
  changing parameters, 142
  clearing screens, 130-133
  const parameter, 143-144
  declaring functions, 146-149
  debugging, 141
  editing variables, 140
  global variables, 144-146
  include files, 386
  libraries, 149-150
  line length, 139-140
  math operations
    integers, 239-242
    real numbers, 244-247

  nested, 376
  parameters, 132
  real number-integer compatible, 248-258
  recursion, 148
  REMINDME program, 453
  SUB project, 129
  typed files, 370-371
  var parameter, 141
  variable precedence, 148
  see also units
subtraction, 117, 231, 240-241
Succ procedure, 241
suspended programs, 119
switches (Boolean variables), 173-176
syntax, 83-84
Syntax Check command (Compile menu), 81
system requirements, 37
System unit, 403

T

tab stops, 270
TabIndex property, 269
tabs, 58-60
terabytes, 15
terminating loops, 224
text files, 347-353
  appending data, 355
  closing, 352-353
  counting words, 409-412
  cryptographs, 359-362
  declaring, 348-349
  disadvantages, 358
  opening, 349-352
  printing, 358
  reading, 355-362
  writing, 353-355
TForm class, 424
thumbnails, 60
Timer unit, 406-407
TObject class, 419

Index

toggling
    Code Editor modes, 65
    forms/units, 53
Top property, 62
Topic Search command (Help menu), 82
tracing, 85-86
tracing code, 135
TRadioGroup object, 271
Trunc procedure, 244
Truncate procedure, 372
tutorials, 82
type checking, 264
type identifiers, 263
type mismatch errors, 104
typecasting
    objects, 424-425
    variables, 271-272
typed constants (units), 399-402
typed files, 367-380
    Catalog, version 1.0, 373-380
    declaring, 368-369
    deleting data, 372-373
    editing, 371-372
    size, 368
    subroutines, 370-371
types, *see* data types
typing variables, 98

U

undefined variables, 122
undo operations, 71
Unit1, 89
units, 41, 78, 385, 388
    bringing to foreground, 52
    circular references, 395-396
    constants, 397-399
    deleting, 46
    designing, 403-406
    extensions, 44
    form units, 89
    GENERAL, 404-406
    GPUNITS directory, 404
    identifiers, 403
    implementation section, 390-391
    interface section, 389-390
    loading, 51
    naming, 389
    Open dialog, 407-412
    project files, 45
    project interaction, 396-397
    scope, 402-403
    selecting, 51
    System unit, 403
    Timer, 406-407
    toggling, 53
    typed constants, 399-402
    Uses clause, 392-395
        calling code, 393
        implementation section, 394
        interface section, 394
        location, 395
    Win API, 393
Units command (View menu), 52
unknown identifiers, 141
unsigned integer variable types, 114
updating labels, 278
user interfaces, *see* interfaces
user-defined data types, 262
    declaring, 262-265
    Ord function, 265-267
    subrange types, 267
Uses clause, 392-395
    calling code, 393
    implementation section, 394
    interface section, 394
    location, 395

V

Val procedure, 159-160
var
    keyword, 100
    parameter, 141

variables, 95
   Boolean data type, 169-176
      comparison operators, 170-172
      declaration, 170
      logical operators, 172-176
      switches, 173-176
   classes, 416
   control variables, 211
   declaring, 95, 99-100
   editing with subroutines, 140
   elements, 262
   file masks, 408
   global, 144-146
   local, 146
   naming, 95-98
      numeric characters, 97
      reserved words, 98
      restrictions, 96-97
   numeric types, 113
   ordinal types, 199-200
   precedence, 148
   preinitializing, 401
   Rand*Seed*, 360
   real numbers, 242
   record conflicts, 311
   Result variables, 149
   scope, 134-136
   typecasting, 271-272
   types
      char, 98
      string, 101-108
   undefined, 122
   unsigned integer types, 114
   see also integers
VBX tab, 59
View menu commands
   Alignment Palette, 58
   Forms, 52
   Project Source, 42, 64
   Units, 52
   Watch, 133

viewing SpeedBar, 51
Visible property, 61
Visual Solutions Pack, 59

W-Z

Watch command (View menu), 133
Watch Properties dialog box, 133
watch window, 133-144
While statements, 219-221
   DICE project, 224-225
   PARSE project, 221-224
whole numbers, 112
Width property, 62
Windows, 16-17
   File Manager, 19-20, 46
   objects, 29-30
Windows API, 393
with keyword, 309-312
word variables, 242
word wrap (labels), 107-108
WordCount function, 406
words (reserved/syntax), 83
wraparound (numeric), 122-123
Write procedure, 353-355
WriteLn procedure, 132, 353-355
writing
   code, 63-71
      editing keys, 66-68
      finding text, 68-70
      replacing text, 70
      undo operations, 71
   strings, 132
   text files, 353-355
   typed files, 369

XOR operator, 172

GET CONNECTED
to the ultimate source of computer information!

The MCP Forum on CompuServe

Go online with the world's leading computer book publisher! Macmillan Computer Publishing offers everything you need for computer success!

Find the books that are right for you!

A complete online catalog, plus sample chapters and tables of contents give you an in-depth look at all our books. The best way to shop or browse!

➤ Get fast answers and technical support for MCP books and software

➤ Join discussion groups on major computer subjects

➤ Interact with our expert authors via e-mail and conferences

➤ Download software from our immense library:
  ▷ Source code from books
  ▷ Demos of hot software
  ▷ The best shareware and freeware
  ▷ Graphics files

Join now and get a free CompuServe Starter Kit!

To receive your free CompuServe Introductory Membership, call **1-800-848-8199** and ask for representative #597.

The Starter Kit includes:
➤ Personal ID number and password
➤ $15 credit on the system
➤ Subscription to *CompuServe Magazine*

Once on the CompuServe System, type:

GO MACMILLAN

for the most computer information anywhere!

MACMILLAN COMPUTER PUBLISHING

CompuServe

PLUG YOURSELF INTO...

THE MACMILLAN INFORMATION SUPERLIBRARY™

Free information and vast computer resources from the world's leading computer book publisher—online!

FIND THE BOOKS THAT ARE RIGHT FOR YOU!
A complete online catalog, plus sample chapters and tables of contents give you an in-depth look at *all* of our books, including hard-to-find titles. It's the best way to find the books you need!

- **STAY INFORMED** with the latest computer industry news through our online newsletter, press releases, and customized Information SuperLibrary Reports.
- **GET FAST ANSWERS** to your questions about MCP books and software.
- **VISIT** our online bookstore for the latest information and editions!
- **COMMUNICATE** with our expert authors through e-mail and conferences.
- **DOWNLOAD SOFTWARE** from the immense MCP library:
    - Source code and files from MCP books
    - The best shareware, freeware, and demos
- **DISCOVER HOT SPOTS** on other parts of the Internet.
- **WIN BOOKS** in ongoing contests and giveaways!

TO PLUG INTO MCP: ➤ **WORLD WIDE WEB: http://www.mcp.com**

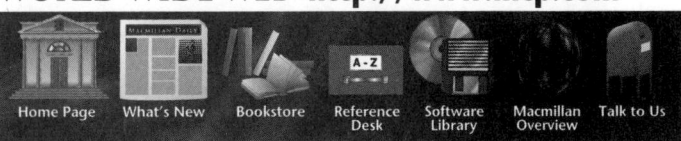

GOPHER: gopher.mcp.com
FTP: ftp.mcp.com